Unamuno's Theory of the Novel

LEGENDA

LEGENDA, founded in 1995 by the European Humanities Research Centre of the University of Oxford, is now a joint imprint of the Modern Humanities Research Association and Maney Publishing. Titles range from medieval texts to contemporary cinema and form a widely comparative view of the modern humanities, including works on Arabic, Catalan, English, French, German, Greek, Italian, Portuguese, Russian, Spanish, and Yiddish literature. An Editorial Board of distinguished academic specialists works in collaboration with leading scholarly bodies such as the Society for French Studies, the British Comparative Literature Association and the Association of Hispanists of Great Britain & Ireland.

MHRA

The Modern Humanities Research Association (MHRA) encourages and promotes advanced study and research in the field of the modern humanities, especially modern European languages and literature, including English, and also cinema. It also aims to break down the barriers between scholars working in different disciplines and to maintain the unity of humanistic scholarship in the face of increasing specialization. The Association fulfils this purpose primarily through the publication of journals, bibliographies, monographs and other aids to research.

Maney Publishing is one of the few remaining independent British academic publishers. Founded in 1900 the company has offices both in the UK, in Leeds and London, and in North America, in Philadelphia. Since 1945 Maney Publishing has worked closely with learned societies, their editors, authors, and members, in publishing academic books and journals to the highest traditional standards of materials and production.

STUDIES IN HISPANIC AND LUSOPHONE CULTURES

Studies in Hispanic and Lusophone Cultures are selected and edited by the Association of Hispanists of Great Britain & Ireland. The series seeks to publish the best new research in all areas of the literature, thought, history, culture, film, and languages of Spain, Spanish America, and the Portuguese-speaking world.

The Association of Hispanists of Great Britain & Ireland is a professional association which represents a very diverse discipline, in terms of both geographical coverage and objects of study. Its website showcases new work by members, and publicises jobs, conferences and grants in the field.

STUDIES IN HISPANIC AND LUSOPHONE CULTURES

Unamuno's Theory of the Novel

C. A. LONGHURST

LEGENDA

Studies in Hispanic and Lusophone Culture 1
Modern Humanities Research Association and Maney Publishing
2014

Published by the
Modern Humanities Research Association and Maney Publishing
1 Carlton House Terrace
London SW1Y 5AF
United Kingdom

LEGENDA is an imprint of the
Modern Humanities Research Association and Maney Publishing

Maney Publishing is the trading name of W. S. Maney & Son Ltd,
whose registered office is at Suite 1C, Joseph's Well, Hanover Walk, Leeds LS3 1AB

ISBN 978-1-909662-14-8

First published 2014

Printed in Great Britain

Cover: 875 Design

Copy-Editor: Richard Correll

CONTENTS

Y un alba se apagó, como se apaga
al asomar el alba allá en la extrema
nebulosa del cielo aquel que nunca
podremos ver recóndito planeta.

(Miguel de Unamuno)

PREFACE

This book has been long in the making. The kernel is to be found in a conference paper given in the University of Salamanca in 2001, later included in the conference proceedings (2003), the expansion of which into book form was encouraged by gracious colleagues. This is my sole justification for engrossing the burgeoning bibliography on Unamuno. I hope all the same it sheds some light on the latter's idiosyncratic fiction. I must make it clear that it is intended as a book on Unamuno, not on novelistic theory. While familiar with much modern writing on narrative theory, what has come to be known as narratology, I cannot say I have been greatly fired by it. Most of it seems to me to be too fond of jargon and too far removed from the novels we read and admire to have any effect on the way we read fiction. Its tendency to reduce narrative to abstract universals effectively kills off even the best novel as a rich, living, dynamic entity. Although it is only fair to add that a reaction to this arid type of literary inquest has clearly set in during the past decade or two, I have tried to avoid an approach derived from contemporary narratology, with but a couple of exceptions, and where abstraction was necessary I have preferred to delve into the kind of philosophical writings that Unamuno himself was familiar with, or else those writings of his near-contemporaries or immediate followers, writers broadly classified as existentialists, whom Unamuno foreshadowed in certain respects.

A work like this could never have been written without the previous work of those scholars who took an interest in Unamuno as a powerful creator of imaginative literature, as distinct from an existentialist philosopher, and who looked into matters of composition, structure, development, etc. and not solely at the philosophical issues contained in his narratives. I am thinking here of pioneering Unamuno scholars in the 1960s and early 1970s such as Ricardo Gullón (1964), Geoffrey Ribbans (1971), R. E. Batchelor (1972), N. G. Round (1974), and David G. Turner (1974). They set the scene for studies of Unamuno's fiction that appeared in the later 1970s and 1980s, such as those by Ricardo Díez (1976), Frances Wyers (1976), John Butt (1981), Paul R. Olson (1984), Isabel Criado Miguel (1986), Robert L. Nicholas (1987), and Gonzalo Navajas (1988). From the 1990s to the present, criticism on the novels of Unamuno has been greatly enriched not only by the many essays in academic journals of repute but by the books of Gayana Jurkevich (1991), Anne Marie Øveraas (1993), Francisco La Rubia Prado (1996 and 1999), Bénédicte Vauthier (1999 and 2004), Alison Sinclair (2001), Paul R. Olson (2003), and Thomas Franz (2003). I should like to express my debt to all these authors and to various others who figure in the (inevitably limited) bibliography. I have learnt much from them although, as is to be expected, my focus, on the whole, will be somewhat different. My purpose is to study the novels collectively, at the same time bearing in mind the essays, in order to inquire into

Unamuno's conception of narrative fiction, what, for want of a better word, I have termed his 'theory of the novel'.

The two books which I think come closest to mine in subject matter are those by Gonzalo Navajas (1988, reprinted under a different title 1992), and Luis Álvarez Castro (2005). The former reads Unamuno from the perspective of post-structuralist theory and comes up with interesting insights that occasionally coincide with my own findings and just as occasionally express an opposite view. By and large I have eschewed post-structuralist theory in favour of seeing Unamuno as the product or outcome of his own readings of eighteenth- and nineteenth-century philosophers, linguisticians, and literary theorizers. These readings go a long way towards explaining Unamuno's ideas and attitudes, which in some areas do happen to anticipate those of the late twentieth century. Álvarez Castro has produced a highly useful survey of Unamuno's literary ideas as a whole which should be an obligatory starting point for those conducting further research in this area. My own book, of course, has a narrower focus and is primarily concerned with fictional narrative, that is to say with Unamuno's novelistic praxis considered in the light of his philosophical, psychological, and literary theories. Ana M. Fernández's short study (1991) on novelistic theory in Unamuno, Ortega, and Cortázar is pure summary, while Teresa Imizcón Beunza's somewhat more substantial book (1996) on Unamuno's poetic theory, despite its title, has little in common with Álvarez Castro's or my own (except for certain source material found in Unamuno's essays which we all use). Nor, rather more surprisingly, does Francisco La Rubia Prado's second book on Unamuno (1999) have anything much in common with mine, despite his interesting comment in the introduction that 'Unamuno acaso sea el autor más consciente y consistentemente teórico de la literatura española'. Perhaps the difference arises from the fact that he, in common with virtually all other scholars, studies individual novels as discrete works and comes up with a particular interpretation in each case (e.g. *La tía Tula* is for him a Lacanian case of 'inauthenticity'). My approach in this book is based less on the study of individual novels as self-contained works and more on certain elements that turn up repeatedly in Unamuno's fiction and which therefore should tell us something significant about his conception of the art of novel-writing.

The research for this book, carried out partly in the Casa-Museo Unamuno in Salamanca, was helped enormously by a Leverhulme Emeritus Fellowship held at King's College London in 2006–07. I should like to express my gratitude to the Leverhulme Trust for making the award, to colleagues in the Department of Spanish, Portuguese and Latin-American Studies at King's for encouraging my application, and to Professors Nicholas Round and Eamonn Rodgers for writing in support. My thanks also go to Ana Chaguaceda Toledano and her team at the Casa-Museo Unamuno for their perennial friendliness and help. The eventual publication of the research project has been made possible by further support provided by the Department at King's College London in the form of a generous publication subsidy.

I should also like to record my thanks to the editors and publishers at the University of Glasgow, the MHRA, and Queen Mary, University of London, respectively, for permission to re-use some material from my previously published articles, as follows: 'Telling Words: Unamuno and the Language of Fiction', *Bulletin of Spanish Studies*,

83.1 (2006), 125–47; 'Unamuno, the Reader, and the Hermeneutical Gap', *Modern Language Review*, 103.3 (2008), 741–52; 'Unamuno on Identity: Personal and National', *Hispanic Research Journal*, 12.1 (2011), 48–62.

Parts of this book were to have been written in collaboration with James G. Longhurst, a medical psychiatrist and lover of good literature. Sadly, his early demise frustrated the plans and the book is no doubt the poorer for it. To Jennifer go my heartfelt thanks for once again wading through a manuscript and spotting the many errors that had escaped me.

C. A. L.

A NOTE ON THE EDITIONS USED

For reasons of accessibility the edition of Unamuno's works used in this study is the Biblioteca Castro *Obras Completas*, Volume I of which appeared in 1995 and Volume X in 2009. Unfortunately the project seems to have undergone a hiatus, and, although the bulk of Unamuno's works have been covered, a significant amount of his production awaits appearance in further volumes.

Well-stocked academic libraries are likely to have one of the two earlier versions of the *Obras Completas*, either the Afrodisio Aguado/Vergara edition (Barcelona and Madrid, 1958) or the Escelicer edition (Madrid, 1966). These editions, however, have long disappeared from circulation and are not available to the individual researcher except in well-established academic institutions (and not always so: the British Library only has volumes I–V of the nine-volume Escelicer edition). One can only hope that the Biblioteca Castro will quickly resume the project of making the entirety of Unamuno's work available at reasonable cost and in a more logical arrangement than in the two previous versions of the *Obras Completas*. In the meantime one is obliged to refer to one of these other versions in the case of writings still to appear in the Biblioteca Castro edition.

In the present study, all in-text references to Unamuno's works are to the Biblioteca Castro edition of the *Obras Completas* and are given parenthetically by volume and page number. Because of its importance in Unamuno's production, quotations from *Del sentimiento trágico de la vida* carry, in addition, the letters *DSTV*.

Also given parenthetically in the text are references to *Alrededor del estilo*, ed. by Laureano Robles (Salamanca: Ediciones Universidad de Salamanca, 1998), since this is a useful, carefully edited compendium of Unamuno's articles on style and is still available.

All other references to Unamuno's writings (those not available in the Biblioteca Castro or in *Alrededor*) are to the Escelicer edition and are given separately in the endnotes with a clear indication to this effect.

INTRODUCTION

Unamuno's Ideas on the Novel

Poet, novelist, dramatist, essayist, political commentator and existentialist philosopher, as well as devoted educationalist throughout his professional life, Unamuno's polymathic output poses a real problem to would-be interpreters, that of deciding where to begin to tackle a writer of such bewildering versatility. In terms of his production of imaginative literature, critical preferences have been clear. Unamuno's substantial poetic production looks staid in comparison with the exciting developments that were going on at the hands of younger poets, the so-called Generation of 1927; which is not to say that Unamuno's poetry is not deserving of far more attention than it has to date received. Unamuno's plays, it has often been pointed out, are too abstract to captivate any but the most intellectually driven of theatre audiences. Unamuno's fiction, on the other hand, has attracted both a wide readership and a devoted and persistent scholarly following in the last fifty years.[1] *Niebla* (1914) still sells profitably one hundred years after its first appearance and has become the second or third most studied novel in Spanish literature (after *Don Quixote* and possibly *Lazarillo de Tormes*). It has also exerted an incalculable impact on modern Spanish fiction, from the vanguard novel of the 1920s right down to our own time, as witnessed by Carlos Cañeque's Nadal-winning *Quién* (1997) or Jon Juaristi's *La caza salvaje* (2007), winner of the Premio Azorín, to mention but two among many possible titles. Where Unamuno failed as a dramatist he clearly succeeded as a novelist. This book is not, however, concerned with explaining this discrepancy, but rather with explaining his cultivation of the novel genre from the point of view of the ideas he brought to bear on his practice.

The early twentieth century was a time of much theorizing about the craft of fiction following the breakdown of the Realist and Naturalist paradigms. In Spain (as indeed in Europe as a whole) there was a continuing debate about the nature, state, and future of the novel, carried on in the press, in prologues, and in essays (Fernández Cifuentes, 1982). This debate affected both practitioners and critics. It is not uncommon to find, throughout the twentieth century, novelists who have written on the art of fiction, and conversely literary theorists who have tried their hand at writing novels. I am thinking of names such as E. M. Forster, André

---

[1] In his pioneering work *Niebla y soledad* Geoffrey Ribbans was still able to write that Unamuno's novels 'no han sido muy estudiadas, aunque quizá sea cierto que el interés por ellas va en aumento [...] porque se van apreciando más las calidades intrínsecas de las obras de ficción' (Ribbans, 1971: 83). These words were to prove prophetic.

Gide, or Milan Kundera among the former, and Malcolm Bradbury, David Lodge, or Umberto Eco among the latter, although one could easily produce a wholly different list. Among Spanish novelists who have ventured onto the minefield of theory one could mention Ramón Pérez de Ayala, Francisco Ayala, or Manuel García Viñó. Unamuno on the other hand never wrote anything approaching a treatise on the novel, for his *Cómo se hace una novela* certainly does not qualify as such, title notwithstanding.[2] His reluctance to engage in theoretical expositions was simply explained: 'Siempre he creído que los escritores y los publicistas debemos ser muy sobrios en hablar de las cosas del oficio, de procedimientos o de técnica del arte de escribir para el público. Con facilidad se olvida uno de que al público le importa muy poco cómo estén hechas las cosas, con tal de que le sirvan para algo' (VIII, 693).

This reticence did not, however, stop him from often making passing or opportunistic theoretical comments in prologues and epilogues, although these do not help us to decide whether the praxis obeys the theory or the theory arose *post factum* to underpin the praxis. The pattern of Unamuno's novels does strongly suggest that he held particular views about the genre, but these views are implicit in the works rather than explicit in his comments. Nevertheless such extra-novelistic comments as there are need to be borne in mind; hence the advisability of commencing our inquiry with an exposition of Unamuno's stated ideas on the novel.

In two articles of 1902, 'De vuelta' and 'Escritor ovíparo',[3] Unamuno distinguishes between two types of writers: oviparous and viviparous, the former incubating their ideas and collecting the necessary material before commencing to write, the latter giving birth to the work without plan or documentation and no very clear idea of where they are heading. Although his articles, he says, are normally written without a previous plan in order to clarify his ideas, they are subsequently expanded in more substantial essays and thereby follow an oviparous process. His long novel *Paz en la guerra*, which he patiently nurtured over a good many years and which required the accumulation of data over a long period, classifies him, he tells us, as an oviparous writer. Two years later, in 'A lo que salga' (VIII, 693–705), Unamuno declares that he has abandoned oviparism and is trying to become a viviparist writer. The major drawback of oviparism is encumbrance or superfluity, the writer finding it difficult to sacrifice the ideas and details so laboriously collected over the incubation period. For this reason he is now experimenting with writing spontaneously, starting from the kernel of an idea and no further preparation. In fact Unamuno's viviparism has proved to be something of a red herring and has led some critics to assume that from this point onwards all Unamuno's works were unplanned. But it is obvious that many post-1904 novels and plays were not viviparous at all. Their long genesis alone precludes that. We also know that Unamuno planned many of his works beforehand because the notes for them have survived. Spontaneity is therefore relative, and most of his longer works did not follow the pattern of his brief newspaper articles but

---

[2]   In the prologue to *San Manuel Bueno, mártir y tres historias más* Unamuno calls it 'el más entrañado y dolorido relato que me haya brotado del hondón del alma' (II, 310).

[3]   Not so far included in the Biblioteca Castro *Obras Completas*, I–X. They can be consulted in the Escelicer edition of the *Obras Completas*, VIII, 206–07 and 208–10.

were incubated over a long period. For our purposes, rather more interesting than his comparison of the creative process with incubation and live birth, is his passing comment to the effect that spontaneous writing is 'lo más orgánico', whereas writing to a prior plan is 'mecánico' (VIII, 694). The implication of this is clear: Unamuno values organic growth over mechanical assembly. What this reference to writing as organism tells us is that Unamuno has been reading the German and English Romantics, who were respectively the originators and propagators of the concept of organicism in literature in the late eighteenth and early nineteenth centuries. This will become a foundation stone in Unamuno's ideas on the novel and creative writing in general.[4]

Unamuno's next significant comment on novel-writing does not come until 1920, in the prologue to *Tres novelas ejemplares y un prólogo*, which contains his best-known declarations on the art of fiction. Although Unamuno says that this prologue is 'la explicación de mi novelería' (II, 192), the explanation is limited to just four points:

(1) In a creative or poetic novel — Unamuno has in mind the greek *poiesis*, creation — the significance does not lie in the external details of the narrative but in the personal vision of the poet or writer. A writer who lacks that vision will be incapable of writing 'poetically'.

(2) This personal or creative vision, driven by the writer's ambition to overcome or repudiate the limitations of his being and circumstances — what Unamuno terms the 'querer ser' or 'querer no ser' — gives rise to fictional characters who are in some way symbolic of an intimate or inner reality.

(3) This inner reality, reflected in the drama of the fictional characters, is derived from the writer's own conflicting emotions, contradictory impulses, and potential for both good and evil.

(4) A poetic novel extends an invitation to the reader to re-create the artistic experience by seeing the characters as symbols or representations of what each reader potentially carries within himself.

Although these aspects are of significance, they are neither especially original nor specific enough to offer much in the way of explanation of Unamuno's highly personal and richly complex world of fiction. Several of these points re-appear, expressed in slightly altered form, in subsequent prologues and epilogues. For example, the idea that the fictional characters are the natural offspring of the author

---

[4] Francisco La Rubia Prado sees 'A lo que salga' as definitive proof of Unamuno's acceptance of Coleridge's theory of organicism (La Rubia Prado, 1996: 81). But this is because La Rubia Prado identifies oviparism with mechanicism and viviparism with organicism. This is not really justified. Unamuno in his two earlier articles is talking about methods of writing, not about aesthetics or literary theory. An egg after all is a kind of seed, and growth from a seed is the basic image of organicism. Oviparism has nothing to do with mechanicism. Mechanicism is a deterministic concept derived from the physical laws of Newton; in literature it refers to writing according to pre-established rules. Nevertheless, La Rubia Prado is undoubtedly correct in pointing to Coleridge (or more generally the German and English Romantics) as the source of Unamuno's theoretical organicism. Gayana Jurkevich also studies what she calls 'Unamuno's gestational fallacy' (Jurkevich, 1990).

re-appears in the 1928 prologue to *Abel Sánchez*. The prologue to *San Manuel Bueno, mártir y tres historias más* (1932–33) also harks back to the prologue in *Tres novelas ejemplares* and makes similar points:

(1) Any narrative has its own point to make, an outlook or philosophical stance: 'todo relato tiene su sentido trascendente, tiene su filosofía' (II, 302).

(2) For a 'verdadera novela', the plot, the external appearance of the characters, and the setting or external environment are the least important aspects. (This point re-appears in the epilogue to *La novela de don Sandalio* (II, 382))

(3) The truly important point is the inner drama of the character, and it is this aspect which a reader should grasp and make his own.

(4) What is common to virtually all Unamuno's personages is the preoccupation with the nature of personality, of one's being.

I said earlier that *Cómo se hace una novela*, written during Unamuno's exile in France, is not a treatise on the novel. Nevertheless it does contain certain points which need to be borne in mind:

(1) A novel is in some sense the writer's life because the writer's life is, *qua* writer, his mental life. That mental life, revealed through literary images, takes precedence over purely material aspects.

(2) A book serves as a mirror in which we see ourselves, and this applies to the author, to the reader, and to humanity as a whole, since humanity's awareness of its own existence and history is largely derived from books. A nation's identity, like a writer's, is to be found in its literature.

(3) An authentic novel, one that is truly alive, must remain open-ended, incomplete. It can convey no sense of completion, not least because its reader is very much alive.

(4) A novel is an organism, not a mechanism, and therefore is not governed by the deterministic laws that govern the workings of a machine. Unamuno rejects the emerging fashion of explaining the internal workings of a novel as André Gide has recently done in the *Journal des faux-monnayeurs*. Like life itself, a novel has to be lived, felt, rather than explained.

It might be useful at this point to compare the theorizing of Unamuno with that of two other Spanish novelists of the time, Pío Baroja and Ramón Pérez de Ayala, both of whom made interesting contributions to novelistic theory. In his well-known 'Prólogo casi doctrinal sobre la novela' Baroja makes the following points:

(1) The novel is a malleable genre which admits an infinity of variations.

(2) A novel has a spiritual or symbolic sense in the same way that a flag has.

(3) Authentic style reflects the psychology of the writer, not the writer's rhetorical skills.

(4) Each novel evinces its own technique rather than following a pre-existing pattern.

(5) A novel is almost invariably a mixture of reality and fantasy.

(6) Its reality comes out of what the writer observes in his milieu.

(7) Its fantasy comes out of the emotional make-up ('fondo sentimental') of the writer.

(8) Character creation is far more important than plot construction.

(9) The best modern novels have an overwhelmingly psychological interest.

(10) This psychological interest derives from unconscious forces.

For his part Pérez de Ayala, although adopting a noticeably more detached and 'classical' posture than the two Basques, makes the following points, dispersed in various of his critical essays and works of fiction:

(1) The modern novel cannot keep up with new scientific discoveries.

(2) It should not therefore attempt to treat existing or observed phenomena empirically, as the Naturalists have done.

(3) If it is to survive, the novel must strive sympathetically to capture psychological states in all their incoherence and indefiniteness rather than classify or categorize.

(4) A novelist should be open to the techniques of other arts, e.g. painting and music.

(5) A novel is not a copy of anything, even other novels; it must create its own living microcosm ('un breve universo').

(6) A novelist should as far as possible subordinate description or enumeration to a particular vision or conceptualization.

(7) The novel genre is in a permanent state of 'crisis' (in the Greek sense of judgment or turning point) because its function is precisely to assess and transform itself.

(8) A novel should offer a multi-viewpoint vista ('visión pluridimensional').

(9) This in-depth vision requires the use of perspectivist techniques.

(10) A good novel does not distract the reader but leads him to a 'contemplación serena'; it provides not escapism but insight.

Already we can see how Baroja and Pérez de Ayala, rather different kinds of novelists, nevertheless offer some surprisingly similar views of the genre. By way of comparison, Unamuno's expressed ideas might be summed up as follows:

(1) The realist novel falsifies reality because it deals only in appearances.

(2) A novel should be like poetry — it should offer a poetic substance rather than facts and descriptions.

(3) The plot of a novel should be subordinated to its sense, what it stands for.

(4) This transcendent sense is achieved via the inner life of the characters, which is usually reflected through their internal dialogues ('monodiálogos').

(5) The novelistic character should have a vision, a 'dream' or striving towards.

(6) This vision of the character is a metaphor of the mental life of the author rather than a representation of his or her person.

(7) The reader must share in the creative task of bringing the characters to life.

(8) A novel is not a mechanical artefact fixed for all time but a living organism or microcosm subject to constant re-shaping at the hands of its readers.

That these three practitioners of fiction (Pérez de Ayala was also a literary critic of high repute) should feel the urge to venture into the field of theory is some indication of their concern not just with the novel of their day, but also with the perception of their own fiction. All three were to an extent responding to criticism of their work or to their own dissatisfaction with prevailing practices. Baroja was responding to Ortega and his theories, Unamuno to barbed remarks about his 'eccentricities', and Pérez de Ayala, as his passing remarks let drop, to his own exasperation with the superficiality, sensationalism, and forced plots of much contemporary fiction. What is most interesting about these responses is how much they have in common, for all three appear to coincide on a number of points that one might paraphrase as follows.

The first point of coincidence is that the main function of a novel is not to describe from the outside but to provide some kind of insight into what lies behind the world of phenomena. The novel should not emulate scientific disciplines by dealing with abstractions or general truths; rather should it try to capture the world that lies shrouded or hidden from our normal gaze. Even if the observed milieu cannot be eliminated from the novel, the novel has to imagine the world within, and this has to be done via the creation of particular ways of seeing, it has to be done ontologically and not discursively, as Unamuno wrote elsewhere.[5] The second point in common is an obvious consequence of this, namely, the crucial importance of character-creation, since it is the characters who provide the necessary interpretative or subjective framework, the point of view.[6] In consonance with Ortega's philosophy, the view from nowhere does not exist for us humans, and most contemporary novelists of note would have assented. It is here, a third area of agreement, that the personality or 'mind' of the writer is seen to play a key role, since those imagined characters who drive the novel forward and give it its sense must necessarily emerge from the writer's own psyche.[7] These central characters are not the writer himself, as Unamuno and Pérez de Ayala make clear, but products of the writer's pathos, of his sympathies or antipathies.

The fourth point is an extension of this, namely, that a novel speaks to us in a symbolic way. It creates a universe which conveys a sense of values. It is for this reason that a novel is, like a poem, a unique experience. And fifthly, it is the reader who becomes the subject of the experience, for in the reader is invested the responsibility to read in such a way as to penetrate 'la caverna que tiene dentro sus surtidores', as Baroja put it in his famous prologue. Thus from the creative source

[5] '[...] en el orden del ser intuitivamente reflejado en nosotros, no en el orden del conocer discursivamente expuesto' ('Notas sobre el determinismo en la novela', *Obras Completas* (Escelicer), IX, 771–72).

[6] 'Inhíbete en tu persona de novelista', Don Amaranto de Fraile advises the novelist in *Belarmino y Apolonio*. 'Haz que otras dos personas la vean [the Rua Ruera] al propio tiempo, desde ángulos laterales contrapuestos' (Pérez de Ayala, 1976: 93).

[7] Baroja said that in his case minor characters were observed types, whereas major characters borrowed a great deal from himself.

deep within the writer, via the propelling conduits of the characters, to the flowing stream within the reader, the novel was regarded as a living entity. Not only does it encapsulate a writerly universe, but it also has the potential to help us understand our readerly way of seeing the world.

The foregoing considerations on the theoretical comments of these three novelists seem to point to a strong similarity in their respective notions of the novel, notwithstanding their very different novelistic products. Does this suggest that the theory has a limited impact on the praxis? Does the theorizing amount to the same kind of abstraction, or generalization, that these same writers criticize in pseudo-scientific writing? Or does it genuinely help us to understand what the novels are about and why? For the moment all that can be said about Unamuno's conception of the genre is, firstly, that, judging only by his explicit comments, it is not so very different from that of his contemporaries; and secondly that key points are borrowed from earlier writers and thinkers. Literature as organism and not mechanism is a deeply Romantic notion, while the idea that spontaneous writing — writing 'a lo que salga' or 'sin saber lo que vendrá' as Víctor Goti puts it in *Niebla* (I, 571) — carries greater authenticity and impact is quite simply Unamuno's idiosyncratic rendering of Schopenhauer's views on art.

Schopenhauer had argued that what we appreciate in great art is its inner nature rather than any concept that underlies its composition. Indeed 'a work of art, the conception of which has resulted from mere, distinct concepts, is always ungenuine.' If what a work of art expresses can also be expressed using concepts in the way that a philosopher uses concepts, then that work of art is no such thing. A genuine poem cannot be reduced to an abstract truth. A writer who can explain, before setting out to write, precisely what his work will tell us need not bother to compose it. Only the driving idea, says Schopenhauer (and for him idea is the equivalent of a Platonic 'form'), should precede the work: 'Naturally the artist should think when arranging his work, but only *that* idea which was *perceived* before it was thought has suggestive and stimulating force when it is communicated, and thereby becomes imperishable.' This is exactly what Unamuno says he is practising: 'me pongo a escribir, como ahora he hecho, a lo que salga, aunque guiado ¡claro está! por una idea inicial de la que habrán de irse desarrollando las sucesivas' (VIII, 697). This kernel of an idea will become the 'sentido trascendente' that Unamuno later declares each narrative to possess. Furthermore, the idea (which appears in several of Unamuno's essays and prologues) that an excess of detail or information harms a work of art because it leaves no room for the active imagination of the beholder also comes from Schopenhauer. No work of art exists except through the medium of the imagination, and the imagination, says Schopenhauer, must be led 'onto the right path. Something, and indeed the final thing, must always be left over for it to do. Even the author must always leave something over for the reader to think.'[8] Thus Unamuno's notions on writing spontaneously, from the kernel of an idea, with a minimum of descriptive detail, and allowing the reader the space

[8] The quotations from Schopenhauer are taken from *The World as Will and Representation* (Schopenhauer, 1966: II, 407–09). Unamuno quite possibly took the word *niebla* from Schopenhauer, where it occurs in this same section.

to complete the account, are all to be found in Schopenhauer, arguably the thinker who left the biggest imprint on him.[9]

Unamuno's empathy with the organicists of the early nineteenth century is also easily explained. In his twenties Unamuno had been greatly influenced by Herbert Spencer and Hippolyte Taine.[10] Taine in particular had brought to bear a 'scientific' approach to the study of literature, which he sought to explain in terms of cause and effect according to the principles of Newtonian physics. Literature might appear to be a complex phenomenon, but it could be reduced to essential facts that could in turn be explained by racial, environmental, and circumstantial factors (' la race, le milieu, et le moment' as he said in the introduction to his *Histoire de la littérature anglaise* (1863)). When Unamuno, following a religious crisis, turned against Positivism in the late 1890s, blaming it for supplanting the spiritual view of mankind and its cultural pursuits with a spurious materialism that explained nothing, and savagely denouncing Taine as a fraudster, he found in the organicism of Coleridge and other Romantics a literary poetics that was much closer to his outlook and on which he could draw to justify or explain his own creative endeavours. This has, of course, nothing to do with *how* one writes and everything to do with *why*, with the core impulse to express oneself.

Organicism helps us to understand the basis of Unamuno's poetics, but by no means does it explain the complexities and ambiguities of his stance, a stance provoked not by the discovery of Coleridge but by his rejection of what he termed *cientificismo*, the pseudo-science which he saw as the prime mover of Positivism. It is for this reason that he rejected Zola's brand of Naturalism. What Naturalism did was to falsify art by trying to turn itself into something it could not be: a science based on logical abstraction.[11] The mis-application of science to fields unsuited to its methods, notably the arts, was of course denounced by many in late nineteenth-century Europe. To this has to be added what was a mark of the time, but more especially in Spain: the desire on the part of new writers to break free of the encumbrance of what Eamonn Rodgers has termed the 'ruled-bound mentality with regard to literature' that still prevailed in academic and literary circles in late nineteenth-century Spain: 'The continuing vitality of classical literary theory meant an almost obsessive preoccupation with rules, reflecting in the artistic sphere the hierarchical and authoritarian assumptions that governed both education and political life' (Rodgers, 1992: 121). Liberation from hidebound rules and conventions

---

[9] Unamuno did not acknowledge his debt to Schopenhauer specifically on the subject of aesthetics; but he did declare that Schopenhauer was one of a very few philosophers who had left a deep imprint on him. To his friend Pedro Múgica he wrote in 1890 that Schopenhauer was the philosopher he most enjoyed reading. His own translation of *On the Will in Nature* was published in 1901. In his exhaustive philosophical survey of Unamuno's work, *Las máscaras de lo trágico*, Pedro Cerezo Galán has described Schopenhauer's influence on Unamuno as decisive (Cerezo Galán, 1996: 273).

[10] The influence of Taine on the young Unamuno has been studied by Herbert Ramsden in his *The 1898 Movement in Spain: Towards a Reinterpretation* (Ramsden, 1974).

[11] For the role that the rejection of Naturalism played in the emergence of the new novel see Longhurst, 1999.

is an expressed desire on the part of many writers of the early years of the twentieth century, including Unamuno, Baroja, and Azorín.

As far as Unamuno's recorded statements are concerned, we can provisionally conclude that the debt to Schopenhauer is there, as is his acceptance of the organic view of the Romantics, as well as the striking coincidences with other Spanish novelists' theoretical pronunciations on the novel. But this at best provides only a very partial explanation of Unamuno's highly personal approaches to narrative fiction. In his praxis, Unamuno took these ideas further. It is time to see how these theoretical notions have helped to fashion Unamuno's novels, or indeed how the latter implicitly convey those notions which appear to be built into their fabric. We must start, however, by considering a fundamental aspect of Unamuno's philosophical outlook.

CHAPTER 1

Physical and Mental Worlds

Body and Mind

With typically playful but pointed provocativeness Unamuno reversed the Cart-esian 'cogito, ergo sum'. One doubts, however, if Descartes would have seriously objected to Unamuno's 'homo sum, ergo cogito' (*DSTV*, X, 519), since such a reversal does not negate the Frenchman's contention that being fully aware of his own thinking provided the certainty that he needed in order to convince himself of his existence. Whether such conviction comes from awareness of our own thought processes or simply from an in-built instinct makes little practical difference, and in some respects Unamuno remains a Cartesian. When in 'Civilización y cultura' he writes 'hay un ambiente exterior, el mundo de los fenómenos sensibles, que nos envuelve y sustenta, y un ambiente interior, nuestra propia conciencia, el mundo de nuestras ideas, imaginaciones, deseos y sentimientos' (VIII, 381), he is making essentially the same well-known distinction that Descartes made between *res extensa* and *res cogitans*, even if for Unamuno the dividing line between the two is rather more blurred than for the Frenchman. For Descartes, the mind (or soul), *res cogitans*, is a thinking entity, and a thinking entity is its thoughts and has no existence separate from those thoughts. The body, *res extensa*, is a physical entity, and as such it must have dimension (or measurement, or shape or volume), whereas thoughts do not have dimension. Descartes's distinction can scarcely be more commonsensical, whatever explanation we then go on to favour for the appearance of mind rather than accept his circumstantially 'safe' explanation that God allows it to be self-standing and perduring. But as we shall see, Unamuno's apparent rejection of Descartes is not based on his having found a better explanation for the human person as a thinking being.

Of Unamuno's reversal of Descartes Pedro Cerezo Galán has written: 'Unamuno ha emprendido su propio camino de pensamiento, lo que le permite enfrentarse a Descartes con una agudeza y originalidad incontestables' (Cerezo Galán, 1996: 392). But there is a flaw in Unamuno's confrontation with Descartes which Cerezo Galán fails to mention, namely that the phrase 'homo sum' already contains the concept 'man'. In order to say 'I am a man, therefore I think', one has to think of the idea of man. The problem with Unamuno's approach is that he insists on giving priority to *sentir* over *pensar*, or indeed in employing the former verb where the latter would have been employed more conventionally. In practice the difference between saying 'I feel myself to exist' and 'I think of myself as existing' is nil, since both expressions reduce to self-awareness. If properly understood, the sense of the Cartesian *cogito* ('I do not doubt that I am thinking, and if I am thinking I must be alive') is simply incontestable, and Unamuno's and later Heidegger's strictures on Descartes smack of self-serving sophistry.[1] Even worse, when Unamuno insists that 'pensamos porque vivimos' (*DSTV*, X, 480), he is descending to the level of platitude. Such, however, is his distrust of the unbridled supremacy of reason that he misses no opportunity to remind his readers that they are sentient beings and not merely rational ones. Unamuno's insistence that thinking cannot be abstracted from our total human circumstance is of course a perfectly respectable stance to take, since our intellectual faculty is but a part of our make-up alongside our many other faculties, sensory, motor, emotive, imaginative, or ethical. Thus while Descartes is comfortable in separating his self from his body (the body as *res extensa* is not part of the self but is possessed and moved by it), Unamuno, like Schopenhauer, is not prepared to make such a distinction: 'Es mi cuerpo vivo el que piensa, quiere y siente' (*DSTV*, X, 342). This is another apparent reversal of Descartes: not a case of my immaterial mind or self possessing a body but of my material body possessing an immaterial self as its centre of operations, something which brings Unamuno right up into orthodox twentieth-century views of the mind–body problem. While this view clearly implies that human existence cannot be considered apart from the body, and in this sense is rather different from Descartes's theistic explanation of the reality of things, nevertheless Cartesian dualism is still present in the mind–matter or mind–body distinction.[2]

Reversing the Cartesian *cogito*, as most of the existentialists do, does not reverse its implications. 'I am, therefore I think' is as much an epistemological statement as an ontological one. I am = I know that I am. The starting point may be different, since for both Unamuno and the existentialists existence is prior to thinking. But as Wittgenstein reasoned in the *Tractatus*, if meaning is to exist, logic must precede experience. Since existence is experience, it follows that logic, our disposition to reasoning, must precede existence. What appears to characterize human beings is precisely a heightened awareness of existing. Being and thinking are so closely intertwined that in practice reversing Descartes's reasoning is little more than a tactical shift. The only useful distinction is that in Descartes the self is seen purely as subject and in existentialism the self is seen as agent. But whether this overcomes the Cartesian subject–object dualism, as Heidegger and some others have claimed, appears doubtful. Even if man is seen as a psychosomatic unity, the mind–body

---

[1] Kant called the Cartesian *cogito* tautological (Kant, 1998: 419). If Kant is right, reversing it can make no difference.

[2] Not all contemporary philosophers would accept this. Among the most distinguished, John R. Searle categorically states that he rejects dualism. At the same time he denies that thought is a material product and can be reduced to brain function (neuronal behaviour). In *The Mystery of Consciousness* he replaces mind–body dualism with a dualism of his own: an observer-dependent world and a non-observer-dependent world (force, mass and gravity are his examples of the latter) (Searle, 1997: 3–18 and 189–214). But a nagging doubt remains. How can one tell what a non-observer-dependent world is really like? It does not seem a reassuring notion. Modern physics, after all, allows for the 'observer-effect' in any experiment set up to study scientific phenomena. The properties of nature could well depend on the way we approach her.

problem remains, if not as a dualism then at least as a problem of consciousness, because there is no adequate explanation of consciousness. A body remains a body without consciousness, so we cannot simply equate the two.[3] And this is so despite the existentialists' attempt to subsume all categories including epistemological ones under the single status of 'being-in-the-world'. If we cannot account for consciousness, we cannot account for the mind as we can account for the body. Nevertheless we can observe a significant difference of emphasis between a Cartesian and an existentialist approach, seen at its clearest perhaps in the treatment of the body. To exist is not simply to *have* a body but to *be* a body. When you do not entertain a dualist stance, argues Unamuno, you do not even need a name to refer to the body: 'Tendrá uno que hablar de su cabeza, de sus brazos, de sus manos, de su pecho, de su vientre, de sus pies, de su corazón, de su hígado, de su estómago, y así; pero su cuerpo es él mismo, mi cuerpo soy yo' (*Alrededor*, 57).[4]

Does this make of Unamuno some kind of physical monist? In fact, despite saying that 'I am my body and its states of consciousness', Unamuno was no physicalist in the sense that mental states are seen as simple attributes of a physical entity. For Unamuno the self (strictly the 'yo' or my own self-awareness) is not a physical entity even though it is wholly dependent on such an entity to manifest itself. What Unamuno posits is a dependence rather than a congruence: the mind can only exist as long as the body exists; there is no disembodied 'I'. But if Unamuno does not take up the Cartesian position whereby body and mind are completely different things, neither does he take up the diametrically opposed position of modern neuroscience that holds mind to be no more than the activity of brain cells. If the 'I' is the brain, then the brain is capable of a wide range of states, a happy state, a fearful state, an aggressive state, a relaxed state, a distressed state, and so forth, and it is also capable of states of belief, of expectation, of regret, and so on. How can a physical entity experience and sustain such states? It simply is not known. Moreover the brain can recognize what sort of state it is in, which makes the proposition brain = self even more of a conundrum. The mental is irredeemably subjective; but we cannot explain how subjectivity can inhere in a purely material object. The physiological explanation of the self is for Unamuno no more acceptable than Descartes's view of it. While Unamuno does not accept the free-floating Cartesian ego, neither does he reduce the self to the brain, because such a reduction would be entirely

---

[3]   The problem of integrating the mind and the body, which reduces to explaining consciousness, continues unsolved despite the efforts of 'neuro-philosophers'. In his *The Empirical Stance*, the distinguished empiricist Bas C. van Fraassen has recently written: 'We can dispense with mind–body dualism at once, or so it seems to me. There is a mystery about consciousness, a mystery about how it is possible for flesh and bones to think, feel, and communicate. But how could that mystery be dispelled by postulating a special mental substance as bearer of consciousness? Drop the rhetorically chosen persuasive name of "mental substance", call it "ectoplasm", say, and you see at once that the mystery remains unchanged. It is just as difficult to understand how ectoplasm can think as how flesh and blood can think' (van Fraassen, 2002: 190).

[4]   Wittgenstein made the same point. When we talk of 'my body' the possessive pronoun is misleading and does not prove that there is an 'I' or a self that possesses a body. And before Wittgenstein the point was made by William James and Gabriel Marcel. Nevertheless this does not necessarily mean that all psychological phenomena must have physiological counterparts.

materialist, and what interests Unamuno in human beings are their aspirations and hopes. Could he, then, be occupying that position later to be described as 'neutral monism', one that rejects dualism, materialism, and idealism preferring to see the mental as a transphysical brain state?

Again there is no conclusive evidence that Unamuno subscribed to this kind of monism. He dismisses what he pejoratively labels 'engañifas de monismo' (DSTV, X, 312), but this only really refers to monism as the doctrine of the indestructibility of matter taken as a pointer to personal perdurance. Unamuno, like St Thomas Aquinas, cannot conceive of existing without a body, so being transformed into some other kind of substance such as divine energy is no consolation. If that makes him a materialist, he says, so be it. But it is entirely a materialism based on the hope that God will conserve the reality and integrity of his self-consciousness, since personal survival without self-consciousness is meaningless. It seems likely that Unamuno's anti-Cartesianism developed under the influence of Spinoza, whom he mentions in passing on a number of occasions. At times he does seem to blur the distinction between mind and matter, as when he says 'Nuestro espíritu es también alguna especie de materia o no es nada' (DSTV, X, 312), which is strongly reminiscent of Spinoza's 'the mind and the body are one and the same individual, which is conceived now under the attribute of thought, now under the attribute of extension' (Spinoza, 1996: 48). Spinoza rejected Descartes's two distinct and separate kinds of substance (res cogitans and res extensa, though it would be more correct to say that Descartes was referring to properties rather than what we understand by substances) in favour of two ways of apprehending the objects of nature, and Unamuno's position is very close to this. In the sentence just quoted, the phrase 'some kind of matter' is unhelpfully vague, but the statement does seem to suggest that there are not two fundamental ingredients to existence but only one. On the face of it, therefore, Unamuno may be reverting to Spinozism and proposing the ultimate identity of mind and matter, just as in Spinoza thought and extension are two different expressions of a single being or nature, a view that is a clear forerunner of the neutral monism favoured by modern philosophers such as Bertrand Russell and Thomas Nagel, namely that mind cannot be reduced to matter nor matter to mind but that both are the result of a common, as yet unidentified, agent. Unamuno appears to agree with Spinoza that body and soul are the same thing looked at from different perspectives. Unlike Spinoza, however, he does not say that mind and matter are different modes of manifestation of an underlying reality, call it God or Nature. What he does say is that they are not separable; but not how one gives rise to the other or a third to both.

In Unamuno, then, as in philosophy and psychology at large, the perennial problem of consciousness essential to the concept of mind remains prominent and unresolved. Consciousness does not fit in comfortably within a physical world, despite being an essential aspect of our existence. Until we understand what it is or how it comes about we will be unable to solve the mind–body conundrum or provide a satisfactory alternative to Cartesianism. One wonders what Unamuno would have made of later twentieth-century materialist theories of the mind which either identify a mental state with a neural state (type-identity theory), or even more radically discard so-called mental events, beliefs, desires, anxieties, etc., as nonsense (eliminativism). At any rate we can safely say that Unamuno was no epiphenomenalist: for him mental events were certainly produced via a bodily entity, but belonged to a self-conscious entity capable of exercising control over the body.[5]

It is possible that Unamuno's concept of mind was to a degree influenced by Plato, familiar as he necessarily was with this classical thinker through his professorship of Greek at the University of Salamanca. We need to remember Plato's well-known distinction between desire and reason. The mind, though usually moved by rational thought, can overcome the desires of the body if it sees fit to do so without need of a rational or known motivation for so doing. It is free to act of its own accord. In the *Theaetetus* Plato presents Socrates arguing that the mind, far from being subservient to the body, has the capacity to follow its own path. The sensory perceptions that we receive through our body and the knowledge or judgments that occur in our mind need have no connection (Plato, 1997: 182, 203–07). The mind can consider aspects which do not come to us through the senses. So it can work in tandem with the body or independently of it, discovering things in which the body has no interest. This was a point grasped by Descartes and developed into a full-blown distinction between our bodily self and our thinking self. In Descartes a person is therefore a result of an interaction between a material entity and a non-material entity, though the nature of this interaction is not really explained. In Unamuno, however, a person is a material substance capable of non-material states, of which he consistently emphasized *querer, amar, sentir,* and their corresponding nouns *voluntad, amor,* and *sentimiento.* These were for Unamuno transcendental states that go beyond bodily pains, pleasures, and appetites. Among his favourite words are *alma, espíritu,* and *verdad* (the last not with a logical but with a moral sense, having more to do with sincerity than with logic), words which he used (and abused) not just when discussing religious matters, but just as often when discussing historical phenomena, thereby revealing an aspiration to penetrate the phenomenological veil. Where Unamuno really does differ from Descartes is in not accepting the latter's view that one's self is revealed by introspection. Too much introspection, according to Unamuno, reveals precisely nothing. We do not have an objective view of our own selves. 'I' appears to be a form of identity as are 'you', 'he', 'she', or 'they'. What we can attach to this 'I' by way of characterization comes not from within but from what we observe outside of us. The reason why Unamuno does not see himself as a Cartesian is that he believes the 'I' to arise from a reciprocal I–You system. In Descartes the 'I' is self-standing; in Unamuno the 'I' exists in relation to the 'You'. By recognizing that others are aware of me I become aware of myself,

---

[5] For a comparison of Unamuno's views on the mind–body problem with those of late twentieth-century analytic philosophers see Barry J. Luby, 2008. Luby is excellent on comparisons, but his insistence on seeing Unamuno as precursor of a whole range of late twentieth-century and twenty-first-century thinkers makes him disregard the eighteenth-century and early nineteenth-century thinkers on whom Unamuno's thought is very largely based. There is for example no mention of Schleiermacher or Humboldt, from whom Unamuno took most of his ideas on language. And there is only a single (and highly debatable) passing mention of Schopenhauer, the philosopher who made the greatest impact on Unamuno.

as well as contributing to others' awareness of themselves. Naturally this mutual reinforcement requires that there be a strong mind–body association, since what others see in me and what I see in others is first of all a body, and in that body we recognize a state of consciousness. An identity is thus a communal, not simply an individual, phenomenon. 'Yo y el mundo nos hacemos mutuamente' (VII, 381) is one of the key statements that Unamuno several times made in his essays. There is no clear dividing line between the inner and outer worlds. Each is a product of the other.

The inner world, then, is in part produced by the outer world; but that outer world is of course composed of other people, who will have their own inner worlds. Unamuno appears to be a materialist and an idealist all at the same time, tending towards one or the other depending on his particular comments. His attempt to source the 'I' in either the mental or the physical realms is inconclusive. What he is left with is an inter-subjective relationship in which identity or self is made up of an I-in-you or mirror-phenomenon, my 'I' being founded on my reaction to others' views of me. We do not grasp our nature a priori, but only as part of a network. But this, as we shall see, is not without its problems.

In part at least, Unamuno's uncertain position between dualism and monism, and between materialism and idealism, is due to his overriding interest in personality, in what makes us what we are or the way we are, and the *idea* of person is inextricably connected to the question of mind and cannot simply be a matter of physiology. It is also a matter of judgment. It was Schopenhauer who pointed out (in his *Essay on the Freedom of the Will*) that we tend to judge persons by what they are rather than by what they do: 'The deed together with the motive is regarded here merely as evidence of the character of the doer; it is looked upon as a sure symptom of the character by which the latter is established irrevocably and for all time' (Schopenhauer, 1999: 94). We judge a person by his or her actions in the broadest sense because to these actions, comportment, or attitudes, we ascribe intentions. The problem now becomes how to reconcile intentions with the physical, since the intentional state does not readily appear to be attached to material states, indeed can arise from false, therefore non-factual, assumptions. The concept of personhood, closely connected to intentionality, becomes enormously complex and perhaps ultimately inapprehensible.

If we accept Franz Brentano's view that the defining characteristic of mentality is intentionality, the idea of person must be closely connected to the question of mind, since we observe intentions in a person. A person is an agent capable of intentions and decisions: the agent's state of mind is 'directed at' something. Are these intentions and decisions brought about by an elementary consciousness (including unconscious drives, like those of an animal driven to look for food or drink) or is some higher-level consciousness, self-consciousness or self-identity, also necessary? Clearly a person's intentionality covers a vastly greater and more sophisticated range of potential targets than an animal's. Unamuno's concept of 'querer ser' or will-to-be, is in some ways similar to Brentano's intentionality (covering all intentional states such as desires, beliefs, hopes, fears, etc.) and suffers from the same perplexing feature. The person we aspire to be does not exist; or at least can only have a noumenal, not a phenomenal existence.[6] Since I can easily conceive of the non-existent, desire the impossible, fear the unreal, and so on, how do I explain the relationship between my mind, which I deem to exist, and something that does not? Indeed it is this impasse that has persuaded some philosophers and psychologists to deny the existence of minds. But this of course is not in itself satisfactory, for, as Paul Feyerabend reminds us in a posthumously published work, if we consider that the 'real is what plays a central role in the kind of life we identify with', then the real is bound to include non-physical phenomena (Feyerabend, 2001: 201) My intentions must therefore be real, irrespective of whether they are directed at something substantive or not. The problem is how to explain those intentions that have no obvious connection to my immediate needs.

Influenced perhaps by Schopenhauer, Unamuno is at some pains to reconcile the phenomenological and the noumenal; unlike the more extreme idealists he has no wish to devalue the world of phenomena in order to assert the world of pure ideas. Indeed he often asserts the influence of physiology on mental attitudes, for example in *Del sentimiento trágico de la vida* or in *Niebla*.[7] How does the ideal world arise? In Chapter II of *Del sentimiento trágico de la vida* Unamuno appears to argue that the ideal world originates in the instinct to perpetuate the species, that physical love in turn generates ideal love: '¿Quien nos dice que no haya un mundo invisible e intangible, percibido por el sentido íntimo que vive al servicio del instinto de perpetuación?' (*DSTV*, X , 296). This seems to suggest that the world of ideas is a by-product of the material world, but Unamuno does not sustain this explanation for long. Rather does he argue that the world of the mind (or spirit, since he often uses the words interchangeably) is constrained by the world of matter, but not defined by it: 'Hállase el espíritu limitado por la materia en que tiene que vivir y cobrar conciencia de sí, de la misma manera que está el pensamiento limitado por la palabra, que es su cuerpo social. Sin materia no hay espíritu, pero la materia hace sufrir al espíritu limitándolo' (*DSTV*, X, 443). The analogy with language is easy to follow. Since our thoughts, in order to gain form and recognition, have to be expressed in language, they are constrained and shaped by the social medium employed. Unamuno speaks of 'la barrera' that matter places in front of the spirit. He is consequently maintaining a dualist position, but with the important rider that the mental world has to exist in, to come to terms with, the physical world. Spirit is to matter as thought is to language, not congruent with it but delimited by it. As the great nineteenth-century linguistician Max Müller showed, religion, the prime expression of the world of the spirit, is inconceivable without language

---

[6] Unless otherwise indicated, I do not use noumenon in the restricted Kantian sense of thing-in-itself (and therefore not an object of knowledge), but in the more conventional sense of something that exists only in our minds and has no physical counterpart, closer perhaps to Plato's Ideas or Forms.

[7] 'No suelen ser nuestras ideas las que nos hacen optimistas o pesimistas, sino que es nuestro optimismo o nuestro pesimismo, de origen fisiológico o patológico quizás, tanto el uno como el otro, el que hace nuestras ideas' (*DSTV*, X, 276); and in *Niebla* he makes his character Augusto Pérez declare: 'No hay más verdad que la vida fisiológica' (I, 577), although we must be wary of identifying the author's views with the character's.

even though it is not coterminous with it (Müller, 2002).[8] Unamuno is arguing in much the same way, although on a broader front. The world of the mind, of ideas and beliefs, and of our conventions generally, is for us humans as real as the world of matter but does not exist independently of the latter. My mind is consequently wholly dependent on my body.

It is here that once again we observe the different emphasis between Unamuno and the existentialists on the one hand and the Cartesians on the other. In the Cartesian tradition the 'I' appears to be separate from the body in the sense that it belongs to a different realm. Since in Descartes's method the existence of the body was subject to radical doubt, he needed the 'I' to be quite separate from the body, and it is on this point that many have parted company with him. The 'I' was what had thoughts and whose existence could therefore not be doubted because thinking cannot be doubted. This allowed Descartes to establish a clear distinction between what is subject to mechanical forces, the body, and what is not, the mind or soul. One of his intentions was to put an end to the sterile and unsettling debate over the destiny of the body by disengaging the immaterial soul from its material and perishable companion. This made the survival or immortality of the soul that much more explicable. By effectively putting Humpty Dumpty together again Unamuno undermines the case for the survival of individual consciousness, and this has immediate repercussions both on his ontology and, even more obviously, on his religious belief, which he is forced to turn into a paradoxical struggle for belief in something which is manifestly destructible. In existentialism the 'I' is not the pure thinking subject that it is in Descartes. Indeed what Unamuno and the existentialists (notably Heidegger) object to in Cartesianism turns out to be less the dualism of mind and body, or of subject and object, and more the concomitant idea of a pure thinking subject detached from the spatial world. Existentialism repeatedly insists that we are not separate from the world but very much a part of it, a being-in-the-world as Heidegger puts it. A clinical detachment from our circumstances is an illusion, an abstraction. We have to say, in Ortega y Gasset's well-known adage, 'yo soy yo y mi circunstancia'. What we think and what we know are governed by our participation in what is going on around us, and to that extent our mind is not only body-dependent but world-dependent too. Unamuno put it this way:

> Del ambiente exterior se forma el interior por una especie de condensación orgánica, del mundo de los fenómenos externos el de la conciencia, que reacciona sobre aquél y en él se expansiona. Hay un continuo flujo y reflujo difusivo entre mi conciencia y la naturaleza que me rodea; que es mía también, mi naturaleza [...]. Yo y el mundo nos hacemos mutuamente. (VIII, 381)

The mutuality of the inner and outer worlds is thus a key aspect of Unamuno's thought. Unamuno's self-consciousness, 'la conciencia de mí mismo', emerges from the interplay of the inner and outer worlds. Subject and object are inter-dependent, exactly as Schopenhauer said and as Wittgenstein famously repeated in his private language argument, namely that our consciousness needs the outside world in order

---

[8]   Unamuno's ideas on language are derived in large part from Schleiermacher, Humboldt, and Müller.

to operate. The objects of perception need a knower in order to be known; the subject of perception needs objects in order to function at all. No world, no self-consciousness.

This is where mind and body are seen to work in collaboration. The human body is part of the outer world and has developed in order to interact with it. Since consciousness or self-identity needs a body, and since the body is part of and needs a world, it follows that one's awareness of self is world-dependent to the extent that it is formed through interaction. An explanation along these lines is indeed what we find in Chapter V of *Del sentimiento trágico de la vida*, allowing for the fact that Unamuno is there employing the slippery world *alma*, which he uses profusely and with scant precision, ascribing it to individuals, collectivities, and even artistic works. *Alma* stands for something like non-physical identity, whether it be individual, group, cultural, or social, but a fluid rather than a static identity.[9] It is this spiritual quality that Unamuno discerns in human beings and human civilization that needs to have some element of material representation. Unamuno's position on the mind/matter debate appears to be that we are governed by our minds, or *almas*, and that minds need bodies in order to function. It is only his emphasis on the mental that sets him apart from many philosophers of our own day who look upon mental phenomena as an emergent property of the brain. Despite the religious complications which we encounter in *Del sentimiento trágico de la vida* (such as the invocation of the eucharistic doctrine of transubstantiation to illustrate the concept of substance), Unamuno makes it clear that one cannot deduce the substantiveness and permanence of the soul (or self-identity) from the fact that we retain our self-consciousness in time, while our body is undergoing changes. Here is the key passage:

> Es lo corriente que en los libros de psicología espiritualista, al tratarse de la existencia del alma como sustancia simple y separable del cuerpo, se empiece con una fórmula por este estilo: Hay en mí un principio que piensa, quiere y siente... Lo cual implica una petición de principio. Porque no es una verdad inmediata, ni mucho menos, el que haya en mí tal principio; la verdad inmediata es que pienso, quiero y siento yo. Y yo, el yo que piensa, quiere y siente, es inmediatamente mi cuerpo vivo con los estados de conciencia que soporta. Es mi cuerpo vivo el que piensa, quiere y siente. (*DSTV*, X, 342)

States of consciousness, then, belong in, and are wholly supported by, the body. My 'I' consists of my body together with the thoughts and emotions which it entails. Consciousness cannot be separated from Cartesian *res extensa* but functions entirely through it. It is my living body that makes possible my consciousness. But it does not cause my consciousness any more than my consciousness causes my body. Our perception of a self, therefore, comes to us through our body, but is not our body. What, then, is it?

---

[9]   Unamuno does offer a definition in Chapter V of *Del sentimiento trágico de la vida*: 'Lo que llamamos alma no es más que un término para designar la conciencia individual en su integridad y su persistencia; y que ella cambia, y que lo mismo que se integra se desintegra, es cosa evidente' (*DSTV*, X, 338). Here *alma* is equated with consciousness of self.

Unamuno states his agreement with Hume's contention that he was never aware of a self separate from his perceptions, that all he appeared to be was a bundle of perceptions. But Unamuno does not alight on the obvious inconsistency in Hume's position. To whom did Hume appear to be a bundle of perceptions? He is still using the concept of self or 'I' even as he refers to the alleged absence of a self. The problem with Hume's attitude to the unity of the self or personal identity is that he demands an empirical entity, an experience of self apart from all sensation, and this he does not find. Kant on the other hand held that the 'I' should not be seen empirically but formally. The 'I' is a logical necessity whose function is to ascribe experiences to a person; it is not those experiences, but rather an enabling tool or structural device for experiences to take place meaningfully. I have an in-built conviction that my experiences happen to me, what Kant calls the transcendental unity of apperception (or self-perception), that is, not derived empirically but existing a priori. Unity of consciousness, therefore, is a perspective that I simply know to be mine and which exists across my own conscious time. For Kant, then, unity of experience presupposes this unity of apperception, or awareness of self, for otherwise there would be no link between experiences.

The transcendental unity of apperception may answer Hume's paradox, but we still do not know what this 'I', this consciousness of thinking, is, where or how it originates. Kant says that it is not knowledge of the self. Like Descartes, he equates it with consciousness of thinking, yet does not regard it as an object of consciousness: 'I am conscious of myself not as I appear to myself, nor as I am in myself, but only *that* I am. [...] I therefore have no cognition of myself *as I am*, but only as I *appear* to myself. The consciousness of oneself is therefore far from being a cognition of oneself' (Kant, 1998: 259–60, B 157/158). It follows from this that I cannot deduce that I am a substance or anything else. The 'as-I-am' is therefore a thing-in-itself; but this, puzzlingly, does not prevent me from having a consciousness of myself. The 'I', then, is not a substance or anything tangible, yet something I carry around with me, as Kant argues in the third paralogism of the *Critique of Pure Reason* (Kant, 1998: 422–25, A363/366). The 'I' is not so much a part of the world as a look-out on it, an idea taken up by Schopenhauer in an attempt to clarify Kant's rather abstruse treatment of this matter. For Schopenhauer the unity of consciousness is simply the holder of perceptions or representations, including the reflections of the intellect, which he likens to a string holding the range of pearls in a necklace. The intellect is nevertheless not the soul or the inner man; it is no more than the requirement of a complex organism. 'The necessity of consciousness — he explains — is brought about by the fact that, in consequence of an organism's enhanced complication and thus of its more manifold and varied needs, the acts of its will must be guided by *motives*, no longer by mere stimuli, as at the lower stages. For this purpose it had now to appear furnished with a knowing consciousness, and so with an intellect as the medium and place of the motives' (Schopenhauer, 1966: II, 250–51). Self-consciousness is the focal point of consciousness, of the brain's function, which is to generate representations. At our level of activity we humans need to know that we are capable of representations for the representations to work. 'That focus of brain-activity (or the subject of knowledge) is indeed, as an indivisible point, simple, yet it is not on that account a substance (soul), but a mere condition or state' (Schopenhauer, 1966: II, 278). Such a condition or state is a phenomenon and therefore knowable. But our innermost being, what drives us, cannot simply be a phenomenon, like our brains are, since it has given rise to the brain function — the application of time, space, causality — that it imposes on the world. This innermost being must of necessity have an origin or essence, a point which Kant failed to pursue: 'He had overlooked the fact that, although objective knowledge, or the world as representation, certainly affords nothing but phenomena, together with their phenomenal connexion and regressus, our own inner being nevertheless belongs of necessity to the world of things-in-themselves, since this inner being must be rooted in such a world' (Schopenhauer, 1966: II, 289). This world Schopenhauer identifies with the universal noumenon, which he chose to term Will. The mind is thus as much of a function of the universal will of nature as is our body; only in our representations can we separate out the knowing individual from what is known.

When Unamuno says that 'la unidad de la conciencia no es para la psicología científica — la única racional — sino una identidad fenoménica. Nadie puede decir que sea una unidad sustancial. Es más aún, nadie puede decir que sea una sustancia' (*DSTV*, X, 344), he is echoing both Kant and Schopenhauer.[10] What, who, or how I am exists noumenally (in the narrow Kantian sense); that I appear to be is all I can know. But 'I appear to be' must carry intentionality. It thus becomes not a source of enlightenment but of complications, as Unamuno must have realized. In fact Unamuno seems to have been in something of a muddle himself since, having apparently agreed with Kant and Schopenhauer on the non-substantiality of self-consciousness he later goes on to say that 'lo unico sustancial es la conciencia' (*DSTV*, X, 399). The contradiction may to a degree be resolved by saying that what has substance for Unamuno is the search or desire for an enduring self rather than consciousness itself.

There seems little doubt that Unamuno took on board the somewhat puzzling view of self in the *Critique of Pure Reason*, something which is strongly reflected in the recurrent theme of personal identity which is the driving force behind much of Unamuno's fiction (and even theatre) from about 1900 onwards. Unamuno also subscribes to the Schopenhauerian view (and we should bear in mind that Schopenhauer was a thoroughgoing Kantian in all essentials) that consciousness is first and foremost will. In Schopenhauer the will may be identified with a blind force in nature, but it nevertheless applies to humans as part of the natural world. In Unamuno this driving force or will to survive ('voluntad de no morir', *DSTV*, X, 391), also serves to explain the religious instinct, the drive in mankind towards saving its subjective consciousness. The difference is that Unamuno personalizes

---

[10] In fact the quotation summarizes what Kant said in the first and second paralogisms, namely that the 'I' is neither a substance nor of a simple nature (Kant, 1998: 415–22, A349/361). Schopenhauer's version, in which he states that the subject of knowledge is not a substance but 'a mere condition or state' is found in Chapter 22 of volume 2 of *The World as Will and Representation*. For Schopenhauer the ego is simply the universal Will focused on the organism: it has no separate reality (Schopenhauer, 1966: II, 278).

what in Schopenhauer is ascribed to nature as a whole.[11] It is this personalization that is key to Unamuno's distinction between physical and mental events. While he holds that the mind has no separate existence from the body, his strong sense of personhood or self-awareness suggests to him that mental phenomena are dependent on, but not identical with, physical phenomena, that it is his own conscious way of thinking that confers on him his uniqueness irrespective of Schopenhauer's all-pervasive and undifferentiated Will. The modern philosophical concept of supervenience, which posits that the mental is supervenient on the physical but is not reducible to it, is relevant here. In the supervenience hypothesis, the mental is seen as an emergent property of the physical (the subvenient base). In other words, at a certain point psychological qualities that we associate with mental activity emerge over and above the physical or biological properties. If two objects were to be physically identical, say two living organisms whose cells coincided in every detail, then their psychological qualities would be identical too. In *Del sentimiento trágico de la vida* we find a passage that, religious terminology apart, is close to supervenience theory: 'Las células todas de nuestro cuerpo conspiran y concurren con su actividad a mantener y encender nuestra conciencia, nuestra alma; y si las conciencias o las almas de todas ellas entrasen enteramente en la nuestra, en la componente, si tuviese yo conciencia de todo lo que en mi organismo corporal pasa, sentiría pasar por mí al universo, y se borraría tal vez el doloroso sentimiento de mis límites' (*DSTV*, X, 394). Although Unamuno's picturesque expression ('I would feel the universe passing through me') renders him open to the charge of naturalistic mysticism, what we see in his reference to the role of the cells is a clear hint of pan-psychism (the universality of consciousness throughout all matter), even though he is not actually saying that every individual cell possesses mental powers, which would confer on it the capacity to experience subjectively.[12] Perhaps what Unamuno is getting at is simply that each cell, as a living organism, has a role to play in the emergence of consciousness, that the latter could be after all a biological phenomenon. Given Unamuno's interest in and fictional explorations of the phenomenon of 'the double', 'el otro', and his frequent combination (though never identification) of physiological and psychological properties in his characters, and given that on occasion he makes statements positing a correlation between physical and mental states, supervenience is one possible way of describing his

[11] In his edition of *Del sentimiento trágico de la vida en los hombres y en los pueblos y Tratado del amor de Dios*, Nelson Orringer adds at this point the following clarificatory note explaining the difference as follows: 'Schopenhauer sostiene, como Unamuno, que en cada individuo la voluntad-de-vivir se manifiesta tanto como un impulso de autoconservación como un impulso de autopreservación a través de todo el tiempo. Pero en la metafísica de Schopenhauer, la voluntad *universal* es la única realidad; en Unamuno, la realidad es el deseo *individual* de perseverar en el ser y de extenderse a través del tiempo' (Unamuno, 2005: 294, n. 72).

[12] The hint of pan-psychism detectable in Unamuno may well be an echo of William James (James, 1950: 148–49, especially 'consciousness in some shape must have been present at the very origin of things'). Cf. Thomas Nagel: 'If the mental properties of an organism are not implied by any physical properties but must derive from properties of the organism's constituents, then those constituents must have non-physical properties from which the appearance of mental properties follows when the combination is of the right kind. Since any matter can compose an organism, all matter must have these properties' (Nagel, 1979: 182).

somewhat fuzzy treatment of the mind–body problem. One has to add, of course, that supervenience is a minimal theory and tells us nothing about the nature of psycho-physical dependency. All it does, as Unamuno himself appears to do, is to suggest that for every living object, a person in our particular case, the physical presence of that person, including relational and circumstantial attributes, gives rise to mental properties that characterize that person as much as do physical properties. It certainly does not explain why. Nor does this — the explanation of the mind–body dichotomy — appear to interest Unamuno greatly. What does interest him, to the point of obsession, is differentiation, the surprising extent to which people are characterized by their mental make-up, what it is that makes one person so different from another when physically we are little better than sheep. In his fiction Unamuno repeatedly explores this phenomenon within the realm of the mental, rather than the physical, although of course human relations bridge the gap between the two. It is the movement from the physical to the mental that characterizes much of Unamuno's fiction. Indeed he refers to organic beings as striving to achieve plenitude by breaking out of the physical moulds ('romper sus límites'), and he goes on to identify man's philosophical endeavours with this aspiration to transcend the physical world: 'Este proceso de personalización o de subjetivación de todo lo externo, fenoménico u objetivo, constituye el proceso mismo vital de la filosofía' (*DSTV*, X, 389).

And not only of philosophy, we might add, but also of history. For Unamuno uses the same distinction to explain his non-materialist (i.e. non-Marxist) view of history, something he does very straightforwardly in Chapter IV of *La agonía del cristianismo* with reference to the historical Jesus. His starting point is his well-known argument concerning the ascendancy of fictional progeny, such as Don Quixote or Hamlet, over the flesh-and-blood writers who created them. The latter represent the empirical entity; the former their mental representations. The physical reality and the mental projection of a historical individual are two different things:

> Habría que distinguir, ante todo, entre la realidad y la personalidad del sujeto histórico. *Realidad* deriva de *res* (cosa) y personalidad de persona. El judío saduceo Carlos Marx creía que son las cosas las que hacen y llevan a los hombres, y de aquí su concepción materialista de la historia, su materialismo histórico — que podríamos llamar realismo; — pero los que queremos creer que son los hombres, que son las personas, los que hacen y llevan a las cosas, alimentamos, con duda y en agonía, la fe en la concepción histórica de la historia, en la concepción personalista o espiritualista.
>
> *Persona*, en latín, era el actor de la tragedia o de la comedia, el que hacía un papel en esta. La personalidad es la obra que en la historia se cumple.
>
> ¿Cuál fue el Sócrates histórico, el de Jenofonte, el de Platón, el de Aristófanes? El Sócrates histórico, el inmortal, no fue el hombre de carne y hueso y sangre que vivió en tal época en Atenas, sino que fue el que vivió en cada uno de los que le oyeron, y de todos estos se formó el que dejó su alma a la humanidad. Y él, Sócrates, vive en esta. (X, 557–58)

Unamuno here rejects the Marxist conception of history on the grounds that history is made by persons, not by material things. A person is a material entity with a non-material role; and it is this role or persona that leaves its mark on history.

The distinction, then, is between a physiological reality which disappears and a transcendental reality which endures. But this transcendental reality, what Unamuno calls 'personalidad', has been associated with the physical entity in the first place and has taken shape in other minds. This non-physical projection is 'el que vive en los demás, en la historia' (X, 558). A historical person is a creation not just of one but of many, that is to say of an interaction between an originator and his observers. In this sense, Unamuno's theory of history and his theory of personality are indistinguishable.

It is sometimes said that from *Amor y pedagogía* (1902) onwards Unamuno's novels revolve around abstractions, but this is a one-sided view. It would be more accurate to say that they revolve around man's historical striving towards transcending or seeing behind the physical world. For, as Paul Feyerabend reminds us, the idea of reality as something hidden or subjacent underpins both religion and science, especially modern physics (Feyerabend, 2001: 10–11 and *passim*). The phenomenal world is certainly not one that has satisfied all of us all of the time. The role that language plays in this — is it cause? is it effect? — is a moot point, but, as we shall see in Chapter 3, it is given a key role in Unamuno's explorations.

For Unamuno, then, as for most philosophers, save those who are complete physicalists or complete idealists, the dividing line between the physical and the mental is blurred, or more exactly, the status of the latter in relation to the former is far from obvious. We may be able to compile a list of mental states, but we are unlikely to be able to explain the relationship between one mental state and another (e.g. a feeling and a belief), much less account for the connection between the physical and the mental in our make-up, notwithstanding advances in neurophysiological research which point to the important role played by the central nervous system in provoking mental states, for the simple fact is that mental states also bring about physical action. Causation in both directions remains almost as mysterious today as Schopenhauer predicted, and no explanation of how consciousness, feelings, or beliefs arise from our physical nature has succeeded in bringing the puzzle to a close.[13] Unamuno, it has to be said, is not directly concerned with solving the mind–body problem; he *is* concerned with how the mind–body problem impinges upon the person. What is it that gives the body a particular kind of mental life? What is it that makes us aware of our mental life? What is it about personal identity that persists through time? These are the kinds of questions that loom large in both Unamuno's essays and his imaginative literature, questions that ultimately reduce to the nature and the workings of the self.[14]

---

[13] There is no consensus among philosophers on how to establish a clear distinction between mental and non-mental phenomena. The problem appears to be that we seem to be unable to account for much of our experience in physical terms. If I believe, say, in God, how do I provide a physical explanation for my belief? The same applies to all kinds of thoughts and inclinations. Can artistic creativity, for example, be explained physically? Even if we concede that our mental experiences have a physical basis in our brains, we still cannot explain those experiences in the terms that a physicist can explain physical phenomena such as heat transfer, kinetic energy or electromagnetic radiation. For a recent discussion of the problem see Galen Strawson, 2010, esp. ch. 6.

[14] Although I am not overly concerned with influences in this study, it is worth noting that the core of Unamuno's ideas on identity can be found in William James. The latter's explorations of the

Personal Identity

In the concluding and somewhat extraneous chapter to *Del sentimiento trágico de la vida* Unamuno resurrects Don Quixote as the prototypical Spanish hero in order to entrust him with the belligerent defence of eternal values against the encroachment of a quasi-scientific and materialist Northern Europe which was threatening to destroy all transcendental beliefs. He is referring of course to the role he thinks a scientifically backward Spain should adopt as defender of spiritual traditions in the face of a Northern-European rationalism which he saw as potentially impoverishing, because it set aside the spiritual legacy of the many Northern-European authors (German, French, British, Scandinavian) whom Unamuno has cited approvingly during the course of the work. It goes without saying that the role he would assign to Spain is a reflection of the role he has himself adopted in *Del sentimiento trágico de la vida*, that is to say, proclaiming the relevance and universality of the spiritual dimension of man which is an intrinsic part of our traditions. But for a scientifically well-informed individual such as Unamuno,[15] this was a notable challenge. Science is a rationalist endeavour and rationalism is materialist. Science has progressed by setting aside key aspects of human existence. It has concentrated on physical and measurable qualities such as volume, weight, shape, density, and motion. It has paid far less attention to smell, taste, hearing, feeling, emotion, all of which would seem to play a greater role in human life than the more purely physical qualities that are deemed to be more objective. Science has sought the truth in an objective reality that excluded the human viewpoint. For Unamuno, a purely scientific approach to the human situation was unacceptably reductive and impoverishing. Abandoning one's personal perspective was to move away from the truth, not towards it. The danger is not in science itself but in the potential that science carries for destroying the life of the spirit, something which makes the latter turn against science. Consciousness is will, the will to survive; and it is our survival instinct that has developed our senses, so the physiological basis of our senses is undeniable, as Unamuno often reminds us, whether in essays or in works of fiction. But he also argues that our will produces spiritual or non-rational explanations as vital supports and motivations.[16] The conflict between rational needs and affective needs runs deep in our make-up, and it is this conflict or disjunction that Unamuno places at the centre of personality, and not simply in a religious sense, as is mostly the case in *Del sentimiento trágico de la vida*, but in a fully secular and social sense, as is the case in much of his fiction.

'I' and the 'Me' in his *The Principles of Psychology* (1890) appear to have prompted Unamuno's own version of the self and its variations (see esp. vol. I, chapter X). This is not to deny that Unamuno's explorations of the self, of his own and his characters', are perhaps his most valuable and absorbing contribution to the art of fiction.

[15] As Alison Sinclair rightly reminds us in her notable *Uncovering the Mind: Unamuno, the Unknown and the Vicissitudes of Self* (Sinclair, 2001). See in particular Part I.

[16] In *Del sentimiento trágico de la vida* he refers to them as 'sentimientos alógicos', not illogical but outside logic. This is obviously connected to the ubiquitous topic of the 'mentira vital' that crops up in early twentieth-century popular philosophical debates. One of the best literary examples is Pío Baroja's novel *El árbol de la ciencia* (1911), but the debate is still present in Unamuno's *San Manuel Bueno, mártir* (1931).

Irrespective of our religious inclinations or absence of them, it would seem that much of our life is mythical, with no physiological counterpart; in other words we create our own 'realities' over and above our physiological existence. We may treat them as real because of their practical applications — such as days of the week — but they have of course no material reality. Perhaps the greatest myth is the phenomenon that Unamuno refers to as *personalidad*, that is, the idea that a human body is not simply an object in the world but also acts as a projection of a particular mode or quality of being. At its most basic and commonplace we encounter this notion in the question 'what is so-and-so like?', meaning 'how does that person project him or herself?', the formulation of which already implies a metaphysical mode of being. This notional identity exists both as self-awareness and awareness of others. I am conscious of my own agency as well as of the agency of others, something which obtains reciprocally, since each one of us is aware of being perceived by others. My identity is not only a matter of self-awareness; it is simultaneously a matter of my awareness of others' awareness of me. Unamuno coincides with thinkers such as Martin Buber and Gabriel Marcel in emphasizing that the 'I' exists only relative to the 'You'. Identity is a differential phenomenon and I need others in order to know myself. No others, no self. Human identity therefore involves a complex of images. In order to attain full knowledge of myself I need to know the image others have of me, an idea that plays a major role in Unamuno's fiction, notably so in *Abel Sánchez*, but also in *Tulio Montalbán y Julio Macedo, San Manuel Bueno, mártir*, and *La novela de don Sandalio*, an idea that is already present in *Niebla*, where Augusto Pérez, a character in search of an identity, eventually becomes obsessed with his public image. This means, obviously enough, that a human being's identity is dependent not on his individuality but on his inter-relatedness; it is the result of an interaction rather than of genetic make-up and the environment as many nineteenth-century commentators had insisted. It is the end result of an I–you relationship, a social or collective construction, not simply the result of physical factors.

Unamuno distinguishes between individuality and personality. Individuality is what differentiates us from others. It is in a sense a straightforward spatial distinction, although one of course with multiple phenomenological traits. What truly characterizes us, however, is personality. Individuality has a purely external function: we can cultivate it in order to appear different from others. Personality on the other hand defines our inner self-conception and is an altogether richer, more complex, more fluid state. It governs one's capacity to interact, adapt, and change. How does it come about? Unamuno argues that as a result of our acute self-awareness we create a persona (in its root meaning of mask, role, or character on stage) to facilitate our projection. According to Paul Ilie, who has studied the phenomenon in minute detail, the concept of persona in Unamuno serves to open a clear psychological gap between a material conception and a non-material conception of being (Ilie, 1967: 64).

Persona stands for the individual who performs, who assumes a role. We create a personage whose function is to represent us in public, to enable us to be someone or something, as Unamuno himself explains on commenting on the evolution of the word persona, which has moved from meaning an actor's mask in Roman times, through a *dramatis persona* in the theatre, a role on the human stage, and finally a self-projection within our own consciousness (VIII, 216). In creating this persona for ourselves we are expressing a desire to acquire an identity in a conscious and not merely instinctive way, that is to say it is something that we impose on ourselves, a way of filling in a blank, of overcoming the lack of function, other than that of reproduction, or of purposiveness of the human being. It is a wholly non-material striving, although it certainly need not be religious. Indeed the Unamunian concept is not all that far removed from the well-known paradox of the atheist Jean-Paul Sartre, namely that 'man is not the being that he is'. Unamuno had declared that 'según te adentras en ti mismo y en ti mismo ahondas, vas descubriendo tu propia inanidad, que no eres todo lo que eres, que no eres lo que quisieras ser, que no eres, en fin, más que nonada' (*DSTV*, X, 385). It is precisely to combat this sense of nothingness that we create our selves.[17] We are nothing save what we pretend to be in our life-project. It is a simple matter to observe this idea in action in many of Unamuno's novels, in *Niebla* for example, or even more patently in *San Manuel Bueno, mártir*, in which the parish priest of Valverde de Lucerna has to choose between being nothing and being what he is not. It is clear, then, that the role or identity that the self creates for itself is something that lacks materiality in the normal sense of the word, and in the case of several of Unamuno's fictional characters that sublimation or spiritualization of the material body into a life-project reaches heroic levels, although this striving does not thereby cease to be a striving of the will. This is what Unamuno, with characteristic philological quirkiness, termed 'serse', not just to be but to be reflexively, for oneself as well as for others: 'Serse es propio de la personalidad . [...] Serse es ser para sí, y ser para sí es ser para los otros. El que no es en él otro y para los otros, el que carece de representación, no se es, y no es para sí, carece de personalidad. [...] El animal que uno es no pasa de ser; la persona que uno es, se es' (X, 909). 'Ser' is merely to be, to exist. 'Serse' is to will oneself to be, and thus the key to personality.[18]

We can see, then, that *personalidad* is the metaphysical entity superimposed on the biological entity. Even saints, according to Unamuno, have to play their role as saints; and those Pharisees who purport to be scandalized at this are simply playing the role of Pharisees. 'Porque esta tragicomedia de la historia es una pieza en que cada persona lleva su máscara. Y si se la quita, lo que queda es el animal, y nada más que el animal, el individuo' (X, 911). The mask or role is a reflection of our will. This will-to-be ('querer ser') is for Unamuno 'lo fundamental, lo esencial, lo íntimo' (X, 912) of each individual. The most authentic me is the one I strive to create, the one I aspire to be, as Unamuno also says in *Tres novelas ejemplares y un prólogo*, although it remains obscure who this initiating 'I' is. All we can surmise

---

[17] Though nothingness is not an easy concept to get a grip on, in existentialism it is usually applied to an absence of meaning or an absence of self. Death is nothingness (Heidegger), as is absolute contingency (Sartre). For a more positive view of Unamuno's *nada*, nothingness as a powerful emotional tension, see Cerezo Galán, 1996: 101–05.

[18] It so happens that in Spanish using the verb in reflexive form emphasizes active awareness, not just in verbs of action like *comer(se)*, *beber(se)*, *andar(se)*, but also in verbs which already imply reflexion such as *saber(se)* and *pensar(se)*.

is that this 'I' is pure agency, a kind of halfway house between body and mind, a state of consciousness supported by the body but not realized into the abstract entity which that physiological entity seeks to be. Something along these lines seems to be suggested by Unamuno's declaration that 'sólo existe lo que obra', that our actions are a striving towards a mode of being.[19] This mode of being, however, is a goal and will remain as such throughout one's life, in perpetual development, never fully achieved. The self that is our consciousness dons a mask to act out its role in the world. We wear our persona, our mask, consciously: 'mi máscara soy yo' he writes,[20] thereby identifying fully with his created persona. What characterizes this view of personality is, firstly, its extreme degree of self-awareness: my self contemplates itself acting out its role; and secondly, its reflection of my bodily existence: like my body, my persona is subject to development and change. Both aspects raise questions.

The persona or acting self becomes its own observer since it identifies itself with it. But this persona is a social or externally projected self, a psychological entity that undertakes a social role. An outsider will clearly observe the actor or social persona. But what does the actor observe? What is the internal counterpart of that external self perceived by others? The I-as-observer-of-myself obviously will not observe what other people observe, not least because other people's observations can scarcely be reduced to a single image. In fact, as indicated above, the inner perception of the social self requires some kind of reflective consciousness. This is indeed acknowledged by Unamuno in his theory of 'el otro', of the split personality, of one self mesmerized by another self, or as Víctor Goti in *Niebla* sardonically explains, of the 'comedia que representamos ante nosotros mismos, en lo que se llama el foro interno, en el tablado de la conciencia, haciendo a la vez de cómicos y de espectadores' (I, 644). This does not translate simply into the much-commented phenomenon of an autobiographer objectifying, and thereby potentially misrepresenting, his or her self. It has implications, too, for the harmony and stability of one's psychological constitution. That Unamuno believed the self to be more than a single entity is clear from his frequent references to 'yos' (or 'yoes' in more conventional Spanish). But even if we limit our exposition to the two main selves, the acting self and the reflective self, the question of authenticity cannot be dodged: which self controls or contains the other? Indeed is it possible to have one without the other, an acting self but not a reflective self? In some of Unamuno's novels, notably in *Abel Sánchez*, this conundrum lies at the very heart of the work.

The second question is that relating to temporal change. Being a person entails a principle of unity and continuity. A person's body provides unity in space, a person's actions provide unity of purpose. What provides unity in time? Is such unity simply a sustained series of states of consciousness? And since our states of consciousness must undergo change in accordance with our changing circumstances, what provides our sense of continuity? Unamuno is well aware that the psychological

---

[19] 'El viejo adagio de que *operari sequitur esse*, el obrar se sigue al ser, hay que modificarlo diciendo que ser es obrar y sólo existe lo que obra, lo activo, en cuanto obra' (*DSTV*, X, 392–93). The same idea already appears in an earlier article, 'Sobre el fulanismo', of 1903.

[20] 'De antruejo', *Obras Completas* (Escelicer), VII, 1344.

self is subject to change just as is the physical body. It is not something stable but rather in continual development. There is no 'real' self that is there permanently. Personality, that is, consciousness of self, is perceived through the medium of time. What there is, then, is continuity rather than permanence, but continuity accepts change. Unamuno emphasizes the succession of temporal states that we are, or choose to become, as we abandon one to take up another. Existence is thus a series of selves that arise and disappear under a continuity of consciousness. This continuity amounts to an existential self necessarily aware of the passing of time, a form of identity in the midst of change. We retain as it were a nucleus or core that tells us who we are.[21] This nucleus Unamuno associates with memory, although he also refers to it as *alma*. I can say that what characterizes my identity is a continuity of self-consciousness acquired in childhood but subject to constant reinterpretation and reconstruction. Unamuno refers to a self in a continuous process of change over a sedimentary bedrock: 'El sentimiento de personalidad en el hombre individual depende ante todo y sobre todo del de continuidad. Yo me siento ser yo y no otro porque me siento ser el mismo que hace treinta y nueve años fue testigo del bombardeo de su pueblo natal, recuerdo que sirve como cimiento a casi todas mis sucesivas experiencias.'[22] Here continuity is simply provided by memory, although memory of a momentous event. But Unamuno goes a little further. On another occasion he writes: 'El hombre de hoy no es el de ayer ni el de mañana, y así como cambias, deja que cambie el ideal que de ti propio te forjes. Tu vida es, ante tu propia conciencia, la revelación continua, en el tiempo, de tu eternidad, el desarrollo de tu símbolo, vas descubriéndote conforme obras' (VIII, 315). There is an enduring quality, or 'símbolo', which transcends time. Thus the conditions in which the self emerges change, but one still uses 'I' as if it were the same self speaking. This 'I' is one's sense of identity coming through all one's temporal selves, the feeling that I am the same consciousness I was in the past and will be in the future despite my changing circumstances and perceptions.[23] Under the variety of selves that exist in time there is a continuity of consciousness which offers me a grab-handle onto a permanent identity. This is the consciousness that Unamuno refers to as *alma*, although on occasion he speaks quite simply of memory as the basis of self-identity, eschewing the larger question of an enduring self: 'Sin entrar a discutir — discusión ociosa — si soy o no el que era hace veinte años, es indiscutible, me parece, el hecho de que el que soy hoy proviene, por serie continua de estados de conciencia, del que era en mi cuerpo hace veinte años. La memoria es la base de la personalidad individual' (*DSTV*, X, 281).[24] We notice that Unamuno

---

[21] I have here been following Ilie, 1967: 99–103. It should be added that the idea of a social self and a nuclear self comes straight out of William James, *The Principles of Psychology*, vol. I, chapter X. Unamuno is probably elaborating from memory, as was his habit.

[22] 'Sobre la continuidad histórica', *Obras Completas* (Escelicer), IV, 975.

[23] Not everyone would agree that there is a permanent 'I'. Galen Strawson has argued powerfully that the belief in an enduring self has no real basis, that there is no persisting self (Strawson, G., 2009).

[24] The well-known case of one of Oliver Sacks' patients seems to support Unamuno's contention. As a result of Korsakov's syndrome, this patient's memory stopped recording in 1945, when the patient was a young man. Nearly forty years later he still displayed the outlook and comportment

does not set aside the importance of the physical organism; but what he does say is that in itself this does not provide the necessary continuity of consciousness. Amnesia brings about the complete loss of personality because memory is 'la base de la conciencia' (*DSTV*, X, 282). While personality can undergo change, it can only do so within the continuity provided by memory. There is a clear distinction here between what is material (body and brain) and what is spiritual (memory and consciousness). Whether this is a satisfactory explanation of how self-identity comes about is debatable, since memory is an imperfect tool. Evidently I do not lose my personality because I have a poor memory and have forgotten certain past experiences; furthermore, since I am often fully aware that I have forgotten something, my consciousness appears unimpaired by my forgetfulness. And the self must clearly be more than just memory of experiences; it must also be, among other things, expectation of things that have not yet happened and which are not yet experiences. Nor does Unamuno really consider the role played in memory by the capacity of recall, whether conscious or unconscious; indeed unconscious recall, as in the mechanistic tasks we daily perform, probably plays a greater part in our lives than conscious recall. Unamuno rightly points out that amnesia is a key factor in personality disorders, that amnesiac patients who lose their sense of time lose any coherent sense of self, although which is cause and which is effect is rather less clear than Unamuno implies. Can a person without a sense of self have memories? Nor does Unamuno have anything to say on false memories. If personality is as dependent on memories as he avers, what part does the proven phenomenon of reconstructive memories (i.e. imagined past events) play? Do they render one's personality inauthentic? Does it matter whether Unamuno really did experience the bombing of Bilbao if he thinks he did? If personality is a creative striving and memory is the basis of such a creation, is there any point in distinguishing between an empirical past and an assumed or invented past? If my past is a fiction, invented or simply mis-remembered, what difference does it make? To say that self-identity is memory-dependent is also to invite the accusation of circularity. For in order to have meaningful and credible memories, do we not need some element of personal coherence beforehand? Is it our memory that makes possible our identity or our identity that makes memories possible? Unamuno does not consider the latter point. On the other hand he is surely right when he stresses the continuity criterion as an indisputable factor. Without it, personal identity would become incoherent; indeed it can be argued that self-identity is consciousness of continuity in time extending into the past and into the future.

Conclusion

It would seem that Unamuno accepts the irreducible nature of the conscious properties of the mind. Despite identifying himself with his body, he is no physicalist in the sense of holding mental phenomena to be explicable in terms of physical

---

of his youth. His personality had not developed. Unamuno, referring to patients who suffer from severe amnesia, comments that 'sólo le queda al pobre paciente, como substrato de continuidad individual — ya que no personal — , el organismo físico. Tal enfermedad equivale a la muerte para el sujeto que la padece' (*DSTV*, X, 282).

phenomena. He is a physicalist only to the extent that he tries not to separate the two, presumably because our experiences cover both. For him the human entity is an embodied soul or an ensouled body. But as his persistent use of the word *alma* suggests, he gives priority to the world of the mind in so far as it is our convictions, beliefs, and hopes that drive us forward and not just our hunger or our libido. In one sense of course even our knowledge of the world is mental. We are predominantly mental creatures who require bodies to express ourselves, *anima utens corpore*, in St Augustine's famous definition. So for Unamuno rather than the mental arising out of the physical, the latter seems to be a manifestation of something which is intrinsically spiritual. Not so much, then, that the mental must be physical as that the physical must be mental. His psychological emphasis, however, does not appear to be naturalistic, that is, holding to the view that empirical psychology explains that part of the world which, even though not physical, is part of nature. For Unamuno the 'I' is not purely and simply part of the body or brain, even though it cannot exist apart from them. According to Barry J. Luby, 'Unamuno is reaffirming the modern Christian conception of the integrated mind and body' (Luby, 2008: 56). I think this is an over-optimistic reading. What we can say is that Unamuno accepts the whole person as composed of mind and body, but he sees the person rather more as an embodied mind than as an integrated whole. Physiology and mind are very often seen to be pulling in opposite directions. For Unamuno spirit is what governs, or should govern, the person; this is clearly illustrated by the personality disintegration that threatens many Unamunian characters and which is a purely mental, never a bodily, phenomenon.

It would be more correct to say that Unamuno is a dualist, but not in the traditional sense. He accepts the distinction between the mental and the physical, but tries to establish some kind of dependency between the two. Mental processes (thoughts, beliefs, emotions, preoccupations, expectations, anxieties) are not to be confused with physical or physiological processes, but neither do they exist separately from them. Unamuno certainly accepts that all impressions coming from outside are stored in the brain and that the 'soul' or 'spirit' must contain all such experiences, both conscious or unconscious (*DSTV*, X, 435). But unlike most of today's philosophers, psychologists, and neuro-biologists, he did not try to make the connection via reductionism, that is, by reducing consciousness to brain states explicable in terms of neuron activity and neural pathways. If anything, Unamuno moved in the opposite direction. After a youthful stage strongly influenced by Spencer and Taine, when he felt the passing attraction of positivistic and deterministic explanations of cultural phenomena, he underwent a complete turn and sought instead to explain the role of the material in terms of the spiritual: 'El mundo material o sensible, el que nos crean los sentidos [...], no existe sino para encarnar y sustentar al otro mundo, al mundo espiritual o imaginable, al que la imaginación nos crea' (*DSTV*, X, 442). The function of the material world is to make possible the world of the spirit, the world whose existence can only be imagined, not observed. Our imagined worlds thus appear to take precedence over the material world, notwithstanding the physiological urges of the body. In Unamuno's fiction we will repeatedly observe a clash between the urge to satisfy our physiological needs — hunger, sex, maternity, affection, social success — and the aspiration to achieve fulfilment through self-knowledge and self-possession. It is possible that Unamuno, consciously or unconsciously, blamed his painful loss of an unquestioning religious faith on the positivistic writers he read in his youth — his early enthusiasm for Spencer and Taine were replaced by severe strictures — and that his renewed search for enduring values made him consider human life as directed towards spiritual ends. At any rate his adage became 'hay que espiritualizarlo todo'. And this was to be achieved by 'dando a todo y a todos mi espíritu' (*DSTV*, X, 445). This, then, became the writer's mission.

Unamuno was well aware of the role of the body (and its material brain) in consciousness. If in the end he defended the mental and spiritual dimensions of man it was because he was sensitive to the potential dangers of a purely materialistic explanation of our being: the devaluation of our cultural and ethical systems. There was another reason too. Consciousness is a subjective property. It is not an objective, third-person phenomenon; it belongs irremediably to the 'I'. An experience belongs to its own consciousness, or, if we prefer, a consciousness produces its own experiences. It is my consciousness with its experiences that confers on me my uniqueness, my 'I-nature'. Unamuno always made it very clear that what supremely characterized human existence was the consciousness of our own selves. For him his 'I' was far and away his most important possession, not tradeable, even if that had been possible, for any other 'I'. To lose one's individual identity, whether in this life or in the next, was for him the equivalent of annihilation. To be conscious is to be conscious of ourselves in space and in time. To exist eternally, outside of time, was not the existence he yearned: '¡No pongáis a la puerta de la Gloria como a la del Infierno puso el Dante el *Lasciate ogni speranza*! ¡No matéis al tiempo! Es nuestra vida una esperanza que se está convirtiendo sin cesar en recuerdo, que engendra a su vez la esperanza. ¡Dejadnos vivir! La eternidad, como un eterno presente, sin recuerdo y sin esperanza, es la muerte' (*DSTV*, X, 477). Personal identity is our own creation, a mental construct, but one that is more real, more enduring, more precious, than anything else encountered in our material existence, more precious even than the Beatific Vision or return to the godhead through Pauline apocatastasis (*DSTV*, X, 476). It is this supreme self-consciousness that Unamuno frequently transfers to his fictional creatures.

Unamuno's contention that fictional characters are every bit as real as real persons is well known. The standard explanation, based on Augusto Pérez's aggressive declaration to his creator in *Niebla*, is that after death an author (and by extension any real person) becomes an 'ente ficticio' whose only reality is that conferred on him by his readers in exactly the way that fictional characters acquire their 'reality'. In a famous passage from the prologue to *Tres novelas ejemplares y un prólogo* Unamuno repeats the idea ('Don Quijote es tan real como Cervantes; Hamlet o Macbeth tanto como Shakespeare' (II, 193)), placing persons and characters on the same plane. At its most basic this is little more than a truism and scarcely warrants the startled reaction which Augusto's and Unamuno's statements have sometimes received. To say that death reduces human beings to the status of characters in books may be an unconventional way of putting it, but it is not a profound insight. A dead person does not belong to the phenomenal world, the world of appearances, any more than does a literary personage. Yet this is not the whole story. For what really lies behind Unamuno's reduction of persons to fictional status is his conception of personality. If I, as the physiological entity that I am, feel the need to invent or envisage a purely mental construct in order to achieve full human status, am I not thereby indulging in a form of fabrication? What, then, is the status of this notional person? One thing is clear: this image of me that I project, and which other beings both perceive and reflect back upon me, has no physical reality and can therefore survive my physical demise, so long of course as there are minds to recall that adventitious ontological status that I acquired in life.

The complicating factor is that this concept of person is inter-subjective and fluid, as Unamuno realized. There is no one, single, universally agreed version of my persona precisely because it is not a solid object constrained by physical laws. It varies with circumstance and relation, and is subject to manipulation and adjustment in response to the presence of other beings. How does this fluidity apply in works of literature? How can a fictional character adapt? And above all, how can an author manipulate his readers' recreation of a character's persona? It is here that Unamuno's analogy between life and fiction begins to pose intriguing questions.

CHAPTER 2

The Author

The Nature of Authorship

As I mentioned in passing in the preceding chapter, it has become a common-place of criticism on autobiographical writing to say that the writer of the text can never be congruent with the subject of the autobiography: there are always two 'I's at work, the 'I' who observes and the 'I' who is being observed. Unamuno did not write a conventional autobiography towards the end of his life.[1] Yet he often declared that writers, himself included, are in their works, and that novels are in some sense autobiographical: '¿No son acaso autobiográficas todas las novelas que se eternizan y duran, eternizando y haciendo durar a sus autores y a sus antagonistas?', he asks in *Cómo se hace una novela*, a question to which a few lines further on he provides his own answer in a much-quoted passage: 'Sí, toda novela, toda obra de ficción, todo poema, cuando es vivo es autobiográfico. Todo ser de ficción, todo personaje poético que crea un autor [se] hace parte del autor mismo' (VII, 574).

The way Unamuno expresses this is of some interest. He does not say that his fictional characters are based on self-knowledge. In fact in *Tres novelas ejemplares y un prólogo* he repudiates the idea that his characters are veiled representations of himself (II, 196). What he says in effect is that the characters that his imagination creates provide an experience for him, thereby becoming a part of him, as indeed any experience one has becomes a part of one. Gonzalo Navajas has explained it well: 'Unamuno advierte que su yo personal se prolonga en su obra. En esa prolongación se produce una expansión de su personalidad, que se beneficia [de] un incremento de su condición y experiencia. De entidad previamente autosuficiente pero limitada, el yo se transforma en un conjunto de componentes que abarca al yo junto con los integrantes de la significación de la obra' (Navajas, 1992: 77). The work becomes a prolongation or enrichment of the author's experience. It is the experience of the characters that provides the significance. The characters acquire their reality by dint not of their origin deep within the writer's self but of their

---

[1] The nearest he came to writing an autobiography was *Recuerdos de niñez y de mocedad*, which only cover his childhood and teenage years, in effect his early life in Bilbao before leaving for university in Madrid. Though published in 1908, parts of it were written much earlier, when Unamuno was still in his thirties. He later referred to it as an 'infortunado librito' (*Alrededor*: 77) The *Diario íntimo*, the result of a prolonged spiritual crisis, cannot be classed as autobiography in the conventional sense; it is rather a series of meditations.

projection, an idea that has something in common with Unamuno's view of the crucial role that our social self plays in our lives. Just as a social or public self is a persona created by an inscrutable inner self, so a fictional character is a role as much as a human person is a role. The writer *qua* writer is then doing what he or she does naturally as a person. This analogy can be taken further. Unamuno on more than one occasion equated writing with living. In *Cómo se hace una novela*, for example, he deliberately confuses *novela* and *vida* as if these terms were co-extensive and interchangeable. Both are projects, one a life-project, the other a literary project. There is, in *Cómo se hace una novela*, a writer who proposes to write a novel about how to write a novel, and to this end creates a character who reads a novel and sees his destiny mirrored in the work he is reading. For him, reading becomes living; hence the conclusion of the reading act must signify the conclusion of his life. (In one sense this must be so. If one holds, with Unamuno, that one's life is what one makes of it, a life-project, then the moment one stops re-creating oneself in one's life-project one dies.) There are three novels at play in *Cómo se hace una novela*, the last of which has a fictional reader invented by the author in order to read his novel. The interdependence of author and reader within the pages of the book is evident. What Unamuno is doing then is consciously reflecting the writer's creative process; hence the paradoxical phrase with which the account proper opens: 'Héteme aquí ante estas blancas páginas' (VII, 571), a statement which negates itself by the very act of objectifying the author's anxiety about the task facing him.

Unamuno therefore sees the reading act as integral to the writing act, the full implications of which we will pursue in Chapter 4. For the moment, and at the risk of oversimplifying, we shall concentrate on the author figure and his function, for function is indeed what Unamuno attributes to the author-figure he frequently invokes in his paratexts. The starting point is the notion of literature as a projection of personality, a Romantic idea that is still coming through in the theorizing comments of Unamuno cited above. 'Mi biografía está en mis obras', he wrote to Jean Cassou in 1926 (Unamuno, 1991: II, 185). What a writer can communicate is above all his or her own creative consciousness. The work of an author is unavoidably the reflection of the inner life of the person, the perception of the world through innate or borrowed eyes. As Pío Baroja said in *Juventud, egolatría*, 'En toda la obra entera, que cuando vale algo es una autobiografía larga, el disimulo es imposible, porque allí donde menos lo ha querido el hombre que escribe, se ha revelado' (Baroja, 1946: V, 157). A novel is not merely the story of the characters; it is also in some less obvious sense the story of the writer. According to Unamuno, persons for whom writing is a way of life have difficulty in keeping fictional characters and real people strictly apart, or may not even wish to do so. For them life becomes a book; in other words the exercise of the creative imagination takes over as the dominant influence in their lives. The idea that underlies the position adopted by Unamuno is that of the mental existence of the world of phenomena. He starts from the premiss that while a book and the world to which it refers may belong to the realm of appearances — they appear to us as real objects — literature itself belongs to the noumenal rather than the phenomenal world, though perhaps more in a Platonic than a Kantian sense.[2] We know literature as a purely mental event which has no existence outside our thoughts.

We have already seen that for Unamuno mental existence at some point supersedes physical existence, more especially in the case of persons. We could say that the noumenal displaces the phenomenal as we begin to form ideas or images of the person over and above the physical attributes that we perceive through the senses, that is to say ideas or images of the character and personality of both ourselves and other people. And if this occurs in real, extra-literary life, it applies *a fortiori* to the fictional realm, since in real life a mind needs a body while in literature it does not. Literature is in some sense a disembodied mind. This is really what Unamuno is getting at. In the first instance of course that mind can only be the writer's. A novel is in a very real sense the life of the author, since the life of a novelist is, in the novelistic persona, the mental or imaginative life of that novelist. The writings are his or her life, the projection of his or her personality, and they will convey an impression of that personality. But in what way, we must ask, is an author present in the text?

Some late nineteenth-century writers (e.g. Gustave Flaubert, Henry James, and some later modernists such as T.S. Eliot) objected to the excessive cult of the artistic personality typical of the Romantics and tried to counter with the ideal of impersonality, of the self-effacement of the author. The presence of the author in the text was not denied — such a denial would have entailed the sacrifice of artistic talent and merit — but was considered to be latent rather than conspicuous: an author was meant to be an invisible presence throughout the work, breathing life into it while standing back impassively, like a painter stepping back to contemplate the canvas. Other modernists reacted against *impassibilité* by appearing to move in precisely the opposite direction, denying the possibility of aesthetic objectivity and making the writer break obtrusively into the work in what has come to be known as self-reflective fiction. Unamuno, curiously, appears to have a foot in each camp. On the one hand he clearly holds that a work of literature encapsulates both the mind of the author and of the collectivity to which the author belongs in some deep-seated, intangible way; in other words he believes in the immanence of the author as did the Romantics. Yet at the same time he finds it necessary to proclaim his presence as author at every turn, both in prologues and epilogues and even within the text itself (as in *Niebla*), as if immanence by itself were insufficient. Moreover he makes use of the fictitious-author and fictitious-manuscript device, not with the medieval and Renaissance object of passing off as historical what was of course fictitious, but rather to emphasize the writing act as the revelation of a particular consciousness in time.

---

[2] I say Platonic rather than Kantian because Kant denied that a noumenon as an object of reason could ever gain the status of knowledge (Kant, 1998: 339–65, A236/B295 — A260/B315). Unamuno commented, somewhat caustically, that 'el noúmeno inventado por Kant es de lo más fenomenal que puede darse' (VII, 603). Needless to say, Kant would have disagreed. Schopenhauer went even further, alleging that Kant had erred in referring to *noumena* (in the plural), and restricted the use of the word noumenon (in the singular) to the Will or energy of the cosmos. Even our faint awareness of the Will belonged to the phenomenal world.

As we saw in Chapter 1, Unamuno adopts the fairly standard view that it is continuity of self-consciousness that makes possible one's self-identity, acquired in childhood but subject to constant re-interpretation and reconstruction. This process also
operates according to the same principle on a much wider scale. Just as an individual
inherits or derives a self-image from others and proceeds to build on it basing
him/herself on mutual reactions, so may a collective inherit an image of itself and
develop that image in time through the interaction of its members and its symbols.
Thus, if an individual's continuity of consciousness admits of many projections
of the self, a national consciousness admits of many states of expression, which in
the case of Iberia Unamuno equates with its different languages and especially its
literatures, because a nation's distinct style, its way of expressing itself, is captured
in its literature. As in the case of personal identity, national identity is the product
of a continuity in time, of an *alma* that is subject to ongoing re-interpretation
and not simply the result of environmental factors à la Taine, which had been
Unamuno's initial position in *En torno al casticismo* (1895). In moving away from
Taine and his brand of cultural determinism, Unamuno was obliged to shift his
ground and to abandon the kind of pseudo-historicizing we find in that work.[3] His
treatment of Portugal and its writers already evinced a somewhat different approach
in that he did not seek to relate their literature to historical actions and events,
as he had done in the case of Castile in the 1895 work. Unamuno was a noted
Lusophile, rating nineteenth-century Portuguese literature far more highly than
nineteenth-century Castilian literature (the same applied to nineteenth-century
Catalan literature, which he admired, especially the poet Jacint Verdaguer). What
is interesting is to note why. There is a theme running through his comments on
his favourite Portuguese writers: Antero de Quental, Eugénio de Castro, Camilo
Castelo Branco, Joachim Oliveira Martins, Abilio Guerra Junqueiro. The adjective
ibérico keeps cropping up. Thus Guerra Junqueiro is 'el gran poeta portugués, o
mejor ibérico'; and he recalls that Guerra Junqueiro himself allegedly said to him
of Camilo Castelo Branco that 'Camilo es ibérico, no ya portugués, y acaso más
español que no portugués', to which Unamuno adds that 'Camilo refleja no algo
privativo del alma portuguesa, sino lo que ésta tiene en común con el alma española;
refleja el alma ibérica' (IX, 252).

'Alma ibérica'; that is what Unamuno was looking for, using a noun that was
topical in the early years of the twentieth century in Spain. He said this of Portuguese
writers just as he said it of 'el poeta de Iberia', the Catalan poet Joan Maragall. Upon
the latter's death in December 1911, Unamuno wrote: 'España acaba de perder a su
más grande poeta contemporáneo, al que más dentro llegó de sus entrañas. Y llegó
a las comunes entrañas ibéricas a través del alma de su Cataluña. A fuerza de catalán,
era honda, íntima, entrañadamente español' (Unamuno, 1971: 141). For Unamuno,
when Portuguese and Catalans expressed themselves authentically, that is, when
they expressed what they felt themselves to be, they were expressing what they had
in common with Castilians, not where they differed. Each region might have its

---

[3]   But it is important to note that some aspects of *En torno al casticismo* do survive in Unamuno's later
cultural ontology, not least the idea of 'tradición eterna', still present thirty-five years later in *San
Manuel Bueno, mártir*.

own distinct character, but underneath lay common Iberian roots, the Unamunian collective 'alma' or 'tradición eterna'. It becomes evident that a nation's identity in these terms is not so much a historical or materialistic consciousness as a poetic or spiritual one.

Just as each region of Iberia has both its distinct personality and an underlying common core, so an individual author has a unique persona and a common heritage. The analogy is not mine but Unamuno's: 'como cada hombre, cada pueblo tiene su representación propia' (VIII, 72). As an individual, a writer has his or her own representation of self; a people has its own representation of a collective identity. But given that in Unamuno's theory of personality self-identity is an inter-subjective phenomenon, dependent on the external world of others and on our own receptivity to others' views, it follows that an author's fictional creations must also in some sense reflect this interaction or external influence. Unamuno felt justified in looking for the soul of Spain in Don Quixote because, as he said in an essay well before *Vida de don Quijote y Sancho*, 'no es el héroe otra cosa que el alma colectiva individualizada' (VIII, 266), which is a precise reflection of his personality theory, personality as a distillation of many partial constructions. If this is so, an author is not only expressing an own outlook and disposition but also those of the community within which that sense of identity was developed. If our self-identity is as dependent on the external world of others as Unamuno makes out, it follows that Don Quixote or any other hero will embody much of that external prompting. Don Quixote is the real representative, whereas the author is a mere instrument: 'Cervantes no fue más que un mero instrumento para que la España del siglo XVI pariese a don Quijote' (VIII, 751–52). Cervantes as author is reduced here to executor of a nation's will. Yet Unamuno was not content with adopting such a role for himself. He was prepared to be a spokesman for his age, and indeed in the political sphere he sometimes presented himself as such; but at the same time he was not prepared to sacrifice his sense of uniqueness. A role had to be preserved for his intimate being, and this entailed the bringing forth of 'la savia vivificante' to breathe life into his writing. The problem, as we shall see in Chapter 3, was essentially a linguistic one.

For Unamuno, then, although being an author entails becoming the embodiment of a collective outlook, this is not tantamount to adopting the role of intermediary to the exclusion of all else, for whilst a writer necessarily emerges from his community he is also, as a writer, the product of his own sense of self. But neither does this self-awareness imply adopting the cold, superior stance of a demi-urge (as Valle-Inclán pretended to do), conscious of an overweening or determining power over his creatures. Nor is the author seen as an omniscient presence and the source of all semantic authority; indeed Unamuno's texts are semantically inconclusive and deliberately raise interpretive questions. What an author is in Unamuno is above all a role, a persona or mask, and this role is often incorporated into his fictions. By proceeding in this manner, Unamuno is already raising the question that will become central to post-structuralist criticism, of whether an author is the *originator* of a text, as traditionally regarded, or whether he is the *product* of a text. To pursue the matter further, I shall now turn to Unamuno's use of an author figure, or more simply of a writer-figure, in his two best-known novels, *Niebla* and *San Manuel Bueno, mártir*.

Unamuno's first novel, *Paz en la guerra* (setting aside the deliberately unpublished *Nuevo mundo*), gives no indication of his later and complex conception of authorship. In this work, and in the frequent comments about it found in his correspondence of the time, Unamuno sees the authorial function as that of *histor* or chronicler who displays knowledge of the 'facts' such as is found in Tolstoy's *War and Peace*. The presentation of the author as *histor* or recorder is a typically nineteenth-century practice in accordance with the prevailing concept of the novel as a quasi-historical genre aimed at studying the social environment. The implied author's role in *Paz en la guerra* is that of chronicling the third Carlist War of 1872–76, not via political and military figures but via the experience of ordinary folk according to the fuzzy concept of *intrahistoria*, the unreported daily occurrences of historical unfolding that fall into the interstices of the major events that are the staple of historiography. Yet towards the end of the work the historical novel surprisingly turns into a quasi-philosophical and poetic meditation in which the implied author, while reflecting the vision of a character, no longer appears as chronicler but as poet, as visionary. This perhaps is a pointer, though a slight one, to Unamuno's eventual engagement with and manipulation of the concept of author. In his second novel, *Amor y pedagogía*, he begins his jestful use of the author-figure both in the prologue and in the epilogue, in the former by handing over a thoroughly critical commentary on the author and his work to an unidentified outsider, and in the latter by indulging in a spoof discussion of determinism in art in order, allegedly, to satisfy editorial exigencies as to length. Already we can begin to glimpse that an author for Unamuno is a protean mask with diverse faces. It is with *Niebla* that the full intricacy of Unamuno's answer to the question 'What is an author?' begins to emerge.

Modern editions of this work often carry additional paratexts dating from 1915, 1923 or 1935.[4] Unamuno could not resist returning to earlier works in search of a former self and commenting upon them, usually muddying the waters in so doing. While such revisitations can occasionally be useful in tracing the development of Unamuno's ideas, they need to be treated with caution and not taken as the disclosing of some hidden message which had been there all along. In what follows I shall set these later paratexts aside and refer only to the 1914 text, itself a revision of a 1907 unpublished manuscript. There are four authorial appearances in this work, that is to say, the appearance of an author-figure, or character who plays the role of author. The first appearance occurs in the 'Post-Prólogo', which is signed M. de U.;

---

[4]   The new *Obras Completas* published by Biblioteca Castro used here repeat the absurdity of placing Unamuno's prologue to the 1935 edition between the 'Post-Prólogo' and Chapter 1 (where it had appeared in the third — i.e. 1935 — edition), unmindful of the fact that the 'Prólogo' by Víctor Goti and the 'Post-Prólogo' by M. de U. are an integral part of the novel and cannot be interrupted by an extraneous 'Historia de Niebla' of twenty years later. Mario J. Valdés, in his excellent edition for Ediciones Cátedra (1985), rightly placed the 1935 prologue before and apart from the novel proper. Mercifully the *Obras Completas* avoid making the same mistake in the case of *Abel Sánchez*, the second edition of which in 1928 carried a new prologue by Unamuno inserted *after* the brief *incipit* with which the novel opens.

the second, in Chapter 25; the third, in Chapter 31 (and first few lines of 32); and the fourth, in Chapter 33. In addition to these personal appearances of the author-figure, a number of references to him are made by Víctor Goti and Augusto Pérez. These personal interventions and references are discordant in the sense that the rest of the novel is narrated conventionally enough by an anonymous storyteller (the first-person plural of the opening paragraph of the epilogue was a common enough form in realist fiction). We need to bear in mind that these authorial figures are not the author of flesh and blood but a literary simulacrum. What effect do these interventions have? The most obvious one is to draw attention to the manipulative presence of the author. This already applies to Víctor Goti's prologue, which is virtually in its entirety about his friend Don Miguel de Unamuno, his foibles and heterodox ideas. Even where Goti expresses disagreement with Don Miguel it serves to draw attention to the novel's denouement. Whereas Goti's prologue admits to an absence of free will, M. de U.'s own post-prologue points to a contrary state by condemning Goti for electing to disclose private conversations to the public at large. The discrepancy between the two figures is further highlighted by their disagreement over the form of Augusto Pérez's death and by M. de U.s threat to put Goti in his place. Right from the very start the authority (*auctoritas*) of the author (*auctor*) is questioned. Clearly we do not here have a conventional view of authorship, but rather a struggle for supremacy, an author trying to impose his will on recalcitrant characters.

The second intervention of 'yo, el autor de esta novela que tienes, lector, en la mano' (Chapter 25) is another assertion of authority. Here the nameless author once again intervenes to cut Goti short because Goti confesses to indecision, indeterminacy, or lack of absolute control over the characters of the *nivola* that he himself is writing. The author-figure will have none of it; he affirms categorically that he has total control of his own work, that what his characters say and do is simply to execute his mandate and justify his decisions. Be that as it may, the discrepancy between the author's conviction and a character's confession is clear.

The third intervention is the famous confrontation between author and character in Professor Unamuno's office in Salamanca. That the exchange between a trembling Augusto and an initially cocky Unamuno is a veritable *tour de force* is beyond dispute. But this Unamuno, the putative author who claims total jurisdiction over his fictional invention, does not emerge victorious from the exchange. He soon gets rattled by Augusto's persistent probing of his authorial self-assurance. Two points in particular unsettle the author-figure. One is Augusto's response to Unamuno's declaration that he has no existence other than in the author's (and the reader's) mind: 'No sea que usted no pase de ser un pretexto para que mi historia llegue al mundo' (I, 650), which effectively reduces the ontological status of an author to that of a mere function, that of vehicle or facilitator, precisely what Unamuno had done to Cervantes in *Vida de don Quijote y Sancho* and subsequent articles. The other is Augusto's suggestion that an author's ability to decide for his characters is circumscribed by the knowledge of those characters, and such knowledge, based as it must be on the originating self that has given rise to such creations, is impossible to attain fully: '— Pues más difícil aún que el que uno se conozca a sí mismo es el que un novelista o un autor dramático conozca bien a los personajes que finge o cree fingir' (I, 652). Professor Unamuno's decision to kill off his rebellious creature comes about as a result of his frustration and perplexity. In effect he loses his cool because he cannot counter Augusto's sophisticated arguments. The more the author-figure asserts his authority, the more his vulnerability and anxiety show through.

The fourth and final intervention confirms this creeping insecurity. On learning by telegram of his creature's death, the author suffers nagging doubts, and in his subsequent dream his proposal to go back on his decision is resoundingly quashed by the ghostly apparition of Augusto Pérez. What the real Unamuno appears to be suggesting, in the midst of a patently humorous treatment of the subject, is that in the last instance authorial control is a mirage. Or to put in a different way, free will exists as a pre-condition of action, it is a necessary presupposition for human agency, including the agency of a writer wielding the pen. Once that agency has been exercised, free will becomes an illusion. What is perhaps most interesting about this debate over the question of artistic creation — whether an author controls the work or the work controls the author — is the way in which it is here presented. For although it may not be immediately apparent, *Niebla* takes the form of a debate between two writers: a contrafactum of Unamuno himself versus an imagined or fictitious novelist, Víctor Goti. Víctor Goti after all is learning his trade through composing a novel that has much in common with Unamuno's. Reverse the signatories of the prologue and post-prologue, and we would in effect be reading Víctor Goti's novel, not Unamuno's. M. de U.'s threat in the post-prologue to dispose of Goti in the way he alleges to have disposed of Augusto Pérez was never carried out.

The issues that such a self-reflective work raises are ones that carry us well beyond a consideration of authorship. But on the latter subject we can see certain preoccupations at work. The first is that, as Unamuno said ten years later in *Cómo se hace una novela*, 'escribir contando cómo se hace una novela es hacerla' (VII, 565), or, reversing subject and predicate, 'hacer esa novela es contar cómo hay que hacerla' (VII, 578). A novel carries within it its own compositional conception, gestation, and parturition, at any rate as far as the author is concerned: the finished product is simply the reflection of a creative process. In *La novela de don Sandalio, jugador de ajedrez*, Unamuno expressed his contempt for readers who demanded fully rounded and fully resolved novels with carefully worked-out plots where everything fell logically into place at the end. Rather than a fully resolved and closed fictional account, *Niebla* is a highly self-conscious novel in which many of the author's dilemmas are dramatized within the text and absorbed into the plot and the dialogue. Unamuno contrives his story in such a way that the questions raised by Augusto Pérez and his life-experience are just as applicable to the writing of novels. *Niebla* can easily be read as an allegory of the problems of the writer right from the start, when Augusto steps out hesitantly into the unknown, through to the end when he disappears into the mists of non-existence. Each time a decision looms as to the direction the plot should take, Unamuno comically reflects this in the story itself. He does this through questions (e.g. '¿Y ahora hacia dónde voy? ¿Tiro a la derecha o a la izquierda?'); through comments (e.g. 'esto no puede seguir así', when the plot appears to have reached an impasse); or through interpolated disquisitions (e.g. on contingency and necessity, following the barefaced stratagem of making the canary's cage fall from the balcony when the plot seemed to be at a standstill — 'canario providencial' Unamuno terms the serendipitous song-bird). The list of examples of interpolated comments that serve to draw attention to authorial contrivances could be continued at length. We need only recall that the long section devoted to Víctor Goti's novel-writing amounts to a *mise-en-abîme* that André Gide might have been proud of; except of course that it appeared a decade-and-a-half before the now classic examples of *Les Faux-monnayeurs* [*The Counterfeiters*] or Huxley's *Point Counterpoint*. If, as Unamuno contends, an author's life is contained in that author's very writings, then those writings will somehow reflect his or her ideas, anxieties, problems and solutions. That Unamuno in *Niebla* sets out to do this consciously and deliberately, rather than unconsciously or spontaneously, does, however, raise another issue, that of authenticity, the second major preoccupation at work in *Niebla*.

The plot of a novel may be like the plot of a life in the sense that 'el argumento se hace él sólo', as Víctor Goti avers. But since the task, or life, of a novelist consists in designing plots, a plot is necessarily a reflection of what is going on in the mind of a novelist. It is here that Unamuno's metaphor of the mirror comes into play, that is to say the book as image or reflection, what he sometimes confusingly refers to as *autobiografismo*, which encouraged some critics to look for parallels between life and fiction and to entangle Unamuno with his creatures.[5] The problem of the mirror, or of the book as self-reflection, is that it is either a *representation* of an existing inner world, or a *creation* of an inner world that has not up to that point existed. Unamuno was well aware of the complication. The phenomenon of the stranger in the mirror is used somewhat ironically in *Niebla*, when Augusto says that on seeing himself reflected in a mirror 'acabo por dudar de mi propia existencia e imaginarme, viéndome como otro, que soy un sueño, un ente de ficción' (I, 602). The same phenomenon occurs in the case of literature. The problem is one of self-objectification, of contemplating the self that is being created as if it were something external and detached, often embodied in what Unamuno calls 'el otro yo', the image in the mirror, noting that the word *mirror* can be used by Unamuno to mean other, book, or representation, or indeed a combination of all three as in *Cómo se hace una novela*. In Unamuno mirror and writing are closely connected, suggesting that the former is a metaphor for the revelatory or transforming effects of language. By dint of projecting and objectifying their own images in their books, writers create an independent entity, the stranger in the mirror, one Don Miguel returning the gaze of another Don Miguel from the pages of the book. Unamuno had first described the phenomenon in his 1904 essay 'Intelectualidad y espiritualidad', in which he compared reading one's previous work to looking in a mirror and

---

[5]   The danger of seeing the Unamuno of flesh and blood in his fictional creatures was not always averted by Ricardo Gullón in his early book *Autobiografías de Unamuno* (Gullón, 1964), and the title sent many subsequent critics scurrying in the wrong direction, looking in the novels for veiled autobiographical confessions.

seeing a ghostly entity, a writer whom he could not recognize, a disturbing case of *desdoblamiento*. The phenomenon recurs in the 1927 version of *Cómo se hace una novela*, when Unamuno, unable to locate the original manuscript, had to retranslate into Spanish (with additional intercalated commentaries) Jean Cassou's 1925–26 French translation of the original Spanish. Unamuno's reworking, three years later, of the original version is his way of renewing himself, of overlaying one identity over another in a never-ending process of self-scrutiny and self-affirmation. The self of the second version emerges precisely as a result of the dialogue with the self of the first version. We are dealing with selves wholly encapsulated in textual language.[6]

It becomes obvious, then, that in Unamuno's conception of literature as authorial revelation the image of the author is not something that is stable, frozen in time. It is something that is inherent in the creative act, and that creative act is re-enacted afresh in the act of reading. A novel begins as the manifestation of an authorial consciousness, and this consciousness is instantiated in the act of writing (it does not pre-exist that act, something which fits in with Unamuno's belief in organicism). In pouring forth his consciousness, the artist discovers a self in the pages of his or her book, that is to say in the mirror (and we should note that Unamuno's application of the word is rather different from the more conventional one made familiar by Stendhal). This consciousness of self and the world has no previous signification, but acquires signification through the act of reading that the act of writing implies. The experience of writing carries a concomitant experience of reading. A creative writer is first and foremost a reader of his or her own self.

An Author at Work

Víctor Goti is only one of a number of Unamunian characters who turn to writing to express a deep-seated necessity. In the case of Goti it is 'ansia de hacer algo, una comezón muy íntima, un escarabajeo de la fantasía' (I, 577). In the case of Joaquín Monegro (*Abel Sánchez*) it is an unbridled urge to impress his tragic greatness upon others, and in that of Julio Macedo (*Tulio Montalbán y Julio Macedo*) it is the opposite, a wish to tear off the public mask of greatness conferred on him by his biographer. Ángela Carballino (*San Manuel Bueno, mártir*) for her part writes her memoir ostensibly to keep alive the memory of Father Manuel Bueno and convey the extent of his sacrifice or 'martyrdom', while Don Sandalio's unnamed chess partner (*La novela de don Sandalio, jugador de ajedrez*) is the most mysterious writer of all, and in his case what drives him is a relentless obsession with appropriating the image of Don Sandalio by creating his own intimate, imagined, and inalienable version of

---

[6]   Here I have to signal some element of disagreement with Pedro Cerezo Galán, who writes: 'La extrañeza ante la imagen del espejo se debe a la duplicación de sí mismo, puesto fuera y puesto en frente, como un objeto, carente de alma. Se produce así una escisión interna del yo. Se diría que el espejo es metafóricamente la sustantivación de la mirada del otro, que me reduce a objeto visto, robándome, como diría Sartre, mi viviente subjetividad' (Cerezo Galán, 1996: 594). But it is not only the other's gaze, it is also the writer's own written work that stares back at him, and this is certainly not the 'espejo muerto' referred to by Cerezo Galán. It is very much a living and constantly changing image.

the silent and inscrutable chess player. I should like to turn to one of these fictional writers to see what else we can infer about Unamuno's concept of authorship.

San Manuel Bueno, mártir (1931) is the only novel in which Unamuno has taken the decision to cede the entire narrative to a fictional character (apart from the epilogue, which stands apart). *La novela de Don Sandalio, jugador de ajedrez*, another case of personal narrative, is an epistolary novel and first-person narration was mandatory. *San Manuel Bueno, mártir*, on the other hand, could have been written in the third person, but Unamuno evidently chose very deliberately to filter the account through the mind of Ángela Carballino, a latter-day Mary Magdalene taking on the role of evangelist and telling the story of a modern Jesus–Christ.[7] The memoir is presented as the work of Ángela, a highly self-conscious narrator who often refers to her role as both disciple and chronicler. This novella is in fact a remarkable example of the exploitation of the fictitious-authorship device. What does Unamuno's use of Ángela as author tell us?

What Víctor Goti says of his urge to write is seen to be at work in a subtle way in the case of Ángela Carballino. Indeed Unamuno has made motivation a key aspect of Ángela's memoir. Ángela is not sure why she writes, but she calls her memoir a 'confesión íntima de mi experiencia de la santidad ajena' (II, 343), thereby revealing the strongly subjective, deeply personal nature of her account. With this phrase Unamuno indicates from the start that the subject of his novel, that is to say what is written down, is the fictional author's experience and no one else's. The motivation to write can be perceived on various levels, from the narrator's present circumstances to her childhood, adolescence, and what I earlier termed a life-project. Unamuno has placed so much effort in characterizing the I-narrator (confirmed by two mentions of her role in the appended comments from Unamuno himself at the end of the memoir) that one can reasonably say that *San Manuel Bueno, mártir* is as much about Ángela Carballino as it is about Father Manuel Bueno. The question 'Why does Ángela write?' turns out to be richly suggestive of Unamuno's psychological interests and explorations, as well as of his idea of an author.[8]

An ageing spinster looks back upon her life, most of it spent in the company of the village priest to whom she has been devoted from age fifteen right up to the time of his death. Now, alone and with old age approaching, she learns that someone is writing a biography of this saintly and charismatic figure. The mention of this biography being written by a complete stranger both opens and closes the account, providing the circumstantial framework for Ángela's memoir about her

---

[7] The analogy is too close to be coincidence. Just as Mary Magdalene was forgiven by Jesus and became a devoted disciple, so Ángela Carballino is forgiven and consoled by Father Manuel Bueno in her first confession and thereafter becomes his 'diaconisa', devoting herself unswervingly to his cause. Mary Magdalene was cleansed of demons by Jesus and Ángela wonders whether she herself is 'endemoniada'. Mary Magdalene witnessed the death of Jesus and Ángela witnesses the death of Father Manuel. As for the latter, he is consistently depicted by Ángela as a Christ-figure in her 'gospel'.

[8] Unamuno developed an interest in psychology while preparing for *oposiciones* in the traditional subject area of 'psicología, lógica y ética'. Among others he mentions having read Wilhelm Wundt's influential 1974 work *Principles of Physiological Psychology*, later reinforced (and superseded) by William James's *The Principles of Psychology*. Unamuno was familiar with Freud, notably *The Psychopathology of Everyday Life*, a copy of which he annotated.

lifelong experience of Father Manuel Bueno. This gives us the ostensible motive for Ángela taking up pen and paper. Father Manuel is now becoming everybody's San Manuel, not 'mi San Manuel' as she repeatedly refers to him towards the end of her memoir. Whereas towards the beginning we often encounter the first-person plural possessive adjective, 'nuestro don Manuel', this is eventually displaced by the first-person singular possessive adjective.[9] The move from the collective adjective to the personal one is interesting. Significantly enough, the first occurrence coincides with Ángela remembering her temporary absence from Valverde de Lucerna as a young woman. She remembers it as an emptiness in her life. Possessiveness is the mark of Ángela's attitude towards the man who dominated her life. Her memoir is presented as a reaction to an outsider's appropriation of the figure of the priest, as a re-assertion of her property rights. After Lázaro, now dead in any case, Ángela was Father Manuel's closest disciple and collaborator, or so she presents herself, and the thrust of her story is that she and she alone penetrated the inner secret of the saintly priest who preached resurrection without believing in it himself. At the time of writing, she is the only one who is privy to the 'truth' about Father Manuel, for according to her no one else has guessed the tragic secret that he carried within him. The 'real' Don Manuel Bueno is about to be supplanted by the 'spurious' version of the Bishop, this public self of Don Manuel thereby obliterating the private self, the 'mi don Manuel', that Ángela has uncovered. For her, the priest's saintliness lay not in his public profession of faith through good works, but rather in the fact that his good works were freely given, not conditioned by faith in an afterlife and the possibility of a reward. But is Ángela right about Father Manuel's incredulity or is she creating an imagined persona, as any writer is wont to do? The question has no answer, but we can be fairly certain that Unamuno expected his readers to ask it.

The commentary that Unamuno, in his adopted role of intermediary and editor, appends to Ángela's memoir is highly suggestive. Having stated that he does not doubt the reality of Don Manuel *as portrayed by Ángela* (comparing his reality with the 'reality' of Augusto Pérez in *Niebla*), he then rather unexpectedly refers to the epistle of St Jude, verse 9, in which St Michael mildly rebukes the Devil for claiming Moses' body. The reference appears at first sight gratuitous, completely detached from anything else in the commentary. But the closing phrase of the paragraph, 'el que quiera entender, que entienda', a phrase of Biblical origin that functions as an invitation to look beyond the surface of the speaker's words, indicates that the reference to St Jude's epistle is not just deliberate but potentially subversive. There are three entities involved in the Biblical anecdote: St Michael, the Devil, and Moses, over whom the first two are in dispute, since the Devil was claiming jurisdiction over Moses on the grounds of his incredulity about the promised land, a jurisdiction St Michael rejected as being based on malicious insinuation. Now since in Ángela's account Don Manuel has been explicitly associated with Moses; since in his appended commentary Unamuno is explicitly identifying with St Michael

---

[9] Ángela's 'mi don Manuel' exactly parallels the anonymous letter-writer's 'mi don Sandalio' in the almost contemporaneous *La novela de don Sandalio*. There can be little doubt that in the use of the singular possessive adjective Unamuno is signalling the subjective, imagined, creative nature of the portrait offered by each narrator.

(he reminds us that St Michael is his patron saint, and indeed Unamuno was born on the feast of St Michael); and since the only person responsible for transmitting the story of the incredulous priest is Ángela (as Unamuno has just reminded us), the clear possibility arises that Ángela's outlook is being associated with that of the Devil (the association of angels with devils occurs in St Jude's epistle too, and twice in her account Ángela entertains the possibility of being 'endemoniada'). It was the Devil, of course, who had claimed that Moses was a sceptic. In other words it appears that Unamuno is using this episode from St Jude as a symbol of divergence between himself as 'reader' and his narrator or 'author' of the memoir, that he is raising the possibility that Ángela's witness is somehow tainted. But why, one might well ask, raise the issue of a questionable portrayal in this oblique way? We need to consider two aspects: one is Unamuno's concept of authorship; the other is the mind of the writer, in this case the circumstances surrounding Ángela's account of the priest. Let us start with the second.

Father Manuel Bueno is the subject of an inquiry by an ecclesiastical tribunal that will have to sit in judgment and decide whether he is a worthy candidate for beatification. In such a tribunal of inquiry, under the canonical procedure in force at the time when Unamuno wrote, the Church used to appoint a prosecutor (technically *promotor fidei* but more widely referred to as *advocatus diavoli*) whose function it was to oppose the promoters of the beatification process by questioning the evidence put forward for beatification and by looking for contrary evidence. In the case of Father Manuel it is the Bishop (in accordance with canonical procedure) who is promoting the process of beatification and who is writing his life as an example of perfect priestliness. Contrariwise, Ángela, in her testimony, is presenting Father Manuel as a man lacking in faith, and is consequently hitting at the very heart of the case for beatification. In the context of a canonical beatification process, which is the starting point for Ángela's story, Ángela and the Bishop are antagonists. It follows that Ángela is cast in the canonical role of *advocatus diavoli*, the Devil's advocate. That this is what Unamuno had in mind is further suggested by the definition of the Devil which he includes in the same paragraph and which fits in exactly with the role of Ángela as *advocatus diavoli*: 'Diablo quiere decir acusador, fiscal' (II, 345). Just as the Devil in St Jude's epistle has interpreted Moses, the leader of his people, as a man who lacked faith in the promised land, so Ángela interprets Father Manuel as a spiritual leader who lacked faith in personal survival despite encouraging such belief in his people.

It is not Ángela's account itself that the Unamuno of the epilogue is questioning but only its historicity. Ángela's memoir has the truth of poetry, not the truth of history. This is wholly in accord with Unamuno's view of the Gospels not as simple records of fact but rather as personal records of the evangelists' own subjective and imaginative re-creations of their experiences with Jesus interpreted in the light of their own Biblical expectations, and as such more authentic and heartfelt than mere chronicles.[10] Ángela, a modern evangelist recounting the deeds of a modern Christ,

---

[10] Unamuno even includes a statement to this effect in the closing paragraph of *San Manuel Bueno, mártir*: 'no me explico que haya quien se indigne de que se llame novela al Evangelio, lo que es elevarlo, en realidad, sobre un cronicón cualquiera' (II, 346).

does not record an objective truth but *her* truth, her interpretation or re-enactment of Father Manuel's life and personality.

The recovery and preservation of 'mi don Manuel' in the face of a competitive account is the ostensible reason for Ángela's memoir. But Unamuno's contention that all good writing is autobiographical, that literature necessarily reflects the mind of the writer, can also be seen to be at work in *San Manuel Bueno, mártir*. We have seen what prompts Ángela to write. But what sort of person is doing the writing? There are many aspects of her account that serve to characterize her rather than her biographee. Her fatherless childhood, her mother's admiration for Don Manuel, her unusual reading of literary works, her religious anxieties, her mystical inclinations, her aesthetic sensibilities and lachrymose nature, her excessive devotion to confession, and her adamant rejection of marriage on three separate occasions, are details that point to a turbulent inner life, a turmoil that comes through powerfully in her recollection of her life with Don Manuel. There is a recurrent image which Ángela associates with the priest and which strongly suggests that her attachment to him is not simply derived from a religious ideal. She repeatedly casts him in the role of father, not just that of spiritual father which it is Don Manuel's priestly duty to fulfil, but of a rather more concrete paternity or fatherliness which fosters and protects in a more physical sense. The explanation that Ángela gives for Don Manuel's entering the priesthood is that he wanted to look after the children of a widowed sister, 'servirles de padre' (II, 315). She also relates various anecdotes which show Don Manuel in the role of protective parent and as extremely interested in pregnancies and child rearing. This paternal role ascribed to Don Manuel is accompanied by the depiction of virile qualities which enable him to fulfil a masculine role in the community. He engages in manual labour using his physical strength in such tasks as ploughing and cutting logs. In all this there is an easily discernible conception of Don Manuel as a father with the attributes of a dominant and protective male figure. Ángela refers to him not as an 'hombre santo' but as a 'santo varón'. The masculinity of the priest acquires its significance when connected to the narrating consciousness, especially when we consider that Ángela comes very close at times to casting herself in the role of unfulfilled mother. Words and phrases associated with maternity are used by Ángela on several occasions. When she relates the calming effect on her religious disquietude of her first confession with Don Manuel, she uses a revealing phrase in reference to herself: 'empezaba a ser mujer, sentía en mis entrañas el jugo de la maternidad' (II, 323). A little later in the account, the phrase 'se me estremecían las entrañas maternales' occurs in a strikingly revealing context which points to Ángela's infatuation with the priest and consequent rejection of marriage. The passage is worth recalling in full:

> — ¿Y por qué no te casas Angelina?
> — Ya sabe usted padre mío por qué.
> — Pero no, no; tienes que casarte. Entre Lázaro y yo te buscaremos un novio. Porque a ti te conviene casarte para que se te curen esas preocupaciones.
> — ¿Preocupaciones, don Manuel?
> — Yo sé bien lo que me digo. Y no te acongojes demasiado por los demás, que harto tiene cada cual con tener que responder de sí mismo.
> — ¡Y que sea usted, don Manuel, el que me diga eso!, ¡que sea usted el que

me aconseje que me case para responder de mí y no acuitarme por los demás!,
¡que sea usted!

—— Tienes razón Angelina, no sé ya lo que me digo; no sé ya lo que me digo
desde que estoy confesándome contigo. Y sí, sí, hay que vivir, hay que vivir.

Y cuando yo iba a levantarme para salir del templo, me dijo:

—— Y ahora, Angelina, en nombre del pueblo, ¿me absuelves?

Me sentí como penetrada de un misterioso sacerdocio y le dije:

—— En nombre de Dios Padre, Hijo y Espíritu Santo, le absuelvo, padre.

Y salimos de la iglesia, y al salir se me estremecían las entrañas maternales.
(II, 332–33)

The conversation between the two characters is remarkable for the way in which
Unamuno has contrived each sentence so that it hints at something which remains
unexpressed. Whether we like it or not we are dragged into reading between the
lines of Ángela's account in order to make some sense of it. The mixture of religious
and maternal sentiments, right down to the final line which, in its use of the first
person plural, recalls the public emergence of bride and groom after the marriage
ceremony, is a *tour de force* of understated writing. The idea of mystical love as the
sublimation of sexual love (*meterótica* is Unamuno's word for it) is perfectly well
explained in Chapter V of *La agonía del cristianismo* (X, 564–65), where we find the
following: 'Conocer es, en efecto, engendrar, y todo conocimiento vivo supone la
penetración, la fusión de las entrañas del espíritu que conoce y de la cosa conocida'
(X, 565). The use of the word 'penetrada' in the passage above is therefore no
accident; it is a deliberate choice. Ángela's claim to have known Don Manuel's
intimate secret becomes, then, a symbol of her sublimated love for him. According
to Unamuno's metaphor, Ángela can only know the priest if she is penetrated by
him, though in her case it can only be a mystical penetration. Her hankering after
maternity must remain unfulfilled as she chooses to enter 'nuestro monasterio
de Valverde de Lucerna' and place herself 'a los pies de su abad' (II, 322). The
sublimation of her love for Don Manuel takes the form of a mystical devotion to
her village monastery (Ángela is fond of reading St Teresa), but her writing betrays
her natural female instinct of maternal fulfilment.[11]

Ángela's memoir, then, acts as a repository of her deepest feelings, unacknowledged
by her as author yet discernible in the interstices of her account. Indeed there is
much in the narrative that could be interpreted as unconscious revelation, should
one wish to go down the psychoanalytic road. Her attribution of enamourment of
Don Manuel to her own mother, or of a 'grito maternal' to a figure of the Virgin,
both of which could be read as unconscious displacement; or the references to 'hijos
ausentes' of women to whom Don Manuel acts as amanuensis; or the description
of the death of a pregnant woman in the arms of the priest; or the reference to a
recently widowed woman whom Don Manuel dissuades from wanting to follow
her husband; all of which could be seen as unconscious revelations of Ángela's
frustrated motherhood and enforced sterility in the face of her attachment to

---

[11] This is entirely in accordance with how Unamuno saw woman. In 'A una aspirante a escritora' he
wrote: 'La mujer es ante todo y sobre todo madre. El instinto de la maternidad es en ella mucho
más fuerte que el de la sexualidad. [...] La mujer es madre ante todo' (IX, 337).

Father Manuel. In addition, Ángela's declared but inexplicable feelings of guilt, her frequent tears, her mental confusion, taken in conjunction with her references to dreaming, could be seen as the embodiment, in covert form, of the conflict or anxiety which the conscious mind has censored. Such a reading, though possible, is not of course mandatory.[12] But what is at any rate apparent is the proximity of maternal and religious motives in the narrator: in several instances it is impossible to separate them.[13] In her memoir Ángela comes through as an impressionable and sensitive woman with mystical inclinations (even her brother is an 'hermano más que carnal, espiritual'), and one whose sexual and maternal instincts are channelled into an unusual and ambiguous relationship — romantic yet spiritual — with a priest who possesses a dominant personality. She forges a relationship with Don Manuel which on her side if not on his clearly goes further than the normal one between confessor and penitent, or between priest and acolyte. For Ángela, Don Manuel is a father figure with a latent sexual role, a clear case of an Electra complex which would have been perfectly familiar to Unamuno as a professor of Greek literature. Except of course that in this case the role of father is played by a Catholic priest. Just as a nun entering a convent and taking her vows becomes 'the bride of Christ', so Ángela on entering her convent of Valverde de Lucerna becomes in her own imagination, as her writing reveals, the bride of Don Manuel. Psychologically this ties in perfectly with what we learn of Ángela's childhood. The loss of her own father when very young provokes a search for a surrogate father, and, given her mother's devotion to Father Manuel, the child's attention is drawn towards the priest. This initial conditioning is reinforced by Ángela coming under the tutelage of Don Manuel at a particularly impressionable age: she is scarcely sixteen. On returning to the village from her city school she quickly becomes emotionally involved (as is evident from her account of the encounter with Father Manuel) with the figure of the priest whom her mother has for so long held up to her as a father figure; the surrogate father becomes a surrogate husband, and what is recognized by developmental psychology as being only a passing phase in female adolescence becomes, in Ángela's case, a more permanent state of affairs. *San Manuel Bueno, mártir* amounts to a quite remarkable portrait not just of the eponymous character but even more of the fictional author. In trying to prise open the mind of Don Manuel, she has only prised open her own.

The personality and circumstances of the narrating mind affect not only *what* is told but also *how* it is told. In *San Manuel Bueno, mártir* Ángela's account is highly idiosyncratic, and the language used visionary and poetic rather than concrete and

---

[12] For a reading of this novel from the perspective of the psychoanalytic concept of introjection see Julia Biggane, 2005.

[13] The association of sexual love with knowing, and of knowing with the attainment of a higher kind of love, is quite explicit in Unamuno (for example in *DSTV*: 'Porque de este amor carnal y primitivo [...], de este amor de todo el cuerpo con sus sentidos, que es el origen animal de la sociedad humana, de este enamoramiento surge el amor espiritual y doloroso' (X, 383)). Sexuality, however, is not to be confused with eroticism, the deliberate provocation of the sexual urge. There is nothing erotic about Unamuno's writing. He very often invokes sexuality in his fiction, but as a quite straightforwardly biological phenomenon. In women, it is invariably associated with the maternal urge. Furthermore, Unamuno often uses the mother as a symbol of the spiritual, i.e. non-material, dimension of human nature. In *Cómo se hace una novela*, Unamuno recounts that

down-to-earth. I shall have more to say on this aspect in the next chapter. For the moment what I should like to emphasize here is the way in which Unamuno has captured the state of mind of the writer. Two aspects stand out: ambivalence and uncertainty. Ángela's attitude towards the subject of her memoir is ambivalent. For if on the one hand she presents Father Manuel Bueno as in many ways an admirable person, on the other she appears determined to question his outward faith at every turn, to persuade herself (and of course her potential reader) that he was not all he purported to be, that he had something to hide, and that she, Ángela, discovered what it was, as indicated by many phrases and renderings that represent Ángela's interpretation of what she observes or thinks she observes in Don Manuel's behaviour:

> [...] recitábamos al unísono, en una sola voz, el Credo [...] Y no era un coro, sino una sola voz, una voz simple y unida, fundidas todas en una [...] Y al llegar a lo de 'creo en la resurrección de la carne y la vida perdurable' la voz de don Manuel se zambullía, como en un lago, en la del pueblo todo, y era que él se callaba [...] Después, al llegar a conocer el secreto de nuestro santo [...] (II, 318)

> Iba también a menudo a la escuela a ayudar al maestro, a enseñar con él, y no sólo el catecismo. Y es que huía, de la ociosidad y de la soledad. (II, 320)

> Con aquella su constante actividad, con aquel mezclarse en las tareas y las diversiones de todos, parecía querer huir de sí mismo. (II, 321)

> Pero lee [says Don Manuel], sobre todo libros de piedad que te den contento de vivir, un contento apacible y silencioso. ¿Le tenía él? (II, 327)

In these and other instances what we see is quite simply Ángela's subjective interpretation at work. She is in effect reading Don Manuel's mind, persuading herself (and her hypothetical reader, for only an imagined reader can explain the employment of many of the phrases) that Father Manuel carries a secret. She also assumes that Lázaro's version of Don Manuel's beliefs (which of course mirror Lázaro's own beliefs as a complete religious sceptic but a progressive social thinker) is the correct one and that Father Manuel is deceiving all his other parishioners: '¿por qué — me he preguntado muchas veces — no trató don Manuel de convertir a mi hermano también con su engaño, con una mentira, fingiéndose creyente sin serlo?' (II, 344). Since Ángela has already assumed that the priest is feigning in his attitude towards the people of Valverde, she asks why he does not continue his deception, why he ceases to feign, in the case of her brother. The question is thus curiously formulated in the negative (why did he not?), a formulation which serves to reflect her own problem with belief rather than Father Manuel's. The words *engaño* and *engañar* crop up repeatedly in her account:

during the spiritual crisis he experienced in 1897 his wife once found him in a state of prostration and exclaimed: '¡Hijo mío!', words which he found deeply consoling (VII, 594). The episode is recalled by Ángela in *San Manuel Bueno, mártir* (II, 317). The idea of wife-as-mother appears several times in Unamuno's fiction, in *Amor y pedagogía*, for example, and also in Don Avito Carrascal's advice to Augusto Pérez in *Niebla* to the effect that if he wants to recover his mother, recently deceased, he should find a wife. To see the mother in Ángela (the symbolic equivalent of Mother Church), is, in Unamunian terms, to see her caring nature.

> Y ahora, al escribir esta memoria, me digo: ¿Por qué no me engañó?, ¿por que
> no me engañó entonces como engañaba a los demás? ¿Por qué se acongojó?,
> ¿porque no podía engañarse a sí mismo, o porque no podía engañarme? Y
> quiero creer que se acongojaba porque no podía engañarse para engañarme.
> (II, 332)

But who is deceiving whom? The priest his parishioners? The priest his disciple?
Or is the disciple deceiving herself, as she almost comes to recognize at the end?
Ángela states that Father Manuel succeeds in deceiving everyone, except her. And
here we have what amounts to a leitmotif in her account, never explicitly stated
but consistently implied: that unlike the simple village folk she, Ángela, educated
and well-read, was too intelligent for the village priest and saw through his false
front from the very beginning. This ambivalence towards her biographee can also
be detected in the ironic interpolations that occasionally embellish the account and
which suggest latent censure. At the end of her account of Lázaro's public communion
administered by Father Manuel, we find the following interpolation: 'Y entonces,
pues era la madrugada, cantó un gallo' (II, 329). Just as Peter betrayed Christ and
his betrayal was marked by the cock crowing, so the priest and Lázaro are seen by
Ángela to be betraying the beliefs of their people by going through the mechanics
of a religious conversion which is false. On the occasion of Don Manuel's death,
the description of the scene carries a pointed comment: 'Y no hubo que cerrarle los
ojos porque se murió con ellos cerrados' (II, 340), the apparent implication being
that he remained blind to the end. Ángela never condemns Father Manuel overtly,
except perhaps when she refers to Lázaro's communion as a sacrilege; her censure
is implicit and oblique, entirely as if the writer could not quite make up her mind.
What we detect in her account is uncertainty and ambivalence, an ambivalence
exemplified in the contradictory phrase she uses to describe his behaviour: 'piadoso
fraude'. Having left her hypothetical reader in little doubt that Father Manuel's
public profession of faith is a mask, a pretence, she then goes on to label him a saint,
and to suggest that both he and Lázaro were in fact believers without realizing it.
Ángela thereby makes of Don Manuel a complete paradox: he is not what he seems
to the villagers and the Bishop, but nor is he what he seems to Ángela! The memoir
leaves the reader in a no man's land, in an uncertainty created by the biography
itself. Ángela as author is no mere chronicler of events; she is an interpreter of
them, and an interpreter moreover in the light of her own uncertain faith.[14]

The ambiguity of Ángela's account of the priest is explicable not only in terms
of the fictional author's own personality and circumstances but also in terms of

---

[14] Needless to say the creation of the narrator's ambiguous attitude towards her biographee is
ultimately Unamuno's own doing. Towards Father Manuel's behaviour we can adopt one of
two positions. One had been perfectly summed up long before by Father Lasalde in Azorín's *La
voluntad*: 'Consideremos como un crimen muy grande el quitar la fe... ¡qué es la vida!... a una pobre
mujer, a un labriego, a un niño... Ellos son felices porque creen; ellos soportan el dolor porque
esperan' (Azorín, 1972: 149–50). The other was Unamuno's own position in real life, expressed on
more than one occasion (see for example IX, 221), to the effect that his role was to raise doubts,
disquiet, even desperation, in his fellow men even at the expense of spiritual contentment. But
adopting either position towards Don Manuel assumes firm knowledge of his beliefs. Unamuno
provides no such knowledge.

Unamuno's conception of authorship, that is to say as incorporating a collective construction. As we have seen, for Unamuno being an author entails giving expression to an external tradition, the tradition or outlook within which the writer was formed. An author is both a personal creator and an instrument. (This, as we shall see in the next chapter, is a fact of language.) The tradition within which Ángela is writing is that of her own community of Valverde de Lucerna. This tradition held Father Manuel to be a great spiritual leader and protector of his people, a person worthy of the greatest honour the Church could confer. This standpoint is faithfully reflected in Ángela's account. At the same time Ángela is creating her own, highly personal, reconstruction of the priest, what wells up from within her depths, what Unamuno calls 'la fuente interna, la sustancia íntima e invisible' (VIII, 925), and it is this personal intuition that tells her that there was more to the priest than his public role. The 'invisible' side of the priest is what Ángela is creating as it were out of her own intimate resources. It is 'mi don Manuel' as distinct from 'nuestro don Manuel'. Both sides of authorship come through in Ángela, the collective and the subjective.

In *San Manuel Bueno, mártir* Unamuno is certainly faithful to his conviction that a novel is disguised autobiography. But what is remarkable is that this works on two levels. At the level of the author of flesh and blood the story of the sceptical country priest who was a model of Christian behaviour can be seen to reflect Unamuno's own paradoxical position of scepticism towards the orthodox beliefs of Christianity and of deep commitment to the values of that very religion, even while dissociating himself from Don Manuel's public strategy of upholding the beliefs of simple folk.[15] At the level of the fictional author, we can observe how Ángela's memoir and personal re-creation of Don Manuel is equivocal, governed by her own ambiguous attitude towards the priest. As she consigns her memories to paper she appears to be disconcerted by the fact that, having given her life to Father Manuel's spiritual cause, she now finds herself sad, lonely, and more uncertain than ever of her own beliefs. It is evident that Ángela's personal reconstruction of Father Manuel's life, her revelation of his 'secreto trágico' and his 'piadoso fraude', represents a challenge to the orthodox biography that the Bishop of Renada is preparing. Ángela, who has been a doubting Thomas all her life, from the time she started reading her father's books, through her confessions with Don Manuel to seek reassurance, right down to the moment of writing her memoir, makes an even greater one of Don Manuel. The sentiments she puts in his mouth parallel her own present sentiments. When she makes him say 'me figuro ahora que creía entonces' (II, 339), she is echoing her own question to herself *at the moment of writing*: 'Y yo, ¿creo?' (II, 344). When she makes him equate his childhood fate with dreaming, she is reflecting her own tendency *as she writes* to see the past as a dream: '¿Es que esto que estoy aquí contando ha pasado y ha pasado tal y como lo cuento? [...] ¿Es que todo esto es más que un sueño?' (II, 344). The dream-like quality of the account, apparent

---

[15] We can say that Unamuno's own position in life was the precise reverse of Don Manuel's. In public he was held to be a heretic and came very close to excommunication. In private, as we know from his correspondence, he never ceased being a deeply committed Christian and a believer, even when rejecting the Church's dogma. The 'Carta a Juan Solís', for example, shows this clearly.

in the final section of the memoir, completely overwhelms any previous semblance of historicity. As she nears the end, Ángela looks back at her account with some perplexity. She refers to the act of writing no less than five times in quick succession (plus a closing tentative comment on the possible fate of her manuscript), indicating that for her now the only reality is the reality of words, not of events. The truth, her truth, *is in the writing*, for that has now become her life. Ángela's account works as a writer's self-projection. The material events of the past have been displaced by the verbal reconstruction that lies before her. It is as a reader of her own work that she finally looks upon it, and what she sees is something whose significance escapes her.

Unamuno's cession of authorship to a fictitious character in *San Manuel Bueno, mártir* makes little sense unless he wanted to raise questions about the nature of the eponymous character's religious outlook and personality, especially since he does not appear to be wholly comfortable in the use of the constrictive I-narration, for Ángela comes close on occasion to omniscient narration, a quasi-omniscience noticeable in anecdotes such as the one of the judge and the alleged criminal, or in the words whispered by Don Manuel in Lázaro's ear on the occasion of the final Mass and communion, or even in the graphic accuracy with which Ángela recalls the priest's words as reported to her by Lázaro. Is she inventing, supposing, imagining? Or is Unamuno quietly transgressing the bounds of personalized, non-omniscient narration? Whichever answer is correct, his choice of narrator amounts to a deliberate interposition between real author and eponymous character. How do we, how can we, judge another self? The use of Ángela as recorder turns what could have been our knowledge of Don Manuel into speculation or assumptions, suggesting that Unamuno is harking back to Plato's well-known proposition (in the *Theaetetus* and more especially in the *Meno*) that knowledge is no more than recollection. The fact that the personalized narrator ends by questioning her own recollections moves Plato's argument of knowledge-as-recollection onto an even more slippery slope. For if she questions her recollections she is thereby questioning her knowledge. We the readers are in precisely the position of the jury in Plato's *Theaetetus*: our beliefs and conclusions about the defendant arise solely from the persuasive powers of the orator addressing us. But if the self-conviction of the orator ends up by crumbling, our beliefs will cease to have any firm basis. Our judgment of Don Manuel, whichever line we take, will be one more act of faith.

Conclusion

The concept of author, or more precisely of author-identity, has traditionally provided a source of stability in interpretation: we have read or critically interpreted according to what we held to be the author's plans; as Foucault has said, the figure of the author has furnished us with a 'principle of thrift in the proliferation of meaning' (Foucault, 1986: 118). It is clear that Unamuno subverts this traditional notion of the author as the ultimate authority in a text, and he usually does so by undermining the position of an invented author-figure, whether sardonically, as in *Niebla*, or more subtly through the questioning of the truth-value or objectivity of an account (Joaquín Monegro's 'Confesión', Angela Carballino's memoir, the anonymous letter-writer's gaps). All these writers fail to persuade us of the objectivity of their accounts. Their own words betray them, so that intention and execution diverge. These 'authors' are seen not to be in control. One cannot of course simply generalize from fictitious authors to the real flesh-and-blood author, yet at the same time it would be hard to maintain that Unamuno's concern with the author-function has nothing to do with his own position vis-à-vis his creations. What seems to preoccupy him is that the implied author (the author a reader 'senses' when reading) is not an authentic or reliable version of himself. He undergoes the same phenomenon when he returns to his texts as a reader: the authorial projection is not the one he feels himself to be. The question inevitably arises as to who is the more real, the implied author immanent in the text or the historical author of flesh-and-blood, especially of course as there is no doubt as to which of the two survives for longer. The problem reduces ultimately to one of language. Characters in books are linguistic phenomena. The same may be said of the implied author, created by a reader upon the reception of words on a page. The Unamuno of flesh-and-blood and the Unamuno of the 'leyenda', of the reading act, cannot be wholly congruent, for the latter is no more than a linguistic construct, a noumenon devoid of a physical counterpart. For us, his readers, Unamuno may be perhaps simply a 'cosa de libros', but for himself he was both the thinking, sentient being and the image his writings projected.

If Unamuno's novels and his frequent accompanying comments on them pose the question of where an author stands vis-à-vis his or her literary production, of whether indeed an author has authority, this in turn is connected to the question of whether an individual is self-determined or determined by his or her circumstances, including other people. Unamuno always manifested a concern with the image of himself that his writings projected, a preoccupation expressed in a variety of places, notably so in *Cómo se hace una novela*:

> ¡Mi novela!, ¡mi leyenda! El Unamuno de mi leyenda, de mi novela, el que hemos hecho juntos mi yo amigo y mi yo enemigo y los demás, mis amigos y mis enemigos, este Unamuno me da vida y muerte, me crea y me destruye, me sostiene y me ahoga. Es mi agonía. ¿Seré como me creo o como se me cree? Y he aquí cómo estas líneas se convierten en una confesión ante mi yo desconocido e inconocible; desconocido e inconocible para mí mismo. He aquí que hago la leyenda en que he de enterrarme. (VII, 577–78)

The legend is the image he and we read into the writing. Unamuno does not say whether he accepts this image as true or rejects it as false. He accepts it as a fact of writing and is clearly fascinated by the phenomenon, since it plays a key part in many novels (I shall pursue this further in Chapter 5). But the question remains: does 'el Unamuno de la leyenda' have any kind of reality or substance or is he merely 'cosa de libros' as Augusto Pérez vengefully remarks? And if the figure of the author is immanent in his text, who is responsible for its recovery: the reader, the critic, the author himself? Unamuno appears not to distinguish between biographical legend and authorial legend. Biographical legends are those that have grown around their figures with a limited basis in historical fact. Pushkin and Byron are well-known cases. There is also the phenomenon of a mythical author existing alongside the historical one; indeed some authors have created or encouraged the creation of legendary personae that had little or nothing to do with the historical person — in the Iberian world Silverio Lanza, Valle-Inclán, and Fernando Pessoa come to mind. The legend impinges on the authorial presence (as distinct from the biographical or historical one). It is this kind of mythical presence that concerns Unamuno, since his biographical presence based on the humdrum existence of a university professor could hardly be considered engrossing. It is once again the mental image that displaces the material reality. Just as a person is more than an object, so a book is more than an object. It ceases to reside in the external world and assumes instead the consciousness of another.

This consciousness that appears to reside in books must in the first instance be the consciousness of the author. But what is significant in the case of Unamuno is that he equates the act of writing with the act of reading, as if one mirrored the other, the metaphor of the mirror being his favourite way of representing books. Clearly a book can only become a mirror through the act of reading. A mirror makes us self-conscious; so does a book. Artists or writers, struggling to express a vision in a world of words, are the most self-conscious beings of all. As they pour into their books their consciousness of themselves and the surrounding world, writers acquire an identity, a projection of themselves in their own work. It is not simply *escribir* but, as Unamuno might say, *escribirse*. If to be is to be aware of oneself — *serse* and not merely *ser* — to write is to inquire into that self in a highly self-conscious manner. The projection of the self does not have a prior existence, but acquires its contours through the act of reading that accompanies the act of writing. A creative writer for Unamuno is first and foremost a reader of himself.

A literary work preserves the author's identity, the thinking 'I', because every word carries the stamp of the person who wrote it. Unamuno equated *vivir* and *escribir*, so for him writing was living. The writing is an objectification of what went through his mind when he wrote it. In theory the reader thinks the thoughts, or penetrates the mind, of the author. But is the self who comes through in the reading act exactly congruent with the self that went into the writing act? And, more pertinently, is a reader thinking the thoughts of the author, are we taking on someone else's mind when we read? Or can a work of literature be said to have a mind of its own? This, after all, seems to be the implication of the stranger-in-the-mirror effect that Unamuno associates with reading his own works. Is it because his dynamic view of personality as something fluid and in constant re-enactment changes the reader who captures the words on the page? Do we have to agree, then, with Roland Barthes that 'dans le texte seul parle le lecteur'? But before we turn to Unamuno's view of the reader we need to consider his view of the medium, language itself.

CHAPTER 3

The Word

From Community to Poet

Unamuno's retirement speech of 1934, delivered on his seventieth birthday, was devoted to the subject of language and to his lifelong dedication to philology, 'amor de la palabra, del nombre', as he defined it. Towards the end of his speech, alluding to himself in the third person, he said: 'este hombre, a quien se le ha supuesto tan versátil, ha seguido, en su profesión académica, como en la popular, una línea seguida'; and he immediately referred to his passion for words with an exclamation: '¡Siempre el filólogo!' (IX, 1126). Language is indeed a recurring theme in all of Unamuno's work and encroaches into his sorties in other areas such as history, politics, religion, and of course literature.

By and large Unamuno's ideas on language are a reworking of those advanced by the linguistic philosophers associated with the Enlightenment and Romantic periods in Germany, notably Herder, Schleiermacher and Humboldt. What this means in effect is that Unamuno belongs fully to the expressive school of language (in opposition to the designative school, which holds language to be no more than a representational tool used to convey information and knowledge). Whereas in the designative approach to language words are seen to correspond to or define something outside themselves, and are therefore co-extensive with what they stand for, in the expressive school words are seen as creative instruments that reveal our nature, create our meanings and our myths, and articulate our emotions. Language for the German Romantics, and for many linguistic philosophers since, gives us our identity, dominates our relationships, and makes possible our creative endeavours. Rather than a tradesman's tool whose usage is invariant, it is rather a painter's palette that admits of many different tones and shades. The key point is that language is seen as both a formative influence (a sort of 'we are what we speak') and a facilitator of our own uniqueness as individuals, two aspects that are not easily reconcilable. From Humboldt Unamuno picked up the idea (previously expounded by Herder) that a language encapsulates the world-view of the nation that speaks it, and that consequently the way we conceptualize existence is governed by the language that we learn as children and which belongs to our community. From Schleiermacher he learnt that language and psychology are inseparable, that a person's utterances belong to that person's inner constitution, to what Schleiermacher calls the life-moments of the individual. These ideas and others closely related to them form the backbone of Unamuno's frequent pronouncements on the subject of language and inform not only his many essays and speeches devoted to linguistic questions but also his literary ideas.[1]

The point of departure for Unamuno is the communality of language, an aspect that is central to Herder and Humboldt, for as the latter wrote in his 1836 treatise *On the Diversity of Human Language Construction and its Influence on the Mental Development of the Human Species*, languages are 'bound and dependent on the nations to which they belong'. A language is not merely a social convenience, a simple means for human beings to maintain communal intercourse; it is 'a thing lying in their own nature, indispensable for the development of their own mental powers and the attainment of a world-view'. It follows from this that, for a speaker, the language he uses becomes a window on the world, for 'given that a language is a mode of apprehending the whole way of thought and feeling of a people, it must exert its influence on us' (Humboldt, 1999: 24, 27, 42). This belief that language fashions our way of thinking, that this way of thinking belongs to the whole community of speakers of a language, and that the way we look at the world is language-driven, was taken up by Unamuno and repeated throughout his life with endless variations. In *En torno al casticismo* (1895), written during his early, deterministic phase when he came under the influence of Positivism in the shape of Spencer and Taine, he wrote: 'La lengua es el receptáculo de la experiencia de un pueblo y el sedimento de su pensar; en los hondos repliegues de sus metáforas (y lo son la inmensa mayoría de los vocablos) ha ido dejando sus huellas el espíritu colectivo del pueblo, como en los terrenos geológicos el proceso de la fauna viva' (VIII, 94–95). The comparison of language with the fossil records of a once-living fauna suggests that at that stage Unamuno was still applying evolutionary models to language. By 1900 he had reacted against Positivism in general and Spencer and Taine in particular, and was replacing his earlier orientation with a modified one which placed the emphasis on finding the authentic roots of a given civilization in the more purely spiritual or intangible dimension of its past rather than in the impact of physical environment or events. But the centrality of language remains, as we can detect in his 1900 essay 'La fe': 'Escudriñad la lengua, porque la lengua lleva, a presión de atmósferas seculares, el sedimento de los siglos, el más rico aluvión del espíritu colectivo' (VIII, 336). A language, then, is a footprint of its speakers' experience and outlook, a view on the world from the perspective of a collectivity, an idea repeated in one of his key articles, 'Plenitud de plenitudes y todo plenitud' (1904): 'Cabe sostener que hay tantas filosofías como idiomas y tantas variantes de éstas como dialectos, incluso lo que podemos llamar el dialecto individual. Si hay una filosofía alemana, no es más que la filosofía del idioma alemán, y así con las demás. La lengua francesa es la que explica a Descartes' (VIII, 666). According to this view, entirely in consonance with Humboldt, a language not only embodies the way of thinking of its speakers but also serves to differentiate culturally between linguistic communities. Each language has become a sort of Kantian category that enables the speakers to make

---

[1] For a recent study of the influence of nineteenth-century linguistic philosophy on Unamuno see Longhurst, 2011. In this chapter I am concerned principally with the narrower question of the literary repercussions of Unamuno's ideas on language, the main source of which was unquestionably Humboldt, with a significant input from Schleiermacher.

sense of the world as well as to capture and preserve that sense. The idea of language as sedimentary bedrock, as constituting our historical identity and our vital outlook, is so fundamental to Unamuno's thought that he was still enunciating it towards the end of his life: 'Cada lengua lleva implícita, mejor encarnada en sí, una concepción de la vida universal, y con ella un sentimiento — se siente con palabras —, un consentimiento, una filosofía, y una religión', he told the audience who attended his retirement speech in 1934 (IX, 1123–24); and the following year, referring to the difficulty of translating philosophical works, he wrote to a correspondent: 'Cada lengua tiene su filosofía, por lo que cada filosofía tiene su lengua. Es la lengua la que habla universalmente en nosotros.'[2]

Even allowing for Unamuno's characteristic overstatements, the belief that language does our thinking for us carries at least two weighty implications. The first and less surprising is that a nation's language is what guarantees historical consciousness and continuity and therefore its artefacts in so far as these are linguistically driven. Seen in this light, our national language does not just play a role in conferring a mental outlook and therefore an identity; it also fashions our history, it lays down, as we have seen, 'el sedimento de los siglos', and it may even elbow out other powerful attitude-forming influences such as religion and ethnic provenance. Speakers of a language carry their nation's past with them, in other words we are inextricably linked to our past by our language, as Gadamer was famously to insist in his 1960 treatise *Truth and Method* and as had been perfectly well expressed by Humboldt over one hundred and twenty years earlier:

> In it [language] we gain a clearer and more vivid sense of how even the distant past is still linked with the feeling of today; for language has traversed through the experience of earlier generations and preserved a breath of this; and these generations have a natural and family kinship to us in these same sounds of the mother-tongue, which serve to express our own feelings as well. (Humboldt, 1999: 62)

The idea of language — more precisely its written form and in particular imaginative literature — as encapsulating a nation's past is one that turns up with some frequency in Unamuno in a variety of guises. Essentially what he argued was that the authentic Spanish spirit was condensed in its literature.[3] In Chapter IV of *En torno al casticismo* he argued that the essence of Castile at the time of her greatness is to be found in the writings of the mystics. Spain's Golden-Age theatre, he wrote in 1896, is 'la expresión más genuina de la conciencia colectiva del pueblo' (VIII, 231). In *Vida de Don Quijote y Sancho* (1905) he discerned the greatness of the Cervantine work in its assimilation of the Castilian spirit, seeing the work's co-protagonists as a paradigmatic manifestation both of Spain's nobility of spirit and of her inadequacies, a 'Biblia nacional' as he refers to it in one of his essays (VIII, 749). This Unamunian notion that a literary work is capable of capturing the way a nation or a people feels is scarcely a new one, since Johann Gottfried von Herder had said well over

---

[2] *Obras Completas* (Escelicer), IX, 560–61.

[3] An argument found not only in Unamuno. The idea is present in, for example, Ángel Ganivet's *Idearium español* when he says that Spain's '*summa* teológica y filosófica' is to be found in her *Romancero* (Ganivet, 1961: I, 160).

a hundred years earlier that the literature of a nation must be true to the inherent character of that nation, an idea that is echoed in Humboldt's contention that a language and its literature reflect a people's aspiration to attain a higher state. Unamuno believed, then, with Humboldt, that language is 'the outer appearance of the spirit of a people; the language is their spirit, and the spirit their language' (Humboldt, 1999: 46). He even follows Humboldt's description of languages as 'a work of the spirit' when he repeatedly associates the word *alma* with the three main literatures of the Iberian Peninsula, Portuguese, Catalan, and Castilian: each had its own *alma* given to it by its particular language, but beyond that they also evinced a common outlook derived from a common root, the *alma ibérica* or Iberian spirit which Unamuno found in a variety of writers from Portugal, Catalonia and Castile. What this must inevitably mean is that the work of a poet, dramatist, or novelist is not just an individual creation but also a collective one. Language has its own spirit or interiority, but it is an interiority that belongs to a cultural collective, not to an individual. This idea comes across powerfully in Unamuno's treatment of Cervantes's *Don Quixote*, in which he looked for the soul of Spain because, as he said in 'El caballero de la triste figura', 'el héroe es el alma colectiva individualizada' (VIII, 266). But there is more to it than a particular writer's creation of a symbolic figure. As Unamuno wrote in another essay, 'Sobre la lectura e interpretación del *Quijote*', 'no puede decirse que Don Quijote fuese hijo de Cervantes; pues si éste fue su padre, fue su madre el pueblo en que vivió y de que vivió Cervantes, y Don Quijote tiene mucho más de su madre que no de su padre' (VIII, 751–52). Don Quixote is thereby seen as the distillation of a whole race, not of a single mind. This, then, is the first implication of the view that language is inseparably entwined with the community that speaks it: that a work of literature belongs irremediably to that community, that it is, in a metaphorical sense, its intellectual property.

The second implication, already present in the immediately preceding quotation, is, for a living writer at any rate, much less comfortable. In Chapter 1 we noted the difficulty of explaining mental phenomena in purely physical terms. The problem is further complicated by the influence of language upon our thought, something on which Unamuno often insisted.[4] Our thoughts (including beliefs, emotions, desires) exist in our own individual minds. Language on the other hand is common property. To the extent that our thoughts are shaped by language, they are not simply private mental events. If one's thinking is as overwhelmingly dominated by one's language as the Humboldtian tradition would have us believe and as Unamuno staunchly accepts, this rather devalues the creative thrust of the individual writer, who is simply instantiating a pre-existing concept. Few poets would wish to accept that they were simply agents voicing thoughts already inherent in the language they were using, and Unamuno the poet — for it was primarily as a poet that he saw himself, whether writing in verse or prose — had to struggle to find a solution that would allow him to assert his individuality through language. The basic premiss,

---

[4] Statements of the kind 'el lenguaje y el pensamiento van indisolublemente unidos, puesto que son en el fondo una sola y misma cosa' (VIII, 466), or 'Se piensa con palabras o con otros signos de expresión [...] y sin esos signos no se piensa (*Obras Completas* (Escelicer), IX, 871) are legion in Unamuno.

nevertheless, remained unquestioned: because culture and thought are language-dependent, individuals who inherit a language are ineluctably absorbing a culture and a way of thinking. The writer simply cannot avoid being the inheritor of a cultural tradition. In the first place Unamuno tried to reconcile himself to this state of affairs by claiming the status of a spokesman for his age. Of his novel *Paz en la guerra* he said that it gathers not only 'recuerdos de mi vida' but also 'de la vida del pueblo en que nací', so that he can conclude by saying that 'esto no es una novela; es un pueblo' (I, 5–6), while he saw *Abel Sánchez* as reflecting the 'vida social' of the Spain of his time and of the Spain of the past, with the protagonist conceived as a heroic version of the 'envidia colectiva' which tormented the Spanish people in much the same way as Don Quixote had been seen as the embodiment of Spanish ideals.[5] But such a defence of literary production could not by itself have satisfied Unamuno, for whom the writer's uniquely personal voice was always what was most attractive, and he sought to reconcile Humboldt's linguistic philosophy with his own powerfully driven curiosity about the world of the mind and the emotions, in a word about himself. For it was language's, and hence literature's, potential to serve as a tool of self-cognition that interested him above all.[6]

Humboldt had not denied the roles of individuals, but he limited their efficacy to the degree to which their actions or ideas coalesced with the sentiments of the community:

> In virtue of the connection here in view between the individual and the mass surrounding him, every significant activity of the former belongs, albeit mediately only, and in some degree, to the latter as well. But the existence of languages proves that there are also mental creations which in no way whatever pass out from a single individual to the remainder, but can only emanate from the simultaneous self-activity of all. In languages, therefore, since they always have a national form, *nations*, as such, are truly and immediately creative. (Humboldt, 1999: 42)

This is the notion that lies behind Unamuno's attributing *Don Quixote* to the creativity, not of Cervantes, but of the Spanish people. Yet there is obviously a tension at work here. Humboldt was engaged in an exercise in linguistics, and he wished to sustain his view that languages reflect 'the mental power of nations' (Humboldt, 1999: 48), and hence their different stages of intellectual development. Indeed he often referred to the mental individuality of nations as if nations were capable of undergoing spiritual experiences. At the same time he was not oblivious of the simple truth that ideas, feelings, and aspirations are really experienced and expressed by individuals. There is no such thing as an objective thought, feeling, or expectation since they are experienced subjectively. All Humboldt could offer by way of solution is to say that while languages are the work of nations they nevertheless still retain the possibility of self-creation for individuals 'in that they can be produced solely in each individual, but only in such fashion that each presupposes the understanding of all, and all fulfil this expectation' (Humboldt, 1999: 44).

---

[5] In the prologue to the second edition (Madrid: Renacimiento, 1928), reprinted in Unamuno, 1995b: 5–6.

[6] Unamuno's views on language as cognition have been splendidly studied by Paul Ilie, 1987.

The inadequacy of this explanation of artistic endeavour — it is little more than a concession — obviously struck Unamuno, obsessed as he was with 'uncovering the mind', to borrow the title of Alison Sinclair's stimulating probes into the fictional ontologies of Unamuno (Sinclair, 2001). Unamuno was well aware of the limitations of language for probing the depths of the soul: '¡Miserable menester el de escribir! ¡Lastimoso apremio el de tener que hablar! [...] ¡Si fuera posible ir creando el lenguaje a medida que se habla lo pensado!' (VIII, 611). This expression of regret he wrote upon the occasion when he realized that the words he had earlier written conveyed a different impression from the one he had wanted to communicate. Here we find Unamuno regretting the power that language exerts over our thoughts in accordance with the Humboldtian doctrine that any thought we care to formulate must of necessity be clothed in worldly garb, those words, images, and concepts which are our common heritage. Unamuno could never be content to act as spokesman or medium for the world out there. Something had to be found that would express his intimate being, what he calls a life-giving sap: 'la savia, esa savia vivificante que desde las raíces sube a mis frutos, esa savia que no se ve, ésa es mía' (VIII, 925). He found the answer in an aspect of language on which Humboldt had had little to say: style.

It is here that another of the great German linguisticians of the Romantic period, Friedrich Schleiermacher, whom Unamuno read in the 1890s, played a role in shaping Unamuno's approach. Although Schleiermacher shared Humboldt's view, inherited from Herder, that a language was a communal form of expression developed to voice that community's enterprise and outlook, he also insisted, crucially, that a knowledge of the grammar that governs a language is not enough to grasp the sense of a text or an utterance. We also need to interpret psychologically (which he at first called 'technical interpretation'), that is to say, we need to be aware of the circumstances of the text or the utterance, which involves knowing something of the state of mind of the writer or speaker as well as of the readers or audience to whom the text or utterance was addressed. Schleiermacher goes even further in pursuit of the psychological dimension of a text, recognizing that an author is not a fixed entity, but rather a dynamic spirit who evolves and changes. Hence in order to capture the sense of an utterance we must be aware, firstly, of the sense inherent in the language inherited by the author, and secondly, of the psychological origins of the utterance, that is to say, of the authorial act that achieves concrete linguistic expression. According to Schleiermacher, a language is certainly an interpersonal system, but each person uses it in his or her particular way. Psychology and language are therefore interdependent, and the style of an individual is not simply a matter of the way in which he or she handles the grammar or lexicon; it is also a distinctive trait of that individual.

Schleiermacher's idea of style, far more developed than the famous declaration of the French academician Buffon, 'le style c'est l'homme même', passed on to Unamuno and can be found in a number of his essays. But it also carries implications for the novels. In Schleiermacher's hermeneutic system, an utterance or a text is regarded as an intrinsic aspect of the mental or spiritual circumstance of the person who is speaking or writing, a principle that we can observe to be at work in some of Unamuno's best-known novels. If it is true that the psychological state of a person, the 'life-moment' as Schleiermacher calls it, is held in that person's way of expression in words, so that we cannot separate language from psychology, is not this principle illustrated in the way that those wayward, anguished, solitary, or perplexed characters that are Gertrudis, Augusto, Joaquín or Ángela express themselves? For there can be little doubt that Unamuno is characterizing these personages more than anything by the way they express themselves. Not by what they do, but by what they say; what they say to others and to themselves (and of course what they write, since Joaquín and Ángela write their own memoirs, and Augusto is something of a poet). Unamuno endows his personages with a distinct manner of addressing the world, thereby revealing their intimate being. For Schleiermacher, understanding a person is tantamount to understanding how that person expresses him or herself, and this interesting intuition, perhaps Schleiermacher's best-known contribution to the hermeneutic tradition, is likely to have made a lasting impression on Unamuno, since, as he often maintained, the interior and the exterior of a person exert a mutual influence and cannot be separated. Even dissimulation can be revealing, as was argued by Wilhelm Dilthey, Schleiermacher's biographer and commentator.

Adapting Schleiermacher's psychological interpretation of style, Unamuno converted the subject of style into a pillar of his theory of creative writing. A writer may not be able to choose his or her own language but can nevertheless develop his or her own style. Such importance did Unamuno attach to the concept of style that when exiled on the island of Fuerteventura in 1924 he conceived the idea of recycling his past comments on style and adding further thoughts on the subject with a view to publishing the material in a single volume under the title *Alrededor del estilo*, although the planned book never saw the light of day in his lifetime.[7] In effect Unamuno is introducing a difference between language and style, between the writer as product and the writer as producer. An author cannot help being a product, but style will ensure that he or she will also be a producer. As we shall see, style stands for many qualities, but above all it stands for the personality of the writer.

Unamuno's meditations on style have, typically for him, an etymological starting point. Style comes from stylus, a writing and engraving implement which leaves an impression. Using a stylus is a craft that has to be learnt. Likewise style does not arise spontaneously; it comes through learning and with practice. Here Unamuno uses exactly the same argument he uses in the case of personality. Just as we acquire our own sense of identity through others, so a writer acquires his or her own style through observing the style of other writers. Those writers who are insensitive to style in others will fail to develop their own; and those who are content to copy

---

[7]   The project finally came to fruition in 1998 with the publication of Miguel de Unamuno, *Alrededor del estilo*, ed. by Laureano Robles, although all of the articles bar two can also be found in the Escelicer edition of the *Obras Completas*, IX, 885–947; and of the two missing ones, one appears under a different title at (Escelicer) IX, 881–82. Most (not all) of the articles in this collection were written in 1924 and published that same year in *Los Lunes del Imparcial*, but they incorporate material going back many years.

someone else's style will not be true to themselves. In the first case personality will be absent because those who 'carecen de estilo [...] carecen de personalidad' (*Alrededor*, 35); and in the second because a borrowed style, like a borrowed dress, will not fit the body that wears it: 'se ve que el remedo no es estilo, y que aquí no hay personalidad alguna' (*Alrededor*, 35). Style may indeed be seen as a dress, as something crafted or fashioned, but 'el verdadero traje, el traje espiritual, se lo hace el que lo lleva' (*Alrededor*, 50). Style, then, is nothing less than the expression of personality in writing, 'su forma suprema, su sello eterno' (*Alrededor*, 149); it is like the pulse of the heart, carrying the life-blood of the writer, not merely a way of expressing thoughts and feelings but actually a way of thinking and of feeling. Unamuno does not deny that style is expression, but it is the expression of personality and therefore can neither be classified nor defined, and indeed Unamuno's approach to the subject is strongly metaphorical. In an interesting article on Benito Pérez Galdós, whom he confesses he only came to appreciate during his 1924 stay in Fuerteventura, he criticizes the Canarian writer for his confused view of style. Through the character Máximo Manso in *El amigo Manso*, he writes, Galdós equates style with oratory, with wordiness, with outward appearances, and a lack of style he equates with a reduced vocabulary:

> Pobre y triste concepto del estilo, que se reduce a algo accidental y muy exterior. [...] El amigo Galdós, como los meros y netos creadores, confundía la pobreza de estilo con la pobreza de vocabulario, sin comprender que cabe un estilo riquísimo, la expresión de una personalidad riquísima — que siempre será una expresión riquísima — con un vocabulario pobrísimo, con unos centenares de palabras. (*Alrededor*, 110)

Style in Unamuno's conception must not be confused with diction or vocabulary. To speak of the style of such-and-such a writer is simply to speak of that writer. What characterizes a great writer's work is that writer's style, the stamp of a personality, and it is style that gives unity to a work of art, an intimate organic unity. Style wells up from the depths of the writer's psyche, it is a search for self, it is, in that characteristically Unamunian expression, a 'querer ser'.

But if style is a willed phenomenon in the first place, in the fullness of time it takes over the writer's being. 'El estilo se va haciendo, y es porque el artista se está buscando a sí mismo. ¿Se encuentra? Aquí está su tragedia. Y cuando se encuentra es que ha encontrado su obra; es que su obra le ha hecho a él' (*Alrededor*, 101). What we have here, of course, is a reformulation of Unamuno's theory of personality. A persona is the public role or presence that we develop on the basis of our interaction between self and others; it becomes our personality, our identity. Style is what a writer develops on the basis of an interaction between the writer's self and his or her works. Once that style has been forged we can indeed say with Unamuno that 'su obra le ha hecho a él', that the writer is the product of his work. But this is more than just a theory of style; it is at the same time a theory of reading. Indeed Unamuno virtually says as much, if not explicitly then at least indirectly. Referring to the reader who, on being asked if he wrote, replied 'Yo produzco consumo. Escribo lo que me dan a leer', Unamuno comments: '¿O es que crees, lector, que yo no sé que estás escribiendo conmigo esto que los dos leemos?' (*Alrededor*, 127).

Writing and reading cannot be separated. Unamuno the writer is as much a reader as his readers. As he quarries within himself he is placing himself in the reader's position, reading his own mind, his sentiments, his disposition. Style thus becomes a crystallization of the writer's self, so that Unamuno can happily equate style, that is self-expression, with biography, and biography with autobiography. But we must be very clear that this is a phenomenon of writing, not of living. What counts is not the writer's subject but the writer's style. In a writer with style, any subject becomes autobiographical, even biography itself:

> Biografía no es [...] biología. Biografía es cosa de estilo y la más íntima del estilo. Todo estilo que lo sea es biográfico, describe una vida. Y aun mejor, es autobiográfico, describe la vida de aquél que lo tiene, del hombre cuyo es el estilo. Y de aquí que todo biógrafo con estilo, que todo hombre biógrafo — llamémosle si se quiere novelista — , es un autobiógrafo, se describe, se expresa a sí mismo. (*Alrededor*, 69–70)

And not just a man, we might add, recalling how Ángela Carballino cannot help but reveal her own intimate being in her biography of Don Manuel Bueno.

For Unamuno, then, style was directly linked to the deepest being of the writer, and, as Schleiermacher had taught him, encapsulated the life-moment of that writer. But this still leaves one question outstanding, a question that did not escape him, especially in view of his insistence that language and thought are so interwoven as to be virtually inseparable. Style is attached to a language, and a language belongs to a community of speakers. Does a community therefore have a style, and is this style passed on with the language? Unamuno was thoroughly disgruntled with the kind of written Spanish cultivated in Restoration Spain, which he described as some kind of disease, *literatismitis*, or style for style's sake, the kind of writing that disguised an inability to come up with fresh ideas, vacuity of expression being the clearest symptom of Castile's *marasmo* or stagnation. Such a *castizo* brand of Spanish, based on rhetorical clichés, was for Unamuno wholly unpalatable, as well as an obstacle to cultural renewal, utterly incapable as he saw it of expressing the deep and vibrant culture he sought to promote.[8] It was not the Spanish language itself which was lacking but rather the way it was cultivated by Castilian men of letters, a habit that got in the way of an authentic form of expression, and hence Unamuno's advocacy of the *americanización del castellano*, a view explained by his admiration for the style of writing of the Peruvian Ricardo Palma, the Uruguayan Juan Zorrilla de San Martín, and various other Spanish-American authors. Unamuno's strong distaste for the bombastic and circumlocutory Castilian style also explains his urging of Catalans to write in Spanish, not because he belittled Catalan, but, on the contrary, because he saw in the Catalan *Renaixença* a vibrancy which was missing in nineteenth-century Castilian culture. Catalans, and indeed Basques, when they expressed themselves in Spanish, struck a different tone, because their diction and syntax were different, and according to Unamuno much more transparent to, and therefore more in harmony with, the thought inherent in them.

---

[8] It should be said that Unamuno was not alone in denouncing nineteenth-century Castilian Spanish. Baroja and Azorín did much the same, if perhaps not as stridently as Unamuno.

Since Unamuno deplored the *castizo* way of expression of Restoration Spain and contrariwise commended that of the non-Castilian regions, it is obvious that he admits the phenomenon of style at the level of a community of users; yet as we have seen he also wishes to claim style as the creative writer's 'savia vivificante', the nourishing sap that rises from the roots and gives the fruit of his endeavours its particular flavour, in Unamuno's organic terminology, that is to say the individual writer's personal contribution to the organism that is a living language. There is much the same tension at work here that we noted earlier in Humboldt's position, except that the situation is the reverse. For Humboldt what was important was to retain the community's hold over language so that he could argue his thesis of national development; for Unamuno what is important is to claim the preponderance of the individual while acknowledging the communal nature of language. He is quite clear that a language carries its own style: 'El lenguaje tiene su estilo; el lenguaje es estilo, puesto que es un pueblo, y un pueblo es un hombre' (*Alrededor*, 73). As in Humboldt, we find the same tendency to individualize a nation. A people has its own style, just like an individual citizen, not least because the latter is a condensation of the entire collective in which he or she has developed. But if there is a collective style attached to a language, or, more narrowly, to a community of speakers, how can style be deeply personal? Does not a linguistic community also have its own characteristic personality? Unamuno is keenly aware of the potential contradiction in claiming both a collective personality and a distinctive individual personality derived from one and the same language and admits so quite openly:

> Y esto de la personalidad colectiva, y, por lo tanto del estilo colectivo, del estilo de muchos y de nadie, es la cruz de esta errabunda indagación. Ello parece echar por tierra cuanto hemos dicho acerca del estilo.
>
> Porque si hay un estilo español, y francés, e italiano, e inglés, y alemán, y griego, y latino..., y así siguiendo; y si hay un estilo del siglo XIII, y otro del XVI, y otro del XVIII, y otro del XX, en las distintas expresiones del espíritu humano, entonces se nos hunde cuanto hemos dicho. (*Alrededor*, 151)

Unamuno's way out of the quandary is to distinguish between two kinds of style. There is a style which is often associated with a time or a place, say in architecture or painting, or even dress. Unamuno calls this style a type by analogy with typefaces. There are many types (as there are many typefaces), each type being typical of something (an age, a place, a nationality). Type is a broader concept of style than that other concept which Unamuno reserves for the creative individual. This personal style can operate perfectly comfortably within the larger type, fashion, or manner which characterizes a community, a nationality, or an age.

Unamuno, then, discriminates between two kinds of style, a personal and an impersonal one; but this is not the end of the road. For here we arrive at the distinction that Unamuno really wants to make and which lies at the core of his disquisitions on style. He equates possessing style with displaying a poetic sensitivity to self and world. When he says 'el estilo es cosa de poetas', he quickly adds: 'Al decir poeta no queremos decir uno que escriba en verso, ¡claro está!, sino, conforme a la fuerza nativa del vocablo, queremos decir un creador, o sea uno que tiene estilo' (*Alrededor* 47). The real distinction is between two kinds of writers: those who write as poets and those who do not. The latter he calls *literatos*, which in Unamuno has pejorative connotations. Style is the preserve of poets, who are not to be confused with versifiers. What *literatos* display is *manera*: 'La manera es cosa de literatos, así como el estilo es cosa de poetas' (*Alrededor*, 47). In 'El arte de escribir', an article written for *La Nación* some years earlier (1920), Unamuno had already made that same distinction. Style is what enables the pen to dredge up and give form to those sedimentary convictions of the writer 'que yacían en las entrañas de su mente sin que él mismo lo supiera de antemano. Lo que se conoce en el estilo. Que no es la manera' (Unamuno, 1994: 53). There is no real distinction to be made between the what and the how, between content and form or *contenido* and *continente*, because 'el estilo de un escritor es el contenido de sus escritos' (*Alrededor*, 73). Style has nothing to do with genre, form, or even expression in its syntagmatic sense. It has everything to do with the ability to capture linguistically those ideas, sentiments, and visions that Unamuno sees as shaping human existence in its non-physical dimension. He dismisses the *novelas de costumbres* as a mere distraction, void of intensity of emotion and little better than dross. And he is happy to cross generic boundaries and call the greatest novels poems, and the greatest works of philosophy and religion novels: 'Una novela es un poema. Cuando lo es claro. Y cuando no lo es, tampoco es novela' (*Alrededor*, 94). Unamuno argues that a poet does not use arguments but intentions and feelings taken from his own experience of the world. A philosopher on the other hand will usually stay at the level of the language he has inherited. His work is a verbal construct: 'El poeta es el que nos da todo un mundo personalizado, el mundo entero hecho hombre, el verbo hecho mundo; el filósofo sólo nos da algo de esto en cuanto tenga de poeta, pues fuera de ello no discurre él, sino que discurren en él sus razones o, mejor, sus palabras' (VIII, 666). It is language that speaks in the philosopher, not the philosopher who makes language speak. It is this distinction between language as logic and language as poetry that lies behind Unamuno's categorizing of the Gospels as a 'divina novela', in other words as the work of poets. But if the poetic approach is distinguishable from the discursive approach of the disciplines impelled by logic, it is nevertheless still subject to the constraints of language, a limitation of which Unamuno was acutely aware and which surfaces repeatedly in his literature.

From Poet to Community

Unamuno uses the word poet in a very specific sense. He frequently resorts to etymology to explain the nuance he often gives to words, and in this case he is using poet in its original sense of maker or composer working through the medium of language, a maker of worlds that transcend ordinary observation. The poet is the writer who can bring the latent power of words to fruition. It is a creative endeavour firstly, because, as Unamuno liked to say, 'nombrar es crear', and secondly, because it involves trawling the depths of one's being in search of new perspectives on our world. The role of the poet is to receive the traditions inherent in a language and to carry forward that tradition through his or her own personal contributions. Inasmuch as prose fiction is a creative exploration that seeks to expand our horizons, it is a poetic form of cognition. Its effectiveness is acutely dependent on style, that is to say on the poet's personal vision as evoked by his particular use of words. Style is self-expression, but this is not the end of the story, for self-expression is fraught with difficulties and conundrums, as we can observe in Unamuno's constant preoccupation with the language question. In his essays Unamuno several times acknowledged the difficulties involved in crystallizing his thoughts, not least because once we have expressed an idea whose pre-linguistic existence was an indistinct nebula, words seem to take over completely and escape from our grasp. That intimate style that according to Unamuno characterizes the poet, can lead, paradoxically, to estrangement.

In the essay 'Intelectualidad y espiritualidad', aptly written in third-person throughout, as if Unamuno were alluding to a person other than himself, we find an exploration of verbal alienation, in which a writer returns to an earlier work of his and does not recognize his earlier intention. Unamuno here writes using *style indirect libre*:

> No, aquello no era suyo, aquello no había querido él escribirlo, no era aquello lo que había pensado y creído, no era lo que había escrito. Y, sin embargo, no cabía duda: aquello, aquello que veía ahora tan extraño, aquello fue lo que escribió y con lo que más renombre había ganado. Volvió a leerlo.
>
> No, no comunica uno lo que quería comunicar –pensó–; apenas un pensamiento encarna en palabra, y así revestido sale al mundo, es de otro, o más bien no es de nadie por ser de todos. La carne de que se reviste el lenguaje es comunal y es externa; engurruñe el pensamiento, lo aprisiona y aun lo trastorna y contrahace. No, él no había querido decir aquello, él nunca había pensado aquello. (VIII, 609)

On returning to the earlier work, the writer does not recognize the intended message, or, what comes to the same thing, he does not recognize himself. The phenomenon leads, almost inevitably, to questioning the integrity of self: '¿No habría en él más de un sujeto?' (VIII, 609). The problem arises precisely because Unamuno is trying to convert what developed as a tool of social communication into an instrument for self-cognition. In accordance with the linguistic philosophy of German Romanticism, he sees language as the main source of identity of a people, and then insists on applying this principle to the individual. But to differentiate the self linguistically, to attain what Unamuno calls style, personality in writing, presents an enormous challenge, for words have the power to dissimulate as well as reveal. It is this struggle with words, with their power to beguile and their power to mislead, that amounts to one of the most original aspects of Unamuno's fiction. Can words be a way of cognizing self? Or of cognizing other? The language doubt is ingeniously at work in *Niebla*.

Niebla is a study in self-discovery. Having lived under the protective tutelage of his mother, Augusto Pérez's mission is as much to find himself as to find a surrogate mother in the form of a wife, or, as Alison Sinclair has put it in an indispensable essay, to achieve self-definition (Sinclair, 1987). In presenting him stepping out into the world at the very start of the novel and disappearing into the mists of nothingness at the end, Unamuno is making him into a symbol of the human acquisition of self-awareness. Augusto is a person in search of a role, an identity. To this end he employs two strategies: the physical and the verbal. Unamuno introduces this distinction in a quite deliberate manner. Don Fermín tells Augusto that 'el único conocimiento eficaz es el conocimiento *post-nuptias*'. [...] Y créemelo, no hay más conocimiento sustancial y esencial que ése, el conocimiento penetrante' (I, 519). Augusto will later repeat this when, driven by sexual instinct, he grabs hold of Rosarito, the laundry girl, and presses her against his body. 'No hay más verdad que la vida fisiológica' he tells himself (I, 577). Language, by contrast, is a fantasy, a misrepresentation, a lie. 'La única verdad es el hombre fisiológico, el que no habla, el que no miente...' (I, 578). The experience is resumed later when he indulges in sexual foreplay with Rosarito, lays her on the sofa, and seems on the point of achieving Don Fermín's brand of knowledge, encouraged by the flushed and ardent girl. But at the last minute, to the alarm of his eager companion, he pulls back, bewitched by his own image reflected in her eyes, and returns to his world of words, unable to fulfil his physiological desires or to satisfy a woman's erotic craving.[9]

The materialistic piano teacher Eugenia, who hates music but needs money, realizes that Augusto, with his poems and his philosophizing, is something of a verbal wimp, and once her mortgage is redeemed chooses to throw in her lot with the penniless but sexually attractive Mauricio. Augusto loses out on both counts, matrimonially and ontologically, since his verbal explorations lead to an impasse. 'Inventar un género no es más que darle un nombre nuevo', says Goti (I, 573), and while we may take it that this is a tongue-in-cheek justification of *nivola* on the part of Unamuno according to his axiom 'nombrar es crear', the fact remains that in resorting to endless dialogue with others and with himself (or with his dog, which boils down to the same thing), Augusto encounters nothing but contradictions, which ultimately prevent him from understanding anything useful about himself. As Paul Olson has explained, language ends up by losing the subservience to its referent and acquiring its own autonomy (Olson, 1984: 91). Ironically, the only disinterested view of language in the novel comes from the mouth of one who cannot speak, Augusto's dog Orfeo, who lacks man's capacity to dissimulate through language.[10] The dog's funeral oration brings home the lesson (but to a now dead Augusto) that language cannot be used as a tool for self-cognition because, like barking, it is directed outwards:

> [El hombre] ladra a su manera, habla, y eso le ha servido para inventar lo que no hay y no fijarse en lo que hay. En cuanto le ha puesto un nombre a algo, ya no ve este algo, no hace sino oír el nombre que le puso, o verle escrito. La lengua le sirve para mentir, inventar lo que no hay, y confundirse. (I, 668)

This view of language, which to an extent coincides with statements made by Unamuno in his essays, suggests that ultimately it is but a surrogate, and that it

---

[9] The reflection in another's eyes is of course a reminder of infancy, when the baby looks into its mother's eyes. Augusto constantly thinks of his mother and of the fact that 'la fisiología le causaba horror' (I, 508). His father, Augusto associates with vomiting blood. The contrast between the two poles, the rarefied and the physiological, is again present in the contrast between the mother and the father, one associated with the spiritual, the other with the physiological. In other words, we inhabit two worlds, Cartesian dualism in another form.

[10] In connection with Orfeo's role and its relation to the broader context of the ideas on language in *Niebla*, see Marsha S. Collins, 2002.

cannot lead us to the truth about ourselves, because it points to a non-existent world, a world that is born of convention, of the need for dialogue, whether with others or ourselves. Our own existence cannot be underwritten by words, not least because words require an interlocutor who is the ultimate interpreter of what we say, and absolute certainty is thereby lost. It is the receptor, not the originator, who is ultimately responsible for the meaning of words.

Unamuno's fondness for quoting the opening words of St John's Gospel is a mere indication of his view that language arose to talk to God, but since God is not a real interlocutor, we are in effect talking to ourselves. But who is the receptor of our prayers? When we dialogue with ourselves we are creating a ghostly entity. This at any rate seems to be the inference to be drawn from Orfeo's canine 'speech', a speech which can only be thought, not spoken in human language, and which is addressed to no one, since there is only a corpse present. Orfeo's God, whom he had thought immortal, is now dead. Interestingly Orfeo brings us back to the physiological theme at the very end of the novel. He learns of Augusto's death through the sense of smell: 'olió a su amo muerto, olió la muerte de su amo' (I, 667). Upon Augusto's death, the narrator dismisses the sentiments of Augusto's friends and acquaintances as irrelevant, but makes an exception of the dog. He is the only figure who can express himself with complete sincerity because he does not speak like a man. The scission of existence into the physiological and the verbal — the two worlds which we inhabit, the physical and the mental — which is such a prominent aspect of *Niebla*, is cleverly invoked in one of the poems from *Rimas de dentro* (1923):

> Cerré el libro que hablaba
> de esencias, de existencias, de sustancias,
> de accidentes y modos,
> de causas y de efectos,
> de materia y de forma,
> de conceptos e ideas,
> de números, fenómenos,
> cosas en sí y en otras, opiniones,
> hipótesis, teorías...,
> cerré el libro y abrióse
> a mis ojos el mundo.
> Traspuesto había el sol ya la colina;
> en el cielo esmaltábanse los álamos
> y nacían entre ellos las estrellas;
> la luna enjalbegaba el firmamento
> cuyo fulgor difuso
> en las aguas del río se bañaba.
> Y, mirando a la luna, a la colina,
> las estrellas, los álamos,
> el río y el fulgor del firmamento,
> sentí la gran mentira
> de esencias, de existencias, de sustancias,
> de accidentes y modos,
> de causas y de efectos,
> de materia y de forma,

> de conceptos e ideas,
> de números, fenómenos,
> cosas en sí y en otras, opiniones,
> hipótesis, teorías,
> esto es: palabras.
> Sobre el libro cerrado
> que yacía en la yerba,
> por la luna su pasta iluminada,
> mas su interior a oscuras,
> descansaba una rana
> que iba rondando su nocturna ronda.
> ¡Oh Kant, cuánto te admiro! (IV, 571)

The poem is based on the ingenious contrast between the poet's world of words and abstract concepts on the one hand and the frog calling for a mate on the other. It clearly suggests that human language is one thing and the world quite another, but, more than this, that to describe the world which surrounds us through the linguistic medium is radically to misrepresent it. Language and the concepts which it holds are 'la gran mentira'. The reference to Kant's first *Critique* is presumably an allusion to the latter's contention that logical reasoning cannot bring us to the truth of those things, such as religious belief, that are most dear to us. The somewhat ironic froggy ending that Unamuno gives his poem points to the fact that the world, or nature, cares not a whit for man's linguistic lucubrations, Kantian or otherwise. This poem comes very close to re-stating Augusto's insight, which he had gone on to forget, that man deceives himself through language: 'el hombre en cuanto habla miente, y en cuanto se habla a sí mismo, es decir, en cuanto piensa sabiendo que piensa, se miente. No hay más verdad que la vida fisiológica' (I, 577). In this poem the poet is forced to recognize that the language of books (i.e. of the intellect, of ideas) is artificial. The only real language is the language of the frog as he goes about his nocturnal business in search of a mate. This, of course, amounts to one of the greatest paradoxes of a man whose business was words. If only the natural world is real, words are superfluous, a mere distraction; yet, it is language that makes us what we are, that gives us our sense of belonging.[11]

Unamuno's other novels do not give prominence to the theme of language in such an explicit manner, yet the presence of a linguistic fabrication within the plot is a frequent technique. In addition to speech acts there is as it were a 'language act' within the fiction, and this language act has an ostensible function and an underlying motive. If in *Niebla* Unamuno makes ample use of interior monologue, in *Abel Sánchez* he goes one better and adds, in what is a third-person narrative, fragments of an autobiography. Joaquín Monegro declares that he is writing his

---

[11] The philosophy which the poem projects and which is found *en passant* in the novels is Schopenhauerian through and through, right down to the admiring exclamation at the end. For Schopenhauer, our physiological urges, and notably the sexual impulse, are a pointer to the ultimate reality or underlying noumenon, the unstoppable Will of Nature. By contrast the aesthetic realm, which offers us objects of intellectual contemplation, gives us a means, temporary though it is, of seeking relief and consolation from the burdens of a violent and predatory existence (Schopenhauer, 1966: I, §38).

confessional memoir 'para que ella [his daughter Joaquina], después de yo muerto, pudiese conocer a su pobre padre y compadecerle y quererle' (I, 719). In other words, it is written as a justification for the bitterness caused by the betrayal, as Joaquín sees it, which he had suffered at the hands of Abel and Helena. Since we learn that Joaquín had earlier told his daughter about the source of his pain, his self-justification appears to be either disingenuous or tantamount to self-deception. The secret memoir, instead of revealing that inner self that Joaquín longs to identify and understand, serves instead to frustrate his search. What is especially interesting about Unamuno's technique is the way in which the main, third-person, narration appears to contradict the character's autobiographical explorations, not in the basic facts of his life but in the motives that drive the personage. In his autobiographical inquisitions Joaquín Monegro makes judgements, both about himself and about others, but these judgements are not validated in the main part of the narration. Joaquín's memoir is not an explanation or an unburdening, as he says, but rather the verbal equivalent of Abel the painter's self-portrait: an attempt at self-objectification and claim to public fame. That is why he is also planning to write the 'Memorias de un médico viejo'. What Joaquín craves is Abel's popularity and public applause, even if in his memoir he refuses to admit it. On one occasion he exclaims to himself that he would gladly exchange his life for someone else's, the implication being that he is thinking of Abel. But in his confession he contradicts this, insisting on the need to fulfil his tragic destiny. His portrait of Abel in the confession is that of an insensitive, calculating and utterly selfish individual; yet the Abel that we observe in the main narration is sensitive to Joaquín's suffering, never speaks ill of him, defends him in public, and appears to be genuinely moved by his eloquent speech at the celebration of his Cain and Abel painting. It is not a matter of one narrative version being objective and true and the other subjective and false, since the two versions are not mutually exclusive. It is rather a case of watching how the personage creates himself while others are creating him. Joaquín's verbal construct is an attempt to forge an identity for himself, a kind of Byronic tragic role; it is neither less nor more real than the various identities attributed to him by others: his wife, his daughter, his son-in-law, Abel, Helena, his patients, his fellow academicians. What is different about his self-portrait is that it is reflexive. Joaquín's all-consuming envy is spontaneous, unreflective; but once he objectifies and names it (literally as well as metaphorically, e.g. 'ese hediondo dragón que me ha envenenado y entenebrecido la vida' (I, 698)), his malady becomes a topos, a motive, a pseudo-identity, in effect a self-defence. Language becomes a smokescreen. It reveals not his real self, but his self-delusion. The linguistic phenomenon is exactly that described by the dog Orfeo in *Niebla*.

Even more intriguing, although perhaps more artificial, is Unamuno's use of autobiography in *Tulio Montalbán y Julio Macedo*, for here the autobiography is merely mentioned, never quoted, and we only learn of its existence near the end of the novelette. Why introduce this device? *Tulio Montalbán y Julio Macedo* is precisely about identity in writing, whether such identity is authentic or fabricated. It revolves around the historicity or otherwise of a biography of the legendary patriot and liberator Tulio Montalbán. This biography, 'The Life of Tulio Montalbán', is the work of a historian, Henri Jacquetot, Montalbán's father-in-law, and was written as a tribute to the liberator and his wife, Elvira Jacquetot, both tragically dead at a very early age. Tulio Montalbán is nothing but an image, a verbal existence, 'cosa de libro', as Unamuno would say. Introduced as the creation of the writer Henri Jacquetot, his is a public persona, a mask known to all, the public property of a nation, of a chronicler, and of a readership. If he has a truth, it is the truth of myth, of literature.

What is especially interesting is that Julio Macedo, on reading Jacquetot's biography, is unable to recognize the Tulio Montalbán that he knew intimately. He attempts to counter it by writing 'The Memoirs of Julio Macedo'. He, too, resorts to words in an attempt to locate and crystallize Montalbán's true self. His epigraph, borrowed from Lucretius, 'eripitur persona, manet res', indicates his wish to tear off the mask, to revert to a pristine state, a thing-in-itself, uninterpreted and uninterpretable. He fails of course, and the autobiography of Julio Macedo will be cast, unread, upon the flames, alongside the fatal biography of Tulio Montalbán. Words have failed both Tulio and Julio.

The theme of falsification through language is also prominent in *La novela de Don Sandalio, jugador de ajedrez*, which is simultaneously a biography and an autobiography (as indeed Unamuno himself speculates in the epilogue). It purports to be the story of Don Sandalio, but Don Sandalio remains an enigma; on the other hand we do learn something of the author of the twenty-three letters, especially his state of mind and peculiar obsession. In *La novela de Don Sandalio* much of the text revolves around saying or not saying, around listening or refusing to listen. Unamuno is here focusing on the linguistic act, whether written or spoken, something he does, if not quite so tenaciously, in much of his fiction. Words are not the conveyors of fixed truths but of half-truths or non-truths, their referential value having been attenuated. Words have become that 'insondable tontería humana' which the letter-writer abhors but in which he cannot help indulging, as when, much to the horror of his enviably silent Don Sandalio, he harangues the latter with a pedantically erudite dissertation on the bishop during an interval in their chess games. When Don Sandalio falls ill, his substitute at the chess table is a talker who spoils the game of chess (i.e. game of life) by his incessant chatter, described by the letter-writer as 'algo insoportable. ¡Que diferencia con las partidas graves, recogidas y silenciosas de Don Sandalio!' (II, 366). But even the silent chess player, Don Sandalio, it transpires, was a talker, who often spoke of his chess companion in the privacy of his home. This garrulous Don Sandalio is anathema to the letter-writer, who promptly rejects as unacceptable the image of this more caring figure provided by the son-in-law. The letter-writer's linguistic phobia is observable too in his scathing comments about all speakers, whether onlookers at the chess games, card players making their bids, or simply groups of *tertulianos* in the club and conversationalists in the hotel. The letter-writer is repelled by language, including the language of newsprint and of advertisements. Language leads to insanity and falsehood. All the humanity he will tolerate is one at a pre-linguistic stage, 'a lo sumo algún niño que no sepa aún hablar' (II, 352). When Don Sandalio dies all he can think of is that he will never be able to hear his silences again. It is this linguistic repulsion that makes him reject all explanations about Don Sandalio's family and fate: 'No, no quería que me colocase la historia del hijo de Don Sandalio. ¿Para qué? Tengo que mantener puro, incontaminado, a mi Don Sandalio, al mío' (II, 361). Language contaminates, debases, destroys. Even the young woman on the beach is portrayed as meticulously shredding a letter into fragments. The paradox is, of course, that the letter-writer cannot avoid using language. Even the rejection of language is made through language. The letters which he writes to express his sentiments are a dialogue not merely with the ghostly entity Felipe, but also with himself, since they are as much diary entries as a collection of letters. In the end the letter-writer announces that he is to stop writing, but only in order to resume an oral dialogue with Felipe about the enigma of Don Sandalio. Language may poison our existence by trivializing and distorting, but it is an addictive poison that compelled Unamuno to endless involutions of his tortured yet inventive self. To all those various café games that the letter-writer mentions in the course of his correspondence has to be added the most distinctively human of all: the language game. Language may be used to declare or to conceal, but even with a mask on, the writer's presence is inescapable.

San Manuel Bueno, mártir has in common with *La novela de Don Sandalio* the use of a personalized narrator. In the preceding chapter we saw that Ángela Carballino's *biography* of Father Manuel Bueno can at the same time be read as an *autobiography*, entirely in consonance with Unamuno's belief that all biographers are autobiographers. In *San Manuel Bueno, mártir* style plays a key role. How has Unamuno clothed the account constructed by this very specific narrator? The answer is not hard to find: Ángela's account is clothed in (1) emotive language, (2) poetic imagery, and (3) biblical allusion. The language is noticeably different from that used in *Abel Sánchez*: the medical metaphors employed by Joaquín Monegro to encapsulate his diseased mind are here replaced by mystical language, in accordance with the basic situation of the novel, in which a female disciple recalls the sayings and actions of a religious leader, thereby bringing to mind the relationship of Mary Magdalene to Jesus, about which speculation has never ceased. Mary Magdalene was forgiven her sins by Jesus, became a frequent companion, was present at the crucifixion, went to his tomb, was the first to learn of his resurrection and the first to whom Jesus appeared, and joined his mother after his mission was completed. There is even a Gospel according to Mary Magdalene, though whether Unamuno had learnt of the discovery in 1896 of fragments of this lost work is not known. The parallels with Ángela Carballino, Don Manuel's 'diaconisa', are abundantly clear. Is it any wonder, then, that Ángela's account appears to take the form of a gospel?

In this respect the language bestowed by Unamuno on his narrator is of course crucial. Indeed it is no exaggeration to say that the language is the woman.[12]

---

[12] The language of the novel has merited some excellent critical pages in Butt, 1981: 40–44. On one point, however, I have to signal my disagreement with John Butt. He says that the language 'is not what one might expect from a country girl like Ángela Carballino' (40). But Unamuno has anticipated this potential objection. Ángela, like her brother Lázaro, is not simply a country girl. She is a semi-outsider, the daughter of a stranger who brought a library with him. Ángela has left the village and attended school in the city until almost sixteen, and she has read adult books as a girl ('devoré yo ensueños siendo niña'). All this would be unnecessary information if it were not

Emotive language is used in matters pertaining to personal relationships, from her school friend ('firmando el juramento con nuestra sangre' (II, 314)), and her brother ('¡Ay, Lázaro, Lázaro! ¡Que alegría nos has dado a todos, a todos [...]!' (II, 329), or '¡Lázaro!, gemí' (II 330)), to Don Manuel, and it is especially noticeable in the case of the latter. A small selection of the many examples must suffice:

> [...] sentía en mis entrañas el jugo de la maternidad, y al encontrarme en el confesonario junto al santo varón, sentí como una callada confesión suya en el susurro sumiso de su voz. (II, 323)

> [...] en la ciudad me ahogaba [...]. Sentía, sobre todo, la falta de mi don Manuel y como si su ausencia me llamara. (II, 325)

> Y salimos de la iglesia, y al salir se me estremecían las entrañas maternales. (II, 333)

Emotively charged verbs like *llorar*, *gemir*, *estremecer*, *acongojar*, *conmover*, *temer*, *temblar*, and nouns such as *alegría*, *corazón*, *temblor*, *tristeza*, *lágrimas*, recur with some frequency, indeed *llorar* is so overworked that hardly a page goes by without the reader encountering the verb and its cognates. Ángela is much given to weeping and in her memoir ascribes the same emotional discharge to others.

Poetic imagery makes use above all of natural objects, especially those associated with landscape. *Lago* and *montaña* are of course the two recurrent poetic symbols strongly associated with Don Manuel, and yet, as John Butt has forcefully argued, however much we speculate about the meaning that these symbols enshrine, their precise semantic value escapes us, for 'the important thing is that they should deliver their emotional charge to the reader by a process of suggestion' (Butt, 1981: 38). To this end Unamuno invests his narrator with the ability to invoke a mysterious world through the use of poetic images as well as expressions redolent of mystical writings:

> Su canto, saliendo del templo, iba a quedarse dormido sobre el lago y al pie de la montaña. (II, 316)

> — Cree en el cielo, el cielo que vemos. Míralo. Y me lo mostraba sobre la montaña y abajo, reflejado en el lago. (II, 324) .

> [...] don Manuel, tan blanco como la nieve de enero en la montaña, y temblando como tiembla el lago cuando le hostiga el cierzo [...]. (II, 328)

> '¿Has visto, Lázaro, mayor misterio que el de la nieve cayendo en el lago y muriendo en él mientras cubre con su toca a la montaña?' (II, 334)

> Desde que se nos murió don Manuel no cabía decir que viviese. (II, 341)

> No vivía yo ya en mí, sino que vivía en mi pueblo y mi pueblo vivía en mí. [...] vivía en ellos y me olvidaba de mí. (II, 343)

All these expressions and countless similar ones serve to underscore the other-worldliness of the narration, thereby emphasizing the longing for a spiritual universe, a kind of ghostly presence hidden in the surrounding world of matter. They become a surrogate for belief.

Unamuno's way of indicating the sophisticated outlook and complex psychology of the narrator. Ángela is culturally split, and she interprets Don Manuel accordingly.

The constant biblical allusions which occur almost on every page, whether through direct quotation, through oblique allusion, or through situational parallelism, most often associated with Jesus Christ and his teachings, not only serve to underline Ángela's role as evangelist, but also link Don Manuel to Christ. John Butt has interpreted this association allegorically, with the consequence that Don Manuel's scepticism about an afterlife is really meant to be Jesus Christ's scepticism, in other words that Unamuno was putting across the view that Jesus had not believed in immortality and was purely a consoler of human beings. This view, however, is dependent on accepting Ángela as a fully reliable narrator, something which Butt himself is unwilling to do, and rightly so, given the idiosyncrasies of the memoir writer. One of these is her penchant for melodrama, and nowhere is this more apparent than in the way Unamuno makes her quote or evoke the Bible. Thus, the refrain '¡Dios mío!, ¡Dios mío!, ¿por qué me has abandonado?' is doubly theatrical: not only does it have a cathartic impact on the audience when Don Manuel takes on the role of the suffering Christ at the Good Friday solemnities, but it leads to a 'triunfo imitativo' (II, 317) every time Blasillo the idiot takes on the role of Don Manuel and repeats the biblical phrase, a phrase which in Blasillo's mouth has the force of rhetoric but no possibility of meaning. Words have become wholly detached from their circumstance. Similarly, when Ángela describes Lázaro taking communion from Don Manuel, we find another biblical reference: 'Y entonces, pues era la madrugada, cantó el gallo' (II, 329), which dramatically enhances the deception perpetrated by the two men but which of course has no literal or referential value, for there is no cock crowing nor does the scene take place at first light. The double death scene, in which we first see Don Manuel in his house with Lázaro and Ángela, and then in church with his parishioners, is a veritable valedictory staging full of symbols (including the six planks which Don Manuel had cut himself, and from which the cross for his tomb has been sculpted, reminiscent of the cross Christ had to carry to his own execution), with references to St John 21.15 and to the Old Testament books of Numbers, Deuteronomy, Joshua and Exodus, with the dying Don Manuel paraded in front of his flock holding a crucifix in one hand and Blasillo's hand in the other, recalling not just St John the beloved disciple but perhaps even the Good Thief at the crucifixion.

The conclusion seems inescapable: Angela's memoir is not a constative report, it is a performative utterance. This is not biography; it is a poetic composition. Ángela, Don Manuel, Lázaro, Blasillo are presented as actors playing pseudo-biblical roles on a symbolic stage. It is worth recalling Victor Goti's words to the humiliated and suffering Augusto:

> — ¡Comedia! Comedia! ¡Comedia!
> — ¿Cómo?
> — Sí, en la comedia entra el que se crea rey el que lo representa. (I, 646)

Performer and performed are fused into one. In the theatre, the actor playing the king may come to believe that he is one. The man and the mask are the same because the role is fashioned by the language. Don Manuel must remain something of an enigma, Christ-like certainly, but in a theatrical way, not so much an individual as a persona, as a role, the role ascribed to him by his evangelist on the one hand

and by the villagers on the other. And Ángela herself, like her more vigorous predecessor, Gertrudis, is a founder of a new religion through the creative power of the word. It is here that language and religion irresistibly converge. For Ángela, for the parishioners, and apparently for Don Manuel, the belief in the reality of words brings with it a belief in a transverbal reality. That is why the priest falls silent during the phrase of the Creed 'the resurrection of the flesh'. But this belief in the dependability of language is precisely what Ángela learns to query as she writes down her experiences, that words are not what they seem, not transparent, that is, upon another reality beyond. As Unamuno learnt from his reading of nineteenth-century theologians and linguisticians, religion is language-bound and has no existence apart from language. When Ángela writes 'Y yo, ¿creo?' and questions her own account, she is giving voice to a radical doubt not simply about belief but about its verbal representation. She doubts not just what she has written but how it will be read.

We find in Unamuno's texts a resistance to closure (as I shall argue in the next chapter), a reluctance on the part of the author to make a dignified exit, return to silence, and leave the book, for better or worse, in the hands of the reader. It seems almost as if to stop writing is to stop living, to lose something precious. This is poetically expressed in *San Manuel Bueno, mártir*, where the fictional author extends her sense of loss to the memoir she is bringing to a close. Ángela's story is one of repeated loss. She loses her father as a young girl, her mother as a grown-up, her surrogate father, the priest Don Manuel, as a mature woman, and her brother Lázaro a few years later. All she has left, as she tells us, is her memories, which is to say her story; but as she nears the end of the story she realizes that she is about to lose this too. The story she has reconstructed through re-living her memories will pass on to others, others who may misunderstand what she has written, as she anxiously confesses. But it is not something that she can forestall. The text must be abandoned to its fate: 'Pero aquí queda esto y sea de su suerte lo que fuere' (II, 345). An author, Unamuno appears to concede, must ultimately be superseded. It is almost as if language must revert to its original owner, the community.

Conclusion

'El estilo nos hace; no hacemos el estilo. [...] Por él, por el estilo, nos descubrimos' (*Alrededor*, 102). For Unamuno to write is to discover oneself. His explanation, derived from Schleiermacher, rests upon the way we use words. Although our language is learned and therefore is not our own, we have an in-built capacity to use it, and this capacity means that there is an element of choice on *how* we use it as individuals. From an initially deterministic position in his twenties and early thirties, Unamuno moved rapidly to a much more libertarian position which emphasized freedom of action, the fact that we feel ourselves to be free to act even though we cannot prove it. In language terms this involved some adjustment to his initial position based on the linguistic philosophy of Wilhelm von Humboldt. While he never deviated from the belief that a language was a communal affair and therefore played a fundamental role in shaping the thinking of its speakers, he nevertheless found a way of asserting the individuality of the speaker or writer. 'Piensa cada hombre dentro del común pensar, pero debe hacerlo por sí, y ha de hablar, en consonancia, dentro del habla común, pero con arte propio', he wrote in 1902 (VIII, 407). This 'arte propio' is something that must be striven for. Just as personality arises from the complex interaction of self and others, so expressing oneself linguistically follows this same path. If we are capable of developing a persona, a public identity, we are capable of developing a style. Writing, like acting, is a 'writing for', and the addressee is the writer him or herself in the first place, and other readers immediately afterwards. Writing is the writer's mirror. What is written and the way it is written — there is no real distinction to be made here — reflects the writer's emergent persona. This Unamuno refers to as style, which develops in tandem with one's personality. Unamuno may well have noted Schopenhauer's assertion to the effect that 'style is the physiognomy of the mind' (Schopenhauer, 1966: I, 446).

Unamuno held that a tradition was not something written in stone forever but rather a dialogue between present and past in constant evolution. Language — including the literature it gave rise to — was the most important tradition of a people, but it had to be a vibrant tradition capable of re-vitalizing itself. Just as he was to say — in *Cómo se hace una novela* — that the novel should be 'organismo y no mecanismo', so he deplored an approach to language based purely on established rules and uniformity rather than on dynamic expression. Linguistic enslavement was a real danger, leading to a fossilized way of thinking. It was here that individuals had an active role to play. Whereas institutions immobilize language, living beings mobilize it. His advice to younger writers was to unravel and adapt language to fit their innermost thought rather than passively adapt their thought to the language (VIII, 409). To this end he advocated the de-Castilianization of Castilian by integrating 'hablas diferenciadas' and allowing it to benefit from the more vigorous forms of Spanish-American expression. 'Las lenguas, como las religiones, viven de herejías', he added (VIII, 495).

This advocation of a fluid, dynamic, 'heretical' concept of language, language as a protean and malleable raw material, is a pointer to an essential, if perhaps somewhat startling, aspect of Unamuno's linguistic philosophy, namely that the greatest value of language lies not in social communication but in self-cognition. He does not, of course, deny that language is a social phenomenon or that meaning is inter-subjective. Indeed he argued on more than one occasion that the cultural shaping of language makes translation from one to another virtually impossible, even if understanding is achievable: 'Las lenguas son, en todo rigor, intraducibles, pero no impenetrables' (VIII, 497). The downside of limiting language to its communal function is that it inhibits cognitive effort: we are constrained by the prevailing conventions of usage, and therefore what we communicate is dictated by norms that are not, for us as individuals, authentic. We use not our language but someone else's. But for Unamuno the real point of writing is to express one's deepest, authentic self. Experience is wholly personal, yet language is communal, and Unamuno refuses to be confined to the communal. It is here that Unamuno runs into problems with words.

'No sé cómo expresarme al entrar en estos escondrijos y rinconadas de la vida del espíritu, y preveo que han de faltarme palabras adecuadas', he confesses in one place

(VIII, 658). When dealing with the inner world, words fail him. This amounts to an admission that language is not up to the task of fulfilling the cognitive function that Unamuno demands of it.[13] The problem is that for Unamuno there are two forms of knowledge, rational knowledge and intuitive knowledge, or as he prefers to say, *saber* and *sentir*. Verbal propositions are for him more than logical judgements; they are also the expression of our feelings and inner convictions, what Unamuno terms *actitudes vitales*. Philosophical reasoning is a purely verbal system, one based on *logos*; different philosophies use different words. But there is another way of using words, which Unamuno calls the poetic way, and whose aim is to reveal a world which is no less real than that of logical reasoning, even if its reality is of a different order. The challenge is how to enclose such 'revelaciones sustanciales' in words (VIII, 667). Moving from the private to the public sphere involves some kind of compromise, and Unamuno's aspiration to 'comulgar' rather than merely to 'comunicar', to engage in communion rather than mere communication, almost invariably leads to frustration. Only the greatest writers — Unamuno often mentions Shakespeare — manage to convey insights that reach beyond the common realm. The poet has to step in where the philosopher has to stop. Unamuno's fictions are poetic explorations of aspects that do not always lend themselves comfortably to logical elucidation. From *Niebla* onwards all the themes of his major works of fiction can be traced back to *Del sentimiento trágico de la vida*, but the language of fiction was to prove as intractable as the language of philosophy.[14]

If to be is to be aware of oneself, to write is to inquire into that self in a highly self-conscious manner. In Unamuno's theory of writing, a truly creative writer is primarily a reader of him- or herself; but Unamuno is also conscious that writing is writing for others, that there is a re-enactment to follow. A book inevitably becomes a collective enterprise. We can see how Unamuno could write in *En torno al casticismo* that 'El espíritu colectivo, si es vivo, lo es por inclusión de todo el contenido anímico de relación de cada uno de sus miembros' (VIII, 195), and how thirty years later he could adapt it to 'historia no es letra, no es documento escrito, no es escritura, antes bien, lectura, lección, leyenda' (IX, 1120), an idea adapted

---

[13] This is an important point that has not always been grasped. For example, Teresa Imizcoz Beunza writes: 'No encontramos en nuestro autor el frecuente problema repetido en tantos poetas: la insuficiencia del lenguaje, la incapacidad de la palabra de expresar todo lo que el poeta lleva dentro, y los límites que ésta pone al poeta' (Imizcoz Beunza, 1996: 228). This is patently wrong. Language for Unamuno is the source of both creativity and limitation. He needs it to uncover, to express his inner being, but it comes to him from outside. It serves both to reveal and to hide. It even masks emptiness. He persistently tried yet failed to equate language and thought in order to give language greater immediacy. In the end he admitted that it was simply a common medium, and that originality and personality lay exclusively in style, i.e. in one's personal conjunction of words.

[14] For Unamuno, if not for many academic philosophers, *Del sentimiento trágico de la vida* was a treatise based on logical procedures or as logical as he could manage. In Chapter IX he warns the reader that, as he had previously indicated, he was trying to 'dar forma lógica a un sistema de sentimientos alógicos' (*DSTV*, X, 440). The subject matter lies outside logic; the approach nevertheless lies within logic. More generally, however, Unamuno saw philosophical or logical expression as self-deceiving in its pretence of objectivity or impersonality. What great philosophy, like great history or great poetry, requires is the imaginative use of language.

from *Don Quixote*, Part I, chapter 50, and first mentioned in *Vida de Don Quijote y Sancho*. In moving from 'escritura' to 'lectura', or 'leyenda', the reading act, the book works equally well as the mirror of a collective entity and as the mirror of an individual searching for his or her identity. The one proviso is that in either case this has to be a shared act, community being a *sine qua non* of identity, whether personal or collective. Unamuno moved from 'we are what we say' to 'we are what we read', but of course saying cannot be separated from hearing, or writing from reading. Both are communitarian activities, and hence literature is a two-way process. Language encapsulates and reveals an individual's identity, but that language was absorbed from the linguistic community to which it belongs in the first place and is redirected at that community, which will in turn transform it hermeneutically. The reader was part and parcel of Unamuno's cognitive pursuits.

CHAPTER 4

The Reader

The Reader as Interpreter

In Unamuno's most famous novel we come across the following passage:

> — [...] es fácil que dijeran los lectores que no pasa nada, y sin embargo...
> — ¡Oh, si pudiesen verme por dentro, Víctor, te aseguro que no dirían tal cosa!
> — ¿Por dentro?, ¿por dentro de quién?, ¿de ti?, ¿de mí? Nosotros no tenemos dentro. Cuando no dirían que aquí no pasa nada es cuando pudiesen verse por dentro de sí mismos, de ellos, de los que leen. El alma de un personaje de drama, de novela o de *nivola*, no tiene más interior que el que le da...
> — Sí, el autor.
> — No, el lector. (I, 645)

This exchange between two fictional characters, Víctor Goti and Augusto Pérez, points to an enduring preoccupation of Unamuno's: the role or reaction of his readers. Readers will only stop complaining that nothing happens when they are capable of seeing inside themselves, says Victor Goti. According to him, characters like himself and Augusto Pérez will have no inner life if their readers do not have one either. To an extent this defensive remark could be explained by the sheer non-conformity of Unamuno's fiction from *Amor y pedagogía* onwards. It is presumably in an attempt to forestall or guide the reactions of those readers that Unamuno so frequently addresses them in prologues and epilogues and even within the narratives themselves. But since Unamuno is still harping on the role of the reader right at the very end of his novelistic career there is clearly more to it than anxiety about the reception of his output.

Unamuno's frequent invocation of a reader in texts and paratexts has been remarked upon by a number of critics. Robert L. Nicholas comments that 'puede verse que el lector, creador hasta cierto punto en cualquier novela, lo es de manera especial en una obra de Unamuno' (Nicholas, 1987: 54). Nicholas limits himself to drawing a parallel between the author–reader relationship and the God–man relationship (who creates whom?), which is certainly one of Unamuno's questions but which does not take us very far in understanding the phenomenon. Gonzalo Navajas offers a rather more unexpected (and supposedly post-structuralist) account of the author–reader relationship from which he concludes that 'lejos de tener como modelo de las relaciones autor-lector un diálogo armónico e igualitario, en su praxis textual la obra de Unamuno se realiza como un discurso individual autosuficiente que se ofrece al lector concluso y sin dejar lugar a modificaciones'.

And he goes on to add that Unamuno's novels 'tienen finales cerrados y didácticos' and that 'tienden a concluir claramente y transmitir un significado inequívoco. De ese modo, el lector ve restringidas sus posibilidades de separación con relación al texto' (Navajas, 1992: 86–87). An Unamuno novel, then, offers no possibility of dialogue; rather is it a closed system with an unequivocal conclusion that admits of no further contribution; what Unamuno produces is the definitive text. Or so it is alleged. My own conclusion will be precisely the opposite: that Unamuno associates closure with death and that his aspiration is to produce texts that are semantically indeterminate and can never be fully accounted for, texts that will perennially demand exegesis. The reader may be drawn in by invitation, so to speak, but is never shown the way out of the labyrinth. Proceeding from his point of view of authorial dominance over an enslaved reader, Navajas is forced to see Unamuno's paratexts as 'una reposesión y, con ella, un intento de detener el movimiento de ficcionalización indefinida, fijar de una vez para siempre su carácter, objetivizándolo con seguridad para la comunidad interpretativa' (Navajas, 1992: 93). This view not only fails to explain the extraordinary interpretative divergency that occurs in Unamuno criticism, but also fails to address Unamuno's explicit statements about literature's need for ongoing interpretation in order to survive.[1] Much closer to the mark seems to me to be Thomas R. Franz's comment to the effect that 'Unamuno is acutely aware that plurivalency is the key to his entire metaphysics, and he deliberately sets out to show how each narrative pulls in many directions on multiple diegetic levels' (Franz, 2006: 59).

The idea that underlies the exchange between the characters in the preceding quotation from *Niebla*, and specifically Goti's contention that as literary personages they are wholly reader-dependent for their personality, is quite simply, as was explained in Chapter 1, that of the purely mental counterpart of the phenomenal world, of the objects and events that are perceived through the senses, and of whether purely mental events gain precedence over the phenomenal world. As we saw in Chapter 2, Unamuno starts from the premiss that literature belongs to the noumenal world, the sphere of thoughts, more in the Platonic than in the Kantian sense, since Kant denied that noumena could be objects of knowledge. This mental or abstract representation does at times appear to take precedence over the physical or phenomenal existence, especially of course in the case of persons, since we habitually form abstract ideas of individuals over and above their physical attributes, whether of others or of ourselves. And if we do so with real people we are bound to do so with characters from books, who do not even have a physical existence. If instead of belonging to the realm of appearances they belong exclusively to the noumenal world, the question arises as to whose thoughts configure the personality or identity of those characters. The author's, as Augusto Pérez believes, or the reader's, as Víctor Goti contends? In Unamuno's poetics of fiction the question is almost constantly present, to judge both by his frequent apostrophes to the reader

---

[1] It even disregards visible pointers, such as Unamuno's frequent use, even abuse, of suspension points. How does Navajas's 'restriction of the reader's possibilities' square up, say, with the suspension points which end *Una historia de amor*, an obvious invitation to readers to supply their own endings?

and by the presence of readers within his fiction. Reader-response is a central consideration and one that is intimately connected to his idea of writing and of literature.

On several occasions Unamuno argued that the mark of great literature is its interpretability, that is to say the degree to which it invites interpretation. The greatest example of this is to be found in the Bible:

> Si la Biblia tiene un valor inapreciable, es por lo que en ella han puesto generaciones de hombres que con su lectura han apacentado sus espíritus; y sabido es que apenas hay en ella pasaje que no haya sido interpretado de cientos de maneras, según el intérprete. Y esto es un bien grandísimo. Lo de menos es que los autores de los distintos libros de que la Biblia se compone quisieran decir lo que los teólogos, místicos y comentadores ven en ellos; lo importante es que, gracias a esta inmensa labor de las generaciones durante siglos enteros, es la Biblia fuente perenne de consuelos, de esperanzas y de inspiraciones del corazón. (VIII, 749)

The reason why the Bible has remained a source of interest throughout the centuries is precisely because it invited interpretation, because it had no final truth, but rather all interpretations were the source of its enrichment. This is the argument used by Unamuno to defend the 'poderosa vitalidad' of Cervantes's *Don Quixote*, its ability to transform itself in successive generations and in different places:

> Cervantes escribió su libro en la España de principios del siglo XVII y para la España de principios del siglo XVII, pero Don Quijote ha viajado por todos los pueblos de la tierra y durante los tres siglos que desde entonces van transcurridos. Y como Don Quijote no podía ser en la Inglaterra del siglo XIX, pongo por caso, lo mismo que en la España del siglo XVII, se ha modificado y transformado en ella, probando así su poderosa vitalidad y lo realísimo de su realidad ideal. (VIII, 748–49)

It was this argument that, shortly afterwards, Unamuno once again invoked in his own defence when he was accused of indulging in a wholly subjective rendering of Cervantes's novel in his *Vida de Don Quijote y Sancho* and in the almost contemporary article, just cited, which appeared in *La España Moderna* in 1905, 'Sobre la lectura e interpretación del *Quijote*'. What he seeks in literature, he argues in a second article of 1905, 'Sobre la erudición y la crítica', is 'una liberación de los tres tiranos del espíritu: la lógica, el tiempo, y el espacio' (VIII, 805). And he then goes on to explain that what attracts him about Cervantes's book is not the work itself, but rather Don Quixote the man. Having devalued the erudite approach to literature as aridity posing as knowledge (erudition is also mocked in *Niebla* through the comic personage Antolín S. Paparrigópulos), he finally comes to the kind of literary commentator he values:

> Hay personas que son ante todo y sobre todo lectores, y su entusiasmo por lo que al leerlo se lo despierta, les lleva a escribir sobre ello, como uno que [cuando] descubre una hermosa vista llama a su compañero, le tira del brazo, y mostrándosela le dice: ¡mira eso! El entusiasmo estético es comunicativo, y nuestro goce de una obra de arte se acrecienta y agranda cuando logramos compartirlo con otros. De aquí nace el buen crítico, el que es poeta a su vez, cante o no poesía. El goce de la poesía es algo activo, y el que se penetra de la hermosura de un poema puede ser por ello mismo tan poeta como el que lo compuso. (VIII, 816)

Once again we see Unamuno invoking the original Greek sense of poet, maker, and now applying it not to the author but to the reader or critic. For Unamuno, then, the best reader is he who 'discovers' the text, who finds in it an experience worth communicating. It is clearly not a matter of approaching a text objectively, but of relating it to oneself or relating oneself to it. It is here that Unamuno is probably reflecting his own reading of the father of modern hermeneutics, Friedrich Schleiermacher.

The idea that to understand a text one needs actively to relate to it is a leitmotif of the German hermeneutic tradition that eventually found in Hans-Georg Gadamer its most explicit proponent: to understand is necessarily to interpret and there can be no understanding without interpretation. This central theme of Gadamer's well-known 1960 treatise *Truth and Method* is not new. Although not expressed as categorically as this, the germ of the idea is to be found in Schleiermacher and in Schleiermacher's pupil August Böckh. For Schleiermacher the 'grammatical' (that is, linguistic) understanding of a text is by itself insufficient; it has to be supplemented by the 'technical' (that is, psychological) interpretation of the circumstances or 'life-moment' that produced the text and gave it its unity or coherence. Böckh emphasized the point, already mentioned by Schleiermacher, that this could mean going beyond an author's intentions, uncovering aspects that might have lain dormant or unconscious. A consideration of both historical circumstances and individual or subjective circumstances was necessary, and the interpreter had to bring to full consciousness what the author of a work might have created unconsciously. Schleiermacher was primarily a theologian preoccupied with interpreting the enigmatic sayings of Jesus. He considered that if we could break into the psyche or ways of thinking of those who listened to Jesus, that is to say his contemporaries to whom his words were addressed, including the evangelists and their first readers, we might arrive at a better understanding of Jesus's words. One possibility therefore open to the interpreter of the New Testament was to consider the reception of the original readers of the Gospels. Knowing what kind of readers (or audience) a writer (or speaker) was addressing was considered essential to a proper understanding of a text (or enunciation). The problem for nineteenth-century biblical exegetes was that the only way to characterize those readers was through the writing itself. This was part of the infamous hermeneutic circle (understanding as a circular activity) with which nineteenth-century hermeneutics was beset, but which was later to be commended as a 'virtuous' circle (by Heidegger and Gadamer) which it was necessary to break into rather than out of.[2] Although one's reading perspective might well be different from previous ones, it nevertheless formed part of a continuing tradition (Gadamer's constantly shifting horizon), and was therefore not ahistorical but rather profoundly historical. Literary works survive

---

[2] The 'hermeneutic circle' has a long history. In the early nineteenth century it was used by Friedrich Ast and taken up by Friedrich Schleiermacher, from whom it passed on to Wilhelm Dilthey (*Die Entstehung der Hermeneutik* [*The Rise of Hermeneutics*], 1900), Martin Heidegger (*Sein und Zeit* [*Being and Time*], 1927), and Hans-Georg Gadamer in his influential 1960 treatise *Wahrheit und Methode* [*Truth and Method*]. It was applied to literary exegesis by a number of New Critics in the Anglo-Saxon world and by the American theorist E. D. Hirsch.

precisely because of their interpretative tradition, not in spite of it. Unamuno, despite his debt to Schleiermacher, seems to have grasped the nature of the predicament and turned it to his advantage by insisting not so much on recovering meaning but in creating it. He does not simply wait for his real readers to generate a meaning for his texts but creates his own reader(s) to generate meanings, as it were to set an example. If we, the real readers, identify with those readers, we are already within the hermeneutic circle. The perennial question of whether a literary text has power over its interpreters must in that case be answered in the affirmative, but at the same time Unamuno has neatly avoided the holy grail of the single, originating meaning still believed in by nineteenth-century hermeneutists.[3]

Unamuno, then, following the German hermeneutic tradition, associates literary texts with interpretation, and interpretation with an active, participatory reading. Interpretation is synonymous with creation, it is a creative act requiring an effort of the imagination, although how the latter works in a reader or interpreter is not really explained.[4] What is clear at any rate is that in reading, passive understanding is not enough. Unamuno expects an active input from his reader, an expectation that he expressed on numerous occasions. A letter to Unamuno which is preserved in the Casa-Museo in Salamanca casts an amusing light on the writer's somewhat mischievous attitude towards his readers. A member of the Centro Obrero in Valverde del Camino (Huelva) had written to Unamuno to explain that a heated debate had arisen among a group of friends belonging to the workers' association as to whether Julia, the wife of Alejandro Gómez in *Nada menos que todo un hombre*, had actually committed adultery with the Conde de Bordaviella or had merely pretended to in order to arouse jealousy in her husband. The writer of the letter asks Unamuno to clear up their doubts, as he is the person best placed to do so:

> Esto lo podríamos consultar con personas que seguramente desharían la duda, pero preferimos a V. que por ser el «padre de la criatura» podría con más autoridad que nadie deshacer nuestra perplejidad, que seguramente no tendría fundamento, pero que nuestra escasa cultura no alcanza a ver claro. Poco habituados a profundidades filosóficas, encarecemos una contestación/ orientación clara, precisa, en consonancia con nuestra cultura, y con la cual podamos orientarnos.[5]

Unamuno was evidently amused, and in his reply (dated 8 July 1919) could not resist the temptation to play on the puzzlement of his readers by pretending to lack

[3] And for which Schleiermacher was taken to task by Gadamer and Derrida; somewhat unfairly, it has to be said, since Schleiermacher was well aware of the limitations of trying to reconstruct an author's intention. But even so, the historical reality of Jesus meant that his utterances must have had a historical reality as well, no matter how difficult it might be to recover it.

[4] The concept of imagination in Unamuno remains vague. At times he seems to equate it with intuition, and at times with an almost mystical transcendence of the phenomenal world. But it also clearly stands for verbal inventiveness: 'Los llamados aciertos poéticos suelen ser aciertos verbales' (V, 65). This suggests that our imagination is fired by the language that we encounter. Unamuno did not go as far as Coleridge's primary form of the imagination as the projection of the divine mind, but perhaps was closer to his secondary form as the echo of that divine quality revealed in works of poetic genius. For a good, if inevitably inconclusive, account see Álvarez Castro, 2005: ch. V.

[5] This letter (undated) and a subsequent one (dated 17 July 1919, in response to Unamuno's) are preserved in the Casa-Museo Unamuno, Caja N° 7/84.

reliable sources on the matter:

> No debo negarles, señores míos, que me ha causado sorpresa, y a la vez gusto, su
> carta. Podría yo ahora contestarles, y sería lo más sencillo, que habiendo muerto
> los personajes de mi relato *Nada menos que todo un hombre* y no teniendo yo ni
> cartas ni documentos de ellos más que los que me sirvieron para aquella relación
> ni nadie que supiese de su vida íntima, no me hallo en situación de poder aclarar
> su duda. (Unamuno, 1991: II, 79)

Unamuno, however, who was after all an educationalist, must have realized that
simply poking fun at unsophisticated but committed learners was improper. So,
adopting a more serious tone, he went on to explain that 'prefiero contestarles en
serio y maravillarme de que se discuta si en una ficción, en un relato novelesco,
pasaron las cosas que se callan de un modo o de otro'. Unamuno was here making
the commonsensical point that what is not constatively present in a narrative does
not occur in this or that particular way. But he also knew that what is not expressed,
i.e. 'las cosas que se callan', can be as crucial as what is. Indeed this is what he then
went on to admit by way of a self-contradiction.

> Por mi parte, al idear aquella mi novela no pensé si Julia se entregó o no
> al conde de Bordaviella ni eso me interesaba. Lo dejé así en suspenso y sin
> declararlo por creer que esa omisión le daba más interés — como en efecto veo
> que le da — al relato, pues si en la historia verdadera una puerta de misterio o
> de secreto añade valor, en vez de quitárselo, en la ficción novelesca ha de pasar
> lo mismo. (Unamuno, 1991: II, 80)

Unamuno is here professing ignorance yet pleading guilty. What is not in the text,
he argues, is irrelevant, but he then goes on to admit that authorial silences are
part of the wilful manipulation of narrative, of inciting the reader's curiosity. And
at the end of the letter he allows himself another quip: 'Como verán, no puedo
menos que dejarles en su duda, ya que ella les espolea a bucear en un problema del
conocimiento del corazón de la mujer' (Unamuno, 1991: II, 81). 'Dejarles en su
duda', leaving readers in doubt, I suggest, is a fundamental strategy of Unamunian
storytelling, though whether the real reason is to spur the reader to delve into
psychological questions would need further elucidation. Leaving the reader in doubt
is in any case a central tenet of Unamuno's fictional poetics. And not just leaving his
readers in doubt but leaving the door open to contestation and polemics.

Those familiar with Unamuno criticism will be well aware of the critical controversies that have arisen among the interpreters of Unamuno's fiction. The death of
Augusto Pérez, the character of Aunt Tula, the behaviour of Raquel in *Dos madres*,
the beliefs or unbeliefs of Father Manuel Bueno, the authorship of the letters about
Don Sandalio the chess player, and even the authorship of the narrative in *Abel
Sánchez*, have all been the subject of speculation and discrepancies, prompting
some commentators to dismiss the whole debate as simply the result of Unamunian
obfuscation.[6] Unamuno's reply in the letter we have just seen hints not at deliberate
confusion but at reader involvement. Apostrophes, or sometimes simple references,

---

[6] Most of these controversies have a long history in Unamuno criticism. The narrative in *Abel
Sánchez* has been imaginatively attributed to Abel Sánchez himself in Sinclair, 2001: 188–89.

to the reader, are a characteristic feature of Unamuno's writing, and on one famous occasion he addresses his reader by specifying what the role of a reader has to be:

> Y yo quiero contarte, lector, cómo se hace una novela, como haces y has de hacer tú mismo tu propia novela. El hombre de dentro, el intra-hombre, cuando se hace lector, contemplador, si es viviente ha de hacerse lector, contemplador del personaje a quien va a la vez que leyendo, haciendo, creando; contemplador de su propia obra. El hombre de dentro, el intra-hombre — y éste es más divino que el tras-hombre o sobre-hombre nietzscheniano — cuando se hace lector hácese por lo mismo autor, o sea actor; cuando lee una novela se hace novelista, cuando lee historia, historiador. Y todo lector que sea hombre de dentro, humano, es, lector, autor de lo que lee y está leyendo. Esto que ahora lees aquí, lector, te lo estás diciendo a tí mismo, y es tan tuyo como mío. (VII, 613)

Just as an actor has to interpret and thereby appropriate the role which the author of the play has provided, so a reader has to interpret and appropriate the roles of the characters the novelist has offered him.[7] The sentiment 'es tan tuyo como mío' is articulated with some frequency and in a variety of guises, for example in *La novela de don Sandalio*, where the letter-writer tells the reader of the letters:

> Ahora te me vienes con eso de que escriba por lo menos la novela de don Sandalio el ajedrecista. Escríbela tú si quieres. Ahí tienes todos los datos, porque no hay más que los que yo te he dado en estas mis cartas. Si te hacen falta otros, invéntalos recordando lo de nuestro Pepe *el Gallego*. Aunque, en todo caso, ¿para qué quieres más novela que la que te he contado? En ella está todo. Y al que no le baste con ello, que añada de su cosecha lo que necesite. (II, 379)

Once again, as in the case of his letter to the workers of Valverde del Camino, we observe Unamuno riding two horses. The work is complete, but it is nonetheless reader-dependent. There seems to be a compensatory mechanism at work here. Since he acknowledges that he loses control of his work once it is written, he will try instead to control the reader, and this he does by making the latter read in a highly conscious way, by drawing attention to the importance of the reading act. Now in order to be able to fulfil the role that Unamuno is assigning to the reader, the latter needs a degree of operational latitude, what we might call a hermeneutical space. How does Unamuno set about creating such a space?

There is not of course a single answer to this question, since it is bound to depend to some extent at least on the situation a particular text describes, but the basic ingredient is that of contriving some kind of existential choice for the character and by implication — even at times explicitly — for the reader. A well-known example is Augusto Pérez's quandary when faced with the choice between Eugenia and Rosarito, which encourages the reader to interpret some of the inter-calated novelettes in terms of parables, parables being an essential component of the hermeneutic tradition that arose in Biblical exegesis, a tradition with which Unamuno had become well acquainted via his reading not only of Friedrich

---

[7]   Unamuno is of course exploiting the close connection between *autor* and *actor*, which in Golden-Age Spanish theatre was more than purely philological, since the *autor* was the impresario or leader of the theatre company who commissioned plays from playwrights (and often tinkered with them) and who was likely to be an actor as well.

Schleiermacher, but also of Albrecht Ritschl, Ernest Renan, Adolf von Harnack, and others (Orringer, 1985). A related technique is that of turning his personages into readers, who then react to what they read. In *Niebla* a reader is invoked on the very first page, in Goti's prologue. This reader becomes that nebulous figure, M de U, who proceeds to offer us his reaction in the post-prologue. From here on the reader becomes a kind of incorporeal presence, invoked by 'el autor de esta nivola', as the narrator refers to himself at the end of Chapter XXV, and again in the resigned yet rebellious declaration of Augusto Pérez when he predicts the death of Unamuno's readers at the end of the famous interview in Salamanca; in addition to which there are other readers in the novel, all of whom react in a personal manner to the accounts that they read or hear being read. Thus Augusto listens to Goti reading an extract from his novel, and also reads the farewell letter that Eugenia writes to him; Eugenia herself listens to the verses read to her by Augusto; and the Salamanca professor reads a telegram from the previous day's visitor which leaves him perplexed. All of these readers are interpreters of texts, each one in his or her own way.

This intra-novelistic interpretation in *Niebla* (which, as we shall see, exists in other Unamuno novels as well) has been faithfully reflected *ad infinitum* in real life, since this novel has become an irresistible object of hermeneutical exploration within the academy. And not just of exploration but even of uncompromising critical conviction. Let us consider one of the worthier examples of this phenomenon. Francisco La Rubia Prado has made a valuable contribution to our knowledge of Unamuno's partiality to the Romantics' theory of organicism in art. Having established the connection he then proceeds to use the theory as a template and to insist that Unamuno's novels must be read 'organically'. In *Niebla*, he contends, Augusto Pérez must be responsible for his actions because in an organic novel 'los personajes son sus propias acciones y en ellas, de las que son responsables, crecen; si se acepta que Augusto se suicida puede considerarse que *Niebla* tiene éxito como novela orgánica' (La Rubia Prado, 1996: 185). But La Rubia Prado appears to forget that Unamuno as another intra-diegetic character must, by the same token, also fulfil the requirement of being responsible for his own actions, one of which is killing off Augusto. Yet for La Rubia Prado if Augusto is killed rather than killing himself, if his death 'ha sido impuesta por el autor mecánico, entonces la lógica propia del personaje no se impone y lo que tendríamos en *Niebla* es un triunfo del mecanicismo' (La Rubia Prado, 1996: 187). In order to discredit this allegedly mechanistic reading, the critic goes to great lengths to prove that Augusto Pérez commits suicide and concludes uncompromisingly that 'dicha muerte no es otra cosa que un suicidio' (La Rubia Prado, 1996: 190). In so doing he is effectively falling into the trap laid by Unamuno: demanding a clear-cut resolution; and since Unamuno is no longer around to fulfil our pleromatic longings, the critic will effectively complete the novel himself and provide the proper ending. But conducting a virtual autopsy of the character to establish the cause of death is self-defeating since the real Unamuno of flesh and blood deliberately and provocatively took no decision as to who or what killed Augusto, and this is so irrespective of mechanistic or organicist ideologies. That Unamuno was sympathetic to and indeed absorbed the Romantic doctrine of the organic unity of the work of art because it fitted in with his anti-determinist turn does not mean that such a doctrine dictates his writing strategies. Indeed the plot of *Niebla* relies as much on contingent events as it does on 'organic' growth, and Unamuno is fully aware of (and makes ironic comments on) the part that 'chance' plays. Rather than organic, the outcome of the novel appears deliberately improvised, like so much else in it. The fact remains that we are given not two but four possible causes of Augusto's death, each one as likely or unlikely as the other three: suicide by self-suggestion, murder by decree, death by edacity, and death by cardiac arrest (the last-mentioned being the doctor's diagnosis). To argue the truth of one over the other three is to fantasize. One wonders of course whether this was the creative reader Unamuno was hoping for.[8]

From *Niebla* onwards the rhetorical use of the figure of a reader gains in originality and effectiveness. In *Abel Sánchez* Joaquín is first a reader of Byron's work *Cain*, whose cry of protest in favour of the murderer of Abel leaves him deeply affected; he later becomes a writer of his own confession, of which we ourselves become the readers. It is entirely as if one reading leads to another: as a reader Joaquín identifies with Cain, and as a writer he seeks for his readers to identify with him, a modern Cain. In *La tía Tula* Gertrudis is a devoted reader of Saint Teresa of Avila and is allegedly influenced by her, and since Saint Teresa was — in Unamuno's conception — a kind of feminine Quixote in pursuit of an ideal, Gertrudis's reading of the saint can be seen as an indication that her quest, too, is the pursuit of an ideal, the ideal of a spiritual community, if an extra-mural one. In *Tulio Montalbán y Julio Macedo* the act of reading gains in complexity, for here all three characters are readers and interact through their different readings of one and the same book, the biography of the liberator Tulio Montalbán written by the historian Henri Jacquetot. Don Juan Manuel Solórzano, a positivist historian who deals in genealogies, dates and documents, reacts to Jacquetot's biography of Montalbán with distrust because the historian has not included the supporting documentary evidence. His romantically inclined daughter Elvira Solórzano reacts with complete faith because the biography has aesthetic coherence, it is psychologically convincing, and that assures her of its truth. Interestingly these two readers employ the two methods advocated by Schleiermacher in textual exegesis, the philological or scientific one and the psychological or intuitive one based on the unity of the work. But Unamuno goes beyond this and includes a third reader, a reader who is an exact contemporary of the events described by the historian, the inscrutable Julio Macedo. This compatriot and fellow freedom-fighter of Tulio Montalbán, who fought the liberation wars alongside him, totally rejects the biography of Montalbán, not because it lacks documentary evidence, nor indeed because it is aesthetically incoherent, but because it usurps the identity of Montalbán, because, that is, the biographer has interposed his own vision and created a Montalbán who is a romantic myth, whom Macedo refuses to recognize. And it is for this reason that Macedo decides to write his own version of the liberator, 'The Memoirs of Julio Macedo'. Once again

---

[8] For a very recent exploration of Augusto's demise, with appropriate references to previous forensic critics, see Álvarez Castro, 2012.

reading begets writing. Here we can appreciate how in his writing Unamuno goes one step beyond what he had absorbed in his reading, something that characterizes his entire *oeuvre*.

Unamuno's view of the powerful position of the reader in establishing the meaning of a text makes him look more modern — that is, late twentieth-century — than perhaps he is. At the time when Unamuno was writing, criticism was still very much centred on the figure of the author, and works were analysed in terms of authorial circumstance and intention. The 1920s and 1930s saw the rise of 'New Criticism' in which authorial intention was bracketed as unknowable and the text seen as the only source of meaning. This approach was eventually superseded in the 1970s and 1980s during the age of post-structuralism, in which the reader was king. In the space of half a century criticism had moved from author-centred theoretical assumptions to text-centred ones and then to reader-centred ones. While there has been no agreement about just how far textual meaning is centred on the reader, there is no doubt that in critical debates the latter occupied centre stage for the last three decades of the twentieth century. From a convention in which a work was considered the revelation of the author's mental world and the reader a passive receptor of it, we had progressed to one in which the work depended exclusively on the reader's re-enactment of it. Indeed in some of the more radical formulations of reader-response theory, such as those of Roland Barthes or Stanley Fish, the reader came to be regarded as the sole progenitor of meaning and the author was cast aside as a figure of no consequence. Even among more circumspect theorists the thrust has been in the direction of explaining texts in terms of consumption, not in terms of production: it is the consumer who holds the whip hand. From Wolfgang Iser onwards the effort of theorists has focused on pinning down the subjective processes by which readers make texts meaningful. Thus we have had reader-response theories based on Hans Robert Jauss's 'horizon of expectations', Stanley Fish's 'affective stylistics' in which literature is reduced to the experience of a reader, and his subsequent refining of that experience as a 'reading strategy', Jonathan Culler's system of assimilated codes of reading competence, Norman Holland's psychoanalytic theory of unconscious response, David Bleich's subjective response of an independent self, Steven Mailloux's reinsertion of authorial intentions embedded in the text as part of the lines of communication between author and reader, and Peter Rabinowitz's reading conventions which enable authors to force their readers' hands. From the author being banished to the wilderness we seem to have come almost full circle to the view of literature as a pact between producer and consumer.[9]

When we compare Unamuno we observe that he too places the reader centre-stage, and, not unlike Iser, sees that reader as co-creator. Indeed he stated as much: 'Me empeño en que el lector colabore conmigo', he wrote to Clarín in 1895 (Alas, 1941: 52). Clearly Unamuno has no direct control over a real reader; but what he

[9] My references are to the following: Hans Robert Jauss, 1970 and 1982. Stanley Fish, 1972 (esp. the appendix, 'Affective Stylistics', reproduced in Jane P. Tompkins ed., 1980) and 1980. Jonathan Culler, 1975. Norman Holland, 1968 and 1975 (reproduced in Jane P. Tompkins ed., 1980). David Bleich, 1978. Steven Mailloux, 1982. Peter Rabinowitz, 1987.

tries to do, apparently quite successfully, is to bring the reader into the text, not as some distant and unpredictable consumer far beyond the production line, but as part of that very production process. He constantly forces us to make choices rather than read passively. In this respect he is an excellent illustration of Terry Eagleton's dictum that 'consumption, in literary as in any other kind of production, is part of the process of production itself' (Eagleton, 1996: 73). In a text such as *Tulio Montalbán y Julio Macedo*, the use of two intradiegetic readers makes us ask questions about the 'correctness' of their reading. Interestingly, Unamuno *qua* narrator does not take sides. Both readings are shown to be wholly subjective, each reflecting the interpretative choice of the particular reader, but they are also shown to have consequences for the readers — in this case tragic ones — far beyond the act of reading. Reading, Unamuno seems to be saying, is not a neutral, inconsequential activity; it involves existential choices, and it bounces off the text like an image off a mirror. Which of course raises the obvious question: where do we, the real flesh and blood readers, stand? What is our role?

The fact is that we too exercise a choice, perhaps unconsciously. *Tulio Montalbán y Julio Macedo* provides a good example of the reader's input. Unamuno might just as easily have titled his novelette 'Tulio Montalbán *o* Julio Macedo', for it is ultimately we ourselves who confer identity upon the character. That is to say, he depends on us as much as we depend on others for our identity. Is he Julio or Tulio? It is we who decide that Julio Macedo is indeed Tulio Montalbán under an assumed name. If we look for clinching evidence we will find none. The narrator never says that Tulio Montalbán and Julio Macedo are one and the same person. Yet as readers we assume that they are; in other words we go beyond the text. And it is a safe bet that we reach that conclusion quite early on in the story, certainly by halfway. We then feel vindicated when at the end we read that after Julio Macedo's death they found among his personal effects a photograph of Tulio Montalbán's wife and a love letter from her. We conveniently ignore that this proves nothing, since those artefacts could have been appropriated by Montalbán's killer or by a fellow freedom-fighter, which is precisely what Macedo claims to have been. In the absence of a higher authority we privilege a particular reading, and convince ourselves that Tulio/Julio is a single person even though we have no proof. The author does not have to complete the story; we do it for him. And not only do we interpret at the level of plot, we interpret too at the semantic level. When the newly arrived stranger, prompted by an agitated Elvira Solórzano, admits that he, Julio Macedo, killed Tulio Montalbán, we the readers almost certainly do not accept the literal meaning of those words, choosing instead to read metaphorically. We decide that it is not a case of homicide; it is rather, for us, the readers, a case of a change of identity, even though this is not what the text says. It is worth emphasizing that the identification Tulio-Julio is not a requirement of the plot. The plot would be just as logical if Tulio and Julio were not the same person. We seem to be back with Julia and the Count of Bordaviella. What appears to have happened therefore is that Unamuno has arranged his story in such a way that it invites us to go down a particular road in interpreting the narrative signs. What we readers do is not in essence different from what the fictitious readers of Montalbán's biography do: venture beyond the text and confer a specific reality on something that only has it potentially, not actually. But why? Is it because, as Roland Barthes and others have insisted, the reader is the measure of all things? Or is it because a writer like Unamuno knows how to anticipate his readers' reactions? I would not wish to argue that meaning is embedded in the text, since meaning belongs in minds, not books, but simply that a reader-oriented text is nevertheless the creation of the writer as much as of the reader. It is true that a reader does not extract meaning but rather inserts it; yet that hermeneutic gap has been fashioned by the writer, a writer highly conscious of the role of interpretation.

The Hermeneutic Tradition and Beyond

The example of *Tulio Montalbán y Julio Macedo* is a good illustration of the reader's (probably unconscious) input, though not of the interpretative polarities which have arisen in Unamuno criticism. But these polarities or discrepancies are not to be attributed to the disputatious spirit of Unamuno critics. It is ultimately the result of the writer's strategy, a strategy aimed at opening, not closing, his texts semantically, at creating that hermeneutic space in which a reader can use, indeed is called upon to use, his interpretative capacity. And we are not dealing solely with the meaning or message of a work *in toto*, for often it is details in the narrative that cry out for explanation. For example, in *La novela de don Sandalio*, how should we interpret the scene at the beach in which a young woman tears a letter to shreds and throws the bits of paper in the sea (letter 14)? What is the function of this scene which appears to have nothing at all to do with Don Sandalio or the author of the letters? There are innumerable such details in Unamuno's narratives. Indeed in *La novela de don Sandalio* virtually every detail is crying out for interpretation, from the identity of the letter-writer to the imprisonment and death of Don Sandalio. Or if we take *San Manuel Bueno, mártir*, what is the significance of the desiccated carnation found in Father Manuel Bueno's breviary after his death? Or of the six planks on which he slept both in life (his bed) and in death (his coffin)? Or why precisely does Unamuno include an epigraph from St Paul I Corinthians 15. 19? Does it imply a rejection of the religion of Don Manuel, or rather does it show up St Paul's narrowness of outlook since after all Don Manuel's Christianity is exemplary? And who is 'acaso el mayor [de los santos]' who had no belief in life after death? St Paul, St Peter, Christ himself? Even in a text such as *Niebla*, pored over and analysed to death by the community of *unamunistas*, there are still many questions that resist hermeneutical subjugation and which facilitate its regular resurrection.[10] I am not referring to Augusto's demise, since this would be a naive question, comparable to that asked by the readers from Valverde del Camino, but rather to questions such as these: how far is Víctor Goti's novel a reflection of Unamuno's novel? What is the connection between Augusto's erotic awakening ('no hay más verdad que la vida

---

[10] As well as the never-ending stream of articles, two comparatively recent book-length critical explorations of *Niebla* bear this out: Bénédicte Vauthier, 1999; and Thomas R. Franz, 2003. Both studies contribute new insights. And the centenary of *Niebla* is resulting in a surge of new exegetical contributions. Unamuno should be well satisfied.

fisiológica' (I, 577)), and his search for identity, and what in turn is the connection between this and Víctor Goti's exposition of the theme in his prologue? How are we meant to see Augusto Pérez: as 'un pobre panoli que vive en Babia' (I, 526) or as a symbol of an errant humanity whose search for purpose invariably ends in frustration? And why does Unamuno, through his characters' constant questioning of words and utterances, undermine our faith in language, on whose effects he is after all wholly dependent? These and other questions posed by the text seem to remain as a permanent challenge to the reader.

Occasionally Unamuno even robs us of a denouement. In *Una historia de amor* the closing phrase, 'desde aquel día', leaves the reader to imagine what happens beyond that day in which the long-separated lovers, now in holy orders, come across each other and realize their love is still extant. In *El marqués de Lumbría* there is not even the hint of a denouement, since the reader — like the townspeople — has guessed the story of Pedrito's birth. The developing Cain and Abel myth is suddenly abandoned as Pedrito simply replaces his half-brother in primogeniture and we learn no more of Rodriguín. In *Dos madres* not only does Raquel's determination to get Juan to impregnate Berta require a psychological diagnosis of some complexity,[11] but the closing lines raise the question of how Juan and Berta's two children will fare under different mothers. Will they learn that they are siblings? Will one become envious of the other's wealth, or of the other's authentic mother? The text stops; its possibilities remain open to the reader. Narratives cannot of course be fully determinate; but in the case of Unamuno's their indeterminacy appears to be part of the strategy. This indeterminacy is thrust upon us with a vengeance in *La novela de don Sandalio*, arguably Unamuno's clearest statement of a poetics of fiction and one of his feeblest efforts at novel-writing.

In *La novela de don Sandalio, jugador de ajedrez* the chess board becomes a symbol for the hermeneutical game that Unamuno is playing with his reader. Once again he invites us to search for meaning through his use of symbols, and many of us willingly oblige. The recurrent linguistic signs this time are made up of a chess game, a hollow tree, a house in ruins, and the sea, all of which, given the letter-writer's poor state of health, can be plausibly connected to a fear of death, a fear which comes out in his chess dream, in which he is in imminent danger of being devoured by an opposing black knight as he fights desperately to keep his white king alive. But what is self-evident is that these linguistic signs are mere shells, that they acquire meaning only by virtue of the hermeneutical excursions of readers determined to penetrate the veil of the fiction. The signs by themselves are devoid of meaning, they have at most a potential for signifying. Yet this is the point that the story of Don Sandalio, a mere accretion of signs, or in this case of letters, is making. In Saussurean language, the nature of the story is as arbitrary as is the nature of the sign. In terms of positive knowledge, everything we know of the two central characters is countered by something which we do not know. To put it another way, we are given effects, but not causes. The letter-writer is running away from something, but from what we are not told. He is experiencing a deep

[11] And indeed there have been such diagnoses. For one of the most imaginative see Sinclair, 2001: 153–69.

crisis, but we are privy to neither its nature nor its origin. His sense of bitterness is ascribed to 'esa pérdida de mi hogar' (II, 368), but we learn nothing of the circumstances of that loss. He has retired to a place where he is unknown, but why he does not say. He admits he is driven by misanthropic sentiments, but the cause of his misanthropy remains shrouded in mystery. And most baffling of all, he wishes to befriend Don Sandalio and admits to being intrigued by him, yet he flatly refuses to learn anything about him. Of course Unamuno is using epistolary form, which serves both to communicate and to hide, under the pretext that the letter-writer's correspondent can be deemed to be familiar with his past life. In the case of Don Sandalio we know a little more, but again each piece of information has a corresponding unanswered question. Is the illness which appears to affect him physical or mental? What does his son die of? What crime has he committed to warrant being thrown into jail? What brings about his death while there? In what way is his son-in-law implicated?

It must be emphasized that these questions about Don Sandalio, and others in the form of the letter-writer's musings, are voiced within the text. Unamuno therefore is consciously playing a game with his readers, as is amply confirmed in the final letter and the 'Epílogo'. La novela de Don Sandalio is a deliberately teasing novel, not just for the flesh-and-blood reader but for the intradiegetic reader, Felipe, who asks the letter-writer to make enquiries and get at the truth about Don Sandalio and his family, only to be unceremoniously rebuffed and branded a reader of potboilers. The mystery of Don Sandalio is not the traditional one created by complex plotting, since the plot in this case could hardly be simpler. The mystery is the mystery of incompletion, of non-closure, or as Unamuno himself, through his narrator, mischievously suggests, of an 'esfinge sin enigma' (II, 378). Is then the 'crude puzzle' label justified in this case?[12] A realistic approach certainly yields no fruitful results since no explanation is forthcoming as to the irrational behaviour of the letter-writer, who rejects all logical explanations of Don Sandalio's situation. What, then, are we left with?

In broad terms there are, I suggest, three possible exegetical approaches to this novel: the linguistic approach (language as fabrication, already explored in the preceding chapter), the personality-based approach (which will be considered briefly in the next chapter), and the reader-response approach, with a porous frontier between the three. The reader-response approach is of course governed by Unamuno's persistent invocation of a reader or readers in his work. The commonly occurring phrase 'mis lectores' (with its many variations) indeed appears in the epilogue to La novela de don Sandalio. Unamuno recognizes what will later become a commonplace in reception theory, namely that the author loses ultimate control to the reader, 'dans le texte seul parle le lecteur', in the well-known phrase of Roland Barthes. In this particular text the reader is personified by Felipe, but Felipe is not Unamuno's model reader; on the contrary, he represents the reader who demands works written for the mass market conveniently wrapped in conventional clothes, with rounded plots, clear outcomes and satisfying solutions. Unamuno's

---

[12] A question posed — but ultimately rejected — by John Butt about San Manuel Bueno, mártir (Butt, 1981: 38).

novels by contrast lack closure and offer a different kind of reading experience, not the passive one of traditional realist novels, where the reader is regarded as the mere receptor of information, but an active one in which the reader is offered the opportunity to project his or her own consciousness or mental existence. *La novela de don Sandalio* thus becomes the praxis of which *Cómo se hace una novela* of a few years earlier had been the theory.[13] It should be made clear, however, that despite its title, *Cómo se hace una novela* is emphatically neither a novel nor a treatise on the novel. Although it contains an invented anecdote, the story of the reader Jugo de la Raza, it is in the main a confessional (and at times intemperate) outburst by a lonely individual undergoing a deep and self-questioning crisis during a self-imposed exile. Its theoretical implications for novel-writing are minimal. The chief point of relevance to novelistic theory is contained in a single sentence found in the passage quoted above: 'El hombre de dentro, el intra-hombre, cuando se hace lector, contemplador, si es viviente ha de hacerse lector, contemplador, del personaje a quien va a la vez que leyendo, haciendo, creando; contemplador de su propia obra' (VII, 613).

According to this view, reading mirrors the reader's consciousness. Thus, when Jugo de la Raza, the symbolic reader in *Cómo se hace una novela*, projects his consciousness onto the mirror that constitutes the book, he experiences a heightened self-awareness, becoming acutely aware of the fragility of his own existence.[14] By being the kind of existential reader Unamuno is proposing, that reader is in effect reading himself. The end of his reading, of his self-consciousness, will signify the end of his life, as the book prognosticates. This is what horrifies Jugo, and he throws the book in the river. But he cannot of course avoid the discovery of his finitude; in effect he cannot opt out as he at first tries to do, unwilling to read on. He will search for another copy of the book to satisfy his curiosity, or, symbolically, to confront his fate. Unamuno leaves the story of Jugo unfinished, which we could take to be a symbol of our own position as readers of the book: as long as we read we are deemed to be alive. The key question is whether the reader is 'viviente', capable of making his reading creative and meaningful. The argument that Unamuno applies to the novelist ('al crear personajes se está creando a sí mismo', from the epilogue to *La novela de don Sandalio*) applies equally to the reader.

In *La novela de don Sandalio* Unamuno returns to his idea of what a reader should be. The epilogue, in which Unamuno rejects the kind of reader who demands fully resolved plots and satisfying denouements, could be seen as a rather smug justification for the incompleteness of the account. Unamuno aggressively counters possible reader dissatisfaction by associating such a reaction with materialistic —

---

[13] This assumes that *Cómo se hace una novela* was written before *La novela de Don Sandalio*, but it could have been the other way round. The latter was published in 1933 but had been written earlier and remained unpublished until it appeared alongside *San Manuel Bueno, mártir*. The twenty-three letters that make up the novel are dated from 31 August 1910 to 28 November 1910, while the epilogue is dated December 1930. This suggests a possible completion date for the novel, but the epilogue could also be a late addition.

[14] Cf. what Unamuno wrote elsewhere: 'Busco en los otros, pues, mi pensamiento, lo que puedo hacer pensamiento mío vivo, y me siento tanto más a ellos atraído cuanto mejores espejos me resultan' (*Obras Completas* (Escelicer), IX, 861).

and by implication inferior — readers who wish to have everything served to them
on a plate. Unamuno ends the story of Don Sandalio in much the same way he had
ended the story of Jugo de la Raza which forms part of *Cómo se hace una novela*, for
there he had written: '¿Para qué acabar la novela de Jugo? Esta novela y por lo demás
todas las que se hacen, y no que se contenta uno con contarlas, en rigor no acaban
[...]. El lector que busque novelas acabadas no merece ser mi lector' (VII, 603). Here
Unamuno repudiates the reader who wants a finished product, for such a finished
product implies non-creativity, in effect the death of the reader. By contrast his
true readers, 'mis lectores, los míos', those who respond positively to Unamuno's
idiosyncratic tales, do not read him for the plot, 'no buscan el mundo coherente
de las novelas llamadas realistas' (II, 382), for they know that the plot is mere
contingency. These are the readers — and the inevitable apostrophe, '¿no es verdad,
lectores míos?', confirms it — that Unamuno is courting, the readers he says he has
created and who have in turn created him ('los lectores que yo me he hecho a la vez
que ellos me han hecho a mí (II, 382)). It is a teasing argument, though one which
contains an insidious kind of truth, Unamuno's fans being those who, by definition,
read him and therefore for whom he writes. Be that as it may, this addendum or
paratext post-factum to *La novela de don Sandalio* about readers does not add very
much to what we find in the novel proper. It merely repeats more explicitly what is
already implicit in the comments of the letters to Felipe. If in the epilogue we find
a writer and his readers connected by a mutual interdependency, in the story of Don
Sandalio there are likewise a storyteller and a reader. This reader, Felipe, responds
actively to what he reads, and the writer in turn reacts to his reader, though not
necessarily as the reader might wish. The difference between Felipe and the ideal
reader is that Felipe is still learning and is reluctant to accept the letter-writer's
reticence about the facts of Don Sandalio's life and death. He demands explanations.
The letter-writer responds to his reader by trying to educate him, to turn him
from a materialist reader into a creative reader, one who appreciates the potential
for signifying rather than merely relying on the teller's explanation. As far as the
letter-writer is concerned he has provided Felipe with all he needs to interpret the
information as he sees fit, and that is what he advises him to do. What Felipe does
with the letters he receives is, ironically enough, to send them to a well-known
writer to see what he makes of them, in much the same way that, years earlier,
Augusto Pérez had gone to consult that well-known authority Professor Unamuno
to seek advice for his existential problem. Felipe is one of Unamuno's readers and
takes it upon himself to urge the Salamanca professor to carry on writing. So in a
kind of way Felipe 'makes' Unamuno just as Unamuno says his readers have made
him. Unamuno will indeed publish the story of Don Sandalio, as Felipe urges him
to, but like the letter-writer he will not elucidate the events, although he is prepared
to indulge in a variety of speculations in his epilogue. It is an ingenious game, one
in which theory and praxis are cleverly connected. But it is worth noting that the
praxis comes first and the theory follows. The ostensible theme of the work, the
enigmatic personality of Don Sandalio as told by a writer who is equally enigmatic,
is closely allied to the idea that permeates the entire work: the novel as the projection
of the mind of both author and reader, as a kind of creative dialogue.

If we take the date of the epilogue, December 1930, to be not so distant from the year of composition, *La novela de Don Sandalio* marks the furthest point of Unamuno's development as a novelist vis-à-vis his first published novel, *Paz en la guerra*. The latter pays homage to history in a Tolstoyan way; we could call it a quasi-poetic reconstruction of the third Carlist war and the siege of Bilbao of 1874. It was an effort that took Unamuno many years and for which he documented himself thoroughly. In *La novela de Don Sandalio*, far from seeking to reconcile history and poetry, Unamuno actively sets them up in opposition to each other, with a concomitant argument based on the idea of facts versus invention. In the epilogue, he attempts to justify this approach by arguing that authentic history is based not on the external or circumstantial facts of our lives but on our personal identity. In accordance with his view of history as the transmission from generation to generation of a people's spirit, he argues that great novels are a true reflection of their authors because they constitute a spiritual, as distinct from a factual, biography. He then extends the argument to well-known autobiographies — those of St Augustine, of Jean Jacques Rousseau, of Goethe — and puts forward the view that their greatness comes from their being poetic rather than factual, that they are the products of imagination, not documentation. As a mere epilogue, it seems a disproportionately ambitious way to try to justify the letter-writer's idiosyncratic biography of Don Sandalio.

For the letter-writer the facts of Don Sandalio's life are an impertinent intromission which he refuses to investigate. His friend Felipe, intrigued by the strange personality of Don Sandalio, and even more by his unexpected death, wants a much fuller account with all the relevant facts, but the letter-writer will have none of it. 'No me interesa su historia, me basta con su novela' he declares (letter 22), reiterating what he has earlier told Felipe he had said to Don Sandalio's son-in-law: 'me basta con lo que yo me invento' (letter 20). On a pragmatic level we could interpret this as meaning that the author of the letters is in no position to uncover the facts because Don Sandalio is an invention of his. But on another level it is obvious that Unamuno is introducing the topic of what a novel should and should not be. This too seems to be what lies behind the anecdote of the four dandies in the cafe who turn on the journalist quietly making notes. The moral flagrantly tagged on to the story is explicit and amounts to a dismissal of *costumbrismo*; the letter-writer, by contrast with the journalist, has no need to visit cafes in search of copy (letter 19). Exactly the same idea is found in the anecdote of Pepe *el gallego* (letter 15), the translator who complained that the sociology treatise he had been given to translate was a mere compilation of facts and documents with no hint of imagination; were he to author such a book, he declares, he would make sure to use his inventive capacity. Unamuno recycles the idea of Pepe *el gallego* in the closing letter, when he makes the letter-writer tell his reader, Felipe, to invent the missing 'facts' from Don Sandalio's life. This is tantamount to Unamuno urging us, his readers, to complete the text according to our own reading of Don Sandalio's personality. The imaginative contribution that the letter-writer is demanding of Felipe, and by extension Unamuno of his readers, is exactly in line with what Unamuno had said a few years before in *Cómo se hace una novela*, 'has de hacer tú mismo tu propia novela' (VII, 613); in other words, a reader who is alive is a reader who writes the text just as he 'writes' his own life.

La novela de don Sandalio is a kind of manifesto of novel-writing and a challenge to the reader. Unamuno composed a narrative that would frustrate and provoke the reader through the creation of yawning gaps and the absence of closure. The beach scene (letter 14) is an analogy of the whole work: there is neither explanation nor justification for its inclusion; it is up to the reader to search for its meaning or function, and if we read passively it will have none. In case we have missed the letter-writer's closing disparagement of popular realist fiction, associating it with Blasco Ibáñez and mass-produced articles, Unamuno in the epilogue denounces those who prefer perfectly plotted works, who feel lost without the requisite plot summary when going to the opera or the cinema. Unamuno avers that he has no need for such readers; his readers, he says, are those who prefer 'la novela de la novela' (Epilogue) which he has just offered them, a novel that is a skeleton rather than a fully-fleshed entity. To be authentic, the experience of reading has to mirror the experience of life, its uncertainty, its incompleteness, its unpredictability, always subject to the signifying action of the individual.

The fact that Unamuno feels it necessary to add an intrusive epilogue to the story of Don Sandalio in order to make plain what he is about may suggest that he did not fully trust those readers whom he insists on calling 'mis lectores'. These frequent appeals to readerly interpretation are often reinforced by Unamuno's habit of re-opening in the paratexts questions which one might have tentatively resolved while reading the text.[15] The prologues added by Unamuno to the third edition of *Niebla*, or to the second edition of *Abel Sánchez*, or to *La tía Tula*, and the epilogues to *San Manuel Bueno, mártir*, to *La novela de don Sandalio*, or, more incongruously, to the comic novelette *Un pobre hombre rico o el sentimiento cómico de la vida*, are all examples of his determination either to open new vistas on his work or to make his readers rethink their interpretation after the reading. In *San Manuel Bueno, mártir*, the cryptic reference to the epistle of St Jude, with its disputation between St Michael and the Devil over their rights to Moses' body, and the statement that it is actions that count because 'las palabras no sirven para apoyar las obras' (II, 346), force the reader to go back to Ángela's interpretation of Don Manuel and to test those suggestions against her account of the priest. In *Don Sandalio* Unamuno goes so far as to discuss a typology of readers and writers, thereby posing the fundamental question of what a reader expects from an author and of how we function as readers according to those expectations, anticipating the 'horizon of expectations' theory that Hans Robert Jauss was to make famous four decades later. *Don Sandalio* is of course, in a formal sense, about a writer and a reader, but it is clear that this is no more than the culmination of Unamuno's long preoccupation with the author–reader relationship. 'Mis lectores están ya acostumbrados a mis libertades' he had written eighteen years earlier, going on to add:

---

[15] These paratexts are usually but not exclusively epilogues. Unamuno also makes use of prologues, epigraphs, digressive insertions within texts, and references to the text in subsequent but wholly different texts as well as in the prefaces to later editions of the same text. For a highly useful guide see Franz, 2006.

Si yo no os dijese algo que, sin vosotros saberlo, esté escrito en el fondo de
vuestras almas, no me leeríais. Pues tengo la pretensión de dar forma a informes
y oscuros pensamientos vuestros. (Unamuno, 1985: 73)[16]

But what Unamuno is doing is not so much reading his readers' minds as inviting
them to read his. A novel is thereby conceived as a hermeneutic exercise. In effect
Unamuno sets out to create an interpretative space into which he entices his readers.
Most often this takes the form of periodically formulating questions that refer back
to a character's motives, irrespective of whether the character is aware of it or not.
Some characters are made more aware than others, e.g. Tula or Joaquín Monegro,
and these tend to be the more challenging and the more controversial ones among
'professional' readers. The questions posed naturally serve to enlarge or advance
the theme or problem which forms the basis of the particular book; but Unamuno
goes further than this, for he habitually requires the reader to revise or reconsider
his or her views, not least by raising new issues in epilogues and addenda. The use
of intradiegetic readers (or listeners, as when Augusto Pérez listens to Víctor Goti's
nivola and reacts to what he hears) is one technique that serves to emphasize the
reading role, as do Unamuno's frequent appeals to the reader, the reader whom he
is grooming as he writes. For Unamuno, therefore, the reader is implicit in, and
inseparable from, the writer, or perhaps more accurately from the text. He conveys
a strong sense of the *lector in fabula* later explored by Umberto Eco and others (Eco,
1979). Nor is it simply a case of the use of the rhetorical devices of narratee and
implied reader beloved of narratologists, although narratees and implied readers are
no doubt to be found.

Unamuno's praxis seems to anticipate later theoretical developments in two
ways. Firstly, it grants the reader pride of place by recognizing that the life of
the text ultimately belongs to him or her alone. This view is formulated at least
as early as *Niebla* (ch. XXX), when Víctor enunciates the doctrine that a literary
personage has no inner life save that accorded to it by the reader. Secondly, it
uncannily prefigures the position of those theoreticians who have sought to place
some kind of constraint on the dangerously destabilizing freedom that Barthes and
some poststructuralists had conferred on readers as individuals by introducing the
notion of 'interpretive communities'.[17] While such a notion in no way displaces
the individual reader as a generator of meaning, it does on the other hand insist
that readers have shared values that make for common ways of reading. There
may not be one single community of readers, but each community will have its
own typology, e.g. the academic community, something which ensures a degree
of stability and meaningful exchange. Unamuno creates his own ideal community
of readers by bringing the latters' interpretative function to the fore, either by
creating intradiegetic readers, or by forcefully reminding the real readers of their
essential role in penetrating the veil of the fiction, or by bombarding them, via the
characters, with questions that require urgent answers. That we, the community

[16] From 'Una entrevista con Augusto Pérez', *La Nación* (Buenos Aires), 21 November 1915,
reproduced by Valdés in his edition of *Niebla*.

[17] I am thinking here of the later work of Stanley Fish in particular (from whom the phrase is taken),
but also of Jonathan Culler and David Bleich.

of reader-critics, have so often taken the bait and acquiesced in providing our own answers is testament to Unamuno's strategic success. In filling that hermeneutical gap we are indeed, to paraphrase him, 'sus lectores, los suyos' to an unusual degree. It is entirely as if Unamuno had us in mind when he wrote his quizzical texts.

Influenced in all probability by the German hermeneutic tradition begun by Schleiermacher, whom he read in the 1890s, Unamuno came to see the reading act as intimately bound with the art of interpretation.[18] Reading as interpretation is variously reflected in the challenges he directly issues to his readers inviting them to read creatively, in the way many fictional characters become readers, but above all in the way that the psychology of central characters is obliquely hinted at yet never directly explained, often being left to other characters to interpret. Interpretation, and the pitfalls involved therein, is the key to most of Unamuno's novels. Indeed the influence of Schleiermacher's hermeneutics appears to be so insidious that it is still present in Unamuno's final work of fiction, *San Manuel Bueno, mártir*. Schleiermacher had tried to systematize hermeneutics as a result of his studies of the New Testament, so that the interpretation of the latter lies at the heart of his ideas, and allusions to its various texts are frequent. *San Manuel Bueno, mártir*, of course, takes the form of a modern gospel, and like Schleiermacher's founding text, makes constant allusion to the real ones. It is therefore worth considering it in the light of Schleiermacher's hermeneutics.

At one point in his treatise, *Hermeneutics and Criticism*, Schleiermacher writes that 'in the assertion that we must become conscious of the language area as opposed to the other organic parts of the utterance also lies the fact that we understand the author better than he does himself for in him much of this kind is unconscious that must become conscious in us' (Schleiermacher, 1998: 33). In Unamuno's novel, the priest Don Manuel declares: 'No debe importarnos tanto lo que uno quiera decir como lo que diga sin querer' (II, 318). Though it may sound quasi-Freudian, this warning about unconscious self-betrayal in making utterances is derived from Schleiermacher, sensitive to the fact that significance did not necessarily lie on the surface of an utterance. If we apply Don Manuel's dictum to the narrative, interpretation might seem not just challenging but despairing. For what has the narrator told us unwittingly, 'sin querer'? The situation is perhaps not quite so hopeless, for the one thing we notice about Don Manuel is that, *within the text too*, he becomes an object-of-interpretation. Thus the villagers have one view of him: they see him as a father-protector; the diseased and disturbed have another view: they see in him a source of healing; the Bishop, a somewhat different view: he sees him as a model for the Church; Ángela, a different view yet again: she sees him as a dedicated pastor, but one riven by doubt or worse; and Lázaro has a view

---

[18] There can be little doubt that Unamuno was familiar with Schleiermacher's *Hermeneutics and Criticism*, since the treatise was published alongside his theological writings in the only nineteenth-century edition of his works. Thus, even if Unamuno was initially interested in Schleiermacher as a Christian theologian, since Schleiermacher's New Testament work was what he was known for before Dilthey popularized his hermeneutics, he would necessarily have come across the hermeneutics. Much has been made of Unamuno's reading of Kierkegaard, but he read Schleiermacher long before he read Kierkegaard, as is evident from his correspondence with Clarín. See Alas, 1941.

different from his sister's: he sees in him an unbeliever who uses others' beliefs for purely humanitarian ends. This, I dare to suggest, is where Unamuno's hermeneutic invitations are primarily located: in the knowledge and judgement of personality, that of others and of ourselves. When we judge others, we are judging ourselves, as Don Manuel himself warns citing St Matthew 7. 1. And Ángela Carballino ends by asking questions not just about Don Manuel, but about herself too. This in turn raises an interesting question about her role and function.

Ángela Carballino's memoir takes the form of a testimony in much the same way as each of the testimonies of Matthew, Mark, Luke or John. Before her death Ángela wants to leave a record of her experience of Father Manuel Bueno's life, acts and teachings. The parallel with the Gospels is obvious, but this does not explain why Unamuno chose a female evangelist, something altogether unusual. He could just as well have chosen Lázaro as the memoir writer, since he was after all Father Manuel's 'más asiduo colaborador y compañero' (II, 333). Had Unamuno heard of the (apocryphal?) Gospel of Mary Magdalene, fragments of which were discovered in Egypt in the 1890s? This seems highly unlikely, for information about this find was only disseminated some forty years later. But there is another explanation.

Critics of *San Manuel Bueno, mártir* usually refer to the priest as the protagonist of the novel. This is not how Unamuno saw it. In the prologue (1932) to the book edition of 1933, which followed the publication in the collection 'La Novela de Hoy' in 1931, he speaks of 'los tres protagonistas'. What this tells us of course is that Unamuno regarded the roles played by Ángela and Lázaro to be as important as the role played by Father Manuel. And the role of brother and sister is to act as transmitters. How do they function? The first clue may well be contained in the very title of the book, which on the face of it is something of a puzzle, since Don Manuel is neither a saint nor a martyr in the accepted meaning of these words. Certainly Unamuno's own attitude towards the religious belief of his fellow-Spaniards was very different from the priest's. He made it very plain that in his view a simple, unquestioning faith was no faith at all, and that his own role was to force people to think about their faith and confront the problem, that is the nature, of belief. He cared, but in a very different way from Don Manuel, so for him the priest was not a model to be emulated. As for martyrdom, one can hardly say that Don Manuel dies for his beliefs. But these labels, which make little logical sense, acquire a different nuance if attributed to those who originate them. One of the things that Schleiermacher insisted on was that, although language is a universal phenomenon which modifies the mind, an utterance itself belongs to the mind which makes it; hence it carries both a grammatical and a psychological dimension. 'Santo' is the label that the unbeliever Lázaro attaches to Don Manuel ('es un santo, hermana, todo un santo' (II, 330)), and it is not difficult to see why, since Don Manuel puts the welfare of the community first and thereby fits in with Lázaro's own political ideals. In the case of 'mártir', it is Ángela who mentions martyrdom when she says '¡Qué martirio!' (II, 331) referring to Don Manuel's public role taken on at the expense of his private beliefs. So it is Lázaro who dubs the priest a saint and Ángela who dubs him a martyr. Don Manuel Bueno, in his role as saint and martyr, is thus their creation. They have read Don Manuel according to their own personal viewpoints. Lázaro is a socialist; so he makes of the priest a socialist saint. Ángela is a doubter who forces herself to believe and suffer her doubts in silence; so she makes a martyr of Don Manuel for exactly the same reason. The title is one more interpretation (or more correctly two) among many interpretations of Don Manuel.

In Chapter 2, I suggested that what characterizes Ángela's testimony is above all her discovery of the secret of the parish priest of Valverde de Lucerna. She is, according to her own declaration, the only person who discovered Father Manuel's secret (in the case of her brother it was the priest himself who told him). This insight on the part of Ángela forms a kind of leitmotif in her account. Unlike the Bishop or the rest of the inhabitants of Valverde, she it was who learnt to read the mind of Don Manuel, to decode his language and his silences, and thereby uncover the truth of his personality. This divining of the secret of the priest is something which Unamuno makes his narrator insist upon, but insisting upon it in a singularly suggestive way:

> Bien comprendí yo ya desde entonces [...] que algún pensamiento le perseguía. (II, 319)

> Y más tarde [...] he comprendido que la alegría imperturbable de Don Manuel era la forma temporal y terrena de una infinita y eterna tristeza que con heroica santidad recataba a los ojos y oídos de los demás. (II, 321)

> [...] sentí como una callada confesión suya. (II, 323)

> Me retiré, pensando no se por qué, que nuestro Don Manuel, tan afamado curandero de endemoniadas, no creía en el Demonio. (II, 324)

> Leí no sé qué honda tristeza en sus ojos, azules como las aguas del lago. (II, 324)

What we observe in all these examples is not Don Manuel making any kind of explicit admission, but Ángela *reading* the mind of the priest. It is clearly intuition, not factual evidence, that allows Ángela to read the mind of Don Manuel and guess his tragic secret. And it is this feminine intuition that could well have been suggested to Unamuno by his reading of Schleiermacher.

In his *Hermeneutics and Criticism*, Schleiermacher distinguished between two kinds of psychological interpretation, which he called the male way and the female way. We can try to arrive at a psychological understanding of a text (what moves a writer to making the utterance under scrutiny) by using the comparative method, which consists in identifying what is most characteristic of an author and comparing him with other authors, that is to say comparing an individual measure with a standard or universal gauge. This is the masculine method. Or we can try to arrive at a psychological understanding by using the divinatory method, which is based on the assumption that each person carries within at least a small part of other people and can therefore put himself or herself in the place of the other person. This is the feminine method.

> The *divinatory* method is the one in which one, so to speak, transforms oneself into the other person and tries to understand the individual element directly. The *comparative* method first of all posits the person to be understood as something universal and then finds the individual aspect by comparison with other

things included under the same universal. The former is the female strength in knowledge of people, the latter male. Both refer back to each other, for the first initially depends on the fact that every person, besides being an individual themselves, has a receptivity for all other people. But this itself only seems to rest on the fact that everyone carries a minimum of everyone else within themselves, and divination is consequently excited by comparison with oneself. (Schleiermacher, 1998: 92–93)

In *San Manuel Bueno, mártir* Lázaro interprets the priest using the masculine method, that is to say the comparative approach, seeing Don Manuel, first of all, as just another priest like so many others, 'un ejemplo de la oscura teocracia en que él suponía hundida a España' (II, 325–26), but later as a priest wholly different from the rest, 'no es como los otros' (II, 326). In Ángela, by contrast, Unamuno has given us a perfect example of Schleiermacher's feminine method of divination, of what we can intuit before we resort to comparisons. Interestingly enough, Lázaro himself refers to Ángela's capacity to 'adivinar' (II, 329). Why is it Ángela, a woman, who guesses the secret of Don Manuel? Because she shares the same religious doubts, the same anguish, or, as Schleiermacher would say, because she recognizes in Don Manuel the symptoms of her own mental state, since 'divination is excited by comparison with oneself'. Ángela, a product of the reading of those books which her father, the outsider, brought to Valverde de Lucerna, confesses to harbouring from a tender age 'curiosidades, preocupaciones, inquietudes' (II, 314), and when she comes into contact with the priest, she says, 'me animé y empecé a confiarle mis inquietudes, mis dudas, mis tristezas' (II, 323). As a doubter herself, she is able to sense Don Manuel's predicament. It becomes clear that the Don Manuel offered to us by Ángela is a projection of her own psychological condition. Unamuno has taken care to let us glimpse the religious doubts of Ángela before allowing her to give her readers a glimpse of the religious doubts of the priest. When she identifies with Don Manuel, seeing a kind of son in him ('empezaba yo a sentir una especie de afecto maternal hacia mi padre espiritual' (II, 325)), when she interprets the symptoms of his condition, Ángela is conferring upon him her own struggle with her doubts, using her state of mind to read his. We thus have a clear example of the process of divination of which Schleiermacher writes and which he calls the feminine method. Don Manuel, as we can observe, has a very particular way of expressing himself: he does so by means of aphorisms, maxims and allusions. Ángela interprets these utterances of Don Manuel, his personal style of expression, as the revelation of a restless spirit anxious to conceal his torment, and from there makes the imaginative leap involved in occupying the mental space of another being, precisely as Schleiermacher had advocated. In this way she completes the interpretative process described by the German hermeneutist.

Conclusion

Unamuno's texts belong to a hermetic tradition (emanating largely from Biblical exegesis) in which language is as much a source of occultation and simulation as it is of revelation and forthrightness. Whether the sphinx has a secret will depend on the imaginative sweep of the interpreter. Unamuno is not by any means alone. Other more or less contemporary novelists who have practised this paraliptic approach to writing have included Joseph Conrad, James Joyce, Franz Kafka, Jorge Luis Borges, and Samuel Beckett. Their narratives often work by suggestion. They appear to hide as much as to reveal and thereby to invite decoding.[19] It would of course be an exaggeration to say that Unamuno's narratives are Kafkaesque (although the perplexity evinced by some of his characters is undoubtedly a common factor in both writers), but there is a certain degree of hermeticism in them. Orfeo's view of language ('la lengua sirve para mentir', (I, 668)), comes to mind, for it is language itself that is the source of the interpretative problem. Language, as Unamuno repeatedly declared, both helps us to formulate our thoughts and gets in the way of revealing them. For language has the capacity to create its own reality. It is not a consequence of some pre-existing reality but rather constitutes its own reality. Unamuno has this in common with the post-structuralists of the 1970s, but unlike them, he had only needed to read certain nineteenth-century linguisticians to arrive at this point.[20] Unamuno's point is that language has a mediating effect on our thoughts and judgments, and that we cannot rely on it to give us direct access to anything, least of all to the reality of a person. It is here that Unamuno's views of language and of identity converge.

A self has no internal reality, or at any rate it is not something that is directly accessible. It is an interpretation, a construct on the basis of what comes to us from outside. One's reaction to this incoming self is what in turn gives rise to one's own idea of self. If selves are therefore constituted externally they are like texts, which are constituted by readers. The self is like a text that has to be read. It is, like a text, a system of signs. It can only be an interpretation, 'el Unamuno de la leyenda', of the reading act, where reading is equated with interpreting. If reading is constitutive, then it follows that Unamuno's effort is directed at constituting his readers. And if the self is a function of interpretation, it follows that in reading it is the result of interpreting strategies.

But there is more to it than this. For Unamuno personality or personal identity is dynamic, fluid. It survives in time via memory, as we saw in Chapter 1, but it is not static or immutable. Nor is reading. Unamuno often speaks, in essays, prologues and epilogues, of returning to his own texts and discovering in them something he had not seen before. In fact, in *La novela de Don Sandalio* we are given three interpretations. The rather curt prologue explains that the letters were sent to Unamuno by one of his readers, the addressee of the letters, that is by Felipe. The epilogue, written after an alleged re-reading ('la he vuelto a leer una y más veces') gives rise to not one but two quite different interpretations of the letters: (1) that they are the work of Don Sandalio himself who has gone so far as to feign his own death; (2) that they are the work of Felipe, Unamuno's reader, writing some kind of

---

[19] Frank Kermode wrote a fascinating study of this phenomenon, centred on the New Testament (Kermode, 1979).

[20] Fritz Mauthner, too, placed great insistence on this point. But despite his extreme nominalism and the seemingly radical nature of his stance, he was only taking further the ideas found in Schleiermacher, Humboldt and the German hermeneutic tradition in general. Unamuno's position, less extreme than Mauthner's because less systematized, has nevertheless been described as 'radical nominalism' by Mario J. Valdés (Valdés, 1982: 9).

disguised autobiography. Not only do we have a proliferation of interpretations, but each involves the active participation of a reader. No reader, no interpretation.

For Unamuno, then, there can be no such thing as an innocent reader, or if there is, such a reader is a mere 'alma sencilla', a simple soul or mentally immature person as he refers to such readers, with specific reference to *San Manuel Bueno, mártir*, in his 1933 essay 'Almas sencillas'.[21] Blasillo 'el bobo', the village idiot, is just such an 'alma sencilla', lacking the capacity to create worlds beyond the words, and can only repeat Don Manuel's incantations 'como un pobre mono' (II, 316). Reading must be a hermeneutical activity, as Unamuno insists time and again, explicitly in his essays and implicitly in his fiction. He is the reader of his own texts, and he often presents himself as such, that is to say as the receptor of material which he processes and passes on to his readers. Unamuno the 'editor' of *San Manuel Bueno, mártir*, reads Ángela's account; Ángela reads Lázaro's notes; Lázaro 'reads' Don Manuel's utterances; the people 'read' the priest's works and teachings; the bishop 'reads' the people's anecdotes of the priest; we, the real readers, have to make sense of multiple readings and we do so in multiple ways, as the plethora of critical readings so amply demonstrates. The reading or interpretative function clearly occupies a special place in Unamuno's conception of fiction; it is the 'para qué' of writing, a thoroughly teleological conception.

Unamuno thus contrives his texts in such a way as to force the reader to deploy particular reading strategies in order to engage with the text. On the face of it, the author does not substitute for the reader as the generator of meaning but is subservient to him or her. There is no meaning encoded in the text, for the latter is little more than a system of signs.[22] In Unamuno's theory it is the reader whose responsibility it is to make the text meaningful. What Unamuno is doing is assuming a particular kind of reader, grooming him or her to read in a particular kind of way. Of course the reader whom Unamuno addresses is not a specific individual. His reader is simply part of a linguistic community ('mis lectores, los míos'), a sharer in a system of rules, both syntactic and semantic, that any reader could reasonably be expected to have assimilated. It is this reading competence that Unamuno is exploiting, and he is exploiting it to make competent readers into fully self-conscious ones, to read as it were 'existentially', aware of the reading act and its consequences.

Unamuno, then, creates a virtual reader whom he nudges in particular directions. Whether a real reader is thereby encouraged to identify with this shadowy doppelganger presumably depends on the reader, but the device works even if it serves to provoke hermeneutic suspicion. We have to be very clear that this virtual reader is more than Wolgang Iser's implied reader or Gerald Prince's narratee, both of which are necessary consequences of writing and narrating. There is nothing necessary about Unamuno's virtual reader, who is a device to keep his texts on the boil. What Unamuno appears to want to do is to open up — or re-open as his epilogues and prefaces to second editions suggest — the experience offered by his

---

[21] *Obras Completas* (Escelicer), VIII, 1199–201.
[22] Unamuno had been a student of semiology in the 1880s, as is mentioned in his correspondence with Pedro de Múgica, much of which revolves around linguistic questions. See Unamuno, 1965: 14, 100.

texts. What he does not want is closure, even at the expense of making his texts appear indeterminate or unfathomable. It is entirely as if the intellectual restlessness of the author were being communicated to the real readers by preventing them from finally shutting the book in a state of satisfied curiosity or attained knowledge. For if such conclusive knowledge is unattainable in real life, it should be equally unattainable in the life of the novel, that is to say, in the life of the reader. In many of Unamuno's fictions we reach the end with key questions unanswered. And if by chance they seem to have been answered, Unamuno as likely as not will stick his oar in to upset our complacency.

For Unamuno, as for Ángela Carballino, writing is an experience of self-discovery. Each text represents a new discovery. He extends this idea to the reader further down the line by virtually forcing that reader to realize his or her own experience through the act of reading, as Unamuno symbolically narrates in *Cómo se hace una novela*. A text has to become in some sense a cognitive activity, both for authors and for readers. Just as writing was for Unamuno a kind of reading, so for Unamuno's readers reading is a kind of writing. By becoming his readers they are discovering themselves in the same way that they discover themselves via others. Unamuno would surely have agreed with Marcel Proust when the Frenchman wrote, referring to his readers, 'ils ne seraient pas, selon moi, mes lecteurs, mais les propres lecteurs d'eux-mêmes, mon livre n'étant qu'une sorte de ces verres grossissants comme ceux que tendait à un acheteur l'opticien de Combray, mon livre, grâce auquel je leur fournirais le moyen de lire en eux-mêmes' (Proust, 1990: 338).

CHAPTER 5

The Person

The Self and the Mask

In the preceding chapters I have had occasion to mention that Unamuno's thought, whether broadly philosophical or more narrowly linguistic, is closely connected to his interest in personality, that is, in what makes us what we are, what gives us our sense of personal identity and self-awareness, whether this is something real, separable from our body, and even whether it could endure beyond our bodily death. The connection between the self and the book is represented in Unamunian ontology by the symbol of the mirror. Unamuno saw the book (originally of course the Old Testament, although he usually refers simply to 'el Libro') as the attempt of the Jewish people to forge an identity for themselves, and he extended this vision of a nation struggling to find a common identity after the humiliation of enslavement and captivity to literary composition as a whole. What binds together is the spoken language, but once the latter gives rise to a written form it creates an enduring tradition that serves to garner not only a sense of community but also of collective identity.[1] In *Cómo se hace una novela* he wrote:

> Todo es para nosotros libro, lectura; podemos hablar del Libro de la Historia, del Libro de la Naturaleza, del Libro del Universo. Somos bíblicos. Y podemos decir que en el principio fue el Libro. O la Historia. Porque la Historia comienza con el Libro y no con la Palabra, y antes de la Historia no había conciencia, no había espejo, no había nada. (II, 575)

Unamuno makes it sound dramatic, but the basic idea underlying this pronouncement — books as the repository of a nation's temperament and view of itself — is not new. It was essentially Herder's position and from him passed down to Humboldt and various other nineteenth-century thinkers from whom Unamuno picked it up. What is peculiar to Unamuno is that he extends the argument to individuals, and especially to one class of individuals, those for whom reading is a way of life, 'los que vivimos principalmente de la lectura y en la lectura' (II, 575). Literature is not only the repository of a nation's self-consciousness but also of the individual's. A book can be an individual's mirror as much as a nation's. The analogy is not without its logic, for if that individual is a writer he or she will need readers to bring forth his or her identity. A writer is part of a community of readers just as a citizen is part of the community or nation to which he or she belongs. One cannot

[1] Unamuno calls it 'personalidad colectiva' (Unamuno, 1993: 149).

be a self-sufficient point of consciousness quite simply because that is not how consciousness works. I become aware of myself because I notice others are aware of me, and the more I notice the more self-conscious I become. Personal identity is thus a communal affair, and a writer is, *qua* writer, dependent on the community of readers. But just as I can affect, for better or for worse, the impressions others receive of me, so a writer can affect the impressions readers receive of him or her. This, in a nutshell, is the essence of the dialogue that Unamuno constantly established with his readers. It boils down to locating where the writer's identity lies. There are of course corollaries to this, the chief one being that the writer is also a reader of himself, as Unamuno reminds us and as he would have seen in Schleiermacher.[2]

In the latter situation, the dialogue is between the object and the image, if we follow the metaphor of the mirror. Whether writers or readers, we are all reflected in the mirror of the book. But in Unamuno this mirror is not the inanimate article made of silvered glass hanging on the bathroom wall. It has a life of its own and can grip and alter us. 'Una novela [...] tiene que ser [...] organismo y no mecanismo', he declares (VII, 616–17), echoing the Romantic natural philosophers, and thus as a living entity the work of fiction has the capacity to transform. It is not an object of contemplation or abstraction but of interaction, just as one person is the source of interaction with another. The world of the book is the world of the mind, and we interact with it as we do with other minds. It is this interaction between minds that becomes the driving force of Unamuno's fiction and of many of his quasi-theoretical comments on fiction, reflected not only in his dialogues with the virtual reader but most obviously in the obsessive passions that are the hallmarks of his fictional personages. The search for identity is not simply an intellectual pursuit; it involves emotions, desires, instincts, as well as the imaginative faculty, all subsumed under the Unamunian *serse*, or what existential psychiatry was shortly to call a life-project.[3] Unamuno's fiction thus takes the form of an exploration of the self, or, what for Unamuno is the same thing, of search for purpose. If we could only know what our consciousness is for, we would know what our purpose is: 'El mundo es para la conciencia. O, mejor dicho, este *para*, esta noción de finalidad, y mejor que noción sentimiento, este sentimiento teleológico no nace sino donde hay conciencia. Conciencia y finalidad son la misma cosa en el fondo' (*DSTV*, X, 284).[4]

---

[2]   The art of hermeneutics seeks 'to understand the utterance at first just as well and then better than its author. For because we have no immediate knowledge of what is in him, we must seek to bring much to consciousness that can remain unconscious to him, *except to the extent to which he himself reflectively becomes his own reader*' (Schleiermacher, 1998: 23; my italics).

[3]   In Spain, this is the concept used by the Spanish psychiatrist and novelist Luis Martín-Santos, who was almost certainly influenced by Unamuno. See Longhurst, 2008: 47–58.

[4]   Unamuno is here following Schopenhauer, who had argued, following Kant, that finality, purpose, was the work of our intellect and not of nature: 'La finalidad fue primeramente traída a la Naturaleza por el entendimiento, que se asombra luego como de una maravilla de lo que él mismo ha creado' (in Unamuno's own translation of *On the Will in Nature*: Schopenhauer, 1970: 120–21). Schopenhauer goes on to argue that since the Will itself has no finality and is the same for everything and everyone, we must be our own representation, or as Unamuno translates, 'todo ser es obra de sí mismo' (121), since an individual cannot be undifferentiated Will. And if finality is the creation of our intellect, then each being searches for his own finality within himself. Unamuno's debt to Schopenhauer is profound.

To find one's role in life, to recognize and fulfil one's life-project, is thus, to a degree at least, to satisfy the ontological query. The disturbing 'who am I?' question can be replaced by the more practical 'what am I for?'. Identity and purpose are the themes around which Unamuno builds his fictional works, and this applies as much to his comic as to his more serious works. I shall briefly consider two of the former, one early and one late production, before turning to Unamuno's more weighty explorations of the subject of the person.

In *Amor y pedagogía*, ostensibly a skit on Positivism and specifically on the new discipline of scientific sociology, Don Avito Carrascal's life-calling is to breed a genius. He is a man of science, or so he thinks, and his life-project is to nurture an exceptional human being according to the emergent science of sociology which emphasizes the key role played by social factors in fashioning behaviour, and notably the formative impact of education. By following the precepts of modern science in educating his son he believes he will bring forth a genius. The reasons for the failure of Avito's plan for his son are made obvious by Unamuno, even in the title of the book: man doth not live by brain alone; the emotions, too, are critical and need to be recognized. Well before he starts the experiment proper, Avito discovers he has to make a choice (between Leoncia, his original choice, and Marina, his more recent discovery), but he does not choose with his head, reflectively, as he had planned, but with his instinct or emotions, even if at first he pretends otherwise. He is constantly besieged by his secret voice, a reminder that his plan is unnatural, artificially contrived. Avito, however, keeps rationalizing his decisions, and chooses to ignore that inner voice, that 'demonio familiar' or simple instinct that tells him such rationalization is spurious. The novel relies heavily for its comic effect on the deterministic philosopher Don Fulgencio Entrambosmares and the spoof Socratic dialogues between him and Avito, but already we can see Unamuno having a dig at deterministic systems of thought, especially where human beings, with their unpredictable behaviour, are concerned. The subject of how far our character and our actions are predetermined will receive far more serious treatment in *Abel Sánchez*.

Amor y pedagogía undergoes a marked change of direction in Chapter VIII as Unamuno switches his attention from Avito to his son Apolodoro, so we only get glimpses into the former's increasing disconcertment as his project starts to unravel. What the portrayal of Apolodoro clearly shows is that scientific sociology fails to explain the basic urges and the awakening of sensuality that grip Apolodoro in his adolescence. The scientific education his father insists on giving him does not prepare him for life's entrapments. On the other hand, poetic books, Apolodoro discovers, 'lo explican todo, lo hacen sentir' (I, 378). For his part Avito blames 'el fracaso de su hijo' not on his absurd experiment but on others' interference. Previously he had blamed Marina; then he blames Apolodoro himself, a clear case of displacement, of the transference of his own inadequacy onto others. Don Avito, puppet that he is (as Don Fulgencio reminds him), fails to learn. He is stuck in a positivistic rut and sees nothing but deterministic forces which he tries and fails to control. Faced with an unexpected and tragic outcome he ends with a cry of '¡Madre! [...] desde sus honduras insondables' (I, 422), a hint of regression to the maternal womb in the face of defeat. In the grotesque epilogue that Unamuno appends, we see Don Avito planning to go back to his old ways with his as yet unborn grandson.[5]

In *Un pobre hombre rico o el sentimiento cómico de la vida* Unamuno offers us the reverse of a life-project; in effect the absence of one. Emeterio's project is to avoid falling into the claws of the landlady's daughter Rosita, not least because he notices the sardonic looks of other guests at her insinuating moves. But it is an external or artificial project, an evasion, literally as well as metaphorically, since he surreptitiously escapes from his boarding house, incapable of either accepting or rejecting Rosita's advances. Leaving Rosita behind physically solves nothing because he cannot leave her behind mentally. It even increases his anxiety and inertia, unable as he is to bring himself to tear the page on the calendar that carried the date of his craven departure.

Rosita is symbolic of Emeterio's refusal to confront his own reality. His passivity extends to saving obsessively out of habit, without knowing what the money is for. He is, like Augusto Pérez, 'un paseante de la vida', a drifter lacking a life-plan or purpose, and without a purpose he descends to voyeurism, to stalking young lovers and living other people's amorous adventures. Emeterio's friend, Celedonio, explains the former's inadequacy as a lack of commitment: 'La cuestión es pasar el rato, sin adquirir compromisos serios. Y tú siempre has huido de los compromisos' (II, 399). Emeterio becomes a virtual automaton: 'Vivía sin porvenir y ya casi sin pasado' (II, 401). The lack of commitment translates into a lack of self-knowledge: 'Ya no sé quien soy' (II, 401). Had this been a serious work rather than an overtly comic one we would be talking of a neurosis, for that is precisely what Emeterio's symptoms, evasion, helplessness, and obsessiveness, point to. He achieves a cure and recovers his self when he makes a commitment and takes a decision: his commitment is to the by-now widowed Rosita, and his decision is to endow his step-grandson with his wealth. Celedonio jokes to Emeterio that 'hiciste de Celestino de ti mismo' (II, 414), but even Unamuno's ironic joke — in a novel, it has to be said, that is brimming with them, including scabrous ones — is based on the idea that by pursuing his calling he contrived his purpose in life; in other words it contains the essence of Unamuno's philosophy of self-definition through interaction with others.

This is equally true of Gertrudis in *La tía Tula*, which poses rather more challenging questions about the whole issue of personality. On the one hand we can see Gertrudis as a model of selflessness, of sacrifice for others. On the other hand we can see her as carving a role for herself through the manipulation of others. Either way Gertrudis achieves self-expression and self-fulfilment through the presence of others; but we cannot escape the fact that Unamuno's presentation is thoroughly ambivalent, that is to say it offers evidence for different interpretations of the character's motivation, and indeed this is exactly the result produced in critical approaches to the novel. The reactions have been amusingly varied and at times

---

[5] Don Avito's regression to the maternal womb is confirmed during his reappearance in *Niebla*, Chapter XIII. On the other hand he now acknowledges that his life-project had been misconceived, but he makes no mention of his grandson.

extreme, both in defence and in condemnation of the character's behaviour. This was very probably what Unamuno was expecting.

Gertrudis is not quite the tortured soul we encounter in the person of Joaquín Monegro in *Abel Sánchez*, but nor is she a straightforward personage whose character we can simply read off the page. Her determination to remain independent and in control of her — and others' — situation is countered by intermittent self-doubt. She is fully aware of her desires and makes her choices in a thoroughly conscious manner. But what worries her is motivation, what appears to lie deep within her personality that makes her behave as she does. Through Gertrudis's intermittent bouts of uncertainty and disquietude, Unamuno makes it clear that for him the novel is not simply about Gertrudis's self-assertive actions; it is just as much, indeed even more, about her underlying motives and her quest to understand herself.

In her domestic and secular convent Gertrudis's adopted role is that of Mother Superior, and she completely dominates the lives of all who live there, brother-in-law, children, servants. Her life-project is to bring up the children as if they were her own and according to her strict and very personal interpretation of a (female) Christian code of behaviour. Unamuno portrays her both as a deeply caring mother and as a puritan autocrat. Her maternal vocation is never in doubt; what is uncertain is the nature of that maternity. Is it genuine or vicarious? Does she sacrifice herself for the sake of the children who have been left motherless or does she rather appropriate others' children as does Raquel in *Dos madres*? The parallel with Raquel is not especially helpful since Raquel is sterile and there is no reason to believe that Gertrudis is so. Indeed she more than once contemplates the possibility of biological reproduction through marriage with Ricardo or Ramiro, and is outraged by Don Juan's offer of a marriage without the risk of conception. For her, the only possible justification for marriage is procreation, as we see in her encouragement of her sister to add to the family. What, then, lies at the root of Gertrudis's unusual behaviour?

Unamuno does not tell us, but given his presentation of the character and her circumstances, at least three possible answers present themselves. The first is that Gertrudis's devotion to the children is simply the secular equivalent of an unfulfilled religious vocation. Gertrudis is a fan of Saint Teresa and runs the household along the lines of a monastic order. Yet there is no evidence that she ever had a religious vocation in the conventional sense. In fact Unamuno appears to invite us to discard this hypothesis by a series of passing mentions. Firstly, he points to Gertrudis's Catholicism as not being exactly orthodox, for she has religious ideas of her own that strike the good priest Don Primitivo as potentially heretical. Indeed it appears from her comments that the Virgin Mary is for her a rather more important figure than her Son, whom she considers to have addressed his Mother disdainfully (Gospel of St John 2. 4): '¡Hombre al fin!' (I, 872), comments Gertrudis to herself with what appears to be a hint of censure. Secondly, Gertrudis herself rejects the idea that convent life would have suited her. Her objection to marriage to Ramiro suggests to the latter that she should have opted for the traditional alternative of the convent, but Gertrudis will have none of it, which probably reflects Unamuno's own view that a genuine religious vocation has to be exercised in the ordinary world and not out of it. Thirdly, when she discovers an ascetic inclination in Ramirín she becomes alarmed, does everything in her power to deflect him from a religious vocation, and contrives to make him fall for Caridad and to marry her promptly. In some ways Gertrudis is more of a religious rebel than a religious conformist. She regards Christianity as a warped religion through the excessive influence of men, '¡[...] religión de hombres — se decía Gertrudis — ; masculinos el Padre, el Hijo, y el Espíritu Santo!' (I, 872). The vocational hypothesis, then, does not help to explain her actions unless we also stipulate a thoroughly unconventional approach to religion. Her vocation is not conventual in the accepted sense.

The second explanation of Gertrudis's behaviour that is raised in the novel is that she acts out of wounded pride. She maintains a firm attitude towards Ramiro and keeps him at a distance, but privately she experiences what the narrator calls 'una brava galerna' (I, 843). She recalls Rosa's request on her deathbed that she, Gertrudis, should marry her widowed husband (to prevent him looking elsewhere), but is reluctant to take it at face value: 'No, no pudo querer eso; no pudo querer que entre él, entre su hombre [...] y yo se interpusiese su sombra..., no pudo querer eso. Porque cuando él estuviese a mi lado, arrimado a mí, carne a carne, ¿quien me dice que no estuviese pensando en ella? Yo no sería sino el recuerdo, ¡algo peor que el recuerdo de la otra!' (I, 843). Since Gertrudis is perfectly capable of imagining Ramiro as her husband and indeed confesses her fondness for him, the possibility arises that her rejection is motivated by a vengeful pride, a possibility vaguely intuited by the character herself ('«¿no es esto orgullo?», se preguntaba' (I, 850)), and rather more explicitly repeated by Father Álvarez during the course of a confession that has all the appearance of a psychoanalytical session. What Father Álvarez suggests is that the root cause of the penitent's disquietude at her decision to reject Ramiro's proposal of marriage is resentment.

> — La cuestión es si usted le quiere o no. Esta es la cuestión. ¿Le quiere usted, sí o no?
> — ¡Para marido..., no!
> — ¿Pero le rechaza?
> — ¡Rechazarle..., no!
> — Si cuando se dirigió a su hermana, la difunta, se hubiera dirigido a usted...
> — ¡Padre! ¡Padre! — y su voz gemía.
> — Sí, por ahí hay que verlo...
> — ¡Padre; que eso no es pecado...!
> — Pero ahora se trata de dirección espiritual, de tomar consejo... y sí, es pecado, es acaso pecado... Tal vez hay aquí unos viejos celos...
> — ¡Padre!
> — Hay que ahondar en ello. Acaso no le ha perdonado aún...
> — Le he dicho, padre, que le quiero; pero no para marido. Le quiero como a un hermano, como a un más que hermano, como al padre de mis hijos, porque estos, sus hijos, lo son míos de lo más dentro mío, de todo mi corazón; pero para marido, no. Yo no puedo ocupar en su cama el sitio que ocupó mi hermana...
> (I, 851)

It is clear from this exchange that the priest does not understand the penitent's position. His is a male's view. Gertrudis does not deny Father Álvarez's suspicion of jealous resentment. What she does do is to reject his suggestion of marriage to Ramiro, and she does so because it is driven purely by the priest's concern for the latter's welfare, not for hers, yet this tenacity in the face of external pressures does nothing to assuage her turmoil and anxiety. Gertrudis's regret comes to the surface momentarily in Ramiro's deathbed scene, in which both her love for the man she has rejected and her fear of him become apparent. Her capacity for self-analysis is therefore not in doubt, but her anxiety and her self-questioning about her motives remain with her to the end.

The third explanation of Gertrudis's determined avoidance of marriage is a fear of sex. She rationalizes this as a fear of men: 'el hombre, todo hombre, hasta tú, Ramiro, hasta tú, me ha dado miedo siempre; no he podido ver en él sino el bruto' (I, 866). But the word *asco*, which appears several times, seems to point to a more deep-seated anxiety than the fear of male aggressiveness. Indeed what Unamuno appears to be suggesting in a few veiled references is that what Gertrudis fears is her own sexuality. Far from being frigid, she is portrayed as being exceptionally sensitive to matters concerning the sexual act, as Unamuno clearly hints in his description of Gertrudis's emotional state as she orders Ramiro either to marry Rosa or to take his leave: '[...] durante él [el silencio] la sangre, antes represada y ahora suelta, le encendió la cara a la hermana. Y entonces, en el silencio agorero, podía oírsele el golpe trepidante del corazón' (I, 812). This description is repeated when Ramiro, now a widower, speaks to her of her enticing presence, of 'el imán de tu cuerpo': 'Gertrudis, toda encendida, bajaba la cabeza y se callaba, mientras le tocaba a rebato el corazón' (I, 840). Gertrudis does everything possible to avoid having to confront her sexual instinct. As soon as Ramiro leaves the house she opens his bedroom windows to rid it of the male odour she detects. She protects the children from sexual manifestations of even the mildest kind, and gladly helps Ramirín in mathematics but not in physiology or anatomy because 'ésas son porquerías' (I, 879),[6] yet she is only too keen to marry Ramirín off to Caridad, just as she had earlier encouraged Rosa to bed Ramiro as often as she could, going so far as to imagine that Ramiro might have been thinking of her during the act which conceived Ramirín. She will not allow the wet nurse to show her breasts while feeding the infant, yet when she herself bottle-feeds she places the baby's hand on her own breast. It is entirely as if the negation of sexuality were compensated by a vicarious sexual experience, an experience for which Gertrudis seems to yearn yet fear. Her aversion is such that she sees herself as the daughter of her mother and the celibate priest Don Primitivo, whom she regards as a completely asexual figure (wrongly, as we know, for the priest is perfectly well aware of Rosa's sexual charms). Of her biological father she makes no mention.

The rejection of her three suitors likewise constitutes an interesting revelation of Gertrudis's aversion to male attentions, since she rejects the first two on the grounds

---

[6] Interestingly, this applies to Augusto's mother too. It would seem that for Unamuno motherhood and sexual curiosity make poor bedfellows, unless he is ironically reflecting the Catholic Church's traditional abhorrence of matters sexual; but the latter is not likely in the case of Gertrudis, since she is hardly an orthodox Catholic.

that having children of her own would rob Rosa's three children of a mother, and
the third she rejects on the grounds that he is sterile:

> — [...] Y no vuelva a poner los pies en esta casa.
> — ¿Por qué, Gertrudis?
> — ¡Por puerco! (I, 871)[7]

This brutal rejection is eloquent enough. Just as she had earlier refused Father
Álvarez's suggestion, the Church's traditional 'allaying of concupiscence' as one of
the reasons for marriage ('¿Qué es eso de considerarme remedio? ¡Y remedio contra
eso! No, me estimo en más' (I, 854)), she now resents becoming Don Juan's sexual
object. It is of course impossible to tell whether Gertrudis's feminism and cult of
purity are the cause or the consequence of her aversion to sexually active men. We
are dealing with a character from fiction, and since Unamuno does not say we are
none the wiser. Although she eventually regrets her cold attitude to Ramiro and the
unfortunate consequences it brought about, she does so using a terminology which
brings out her persistent horror of the sexual act: *fango, pozo negro, albañal, légamo,
porquería, estiércol, podredumbre*, all words associated with filth and which provoke
repugnance. The traditional cliché of Madonna-versus-whore as characterizing the
female psyche is of course wholly inadequate. Gertrudis is presented as neither. If
we have to resort to binaries, the only one that is relevant is that of materiality/
spirituality, or physical reproduction/spiritual reproduction. Gertrudis veers
between the two poles, but is strongly inclined to reject the material as detrimental
to the spiritual. And this, unsurprisingly, is much closer to Unamuno's own outlook
as found in *Del sentimiento trágico de la vida*.

   The novel, then, inevitably poses the question: which is Gertrudis's real identity
and which is the mask? Is she the Gertrudis whose self-sacrifice and dedication
to her family win her the veneration of those around her, even after her death? Is
she the one she aspires to be, the 'querer ser' that Unamuno had extolled shortly
before in the prologue to *Tres novelas ejemplares y un prólogo* (II, 194), a latter-day
Virgin Mother, creator of a pure, untarnished, fraternal (or sororial) community?
Or is she the one she suspects she might be: a person whose pathological aversion
to the flesh makes her impose her 'idea inhumana de la virtud' (I, 866) on others,
reducing them to puppets? A saint who has produced sinners, as Ramiro says? Or a
sinner who strives to produce saints, as she herself says? Unamuno's portrayal of the
character suggests that Gertrudis is potentially all of these things for it is up to her
and to us to complete the character; but if we do, we shall, in Unamunian terms,
be projecting our own selves, contemplating the image in the mirror.

   Gertrudis is a very good example of the way Unamuno lures us into passing
judgments on the character in precisely the way we do with real people. In one of
the key essays on this novel, Geoffrey Ribbans drew attention to the wide variety
of responses that the character had so far evoked, and concluded that it was an error
to judge her in accordance 'with conventional notions of realism, verisimilitude or

---

[7] Unamuno seems to have had a lofty conception of female purity. In *Dos madres* he makes the
pregnant Berta make a similar utterance to her husband: 'Los hombres sois todos unos cochinos'
(II, 225), a repetition of what Doña Marta had said earlier (II, 210).

social representativeness'; she had to be judged rather 'as a character who within a given human or psychological context is working out a particular aspect of those problems of existence, belief and conduct which obsessed Unamuno' (Ribbans, 1987: 418). Since Ribbans wrote those words the phenomenon of over-reaction to Gertrudis the person has continued to affect even the best scholars. Thus Francisco La Rubia Prado writes: 'Lo cierto es que Tula ha vivido su vida en la mentira', in itself an extraordinary thing to say of a fictional character in a fictitious narrative; and he goes on: 'y [en] la negación de lo que escapa a sus dogmas y percepciones radicalmente monológicas, ni contrastadas ni empáticas con otras voces y maneras de ver las cosas' (La Rubia Prado, 1999: 179). What this verdict on the character shows is that it is the critic who is being monologic by imposing his own view as the 'truth' in contrast to the character's 'false' existence. There is of course no such truth in the novel — neither hers nor his — nor are there 'other ways of seeing things' except those of the male characters who try to pressurize Gertrudis into giving in to their wishes. The critic appears simply to have forgotten his postmodernist stance driven by what he sees as the personage's unjustified intransigence. Contrary to what this critic believes, Unamuno does not make Gertrudis reject her sexuality; what she evidently resists is allowing others to subject her sexuality to their own ends, as is entirely obvious in her rejection of Don Juan the doctor, whose name is scarcely accidental. Gertrudis's life-project is what it is — an attempt to rewrite male Christianity — and the vicissitudes of the plot are subservient to that end. She is very conscious — Kierkegaardianly so — that she has choices and that she could have acted differently. But as she lies dying we, and she, can see that her life-project has been fulfilled, though not without cost to others and to herself. To question that life-project is tantamount to questioning the existence of the novel in our hands or, what amounts to the same thing, Unamuno's novel-writing.

Father Manuel Bueno's life-project, too, is fulfilled, and fulfilled, in Ángela's estimation, at a cost to himself, though not to others. Yet alongside the Raquel of *Dos madres* and Alejandro Gómez of *Nada menos que todo un hombre*, Father Manuel is the one who least wavers in his determination, in his case the determination to protect others from his own existential solitude, from his fear of impending nothingness. Only Lázaro appears to be privy to his angst, but Lázaro is a convinced unbeliever anyway and remains unaffected except in his admiration for the priest. Interestingly, Father Manuel's existential isolation is mirrored in the recessive technique employed by Unamuno to relate his story, for we see him at second or third hand, mainly through the eyes of Ángela and her brother. Since both of these characters have their own highly personal points of view, the 'real' Don Manuel is hidden from us. We may know the facts of his biography but of his motivation we know practically nothing. This, nevertheless has not deterred a large number of critics from analysing his beliefs, behaviour, and convictions. The facts about the priest do tell us something about him, but only at a superficial level which makes any judgment questionable.

Don Manuel is not, apparently, attracted to the priesthood by a strong religious vocation. He becomes a priest for the same reason that Gertrudis appears to sacrifice marriage: in order to help look after the children of a widowed sister, to provide for them and act as father rather than uncle. For this reason he rejects all ecclesiastical preferment and remains in his native village. His dedication to his fellow-villagers is as exemplary as is Gertrudis's to her adopted family. He looks not just after their religious welfare, but after their hygiene, grooming, health, work, physical comfort, and entertainment, with particular attention to children both at school and recreation. Here the parallel with Gertrudis is obvious: Father Manuel has given up marriage but he has not given up children. For Gertrudis her convent and her order are her home and her five children, for whom she provides 'años apacibles y serenos [...], íntima luz espiritual de serena calma' (I, 873), or in other words loving care. For Don Manuel, 'mi monasterio es Valverde de Lucerna' (II, 322). His attitude to his parishioners is protective and consoling. Like Moses, he is their leader both spiritually and materially, wholeheartedly and incessantly devoted to his 'piadosos menesteres' (II, 331–32). Such is his dedication to his village that the villagers give him their absolute loyalty, believing they have a saint in their midst, something that looks like being officially sanctioned in the fullness of time. What does this tell us about the personality of Don Manuel? Clearly very little, apart that is from his supreme devotion to duty. Seen from the outside, as the villagers see him, we have an exemplary pastor whose care of his flock is exceptional and admirable, but little else.

There is an interesting comparison to be made with *La tía Tula*. In the latter Unamuno has given us various perspectives on Gertrudis according to how other characters see her, and what is obvious is that none offers a fully convincing interpretation. Rosa, who is closest to her, finds it strange that Gertrudis should want to precipitate both her engagement and her marriage to Ramiro. And although she appears to glimpse Gertrudis's hankering after motherhood, she does not understand it: she neither understands Gertrudis's refusal to come to live with her and Ramiro, nor realizes, just before her death, that Gertrudis is not acceding to her sister's petition to marry Ramiro. Ramiro for his part sees Gertrudis as stubborn but fails to understand her resistance, why she is willing to live in his house and look after his children but not accept him as husband. Ricardo interprets Gertrudis's courteous and sensitive letter declining his approaches as a sign that she is counting on marrying Ramiro. Don Juan is of the same opinion, and later makes things worse for himself by his maladroit offer of marriage, entirely misreading Gertrudis's love for her nephews and nieces. Father Álvarez is equally insensitive to Gertrudis's feelings in his attempt to persuade her to accept Ramiro's proposal. First he suggests that living in a widower's house provokes gossip, failing to foresee that such considerations can only incite contempt in a person as independently minded as Gertrudis. Then he advances the idea of an old jealousy, without allowing that affection for a person of the opposite sex need not imply sexual acceptance. And finally he provokes Gertrudis's wrath by suggesting that she should offer herself up as the solution to her brother-in-law's sexual appetite. Don Primitivo, by contrast, does not even try to understand Gertrudis: '¿para qué me voy a meter en sus inclinaciones y sentimientos íntimos?', a thought which, exceptionally and tellingly, earns him the complimentary phrase 'con muy buen acierto' from the narrator (I, 806). Despite the variety of critical responses to Gertrudis, no critic to my knowledge has suggested that any one of these characters has the key to Gertrudis's secret. And yet, with very few exceptions, critics in general have taken Ángela Carballino's interpretation of Don Manuel to give us the correct and objective version of the priest's personality and secret. Such, then, is the powerful effect of what David Goldknopf, in a classic study of the 'I' narrator, referred to as 'the confessional increment' (Goldknopf, 1972).[8] Yet the fact remains that in *San Manuel Bueno, mártir* Unamuno has gone even further than in previous novels in masking the personality of the central character. For what we are left with, by and large, is the highly personal view of a highly idiosyncratic narrator who herself has a distinct personality and who finds herself in a situation of some stress and anxiety at the time of putting pen to paper. What we are given in *San Manuel Bueno, mártir* is a character whose personality *has already been interpreted*. We can either accept that interpretation or deconstruct it. But Unamuno still had one further step to take.

Being for Others, Being for Oneself

As I noted in Chapter 4, the ostensible theme of *La novela de don Sandalio, jugador de ajedrez* is the enigmatic personality of the silent chess player. The title already indicates that this is a 'novela' and not a 'cronicón cualquiera' (II, 346), an imaginative or poetic reconstruction of a life, not a listing of biographical facts. The kernel of this strange tale is to be found in a memory of Unamuno's youth, as is evident from one of the articles which he used to write regularly for the Buenos Aires newspaper *La Nación*:

> En mi época de ajedrecimanía solía yo jugar con un ancianito que no parecía vivir sino para el ajedrez. Todas las tardes me pasaba dos o tres horas jugando con él. Y jamás supe sino su nombre, que hoy ya no lo recuerdo. No sé de dónde ni cómo era, ni qué ideas tenía, ni nada de su vida pasada. No nos unía más que la común afición al ajedrez. Y así se ve que dos hombres pueden reunirse todos los días dos, tres o más horas, en torno a un tablero, a comerse caballos y torres y convertir a peones en reinas, y desconocerse profundamente el uno al otro, manteniéndose mutuamente extraños. [...]
>
> Un día falta uno de los jugadores, dura su ausencia unos días, al cabo de ellos vuelve a su hábito, pero vestido de luto y con aspecto de cierta tristeza. En esos días ha quedado viudo. Y puede muy bien ocurrir que su competidor lo ignore.
> (IX, 489)

'Desconocerse profundamente el uno al otro', to remain deeply ignorant of the other, is of course the situation that obtains in *La novela de don Sandalio*. But in composing his novel Unamuno has gone well beyond the anecdote, for now we have not a matter of ignorance but of wilful avoidance of the 'facts'. It is not just Don Sandalio who is a mystery; the letter-writer is one too. For not only is his background mysterious — the snippets of information we get merely adding to the mystery — but his behaviour is even odder than that of his chess partner. In the

---

[8] Among the few critics who have held back from accepting Ángela's memoir as an objective account of Don Manuel one could cite John Butt, 1981, and Reed Anderson, 1974.

club, the letter-writer observes Don Sandalio from the outside and sees a silent, self-contained individual whose whole attention is devoted to the chess board he has in front of him. On this basis he speculates upon Don Sandalio's personality and builds up an imagined picture of him. But when he has an opportunity of finding out about the real Don Sandalio, he deliberately shuns it, refusing to enquire as to his health or his bereavement, and cutting others short when they try to impart information. It is not a case of the letter-writer not being curious about Don Sandalio, since he often formulates questions about him in his letters to Felipe; it is that he adamantly refuses to allow versions of Don Sandalio emanating from other people to intrude into the version he creates for himself. The narrator resents the fact that Don Sandalio is not his property alone, and he reacts by wilfully ignoring and rejecting other people's knowledge of him. As he makes abundantly clear, it is only 'mi Don Sandalio' that he is prepared to accept as authentic. He does at times reluctantly recognize the existence of other versions of Don Sandalio, even as late as in letter 21, after he has refused to listen to the son-in-law. But in letter 22 he flatly refuses to go in search of the real Don Sandalio, as Felipe would like him to, preferring instead to continue his dream-like imaginings of him. The letter-writer begins his account of Don Sandalio by declaring his preference for imagination over information: 'No he podido columbrar nada de su vida, ni en rigor me importa gran cosa. Prefiero imaginármela' (II, 355), and at the end he is still reiterating this idea and advising his naturally curious correspondent to do the same himself. Yet in between, the letter-writer has in fact imagined very little about his man, for despite his determination to invent or imagine Don Sandalio, his powers of invention turn out to be meagre. In the end his Don Sandalio remains something of a hollow shell, a 'sombra enigmática', as the letter-writer himself is finally forced to admit, a personality who hardly exists. But what is the point of creating a void, what Alison Sinclair has aptly termed a 'black hole' into which the character is in danger of falling, never to emerge? (Sinclair, 1999).

In the case of Don Sandalio, if the enigma appears to revolve around his personality, it is only because the narrator or letter-writer so disposes by his refusal to take in others' views. The 'real' Don Sandalio, in so far as there is one at all, need not be such an unknown quantity. His life, his death, his personality, his imprisonment could all have been explicable in conventional terms, but for this we need *external* views, we need to know *about* him, especially about his *relations with others*. We get a faint glimpse of this external Don Sandalio, for despite the narrator's wish to turn him into a sphinx-like figure, there are aspects of Don Sandalio that are entirely natural. He turns out to have a family and a home and he does appear to share his experiences with others. We do not know why he is arrested, but other people do, for they are not surprised by this development: the informant finds it entirely logical: 'Pues claro, ¡en la cárcel!, ya comprenderá usted...' (II, 367). We do not know why Don Sandalio's son dies, but again there was a story behind this, one we are never allowed to hear. Similarly we do not know why Don Sandalio himself dies; but we do know that he was ill. The mystery of Don Sandalio is presented by the novelist as the deliberate creation of a misanthropic and solitary observer who has no truck with others and their views. This observer, in flight from the world and its inanities ('tonterías'), is entirely inward-looking. In effect we are presented with two Don Sandalios: the predominant one, who becomes the subject of the letter-writer's obsessive musings, and a subsidiary, potentially more normal, figure who does not interest him at all and who therefore hardly exists in his account.

What Unamuno has done here is to reverse his oft-repeated theory of personality — that one's inner self is based on one's perception of our public self, of how we stand in relation to others. Seen in this light, *La novela de don Sandalio* is not about Don Sandalio at all but about the fictional author of the letters. Here we have a character who shuns others and becomes entirely inward-looking. The key question in Unamunian personality theory is still conspicuously present, explicitly formulated in letter 10, when the letter writer wonders what Don Sandalio makes of him: '¿Quién seré yo para él?' (II, 362). But the letter-writer fiercely rejects the possibility of finding out *what he is for* that Other. He cannot answer his own question because he is unreceptive to the reality of others. The result of this perverted introspection is that he creates a personality that is an empty shell. The letter-writer and his Don Sandalio are inextricably linked. One personality has become the mirror image of the other, reminding us of Unamuno's warning that the more we look into ourselves the less we will find: total introspection leads to nothingness, 'nonada' (*DSTV*, X, 385).

This emptiness or absence of self can also come about for the opposite reason: not shutting ourselves off from others but instead allowing ourselves to become wholly dominated by others' views of us. In an essay published in 1903 Unamuno commented as follows:

> Nuestra conciencia vive prisionera de la idea que los demás se han formado de nosotros, idea que acaba por imponérsenos. El Juan tal como le creen los demás concluye por formar el Juan tal cual él mismo se cree ser, y este Juan tal cual él se figura a sí mismo acaba por desviar de su dirección primera y de formar a Juan tal cual en realidad es por dentro.
>
> Muy pronto en la vida se nos impone el papel que la suerte nos hace representar en su escenario, y ese papel, al que entramos acaso con toda alma y toda sinceridad, acaba por ahogarnos la sinceridad y el alma.[9]

This problem of evading our own potential self-construction by passively bowing to external views of us is encountered in *Niebla* but is particularly well illustrated by one of Unamuno's short stories, 'Robleda el actor'. Octavio Robleda, suffers from an unusual degree of self-consciousness, and his solution to his syndrome of extreme timidity is to adopt very pronounced roles. He knows how to represent others but not how to represent himself. For him, acting on stage is a way of hiding behind assumed personalities. But it does not entirely work because the theatre-going public recognizes the talent behind the acting and applauds the actor, not the figure represented. Robleda's fear remains, the fear of being nobody, the fear of nothingness. His 'tragedia más profunda' (II, 619), intuited by his audience, is the fact that he lacks a clear sense of identity, that he feels himself to be an empty shell. Yet the narrator, while understanding Robleda's predicament that he is only

---

[9] 'Sinceridad y convicciones' (*Obras Completas* (Escelicer), IX, 835).

the *dramatis persona* that he happens to adopt on stage and nothing in himself, does not see him in quite the same way. For the narrator, that fear of nothingness is itself the deeply characterizing quality of Robleda's personality. Unamuno's Robleda is a perfect prefiguration of the case of David described by R. D. Laing. David was a practised actor who played a variety of roles in order to hide his own inadequate sense of self. 'He found reassurance in the consideration that whatever he was doing he was not being himself' (Laing, 1990: 71). What David developed was a whole series of partially elaborated personalities, 'fragments of what might constitute a personality' (Laing, 1990: 73), divorced from what he referred to as his own self. An individual such as David, comments Laing, 'is invariably terrifyingly "self-conscious" in the sense in which this word is used to mean the exact opposite, namely, the feeling of being under observation by the *other*' (Laing, 1990: 74). Unamuno's Robleda, like David, has only an external self and fails to relate this to his internal self. The letter-writer by contrast cannot relate to his external selves, as symbolically represented by his chess companion Don Sandalio. The latter is made into a projection of his own inner self, and there is no interplay between the outer and inner worlds.

Unamuno's late works, notably *San Manuel Bueno, mártir* and *La novela de don Sandalio* can be seen as extreme or even deviant explorations of his ideas on personality. But it is in *Abel Sánchez*, chronologically at the centre of Unamuno's novelistic production, that we find the clearest example of how Unamuno applies his theory of personality to the creation of fiction, for the novel is built entirely on the protagonist's obsession with the nature and origins of his personality. Although *Abel Sánchez* is Unamuno's most complex and profound exploration of his favourite topic, a familiar pattern can nevertheless be discerned. The basic theme — one insisted on by Unamuno in many non-fictional writings — is enunciated right at the start: 'Aprendió cada uno de ellos a conocerse conociendo al otro' (I, 679). In other words, we can achieve self-knowledge only through the presence of others. Joaquín exists, is what he is, only in relation to Abel. This is part of Joaquín's problem: he needs to penetrate Abel's personality in order to understand his own. He locates his unhappiness in a consuming envy of Abel's character and popularity, and he looks for an explanation both outside and inside himself. But this is not simply a matter of character portrayal, of 'filling-in'; it is part of Unamuno's narrative strategy. Spaced at regular intervals throughout the novel, from early on right through to the very end, we find a series of questions which the character asks himself:

> ¿Pero estoy vivo? ¿Yo soy yo? (I, 696).
>
> ¿Qué es creer en Dios? ¿Dónde está Dios? (I, 710).
>
> ¿Por qué me hicieron? ¿Por qué he de vivir? (I, 716).
>
> ¿Por qué nací? (I, 727).
>
> ¿No es esto que me odio, que me envidio a mí mismo? (I, 741).
>
> Y yo, ¿quién quiero ser? (I, 763).
>
> ¿Por qué me rechazaban? (I, 771).
>
> ¿Qué hice para ser así? (I, 790).

The list is not exhaustive but it highlights the approach that Unamuno is employing, and which consists in creating a character engaged in an ontological quest through persistent self-analysis. The answers which Joaquín seeks are not forthcoming; rather they become subsumed in another more fundamental question. Commentators have taken this novel to be about the phenomenon of envy, and there can be no doubt that the starting point is the Cain and Abel myth as found in Genesis 4. 1–16. But the novel is more than a modern version of a theme from religious literature, and takes us well beyond this particular one of the seven deadly sins. For within the novel itself questions are raised about other characters too, about the way they are or, more precisely, about the way they *appear to others*. Why is Abel perceived as socially attractive, relaxed, seductive, popular? What is he like inside, separated from his public persona?, Joaquín wants to know. Why is Helena a supercilious beauty, elegant and refined yet cold and haughty, physically attractive yet morally repellent? Why is Antonia devoted and self-effacing, or Joaquina self-sacrificial yet assertive? And why is Abelín devoted to his father-in-law yet dismissive of his own father, a situation reversed in his own son who prefers his paternal grandfather to his maternal one? These are all questions that are either explicitly or implicitly raised during the course of the novel, indicating that the underlying issue is one of personality, that non-physical entity that seems to underlie a person's physical presence, its expression and its perception. Joaquín believes in the inner man, the private or core entity that reveals its existence in external actions or reactions. He wants to locate not just his own self ('¿Dónde estoy yo?'), but to uncover the hidden self beneath Abel's easy-going manner. We are back with the thorny question of the relationship between phenomenal reality and a subjacent or assumed noumenal reality.

Joaquín is not only a tortured being, he is also a tortured writer. Some of the questions formulated by Joaquín are raised within his own 'Confesión', which is of course written to be read, so that it becomes a *mise-en-abîme* of the wider book, reinforcing the authorial strategy in the latter. The questions are questions for the reader as much as for the character, for we too face the task of having to make sense of the character, or what amounts to the same thing, of the novel. Joaquín's quest for self-understanding is not so very different from our own natural quest to understand what the novelist Unamuno is driving at. Joaquín's questions appear ultimately to reduce to one: can an individual alter his personality without ceasing to be who he is? I shall have more to say on this aspect in the next chapter, but for the moment what is to be noted is that this question is raised more or less explicitly in the novel. Joaquín is struck by the disinherited Aragonese's expression of desire to cease being the person he is in exchange for becoming Joaquín. This declaration brings home to him that his envy of Abel is there not because he wants to be Abel but because he does not want to cease being Joaquín. It is this impasse that brings about Joaquín's decision to adopt a tragic role for himself, a role which he exploits in his 'Confesión'. Despite wanting to be like Abel, likeable, popular, good-humoured, relaxed, he has been born Joaquín, off-putting, spurned, abrasive, irritable. But playing out his destiny as he sees it does not bring any contentment or sense of achievement in its train. On the contrary: it exacerbates his problem because he creates friction and disharmony by driving himself to hate Abel and by trying to find evidence of the other's reciprocal hatred. It is here that Joaquín descends to the depths of abject behaviour in his treatment of the housemaid and in his attempt to seduce Helena by the delation of Abel's womanizing. Far from becoming the Byronic tragic hero he sees himself as, he becomes a loathsome individual, not least for himself. His life-project becomes warped and debased.

The debate going on within Joaquín is whether he can get rid of his 'demonic' self without losing his integrity or whether he has to accept the Biblical curse put on Cain by God and play out the role fate has assigned to him. Here Unamuno makes his character waver, the same wavering that we observe in Gertrudis but in a much more marked and sombre mood. He rejects free agency and sees himself as a victim of fate. 'No creo en el libre albedrío, padre. Soy médico' (I, 727), he tells Father Echevarría when the latter urges him to make the effort to assume responsibility for banishing the destructive envy that has turned into a consuming hatred. Here Joaquín is engaging in self-justification, in displacing blame for his condition, as we observe when he accuses Abel of being envious, an obvious projection of his own deadly sin, for Abel is portrayed as self-sufficient or indifferent, but hardly envious. Joaquín constantly rationalizes a mite too far, as we see for example in his attempt to explain Abel's passivity in the face of his appropriation of his son, Abelín, by arguing that Abel is only interested in acquiring fame, in living for and through his work as an artist, and not in his descendants. His self-ascribed determinism notwithstanding, Joaquín is shown to be capable of overcoming his animosity. He saves his friend from certain death despite the temptation to let him die through medical inaction: 'Luché entonces como no he luchado nunca conmigo mismo, con ese hediondo dragón que me ha envenenado y entenebrecido la vida' (I, 698), and is rewarded by a sense of achievement: 'Nunca he estado más feliz' (I, 698). This self-overcoming is repeated in the case of the birth of Abelín and the laudatory speech at Abel's banquet, described by the narrator as a heroic act. Given Unamuno's presentation of Joaquín, the fact that he shows him capable of overcoming his 'lepra' and moreover makes him fully aware that it is his responsibility to do so, as Joaquín recognizes in his 'Confesión', why does he make the character fail to overcome his condition?

There are I believe at least two possible answers to this question. One is tied to the longstanding and unresolved philosophical debate of free will versus determinism, which I shall return to in the final chapter. The other is more closely connected to Unamuno's ideas on personality. Unamuno appeared to believe that personality or self-identity is a human construction rather than a phenomenon that arises spontaneously in nature. The basis of this construction is, as he often explained, an individual's perception of how others react to him. If this is so, then Cain was not born envious and fratricidal. He became such because he perceived God's approval of his brother and His disapproval of him. What Joaquín perceives early on is that other people do not react to him as positively and warmly as they react to his close friend Abel. This awareness is confirmed by Helena's rejection of him and acceptance of Abel. On the basis of this perception Joaquín constructs a thoroughly negative view of his own personality. His reading of the Romantic rebel Byron convinces him that he is the victim of a cosmic injustice, the reason for which he cannot fathom. Instead of attempting to improve his outlook and relationships, he builds on his perception of others' rejection of him and creates an image of himself as a loathsome creature repugnant to all, unable to accept that Abel holds him in high regard or that Antonia loves him unconditionally. He becomes so pathologically obsessed with his predetermined personality that he turns his daughter's joy at hearing his optimistic plans for the future into another case of rejection:

> — ¿Te alegra oírme decir que seré otro? — volvió a preguntar el padre.
> — ¡Sí, papá, me alegra!
> — Es decir, ¿que el otro, el que soy, te parece mal? (I, 767)

Even his son-in-law's obvious admiration and affection count for nothing when Joaquín realizes that his grandson has a greater liking for his grandfather Abel. As we approach the dreadful outcome, Unamuno once again makes Joaquín's neurosis come violently to the surface, provoking first Abel's fatal heart attack and then a terrible self-indictment as he nears his own end. Yet even now Joaquín is aware that he had brought his misery upon himself, that there had always been an alternative: 'Si pudiéramos volver a empezar' (I, 790), he twice says, finally recognizing that it was his obsession with his own self and his tragic role that had constituted his malady. This is entirely in accordance with Unamuno's view, expressed elsewhere, that excessive introspection does not lead to self-knowledge.[10] Joaquín, obsessed by the '¿por qué?' question, has forgotten the '¿para qué?' question. His regret at what he is, or rather at what he is forced to be, makes him oblivious of what he is for.

The entire novel is built not just around Joaquín's adoption of the role of Cain but at the same time around Joaquín's error. He is the flawed hero of Greek tragedy, aware of his failing yet caught in fate's web and unable to rise above that destiny that he sees as imposed on him. Though at times he resists, his reaction for the most part is to play out that role, to nurture and enhance it (reminding us of Víctor Goti's contention that 'en la comedia entra el que se crea rey el que lo representa' (I, 646)). Joaquín comes to identify fully with his neurosis, with his hatred. That hatred caused by envy becomes his mark of identity, as he watches himself hating: 'Y vi que aquel odio inmortal era mi alma' (I, 718). His role is to hate, to hate Abel for his alleged treachery and to hate himself for hating. Joaquín's error is not only to see himself as 'un predestinado' when he can clearly act of his own volition, but also to become transfixed by his image of the inner man, or *intra-hombre* as Unamuno calls it in *Cómo se hace una novela*, that nuclear person which reveals its nature in projecting itself outwards through its outlook and performance. In the latter work Unamuno will see that inner man in a more positive, creative light; but in *Abel Sánchez* his portrayal of that inner man is deeply ambiguous. Joaquín identifies fully with that noumenal self, but that self is derived from an extreme self-consciousness, as we observe in Joaquín's reactions to others' often harmless remarks and even in his extraordinary reaction to Abel's painting:

---

[10] For example, 'la introspección engaña mucho, y llevada a su extremo produce un verdadero vacío de conciencia' (VIII, 525); and 'me parece casi imposible que llegue a conocerse quien se encierre en el yermo a pasar los días contemplándose' (VI, 327). In isolation, introspection reveals nothing. Cutting oneself off does not reveal the truth about oneself.

> Joaquín iba a la sala de la exposición a contemplar el cuadro y a mirar en él, como si mirase en un espejo, al Caín de la pintura y a espiar en los ojos de las gentes si le miraban a él, después de haber mirado al otro. (I, 719)

The portrait of Cain killing his brother is for Joaquín a kind of portrait of himself. And even the discovery that there is no intended likeness between Abel's Cain and himself haunts him: '¡Ni siquiera pensaban en mí!' (I, 720). The role that Joaquín assigns to himself and that he consigns to his 'Confesión' is, once again, in line with Víctor Goti's announcement to Augusto Pérez that we are actors watching ourselves acting: 'Es la comedia, Augusto, es la comedia que representamos ante nosotros mismos, en lo que se llama el foro interno, en el tablado de la conciencia, haciendo a la vez de cómicos y de espectadores' (I, 644).[11] If Joaquín identifies with his demonic self, he is also capable of observing that self. He knows that to counteract the hated self he has to create another self, 'ser otro' as he puts it, but this is where Unamuno's strong sense of personal identity intervenes. For one of the things that Unamuno said on numerous occasions and which appears in *Abel Sánchez* is that he could not understand how anyone could wish to be someone else, by which he presumably meant that taking on a different identity in lieu of the current one is the equivalent of death. 'Irle a uno con la embajada de que sea otro, de que se haga otro, es irle con la embajada de que deje de ser él', he had written in *Del sentimiento trágico de la vida* (*DSTV*, X, 282).[12]

As we saw in Chapter 1, Unamuno had already declared in this same work that the deeper we explore within ourselves the more we realize that there is nothing solid within. We become what we make ourselves to be in our own life-project, what we will ourselves to be (which Unamuno termed 'serse'); and this life-project is something creative and ongoing, or as Unamuno referred to it in a letter to Antonio Machado, 'fraguarse día a día su sustancia', constructing one's self as one lives.[13] Joaquín's initial life-project, to devote himself to medical research, is swamped by the onset of his neurosis and turned into the representation of the role of Cain. Though he realizes that his new role can only bring suffering to himself and his family, he will not accept Father Echevarría's recommendation to change his life-project, or as the priest puts it, to sublimate his hateful passion into the noble passion of caring for his patients in his chosen profession. Father Echevarría's advice is entirely in consonance with Unamuno's own proclamation in *Del sentimiento trágico de la vida*, where he had declared that the way to overcome our temporal circumstances, to 'pelear contra el destino', was to regard our civil profession as if it were a religious vocation: 'Todos, es decir, cada uno, puede y debe proponerse dar de sí todo cuanto puede dar, más aún de lo que puede dar, excederse, superarse a sí mismo, hacerse insustituible, darse a los demás para recogerse de ellos. Y cada

---

[11] Augusto had already discovered this: 'Como yo ahora aquí, representando a solas mi comedia, hecho actor y espectador a la vez' (I, 578). One self acts, another self watches.

[12] Identity change (and its implications for personhood) is one of the standard issues that crops up in the philosophy of identity. See for example Derek Parfitt, 1984, esp. Chapters 10–13; and Harold Noonan, 1989, in which the question of identity change is present throughout. Identity change, its possibility or impossibility, is of course the central theme of *Tulio Montalbán y Julio Macedo*.

[13] *Obras Completas* (Escelicer), I, 1156.

cual en su oficio, en su vocación civil' (*DSTV*, X, 488). But Joaquín has discovered the Cain within himself and realizes that to give up the person that he is involves acquiring a new identity, a new self. Instead he perseveres in trying to understand the self that he already is or feels himself to be, the self he has been born with, or in Schopenhauerian terms the *character* that emanates from the Will.[14] But each time he tries to understand himself he effectively creates a new objectivized self, another image in the mirror, as happens to the letter-writer in *La novela de don Sandalio* who feels disconcertment and then panic on seeing the fragmentation of himself into multiple images in the mirrors of a café.[15] We can create images of ourselves, but that 'we' which creates the images, that 'author' that is Joaquín or the letter-writer, must remain tantalizingly out of our reach, beguiling but inapprehensible; or as Unamuno trenchantly said of another of his fictional creatures, 'Bonifacio vivió buscándose y murió sin haberse hallado' (II, 45). Self-cognition as a project becomes a search for the crock of gold at the end of the rainbow. I certainly exist for others. But do I exist for myself?

Interestingly Unamuno makes Abel express scepticism about the reality of the inner self that we think we possess: 'Estoy convencido de que todo hombre lleva fuera todo lo que tiene dentro' (I, 747). Abel's theory of personality, which proposes that there is no difference between the inner and the outer man, between the noumenon and the phenomenon, more or less puts paid to any idea that we act creatively in constructing our own self and other selves, but Unamuno does not appear to offer support for this idea, at least in *Abel Sánchez*. Indeed Abelín's view of his father's indifference raises the question of whether Abel's view of personality is tenable. Abel himself seems almost to belie his own scepticism about the inner self when he senses in Joaquín, under his cold exterior, a man tortured by deep passions, and he goes on to express his desire to capture his soul in a portrait: '¡Si se pudiera captar el alma de Joaquín!' (I, 754). Joaquina, too, distinguishes between body and soul, and intuits a hidden side in her father: 'no sé lo que anda dentro de ti, pero es algo malo' (I, 759). What we can say is that Unamuno proposes both an outer and an inner self. Abel paints a self-portrait; Joaquín offers a written one in his 'Confesión'. The difference is that while the former captures the external personality with his brush, the latter tries to capture the inner personality with his pen. The external personality is the only truly empirical one. The inner remains

---

[14] Schopenhauer distinguished between the *character* of a person, which is conferred by the Will and which he calls original, and what the person learns of himself in the course of experience, which is secondary knowledge. One's character is fixed; all one can change is one's motivation or chosen path (Schopenhauer, 1966: I, §55).

[15] The phenomenon can also be found in Kierkegaard's *Either/Or*: 'Can you think of anything more frightful than that it might end with your nature being resolved into a multiplicity, that you really might become many, become, like those unhappy demoniacs, a legion, and you thus would have lost the inmost and holiest thing of all in a man, the unifying power of personality?' (Kierkegaard, 1959: II, 164). This suggests that Unamuno had been reading *Enter/Eller* (in Danish) not long before composing *Don Sandalio*, which fits in with what he says in the prologue to *San Manuel Bueno, mártir y tres historias más*. Multiple duplication of the self is also found in Dostoyevski's *The Double*: the neurotic Golyadkin has a terrifying dream in which he sees himself pursued by a multitude of look-alikes (Dostoyevski, 1997: 87).

an imagined or noumenal one, and ultimately an enigma for it can never be fully apprehended. Joaquín's quest to get to his 'root self' ends in frustration.[16] But whether this root self that seems to govern our lives truly exists or not, the fact is that we appear to need it. The contemporary British philosopher Galen Strawson has provocatively dismissed as a baseless construction that inner self or 'I' that many have seen as the basis of identity and self-consciousness. For Strawson there is no enduring self, only experiences, which are necessarily subjective and unending; hence there is no persistent self (Strawson, G., 2009). Unamuno does not appear to go quite that far, although he comes fairly close in *Del sentimiento trágico de la vida*, when he says, '¿Qué razón desprevenida puede concluir la simplicidad del alma del hecho de que tengamos que juzgar y unificar pensamientos? Ni el pensamiento es uno, sino vario, ni el alma es para la razón nada más que la sucesión de estados de conciencia coordinados entre sí' (*DSTV*, X, 342). What comes through in his novels, and indeed is suggested in a number of essays, is that the identity that we assign to ourselves is derived from the Other, from our inter-relationship with other beings, that its existence is driven not by any natural phenomenon but rather by our need to identify ourselves and be identified. This social self does clearly have a kind of reality; but whether it is underlain by a deeper self remains unknown. Or more precisely it remains a 'fiction'; for it is only through fiction that it can be explored. It has precisely the existence that we accord the characters of fiction.

Conclusion

Unamuno's fiction could in most cases be described, correctly if tersely, as a search for self.[17] The complexity and scope of this awareness of self or inner person vary considerably, but what is common to the novels is the social context in which it takes place, whether it is friendship, marriage, family or the wider community. We can see it operating at its simplest in *Nada menos que todo un hombre*. In this novel the problem that arises between the spouses is in line with Unamuno's view of the reciprocity of personality construction. Julia's problem, which already exists before she marries Alejandro, is that she feels others only see her external beauty and are content to possess her for that quality alone: 'Se enamoran de mi hermosura, no de mí' (II, 259). Thus Julia distinguishes between an inner and an outer self and fails to integrate them harmoniously. The reason why she gives in to the Count's advances — or appears to, since, as we saw in Chapter 4, Unamuno cleverly avoids confirmation of adultery — is that the Count, unlike her husband, insinuates that he is in love with the inner woman:

[16] I borrow the term from Paul Ilie, 1967: 109–11. William James refers to this core self as the 'central nucleus of the Self' (1950: I, 298–99).

[17] There is a qualification to be made here. I cannot think of myself as 'a self' in Spanish, since the language has no precise equivalent for self. In Spanish one has to resort to 'el ser', short for the quasi-tautological 'el ser que yo soy', or 'el yo'. The self suggests a greater degree of objectification than 'el yo'. Some degree of objectification is provided by the neologism 'yoismo' or 'I-ness', a term which Unamuno does use. It may be significant that philosophical enquiries into personal identity, that is into the self, are very rare in Spanish as compared to English. Philosophy may after all be linguistically driven, as Unamuno proposed.

> — Señor conde..., señor conde, que está usted entrando en un terreno...
> [...]
> — Donde estoy entrando es en tu conciencia, Julia.
> El *tu* arreboló la oreja culpable.
> El pecho de Julia ondeaba como el mar al acercarse la galerna. (II, 273)

Alejandro goes to the other extreme. His '¡Yo no vivo de apariencias, sino de realidades!' (II, 275) indicates that he does indeed value the inner person, but takes it for granted that his wife understands his devotion without the need to make a show of it. While Julia, accustomed to the external reaction of men, seeks the external reaction of Alejandro on which to build her self-confidence, that is, her conviction that it is *she* who is loved and not her physical beauty, Alejandro, utterly convinced of his own worth and loveability, disdains any external show of affection, or as Julia says, '¡Ni siquiera exiges que te quiera!' (II, 278). In the face of Julia's provocation with the Count, Alejandro becomes even more attached to his own conception of himself: 'no conseguirás que yo te regale los oídos con palabras de novela' (II, 281). The mutual incomprehension between the spouses — Alejandro's unwillingness to externalize his love for Julia in order to build up her confidence, and Julia's inability to see through Alejandro's façade of impassivity — is what brings about their estrangement. Unamuno makes this doubly clear by allowing the mask to drop temporarily in the love scene following Julia's release from the mental hospital to which Alejandro has confined her. But the latter reverts to his hermetic coldness and she to a fatal apathy. Her final question, '¿quién eres, Alejandro?', at long last evokes the response that Unamuno held to be the only valid or intelligible one, the person as the creation of others: '¿Yo? ¡Nada más que tu hombre..., el que tú me has hecho!' (II, 291), but it comes too late to save her or him.

The fairly straightforward approach to personality construction that we find in *Nada menos que todo un hombre* acquires much greater complexity in longer novels, notably in *La tía Tula*, and above all in *Abel Sánchez*. The reason for this is readily discernible. Gertrudis and Joaquín are not simply convinced of who they are and merely try to maintain that conviction, as is the case with Alejandro Gómez. They are driven by a desire to locate their real selves, to overcome radical doubts about their motives, to define the role that they see themselves as required to play. This role or life-project is crucial. Augusto Pérez calls it 'un objetivo, una finalidad en esta vida' (I, 529), which he identifies with his wooing of Eugenia. At the beginning of *Niebla* we see Augusto in search of a role. In his case this search is prompted by the death of his mother, a protective and possessive mother who has shielded him from life's vicissitudes and in whose lap ('regazo'), as he himself recalls, he had taken refuge as a child 'por miedo de encontrarse con los ojos devoradores del Coco' (I, 507), a mother who had pre-empted all potential problems and had provided until recently 'una casa dulce y tibia' (I, 507). Precisely at the moment when Augusto falls in love with Eugenia we learn that Augusto's dwelling no longer provides a home. In Eugenia he hopes to recover that home: 'Y ahora me brillan en el cielo de mi soledad los dos ojos de Eugenia. Me brillan con el resplandor de las lágrimas de mi madre' (I, 517). Augusto's falling in love seems entirely accidental; but what Unamuno indicates is that he falls in love thinking of his mother and of the latter's advice to him to marry as soon as possible 'con una mujer de gobierno que sepa querer... y gobernarte' (I, 502). Thus, in giving us an overview of Augusto's life up to the present, Unamuno emphasizes that Augusto lived through his mother even as a young adult. Now he is living through his memories of her, something Unamuno signals through the dog Orfeo. When he first finds Orfeo, what attracts Augusto is that 'el animalito buscaba el pecho de la madre' (I, 509), and on returning home he immediately bottle-feeds the puppy. And he says: 'Si te hubiese conocido mi madre... Pero ya verás, ya verás, cuando duermas en el regazo de Eugenia, bajo su mano tibia y dulce' (I, 510). As if the connection between Augusto's mother and Eugenia were not clear enough, Unamuno drives the point home when he makes Augusto say: 'acaso casándome volveré a tener madre' (I, 555). Augusto had acquired his identity entirely through his relationship with his mother, as he himself recalls while meditating in church after Eugenia's first rejection of him: 'Y repasó su vida toda de hijo, cuando formaba parte de su madre y vivía a su amparo' (I, 547). With his mother dead, he needs to replace that Other that had given him his ontological reassurance, and he will try to do so via Eugenia, or as he says, employing Unamuno's favourite word, 'lo que yo necesito es alma, alma, alma. Y un alma de fuego, como la que irradia de los ojos de ella, de Eugenia' (I, 555). When Eugenia fails him he will be plunged into a crisis of identity ('¡Quiero ser yo, ser yo!') out of which not even his creator will extricate him.

Augusto's case makes for an interesting comparison with Alejandro Gómez's. Augusto complains that his public image has been shattered following the Eugenia debacle, and this leads to a loss of self-regard and the total breakdown of his coping strategies. His own self-image is destroyed by his excessive reliance on others' image of him. The opinion of others is of no consequence whatever to Alejandro Gómez. He knows who he is, and his self-containment is unyielding. He deserves the label 'todo un hombre' in contrast to Augusto's 'un pobre panoli'. Here, then, we have two extremes of reaction to the public self. One is a slave to his social self, the other despises it. Both Augusto's extreme dependence and Alejandro's extreme independence bring disaster in their train.

This social self, this self constructed through others or in response to them, is of fundamental importance, both in a positive and in a negative light. In Unamunian ontology personality develops in a social context as the individual performs his or her role in the collective and establishes a fruitful relationship with it.[18] This social self exists as a subject, but also as an object of the contemplative or inner self. Both have their relevance, and the balanced individual is the one in whom both dimensions or selves maintain a harmonious dialogue. This integrated 'I' is dependent to a large degree on an external or social reality. The 'I' engages in a dialogue with the different sides of the being or selves that the individual carries within. That 'I' hears the Other inside him and responds in the form of what Unamuno termed a 'monodiálogo'. We could say, then, that this internal 'I' that enters into a dialogue with variations of itself is initially conditioned by the

---

[18] Unamuno's idea of the social self is to be found in William James, 1950: I, 293–96. As indicated before, on the question of the self or selves, Unamuno's debt to William James is substantial.

social self whose job it is to enter into a dialogue with other beings; the individual observes and absorbs that external self. And the recognition of that self in turn helps us to maintain our social relationships.[19]

For Unamuno, both an excess of contemplation and an excess of socializing represent a danger to one's equilibrium.[20] If on the one hand a life lived wholly within the bustle of social existence can suppress one's inner self, on the other he who isolates himself totally ends up by looking into a void. In the first case the inner self is displaced by the social self, which so dominates that it distorts one's personality, impeding genuine reflection and forcing one to act in accordance with what Unamuno calls 'la leyenda', the public image. And vice-versa, to give oneself up wholly to self-reflection is to run the risk of creating a fictitious self, a purely abstract entity devoid of real or phenomenal content. This is an alienated self which, in acute cases, detaches itself from the person contemplating himself, becoming a foreign, disquieting entity, the source of anxiety and even terror. It is the famous image in the mirror which terrifies Augusto Pérez (I, 602). The phenomenon denotes the subject's lack of possession of the self, or more precisely of one of his selves, something which results in alienation. To overcome this alienation one has to recover possession of that estranged self, something which, according to Unamuno, can be achieved through pain, because pain is something which can only be experienced in oneself, not something we can, as it were, export.

What we get in some Unamunian characters, notably so in Joaquín Monegro, is precisely the kind of neurosis to which existential psychoanalysis has accustomed us, the neurosis in which the patient has abdicated responsibility for his mental state and places the blame on some environmental cause which he sees as threatening him. The neurotic person projects his fears onto others, often seeing them as the cause of his anxiety. Where the person feels unable to face the world, takes flight into an unreal or ghostly existence, and stops relating to others, psychosis will supervene. This stage, characterized by evasion and a total inability to cope, is not reached by any Unamunian character (with the possible exception of the letter-writer in *La novela de don Sandalio*), but we can nevertheless see that the obsessive search for self of some characters does clearly result in a neurotic state that brings them to something which is akin to the psychoanalyst's couch. Unamuno uses confession, whether it be the sacrament of the Catholic Church (Gertrudis, Joaquín, and in a peculiarly reversed manner Father Manuel Bueno, whom Ángela describes as going to confession with her) or confession to others (Augusto to Víctor, Joaquín to his notebook and future reader, the letter-writer to Felipe), as the character's attempt to relate, to recover that self in danger of being lost through excessive introspection. The solution which Unamuno proposes in his novels is precisely the one we find in *Del sentimiento trágico de la vida* and several other essays: giving oneself to others in

---

[19] This summary is no more than what is to be deduced from the essay 'Soledad' (VIII, 777–95). And in another essay, '¡Adentro!', Unamuno writes: 'Sólo en la sociedad te encontrarás a ti mismo; si te aíslas de ella no darás más que con un fantasma de tu verdadero sujeto propio. Sólo en la sociedad adquieres tu sentido todo, pero despegado de ella' (VIII, 320).

[20] This is the argument running through the essay 'Grandes y pequeñas ciudades' (VI, 324–30).

order to recover their recognition of us, 'darse a los demás para recogerse de ellos', a fundamentally ethical or spiritual therapy.

In several of Unamuno's characters, notably so in Gertrudis and Joaquín, there is a mighty struggle between the 'creerse ser' and the 'querer ser', between the instinctual and the sublimatory sides of personality. In fact Unamuno is starting from the premiss, which developed into a strong belief from at least 1900 onwards, that human beings need to distance themselves from their animal condition (the 'bruto' that Gertrudis still detects in the male of the species) and, without denying natural instincts, must strive to cultivate higher pursuits, whether poetic or religious, both covered by his term *espiritualizarse*. The process of sublimation of base or material instincts can be observed in many of the fictional personages, in Augusto, in Joaquín, in Ángela, and in a quite exceptional way in Gertrudis, the Virgin Mother. This valuing of the spiritual (or poetic) dimension above the material (or physiological) dimension explains not only *Del sentimiento trágico de la vida* (life is a struggle to impose those spiritual aspirations when reason tells us it is in vain), but also the Unamunian concept of *persona* which underlies his fiction, the mask or identity which we adopt in the face of others. The persona is that part of the individual who plays out the life-project we have assigned to ourselves. It constitutes, as Unamuno himself explained, a character who gives us an identity, someone who allows us to act consciously and responsibly and not just instinctively. It is, in the last analysis something that, coming from outside us, we have to learn to impose on ourselves, a way of surmounting the purposelessness that governs our arrival in this world. In this respect, it is the saintly priest of Valverde de Lucerna who is perhaps the clearest indication of Unamuno's dictum, after Lammenais, that we move 'entre el ser y la nada' (*DSTV*, X, 369).

CHAPTER 6

The Double

Doubling the Person, Splitting the Self

The phenomenon of the double, which has been traced back to ancient myth, was exploited in modern times by Gothic fiction writers and by some Romantic poets, and has re-appeared with some regularity from Dostoyevski's *The Double* (1846), through the well-known examples of Stevenson's *The Strange Case of Dr Jekyll and Mr Hyde* (1886) and Wilde's *The Picture of Dorian Gray* (1890) right down, in our own time, to Saramago's *O homem duplicado* [*The Duplicated Man*] (2002). The list of related examples is so long (Goethe's *Faust*, Espronceda's *El estudiante de Salamanca*, Kafka's *Metamorphosis*, among endless others) that any attempt at defining the phenomenon is self-defeating. What can confidently be said is that, in principle, we are dealing not with a psychological phenomenon but with a literary trope that lends itself to an infinite variety of uses. By contrast, the purely critical approach to the literary phenomenon is much narrower in range and more susceptible of orderly exposition. Broadly such approaches can be reduced to one of three, or to a mixture:

(1) The theological approach. This sees the phenomenon as the revelation of a clash between cosmic forces embedded in human nature: good versus evil, the angelic versus the demonic, or even, archetypally, of primitive desires versus civilized forms of behaviour.

(2) The psychological approach. This regards the phenomenon as a clear sign of mental instability, perhaps even of outright madness. In this approach the double is an invasive disease that threatens to destroy the integrity of the self or indeed succeeds in doing so.

(3) The psychoanalytical approach. This has been the most common approach in the twentieth century. The double is interpreted as a sign of repressed anxieties that are threatening the dominance of the ego.

Unamuno's clearest exploration of the phenomenon is his play *El otro*, his best-known and most studied. In the play the problem (or rather the mystery, since Unamuno, like Gabriel Marcel after him, explicitly differentiated between the two) is that of the identity of the surviving twin, but it is a mystery only inasmuch as the two are indistinguishable and the surviving one, traumatized by the death of his brother, refuses to say which of the two he is, Cosme or Damián. We could if we wanted to see the play in terms of Lacanian lack of self-recognition, that is, that the self has changed places with his reflection and no longer feels himself. But in Unamuno the emphasis falls on the irreconcilability of the two selves or twins; they cannot live together but they cannot live apart, as in Edgar Allan Poe's *William Wilson* (1839), the story of the two schoolboys who carry the same name, a story with which *El otro* has at least something in common and which is a clear precursor.[1] As El Otro says, to see an external version of oneself is deeply disturbing: 'desde pequeñitos sufrí al verme fuera de mí mismo..., no podía soportar aquel espejo..., no podía verme fuera de mí' (III, 438). One twin's envy of the other is another version of the Cain–Abel myth Unamuno had already explored in *Abel Sánchez* as well as in 'Allende lo humano' and 'El que se enterró', two short stories which on the face of it can be read as examples of a schizoid split in personality but which Unamuno presents rather as supernatural experiences with no explanation. Furthermore the struggle between the two wives for the surviving twin in *El otro* also harks back to *Dos madres*, as we shall shortly observe, so the play offers little that Unamuno had not already explored.[2] It is the play's obvious artificiality that probably accounts for its failure on the public stage, an artificiality that Unamuno's prefatory apologia does little to justify. The origin of the play, Unamuno's 'sentimiento congojoso de nuestra identidad y continuidad individual y personal' (III, 417), is itself no mystery, and his concomitant 'lo que importa es la verdad íntima, profunda del drama del alma' is not an especially revealing comment on a play that is explicit almost to the point of artlessness. It matters little whether it was Cosme who killed Damián or vice-versa. The theme of the double here is not suggestive but manifest. El Ama's dramatic declaration of lost identity in the Epílogo ('¡El misterio! Yo no sé quién soy, vosotros no sabéis quiénes sois, el historiador no sabe quién es [...], no sabe quién es ninguno de los que nos oyen' (III, 460)) is so overt as to border on banality. Her closing words ('Y los dos mayores misterios, don Juan, son la locura y la muerte') amount to a quasi-philosophical statement that puts a gloss on El Otro's history, thereby ascribing a particular significance to the play and inviting the audience to see it in a particular light.

In the fiction we seldom, if ever, find an equivalent closing statement. We can see the difference in terms of public experience versus private experience, the latter — the act of reading — being not a collectively shared spectacle from which we exit at the end of a performance but a continuing dialogue with our imagined reconstruction of a text. One must be wary of transferring theatrical representation to narrative composition, for it can produce misleading inferences. This occurs, for example, if we read *Tulio Montalbán y Julio Macedo* in the light of the later adaptation for the stage, *Sombras de sueño*. The novelette and the play produce rather different effects, though one work is derived from the other. Where the narrative version is economical, understated and inferential, the expanded stage version is geminative,

[1] Unamuno had a copy of *Tales of Edgar Allan Poe* (1884) in his library.
[2] For the links of *El otro* with other Unamunian texts see Edward Friedmann, 1980. For a helpful review of the various issues posed by the play and its critics see Julia Biggane, 2000. For a detailed study of Unamuno's recycling of 'El que se enterró' in *El otro* see Rebeca Martín, 2007. An early and significant contribution to the theme of the double in Unamuno is that of Frances Wyers, 1976: 40–48, and 82–91.

transpicuous and elucidative. The difference of medium appears to govern our responses to a surprising degree. Whereas the drama unveils an action before our eyes and we are reduced to passive observers awaiting an outcome, the much more condensed novelette raises interpretative questions on virtually every page, leading to a (potentially) more active involvement by the reader, much less certain of what is going on. It is entirely as if what we observe on stage had abandoned all pretence of secrecy (irrespective of whether the staging occurs purely within an imaginary theatre), by contrast with which the novelette hinted darkly at some private communication between storyteller and reader: the narrative text appears to be saying more than it actually says, and we partake of the story not as observers but as addressees.

Be that as it may, the double in Unamuno's fiction is more a matter of composition than of investigation of a supernatural or psychological phenomenon, or to put it another way, it betrays Unamuno's fondness for the trope rather than a determination to discover the roots of the phenomenon, whether religious, psychological, or archetypal. For Unamuno the novelist, the double is above all a useful tool in the broader exploration of personal identity. This, I believe, explains the variations, what is different as we move from one text to another rather than what is the same. Unamuno shows no sustained interest in studying the phenomenon from the point of view of personality disorder, as would a psychiatrist, although we must not forget that Unamuno was an early student of psychology, notably of works by Herbert Spencer, Théodule Ribot, Wilhelm Wundt and shortly afterwards of William James and his monumental *Principles of Psychology*. Thus, if Unamuno's interest lies not in explaining the phenomenon *clinically* but in acknowledging its presence and exploring its manifestations *poetically*, this need not exclude certain psychological ramifications of which Unamuno was very probably aware. By its very nature, the trope of the double offers possibilities which are psychological and suppositional. It is a useful way of evoking unusual mental states.

The doubles in Unamuno's fiction can be classified very broadly under three types, though I must emphasize broadly, since more often than not more than one type is implied:

(A) Extrinsic double.
    The doubling of the personage: the twin syndrome.

(B) Intrinsic double.
    The doubling of the self: the split syndrome.

(C) Linguistic/textual double.
    The doubling or reversal of expression and/or text: the writerly syndrome.

All three can occur in the same text, and a clear separation, especially between A and B, is seldom possible. Indeed A usually implies B. The double certainly serves to complicate Unamuno's treatment of his favourite theme, personal identity, and perhaps even introduces irresolvable contradictions or leads to aporias, but in a fairly obvious sense the concept of a double is already implicit in Unamunian teleology: 'El que uno quiere ser, es en él, en su seno, el creador, y es el real de verdad. Y por el que hayamos querido ser, no por el que hayamos sido, nos salvaremos o perderemos'

(II, 194).[3] If what we are is but a shadow of what we aspire to be, we are condemned to having a split personality from the start. But in the fiction the phenomenon is not so straightforward, not an idealization or sublimation but a fragmentation. It is a literary device employed to express self-division.

Unamuno's use of the double fits reasonably comfortably into the modern history of the trope. In the Gothic novel of the late eighteenth and early nineteenth centuries the narrative still retains something of the supernatural quality it had always enjoyed in myth, but increasingly in the nineteenth century under the effect of a positivistic outlook it became completely secularized and took the form of an extreme objectification of a troubled or disintegrating internal self (e.g. Dostoyevski's *The Double*). It thus came to be seen as a symbol of unreason, of breakdown, of madness, that is to say of mental abnormality as seen from a 'normal' perspective. But equally it can be seen as a manifestation of contradictory tendencies inherent in the human psyche — the theory of complementary opposites — which only in extreme cases leads to mental imbalance. Jung, for example, followed this line of thinking in seeing in the double evidence of primitive impulses or unfulfilled desires the realization of which has been rendered impossible by the imposition of civilized modes of behaviour. Seen in this light the double clearly challenges the traditional view, prevalent in the nineteenth-century realist novel, that a sane person has a coherent, unified, indivisible self, and that only the insane suffer from fractured selves. As D. H. Lawrence pithily put it in *Kangaroo* through his character Richard Lovat: 'The bulk of people haven't got any central selves. They're all bits.' And in *Les Faux-monnayeurs* [*The Counterfeiters*] André Gide denounced consistency of characterization as 'the very thing which makes us recognize that they [the characters] are artificially composed'. Unamuno's literary use of the double or fragmented self belongs very much in this latter tradition in which the dividing line between normality and abnormality is seen as indistinct.

Apart from the play *El Otro*, Unamuno's use of the double is at its most obvious in two short stories which can be read as examples of a schizoid split in personality but which Unamuno presents rather as supernatural experiences with no explanation. They are Gothic tales with the emphasis on the non-rational or unknown and with no precise psychological counterpart. In 'Allende lo humano' the personage tells his friend — who transmits the story — of the experience of confronting his double who had come to visit him and sat in silence before him. The mutual self-scrutiny was immediately followed by a death experience. On recovering consciousness the personage had discovered that he and his double had changed places and furthermore that the one who occupied his chair was dead. The reader does not know whether it is the incumbent or the visitor who has died. Indeed the survivor speaks of examining his own corpse and of disposing of it. His extraordinary experience brings about a 'cambio de carácter' (II, 723), a change confirmed by the narrator. The personage rejects any attempt to label the experience hallucinatory or symbolical, but since the existence of the corpse is not verified the reality of

---

[3] Cf. the even more explicit 'Y el que queremos ser, y no el que somos, es nuestro yo íntimo' ('Nuestros yos ex-futuros', *Obras completas* (Escelicer), 491).

the experience remains unproven. All the personage will admit is that he had been reading works on the sciences of the occult before his experience. The best the narrator can offer by way of explanation is a banal experience of his own in which an umbrella taken on the spur of the moment on a sunny, clear day turns out quite unexpectedly to save him from a downpour. We can of course choose to see the personage's radical change of character with which the story opens not as the consequence but as the precipitating factor in the otherworldly experience. But Unamuno typically does not help his reader; he is using the trope but attaches no particular significance to it. 'El que se enterró' follows the same pattern, with an identical opening, an extraordinary 'cambio de carácter' (II, 531), followed by the personage's account of his death experience to a friend.[4] One key difference is that this time Unamuno makes it very clear that the personage is clinically ill before the otherworldly experience supervenes. The other key difference is that the narrator is shown the buried corpse, so he cannot entertain any explanation in terms of a hallucinatory experience. In other words one key feature cancels the other out. The double is presented as an apparition whose reality can neither be doubted nor explained. Even if conjured up by the feverish imagination of a mentally ill patient, the experience remains real, and in this case real for both teller and told, for the narrator too is made to witness the experience of death by the disinterment of the corpse. The problem is not so much the experience as how to explain it. The moral of the story, in both versions, seems to be that our rational faculties will take us so far and no further, what Unamuno will later dub 'misterio' in the sub-title of *El Otro*. If life and death are inexplicable phenomena, our experience of them must be too. We can of course see these stories in psycho-existential terms as exemplifying the onset of a psychosis. Since the abnormality or signs of instability are mentioned before the supernatural or spectral experience, we can interpret the latter as the diseased person's attempt to overcome the paranoia by 'killing' his threatening self. It is, then, a fear of depersonalization that brings about the split and consequent civil war: one self has to be destroyed. It is, as R. D. Laing called it, 'the denial of being, as a means of preserving being' (Laing, 1990: 150).

Unamuno's incursions into Gothic fiction are rare and limited to the short-story genre, but the use of the double appears in more sophisticated form in several novelettes and the longer novels. Indeed Unamuno's fondness for the trope tends to blur the picture considerably, for the double often consists in presenting two perfectly distinct characters whose fortunes are so intertwined or whose interaction is so intimate as to leave little doubt that in Unamuno's conception they are meant to represent dual facets of the human psyche, facets which usually enter into conflict. Thus in *El marqués de Lumbría* the two sisters, Carolina and Luisa, are characterized by their predilection for *sombra* or *sol* and driven by a competitive hatred for each other as they try to assert their supremacy in the family succession. Both having

---

[4]   I am assuming, following Ricardo Senabre's suggestion as to the early date of composition of 'Allende lo humano', that 'El que se enterró' is the later product (see Unamuno, 1995b: xiii). Indeed it would make no sense for Unamuno to have written the former after the publication of the latter in 1908 since 'El que se enterró' is a slightly more elaborated version of 'Allende lo humano'.

used the same male for the purpose, Luisa succeeds in banishing the pregnant Carolina only for the latter to return triumphantly to assert the succession rights of her son over the son of her rival. The two half-brothers of course reflect the same destructive rivalry as their mothers: one must achieve supremacy by suppressing the other. Pedrito's ascendancy necessitates the banishment of Rodriguín. Here Unamuno's treatment of the double tendency in the human spirit, though not clearly characterized in terms of good versus evil, is implacable: the forces of darkness (*umbría*, as the title indicates) have triumphed over the forces of light.

Equally implacable, though a little more subtle, are the forces acting upon Juan in *Dos madres*. Here Unamuno very clearly illustrates a mental condition which existential psychiatry has referred to as engulfment, a form of ontological insecurity or discontinuities of the self in which relatedness to others is felt as a severe diminution of one's personal identity (Laing, 1990: 43–45). Juan fits the clinical picture perfectly. His attempt to cope with a double relationship, represented by his lover Raquel and his wife Berta, unnerves him. The two women see themselves as his saviours, one from his transient love affairs, the other from the scandal of an illicit relationship. The possessiveness of the two strong-willed women impinges on his autonomy: '«¡Mío!, ¡mío! — pensó Juan — ¡Así dicen las dos!»' (II, 224). The two women, referred to as demonic and angelic, one black-eyed and the other blue-eyed, are, despite their overt rivalry over the soul of Juan, ('robar el alma' is the phrase used by Juan himself), covertly connected. Raquel is idolized by Berta, envied for her power over men, and Berta is envied by the barren Raquel for her fertility. Juan becomes a tool of their machinations but also of their collaboration, as we finally observe in their pact when they contemplate the corpse of the man driven insane by their possessiveness. The title of the story is cleverly ambivalent, for the two children fathered by Juan have no real part to play. It is Juan himself who has 'dos madres', and indeed both women refer to him as their son. As he veers from one to the other, Juan senses an increasing inability to govern his own destiny:

> El pobre Juan, ya sin don, temblaba entre las dos mujeres, entre su ángel y su demonio redentores. Detrás de sí tenía a Raquel, y delante a Berta, y ambas le empujaban. ¿Hacia dónde? El presentía que hacia su perdición. Habíase de perder en ellas. Entre una y otra le estaban desgarrando. Sentíase como aquel niño que ante Salomón se disputaban las dos madres, sólo que no sabía cual de ellas, si Raquel o Berta, le quería entero para la otra y cual quería partirlo a muerte. Los ojos azules y claros de Berta, la doncella, como un mar sin fondo y sin orillas, le llamaban al abismo, y detrás de él, o mejor en torno de él, envolviéndole, los ojos negros y tenebrosos de Raquel, la viuda, como una noche sin fondo y sin estrellas, empujábanle al mismo abismo. (II, 211)

Caught between the bottomless sea and the endless sky, Juan feels himself returning to infancy and at the mercy of the judgement of King Solomon. In effect Juan's self is being absorbed by the double figure outside himself, and he falls into a spiral of self-diminution: '¿Es que soy mío? ¿Es que soy yo?' (II, 216). What is striking is Unamuno's insistence on portraying Juan's predicament as a loss of self, as a descent into a void, something which he does by the reiteration of a few closely-related symbols. Juan's presentiment of death is frequently expressed through the use of words such as 'matar', 'muerte', 'perdición'. 'No soy mío' is uttered twice.

Juan is 'enajenado', aware of an encompassing void which surrounds his mind and sensibilities. The word 'abismo' also appears twice, invoked in the abyssal depths of 'un mar sin fondo' and of 'una noche sin fondo' which entice him into a flight from consciousness. The word 'vacío' appears in a telling phrase: 'un terror loco le llenaba el corazón vacío' (II, 229). Unable to reconcile the two forces which have split his personality asunder, Juan is struck by a 'congoja de muerte' (II, 231), loses all sense of reality ('no sé dónde estoy' (II, 231)), and plunges into the literal and symbolic precipice of self-annihilation. '¿Y tú, Juan, hijo mío, te vas a repartir?' (II, 233), Unamuno makes Raquel say just a few lines before Juan's demise, as if drawing attention to the nature of Juan's severed personality.

In Augusto Pérez we can see a clear precedent of Juan. While *Niebla* is an altogether richer work in its range of ideas, Augusto presents similar symptoms of engulfment. As we saw in the preceding chapter, his mother has so taken over his existence that she has obliterated his selfhood, preventing the development of his personality. Because he has lived through his mother, her death leaves Augusto in a void, with the task of having to develop his sense of self and make his own decisions, something he will never achieve by himself because he lacks self-knowledge. Unable to decide, he drifts through life and becomes the victim of chance or of others' will. Like Juan, he is driven to despair by the behaviour of two women, but unlike Juan his desire to put an end to his inner emptiness is frustrated by a malevolent fate in the shape of an uncooperative creator. Depersonalized by an over-possessive mother, Augusto is left in a non-person state. His ontological insecurity or lack of self-identity leads to his seeing himself as a mere object or plaything of others instead of seeing others as a source of enrichment, as confirmation of one's sense of identity. The extrinsic double in this case is represented by the dog Orfeo, who serves as a mother substitute to whom Augusto takes his uncertainties and insecurities. It is Orfeo who becomes Augusto's other self as he engages in an endless 'monodiálogo', or dialogue with himself, in an attempt to uncover the inner self which he thinks must reveal his identity. Orfeo, as the name clearly implies through its association with the Orphic or mystical, represents the occult or hidden self that Augusto is trying to define. Here we see how the extrinsic double becomes an intrinsic double, or what is ultimately the same, how the intrinsic double is projected outwards and acquires a separate identity. In psychiatric terms Orfeo is the invented persona which the schizoid individual tries to inhabit as a substitute for his weak or absent sense of self. Eugenia, who announces that she will get rid of Orfeo, spells the destruction of the last vestiges of self-respect in Augusto. In Unamuno, the double is, as I have said, a literary device, and in *Niebla* one with an ironic purpose at that, the purpose being to crystallize the ontological void of a person who turns out to be but a character or role in a book and enjoys no autonomous existence

A more realistic — as opposed to metafictional — variant on this is found in *Tulio Montalbán y Julio Macedo*. Here we have a confrontation between a person and his double, Julio Macedo and his book image Tulio Montalbán. The problem for Macedo is that much as he wants to he cannot banish his public persona, the one enshrined in the biography that is in public ownership. The private self and the public self are at odds; there is no harmony. The literary double Tulio Montalbán

— and here we must remember that for Unamuno the book is a mirror — is experienced by the personage as a threat to his self, as obliteration, but he cannot by himself overcome that threat. He needs the confirmation of others, precisely because in Unamunian ontology our sense of self originates with others. The personage's response to the threat from the image in the mirror is to try to create another external self, Julio Macedo, but his failure in persuading others of the authenticity of this inner self results in a loss of identity and leads to self-destruction. In fact the case of Tulio/Julio is easily explained in psychological terms. A split self usually needs a third party, an outside agency, to resolve the issue. This is the case with Tulio/Julio. Curiously he chooses a woman named Elvira for the second time, suggesting that Julio Macedo still carries his former self inside him. Stricken by the loss of his first wife and unable to overcome her absence, he is looking for her all over again. So in a sense Tulio's creation of Julio Macedo is an attempt to return to a former or gestational state, the state he was in before he became a legendary figure and which he associates with his wife, the first Elvira. Julio's problem is that he needs external corroboration to recover that former fulfilled self. But he finds himself trapped by the 'false' image of him projected by his own exploits as freedom fighter. He has become, to paraphrase Unamuno's reference to himself, 'el Tulio de la leyenda'. Unable to destroy that 'past' self, the personage destroys his 'future' self.

It is arguably in *Abel Sánchez* that we observe Unamuno's use of the double at its most complex and suggestive.[5] Abel and Joaquín are incontrovertibly bound together. The title of the novel represents the ruling passion of Joaquín; and the opening lines establish their intimate connection:

> No recordaban Abel Sánchez y Joaquín Monegro desde cuando se conocían. Eran conocidos desde antes de la niñez, desde la primera infancia, pues ya sus sendas nodrizas se juntaban y los juntaban cuando aún ellos no sabían hablar. Aprendió cada uno de ellos a conocerse conociendo al otro. (I, 679)

Unamuno does not present the two central characters exclusively as rivals. In some ways Joaquín and Abel complement each other, as indeed do Cain and Abel in the Biblical myth, even though they are rivals for God's affection. Joaquín and Abel are together *ab origine* and learn to see themselves in the light of the other. This must obviously mean that there is something of Joaquín in Abel and something of Abel in Joaquín. If Joaquín describes Abel as a 'pintor científico', Abel describes Joaquín as a 'médico artista'. Both will compose self-portraits, Abel with the brush, Joaquín with the pen. This Unamunian idea of the complementarity of opposites is reflected in a particular technique employed, which consists in interchanging the traits or beliefs of the two characters, making one absorb the ideas of the other. Abel and Joaquín discuss the difference between art and science, which they each represent in their respective professions. Joaquín tells Abel that medicine is an art; when he later attacks artistic enterprise and defends science as the pursuit of truth, it is Abel who uses Joaquín's earlier argument that the practice of medicine is not a science but an art. Joaquín advises his friend to avoid a literary approach to painting; later

---

[5] The double in *Abel Sánchez* has been interestingly studied from an archetypal (i.e. Jungian) perspective by Gayana Jurkevich, 1991: 106–33.

Abel says he does not attach titles to his paintings because that is mere literary vanity. Yet the one who converts painting into literature is Joaquín, for it is he who, having borrowed Byron's *Cain* from his friend, uses it to interpret Abel's painting; yet once interpreted, it is Abel who confesses to only now having understood the significance of his own painting. According to Joaquín, Abel regards other people as 'a lo sumo, modelo para sus cuadros' (I, 695), but this is in fact what Joaquín's own patients become in his 'Memorias', models or examples 'que había cosechado de la práctica de su profesión de médico' (I, 771). Moreover Joaquín refers to 'desnudar las almas' and to forcing people to see themselves 'al desnudo' (I, 771), which is exactly what Abel had said he had tried to do in his famous painting, 'dos estudios de desnudo' (I, 712); and he aspires to convey in words a portrait of Abel and Helena 'que para siempre habría de quedar [...]. Y su retrato valdría por todos los que Abel pintara' (I, 771–72). As if the parallelism between the cold, scientific painter and the artistic doctor were not clear enough the narrator adds a further detail: referring to Joaquín's new attitude to Abel he says that he looked upon him 'como a un modelo' (I, 773,), which is exactly what Joaquín had criticized in Abel. Joaquín and Abel may see themselves as very different from each other, as indeed do other characters, but what we observe is Unamuno establishing parallelisms between the two, making them express similar ideas and occupying each other's ideological positions. This is true even of the central theme, the story that we find in Genesis 4. 1–16, in which Abel and Cain are by no means confined to the hero and villain roles that have traditionally been assigned to them. Since the myth requires them both, one is as much to blame for the crime as the other.

During their first discussion of the Biblical myth, Joaquín defends Cain and blames both God and the victim for the fratricide: God for having favoured Abel over his brother and Abel for having taken pride in his favoured status. Much to Abel's surprise, Joaquín goes further, widening his attack to include those whom he calls Abelites, whose arrogance and ostentatious self-righteousness are an affront to others and who delight in belittling others the better to savour their own success: 'su goce está en ver, libres de padecimiento, padecer a los otros' (I, 714). This defence of Cain via a frontal attack on his detractors is repeated later on, but the second time around it is Abel, not Joaquín, who defends Cain. He argues that orthodox believers, who hold God to be on their side, persecute the minority of those who entertain heterodox views because they will not tolerate deviance from their own impoverished norms. It is their envy of those who think for themselves that make them condemn their distinctness. This time the one who expresses surprise is Joaquín, who asks if these envious people whom Abel labels conformist, mediocre, and unimaginative do not deserve to be defended. Abel counters with the argument already used by Joaquín in the banquet in honour of the painter: that Cain's envy is not to be confused with that of mediocre mortals led by an inquisitorial fanaticism, those with whom Joaquín is now consorting: 'la envidia de Caín era algo grande' (I, 729), by which he gives us to understand that Cain acted as he did not for petty or egoistic motives but as a universal protest against an unjust fate, a tragic, not a selfish, act. Joaquín's reaction to Abel's argument is revealing: 'Pero este hombre — se decía Joaquín al separarse de Abel — ¿es que lee en mí?' (I, 730). Abel has done precisely what Joaquín had done earlier: interpret the myth from the perspective of a modern individual at odds with a norm of behaviour imposed from without.

It thus appears that, as in the Biblical myth, Joaquín and Abel are conceptually inseparable, and this is reflected in the way that Unamuno makes them swap intellectual positions. The extrinsic double of the Gothic tales, where the two figures change places physically or where one 'kills' the other, survives in *Abel Sánchez*, but without the supernatural or spectral paraphernalia. Instead of one self killing or burying his double we have a scene in which an angry Joaquín, who feels he is being deprived of a part of himself (his grandson), turns on a threatening Abel as if to kill him only to provoke a fatal heart attack in an already susceptible Abel. The latter is obviously meant to exist as an independent character within the fiction and is not solely the imagined projection of a schizophrenic or merely schizoid individual. Yet at the same time the Abel that we learn about exists overwhelmingly as a function of Joaquín. The Abel who exists independently of Joaquín is a shadowy figure about whom we learn comparatively little.[6] Abel, the likable, easy-going, ever-popular character who enjoys success with women and gains the approval of the public without having to make an effort, who has no need of the consoling power of religion, is the person that Joaquín would like to be, but without abandoning his own sense of identity. The brotherliness which unites the two men and to which reference is made several times has a clear symbolic value which, given that most of what we learn of Abel we learn through Joaquín, must mean that Abel is an intrinsic double, an image of another self created by Joaquín to complement the image of the odious Joaquín that the latter carries of himself. The paradoxical and ambiguous expression 'su amigo de antes de conocerse' (I, 720) indicates the intrinsic nature of the presence of Abel.

The trope of the double is nevertheless put to a more complex use in this novel than in the short stories or the play *El Otro*. The two dominant selves of Joaquín, the one he feels himself to be and the one he would like to be, do not appear to threaten each other's existence; rather they seem to co-exist uneasily but reciprocally. Joaquín is to Abel as self-loathing is to self-esteem. Both images would appear to be constructions of a third, unidentified self, the self that oscillates between the two representations of self. This unidentified self is the one who is torn between the attractive Abel and the odious Joaquín, between the 'angelic' role and the 'demonic' role.[7] This nuclear Joaquín whom we hardly see but who could be deemed to be present throughout always keeps the two other versions in play, veering between one and the other, as we observe over Joaquín's public speech in favour of Abel, which he regrets almost as soon as delivered; in other words he alternates between attraction and rejection.[8] The 'querer ser' that is Abel becomes hateful because,

[6] Isabel Criado Miguel has said of the autonomous Abel that he passes into the shade: 'pasa a la penumbra' (Criado Miguel, 1986: 131).

[7] I take the terms from 'Artemio heautontimoroumenos' (II, 615–18). Artemio knows his two selves, the demonic and the angelic, but like Buridan's ass fails to choose one or the other, with the result that he becomes wholly ineffective and hates himself for his indecision.

[8] R. D. Laing explains that 'what at one moment is most dreaded and strenuously avoided can change to what is most sought' (Laing, 1990: 44).

despite its tantalizing proximity, it turns out to be inaccessible. Joaquín believes there must be a reciprocal hatred, but the other's feelings elude him. The fact remains that within the plot of the novel Joaquín cannot break the bond that unites him to the person who stole his girlfriend; on the contrary, what has happened unites him to Abel more closely, so much so that he loses his autonomy in both a psychological and a moral sense. '¡Necesito que viva!' (I, 698), he tells himself, and indeed when Abel finally dies Joaquín will survive him for only a year, dying, as he had lived, from 'una oscura enfermedad' (I, 789). Everything Joaquín does, both good and bad, derives from his intimate bond with Abel. The latter therefore represents that second self that Joaquín carries within and which becomes an overriding obsession. Joaquín has to struggle to assert his autonomy as that other threatens to engulf his life. The double in this case represents an inability to relate to oneself. The individual suffering from this condition tries to defend his identity by a restless activity and contestation.

> Volvía [al Casino] por no poder sufrir la soledad. Pues en la soledad jamás lograba estar solo, sino que siempre allí el otro. ¡El otro! Llegó a sorprenderse en diálogo con él, tramando lo que el otro le decía. Y el otro, en estos diálogos solitarios, en estos monólogos dialogados, le decía cosas indiferentes o gratas, no le mostraba ningún rencor. ¿Por qué no me odia?, ¡Dios mío! — llegó a decirse —. ¿Por qué no me odia? (I, 740–41)

In this context, a comment by R. D. Laing serves to illuminate Joaquín's mental condition: 'The other's love is therefore feared more than his hatred, or rather all love is sensed as a version of hatred' (Laing, 1990: 45). This exactly applies to Joaquín, as he seeks to uncover Abel's (non-existent) hatred of him, and rejects the love of his wife and daughter, ascribing to them (an equally non-existent) feeling of repugnance. To be hated appears preferable to being loved because to be loved would amount to being deleted. The hateful self that Joaquín creates is in effect a defence against engulfment by the other. Like the Biblical Cain, he seeks to kill Abel; instead, at the critical moment, when he has the opportunity to 'haber acabado con él artísticamente' (I, 726), he chooses to consecrate him, figuratively to paint his picture for him, thereby provoking the other's effusive gratitude. What is significant, however, is Joaquin's dual reaction, reconciliation and repulsion all at the same time:

> Levantóse entonces Abel y, pálido, convulso, tartamudeante, con lágrimas en los ojos, le dijo a su amigo:
> — Joaquín, lo que acabas de decir vale más, mucho más que mi cuadro, que todos los cuadros que he pintado, más que todos los que pintaré... Eso, eso es una obra de arte y de corazón. Yo no sabía lo que he hecho hasta que te he oído. Tú y no yo has hecho mi cuadro, ¡tú!
> Y abrazáronse llorando los dos amigos de siempre entre los clamorosos aplausos y vivas de la concurrencia puesta en pie. Y al abrazarse le dijo a Joaquín su demonio: «¡Si pudieses ahora ahogarle en tus brazos...!» (I, 723–24)

To strangle him figuratively is of course what Joaquín, regretting his act of extolment, will henceforth try to do in his 'Confesión' before finally trying to do it literally in a fit of jealous rage.

On one level, then, the symbolical, we can read the novel as heautoscopy, the phenomenon of meeting a duplicated self, and Joaquín's attack on Abel as the consequent autocide, an outcome familiar in imaginative literature but also well documented in medical literature.[9] Since the heautoscopic experience as a clinical condition is associated with feelings of horror and despair and often leads to suicide, such a reading fits in well with Joaquín's state of mind in which he questions his own existence and finally attempts to strangle his double. But we can also read the novel literally, for no matter how extreme Joaquín's obsession may appear to be, Unamuno has not resorted to extraordinary events in order to explain his condition. This is where *Abel Sánchez* scores heavily over some other Unamunian treatments of the double. It is very much a novel about mental disease, or at the very least mental instability, but it explores the subject within the confines of a credible and realistic portrayal. It is neither metafiction, as is *Niebla*, nor Gothic horror story, as are some of the *cuentos*. It is, as Nicholas Round concluded after the most thorough and penetrating analysis to which this novel has been subjected, a 'highly complex account of the inner and outer relationships of the self' (Round, 1974: 92).

Unamuno's last use of the trope of the double can be found in *La novela de don Sandalio, jugador de ajedrez*, although it would be possible to see a faint reflection of it in the two versions of the saintly priest, the public and the private, that we are given in *San Manuel Bueno, mártir*, which I shall consider presently.[10] In the first (and also earlier in terms of composition though not of publication) of these two works, we are virtually obliged to follow this same line in order to make sense of what can appear to be a rather whimsical creation. Unamuno is pointing us in this direction by including veiled references to the letter-writer's state of health, both mental and physical, within the constraints of first-person narration. The letter-writer appears to have lost his family, and he is suffering from a cardiac illness. His behaviour is erratic, as shown by his love-hate relationship with the club and its members, by his solitary walks and his befriending an oak tree hollowed out with age, and above all of course by his extraordinary attitude to Don Sandalio and his fate. The idea of madness is brought into the text sometimes obliquely, sometimes directly: obliquely when first Don Sandalio and later his son-in-law give the narrator a quizzical look that expresses their understandable alarm after the latter's extraordinary outbursts, and also when the narrator evokes the image of the mad Don Quixote being taken home in a cage; directly when he wonders if perhaps Don Sandalio had intuited the truth about him and he was in fact mad, and in his references to himself as a mad bishop. The letter-writer's mental stability is therefore suspect, and this helps explain his extraordinary attitude to his chess partner. In effect he presents us with two Don Sandalios: the one who goes home after the game of chess and there,

---

[9] See for example Peter Brugger *et al.*, 1994: 838–39, which refers to a number of other studies of heautoscopy. The split self has also been ascribed to the independent functioning of the left and right cerebral hemispheres of the brain, effectively giving the individual two minds or, seemingly, two persons in one body. See for example R. W. Sperry, 1968: 723–33.

[10] In addition to what I shall have to say about *San Manuel Bueno, mártir*, one should also bear in mind Gayana Jurkevich's Jungian approach to Unamuno in which she interprets Blasillo el bobo as an *alter ego* of the priest (Jurkevich, 1991: 137).

inaccessible to him, leads a quite separate existence; and the one who is created by the letter-writer on the tenuous basis of his brief and mute exchanges with him over the chess board. And we are left in no doubt that, while the 'normal' Don Sandalio hovers in the background, the mysterious Don Sandalio is a creation of the mind of the letter-writer himself. He even comes close to admitting this when he writes: 'me di casi a temblar pensando si en fuerza de pensar en mi don Sandalio no me había éste sustituido y padecía yo de una doble personalidad' (II, 361). This idea of a double personality is crucial, and once we realize just how closely the narrator's Don Sandalio is modelled on himself, a possibility emerges that, despite its whimsicality, the tale has a logic all of its own.

That the letter-writer is creating Don Sandalio in his own image becomes clear when we consider the number of parallels between the two. Both enjoy playing chess silently, intently, and without onlookers, comments, or interruptions, unlike the other chess players in the club. The letter-writer is a solitary and introverted man; so is Don Sandalio: '¡Le veo tan aislado en medio de los demás, tan metido en sí mismo!' (II, 355–56). The letter-writer is an ailing man, perhaps seriously ill; and he is worried by his health. All this applies to Don Sandalio too: 'Le observo a don Sandalio alguna preocupación. Debe de ser por su salud, pues se le nota que respira con dificultad' (II, 360); Don Sandalio is indeed so ill that a month later he is dead. We know too that the letter-writer has suffered some kind of tragedy in his life; exactly the same befalls Don Sandalio: he loses a son, cannot bear to stay at home, is imprisoned, and the writer even hints darkly at other possible tragedies. Indeed the idea of a personal tragedy in Don Sandalio's life has been present in the writer's mind from the very first encounter — '¿lleva alguna tragedia en el alma?' (II, 356) — which reflects the intrusion of his own personal tragedy into the story he is relating. Don Sandalio, in other words, is made into a tragic figure by the letter-writer's own sense of personal tragedy. It is a kind of catharsis, a relieving of the neurotic state of mind of the narrator by the projection of his own fears and anxieties onto another being, a being created by literary means. At one point the narrator actually acknowledges that his letters provide an outlet for the release of his mental tension: 'un desahogo de carta' (II, 369), he writes. What precisely the anxiety is that impels him to indulge in such unusual epistolary activity we are not directly told, but the references to his failing health all point to an ailing figure who sees the end of his life approaching just as the autumnal season is moving inexorably towards winter. What we have in Don Sandalio, then, is a variation on the classic use of the trope of the double as a harbinger of death. Don Sandalio is, as we saw in the preceding chapter, a hollow shell precisely because he symbolizes the nothingness or obliteration facing the letter-writer. The latter is desolate, prone to collapse, separated from reality, as his preferences for the hollow tree, the ruins, the solitary beach, and of course the silent Don Sandalio seem to indicate. In effect the letter-writer is showing all the symptoms of what existential psychiatry has referred to as an inner vacuum. Such a state can involve the individual in alternate phases of an avid pursuit of social life followed by a total withdrawal from it, as R. D. Laing explains:

This shut-up self, being isolated, is unable to be enriched by outer experience, and so the whole inner world comes to be more and more impoverished, until the individual may come to feel he is merely a vacuum. The sense of being able to do anything and the feeling of possessing everything then exist side by side with a feeling of impotence and emptiness. The individual who may at one time have felt predominantly 'outside' the life going on *there*, which he affects to despise as petty and commonplace compared to the richness he has *here*, inside himself, now longs to get *inside* life again, and get life *inside* himself, so dreadful is his inner deadness. (Laing, 1990: 75)

This process describes the letter-writer's behaviour perfectly, as he tries repeatedly to return to a social life only to withdraw into his shell once again. The double that he creates, who is not only his double but at the same time a double figure, gregarious family man and shadowy, silent chess player, can thus be seen as a clear projection of a personality threatened by implosion.

Doubling the Text, Splitting the Author

If the literary trope of the double is frequently invoked by Unamuno in order to suggest a disturbed mental state in his fictional characters, there is another way in which the device intrudes into the fiction: what I earlier labelled the linguistic or textual double. Just how conscious Unamuno is of his penchant for doubling is impossible to know, but that it is a frequent technique is not to be doubted. The use of the chiasmus in the broadest sense, so well studied by Paul R. Olson, is one clear manifestation of this. Olson sees the chiastic structure — or end-to-end reversal, with a typical structure of ABC:CBA — working on three levels: at the level of the syntax or statement, itself a reflection of Unamuno's way of thinking; at the level of the narrative structure or disposition of particular works; and at the level of Unamuno's overall development from *Paz en la guerra* to *San Manuel Bueno, mártir* (Olson, 2003).[11] The chiastic structure of course implies a doubling, trebling, and so on in a symmetrical pattern, each further statement or view having its own mirror image. A simple example, taken from the novel just discussed, would be 'hay recuerdos de cosas futuras como hay esperanzas de cosas pasadas' (II, 377), in which the paradox is expressed by a clear reversal of the nouns (recuerdos/esperanzas) and the adjectival phrases (de cosas futuras/de cosas pasadas) as well as by the unexpected transposition of the latter. Here I am more concerned with doubling than with reversal, for as we have seen in the case of fictional characters, Unamuno tends to see them as Janus-faced, either because they have a split personality (two or more selves) or because they represent the possibilities of alternative courses of action in an existential sense, that is, they are embodiments of those very alternatives. It is this doubling that seems to affect Unamuno himself *qua* writer. As he makes a statement — or as he develops a narrative — he seems conscious of alternative possibilities, of attacking the problem from the opposite side. At the level of the sentence this reversal is so frequent and intrusive as to be occasionally tiresome. At

---

[11] Another key contribution in this area is Thomas Mermall, 1990. Mermall argues that in Unamuno the chiasmus has a fundamentally philosophical function in exploring the connection between uncertainty and truth.

the level of the narrative, however, it is much less obvious, although some examples have been well studied, notably the doubling that Víctor Goti, the author of the *nivola*, represents vis-à-vis the author of the *novela* and the ensuing confrontation between the two writers.[12] Each person is the other's double in the sense that they both exert an influence over the protagonist, Augusto Pérez, but it is not simply a case of *mise-en-abîme*, since Goti and Unamuno do not see eye to eye. They represent different possibilities, one the idea that a character makes an author, and the other that an author makes a character. The double here reduces to the debate over the question of the ultimate preponderance of author or work.

The double-author syndrome is most interestingly expressed in having a doubling of the text, that is to say where the existence of a second text is invoked either by citation, or by direct mention, or at the very least by implication. In *Abel Sánchez* we have two texts, the 'objective' text of the impersonal narrator and the subjective text of Joaquín himself. This of course raises the (entirely fictional) question of primacy. Which is the primary text, the impersonal account or Joaquín's 'Confesión'? Is the former to be seen as derived from the latter, as a biography of St Augustine might well use and quote from the *Confessions* but be distinct from them? The issue could have been settled in the preface attached to the text, but all that the brief, six-line note does is to prepare the reader for the extracts from the 'Confesión'. There is no indication as to authorship in the case of the impersonal account found among Joaquín's papers. In an attempt to give the story greater verisimilitude, Robert L. Nicholas (1987: 47) suggested that the account be seen as the work of one of Joaquín's grandchildren, but Unamuno has provided no clues. In any case identifying the narrator would solve one mystery only at the expense of creating new ones. We are forced back to the position that the two texts in *Abel Sánchez* represent two perspectives, an internal one and an external one. The two accounts are not incompatible, though they are written from different points of view and seek different effects. Unamuno has not followed Dostoyevski's example in *Notes from Underground* by conveying the entire story in first-person form. He has opted for a double perspective, an inner and an outer one, which, without any glaring factual contradiction, open up different possibilities of interpretation. The discrepancies between the two accounts are subtle, but they are nevertheless there, so the technique allows us to see that Joaquín does not fully understand himself, that he ascribes motives to himself in his confession which the main narrative invites us to see as self-delusion, or indeed as self-creation. The self-creativity of Joaquín in his autobiography parallels that of the impersonal narrator, but it is an alternative, not a confirmation.[13] By allowing the character to address the reader directly, Unamuno makes us see the character not as he is but as *he believes himself to be*. And not only as he thinks he is but also as he would like to be. The 'Confesión' is a self-projection, an attempt to rip off the painful public mask he sees himself wearing by converting it into the tragic role that has fallen to his lot. It is a looking-

---

[12] See for example Anne Marie Øveraas, 1993: 85–92, and Bénédicte Vauthier, 1999: 61–62 and 132–37.

[13] Examples of the discrepancies between the two versions may be found in the Introduction to my edition of *Abel Sánchez* (Unamuno, 1995a: 26–29).

in-the-mirror, a meeting with fate face to face. Both texts are interpretative, since the impersonal account goes beyond the externally observable actions to interpret the character's mind; but it is an external portrait, a what-is-he-like approach. Joaquín's account is an insider's view of himself and those around him, neither truer nor less true than the impersonal account, for all Joaquín can do when he picks up his pen rather than his stethoscope is exchange one mask for another. This, after all, is Unamuno's repeated point, that our relationship with the world and our relationship with ourselves requires a mask, a role.

Tulio Montalbán y Julio Macedo is a variation on the doubling of the text. The narrator refers to two texts that we do not read: the 'Vida de Tulio Montalbán', the biography of the heroic liberator written by Henri Jacquetot, and the 'Memorias de Julio Macedo' written by himself. Although we can read neither text, we can tell that here there is opposition between the public and private versions. Macedo has repudiated the biography as a historical fiction and has produced an autobiography as an 'alegato contra la «Vida de Tulio Montalbán»' (II, 181). The doubling here is complete: two fathers-in-law (one encomiastic, the other sceptical), two Elviras (one devoted to a simple man, the other devoted to a legendary hero), two protagonists (one highly public, the other intensely private), and two texts. It is almost a mathematical equation in which each side cancels out the other. And the story does indeed end in immolation: not just the destruction of the double protagonist Tulio/Julio, but of the two antagonistic texts, jointly consigned to the flames in a symbolic act of liberation from the tyranny of the word.

In *San Manuel Bueno, mártir* we again have two biographical texts, but this time we read one (Ángela's) and not the other (the Bishop's). Not that we need to read the Bishop's biography of Father Manuel Bueno since we know that it will be 'una especie de manual del perfecto párroco' (II, 345) based on the information collected from the priest's devoted parishioners. Ángela's own account — her private account as opposed to the Bishop's public account — must be seen as a response or alternative to this other biography. Ángela, determined to construct her own portrait of the priest, paints a very different picture of his saintliness. Who is right and who is wrong? Again Unamuno shows no interest in this question, except perhaps to suggest that these accounts are constructions which exist alongside their subject but cannot give us full access to the truth of personality. When Unamuno writes in the epilogue that he believes in the reality of Ángela's account of Don Manuel more than Don Manuel himself believed in his own reality, he is of course creating a paradox, but it is a paradox that hides an inevitability. Ángela sees Don Manuel with her own eyes, and her account reflects her vision of a tortured soul just as the Bishop's will reflect his vision of perfect priestliness. Don Manuel's vision of himself is hidden from us, but we as readers will invariably create our own based, as Unamuno says, on the account we read. But Unamuno does not fail to remind us that we could have been reading a very different account, in exactly the same way that St Michael and the Devil interpreted Moses's scepticism about the promised land in different ways. Once again we can see that the technique of doubling serves to underline the uncertainty, ambivalence, or inconclusiveness of any attempt to convert mental realities into words, especially of course where the reality pertains to a person's intrinsicality. The 'realidad' of Ángela's account that Unamuno believes in is the reality of words, not of the person, and words in Unamuno's ontology lose all referential validity when applied to the person as noumenon.

The textual doubling appears too, though more conventionally due to the use of epistolary form, in the unconventional *La novela de don Sandalio*. One set of letters presupposes another travelling in the opposite direction, and of course Felipe, the letter-writer's addressee and correspondent is the shadowy author of letters which we do not read but of whose content we are made occasionally aware, more especially towards the end of the correspondence, where the two correspondents react strongly to each other's letters. Unamuno warns us that what we read are not complete letters but fragments of them, so that an editing process has been at work. The literary trope of the double thus functions at various levels. Firstly, we have a letter-writer and his reader in a symbiotic relationship, each needing the other. Secondly, we have a character with a double personality, that of the silent chess player who abhors humanity and that of the garrulous, home-loving, and sociable family man. Thirdly, we have a provider of copy, who could be Felipe himself, the recipient of the letters, and his own addressee, whom we identify with Unamuno as consumer of the correspondence. And fourthly, we have a prologue and an epilogue in which the various identities and possible connections are mischievously discussed: '¡Figuras todas de una galería de espejos empañados!' (II, 381). The novel has become a game of mirrors in which there is not one object and its reflection but potentially an endless succession of images. The scene in letter 19, in which the letter-writer sees infinite images of himself receding into the distance, is a microcosm of the novel as a whole, that is to say of the art of writing, which commences as a double act — one self projecting another — and ends as a hall of mirrors.

Conclusion

Unamuno's use of the literary trope of the double is both persistent and richly varied. The basic trope, as occurs in literature more generally, is that of the double self, or, as in psychiatry, the split self. This is a useful starting point for Unamuno since it inevitably raises questions of identity, a subject which, as he repeatedly made clear, fascinated him because of its wide ramifications, psychological, philosophical, religious, linguistic, and of course creative. The meeting with the double can occasionally be quite literal, i.e. the doppelgänger or twin phenomenon, but strictly speaking this only applies to a few short stories. More commonly what we get is a doubling rather than a double. Indeed there is hardly a major character of Unamuno's who does not undergo this experience of having a double personality in some form. Even Gertrudis, not so far discussed in this chapter, suffers from the double syndrome. There is the Gertrudis who is deeply in love with Ramiro — Ramiro's death-bed scene leaves no doubt — and who comes close to marrying him; indeed we are left with the strong impression that she might well have done so had he not satisfied his concupiscence with someone else, or even if he had survived the fragile Manuela. And there is the Gertrudis who wants to place her life-project above all else. The fact that Unamuno will not allow his character to reconcile these two perfectly reconcilable tendencies but instead subjects her to the distressing experience of a 'brava galerna' only goes to show just how intent he was in emphasizing the dual-personality syndrome of the personage. This is true of several other characters, including, remarkably, the priest Father Manuel Bueno.

One side of Father Manuel sees religious belief as providing a real communion with a transcendent reality for the person who has that belief, something that he considers both valuable and important and which he does his utmost to uphold. The other side of him tells him that he can entertain no such belief. This is tantamount to saying that I fervently wish you to believe in something that I am not prepared to believe in myself. In other words the Unamunian character is simultaneously occupying two distinct and contradictory positions. Ángela can make no sense of this; hence her paradoxical 'se murieron creyendo no creer [...], pero sin creer creerlo, creyéndolo' (II, 343–44), which posits the possibility of believing in something in which one does not believe. Unless we see Father Manuel Bueno and his acolyte Lázaro Carballino as split selves their position as described by Ángela is not logically tenable: belief cannot be thought of as some medicine that could be beneficial to one person and harmful to another; it is rather a constitutive attitude of one's being. I can doubt the truth of something, which means I am uncertain as to its validity. But belief is either valid or not valid; it can scarcely be both simultaneously for an individual unless he is two distinct personalities. Gabriel Marcel explained it very simply, for as he said of his own previously contradictory stance 'it was anyhow a deep delusion to think that I could really believe in the faith of others if I had none of my own' (Marcel, 1965b: 220).[14]

The split syndrome can also be seen to be at work in Don Avito Carrascal, where his instinctual and intellectual tendencies provoke a state of siege — 'demonio familiar' — in him, although here of course it takes the form of caricature. In Tulio Montalbán the discrepancy between his two selves, one derived from his wife's vision of him, the other from his compatriots' vision of him, provokes agony and flight. In effect Tulio/Julio is an example of reification, where an individual sees himself as becoming a mere thing or object for others and feels that his 'real' self is being cast aside. To a degree this is also true of Augusto Pérez, who declares that he has been treated (by Eugenia and Mauricio) as if he did not exist. The two cases are reversed images. Whereas in Tulio's case the public image is the one that is applauded, in Augusto's case the public image is the one that is derided. But since our own self-image has to accommodate others' image of us, any clash of the two is fatal for the individual's sanity.

The twin syndrome and the split syndrome come powerfully together in *Abel Sánchez*, arguably Unamuno's most profound exploration of the problem of self.[15]

---

[14] It would be a mistake to see Father Manuel Bueno's double stance, if that is what it is, as somehow representing Unamuno's. Here is what Unamuno said in his essay 'A mis lectores': 'Hay que sembrar en los hombres gérmenes de duda, de desconfianza, de inquietud, y hasta de desesperación — ¿por qué no? ¡sí, hasta de desesperación! — y si de este modo pierden eso que llaman felicidad, y que realmente no lo es, nada se ha perdido' (IX, 221). The divergence from Father Manuel Bueno's own philosophy is stark. For Unamuno, belief without doubt is of little value.

[15] N. G. Round's analysis in his Critical Guide to the novel (1974) leaves little room for doubt.

The two major characters are twins in the sense that they grow up in the presence of each other and each is his own self only in relation to the other ('aprendió cada uno a conocerse conociendo al otro' (I, 679)). But read allegorically they are not two separate individuals but two personalities within a single being that provoke discord through an attraction-repulsion mechanism. The Joaquín-person wants to be the Abel-person because he is fascinated by his manner, but hates him because he cannot bring himself to be that person. He can neither get rid of that second self nor allow it to take over the primary self, what he feels is the self he has been born with. The ensuing torture destroys his wellbeing.[16]

In *La novela de Don Sandalio* the two chess antagonists vie with each other for supremacy. While they are strangers over the chess table — involved in a game of life and death — they eye each other with suspicion or even fear ('me miraba asustado' (II, 363)), but above all they speculate about each other's hidden personality and motives, the letter-writer in his correspondence, Don Sandalio at home with his family. The contest ends when one banishes the other and thereby achieves a measure of composure, as occurs at the end of this particular account. In none of these various cases are we dealing with the Freudian *id*, *ego*, or *super-ego*. What we are dealing with is essentially fragmentation or breakdown of the coherent self into its constituent parts, a fragmentation that usually takes the form of a split into two distinct personalities but which can also be represented by the multiple mirror effect of endlessly receding images that sends the character into a spin. For Unamuno, to lose one's sense of self is to lose one's identity in an absolute sense. This is an ever-present danger in Unamuno precisely because he emphasizes the role of the other in acquiring our sense of identity. The flip-over comes if we allow others to take over our sense of self completely. This is what we see happening to Apolodoro, to Augusto Pérez, and to Juan in *Dos madres*.

We can also observe the double at work in quite another sense, the sense in which a character is made to face an existential choice, that is to say a choice that will radically affect that character's life circumstances. The choice may be one of person or of state. Should Avito choose Leoncia or Marina, or Augusto choose Eugenia or Rosario, or Juan choose Berta or Raquel? Should Gertrudis choose marriage or virginity, or Ángela choose discipleship or marriage and family, or Ricardo choose life with Liduvina or life in Holy Orders? All these characters choose, or are made to choose, only to find that the personality they left behind as part of the alternative they did not choose stays with them forever alongside the personality they have become. Indeed some of them, like Fray Ricardo or Gertrudis, will be haunted by this virtual self. Only one or two, notably Emeterio Alfonso in *Un pobre hombre rico*, will manage to turn the clock back and recover what Unamuno elsewhere referred to as a 'yo ex-futuro', the I that I could have been but am not, a shadowy presence that at best distracts and at worst destroys.

---

[16] In the splitting of the self one part usually retains the sense of 'I' and the other part becomes 'him' but still a part of 'me'. The other self can quickly become the basis of hallucination. See R. D. Laing, 1990: 158.

Does Unamuno's use of the double shed any light on his ontology? If we compare the frequency of the literary trope with what he says of himself in some of his essays we can hardly avoid the suspicion — which must remain a suspicion — that the use of the double is a reflection of a state of being in which he genuinely felt himself to be more than one, that is to say, as several points of view incarnate in one individual. His adoption of contrary positions is well known. Expressions of both religious belief and unbelief are disconcertingly abundant and not easy to reconcile. His egotistical desire for recognition was countered by his rejection of personal enthronement. His attacks on the Church and its dogmas were offset by his adamant defence of spiritual values and denunciation of materialism, and so on.[17] He was aware of his inconsistencies and defended them as part of an authentic expression of self. He had to be as much one self as another self, almost as if all his potential selves, or 'yos ex-futuros' as he called them, had a right to life. Nevertheless generalizing from work to person is a high-risk activity, though not incompatible with Unamuno's own view that all literature is covert autobiography.

Unamuno has frequently been seen as possessing an obsessive temperament, especially of course where survival of his ego was concerned. Irrespective of whether such a view is justified or not, he deserves credit for exploiting his obsessions inventively, productively, and through recognizably literary or meta-phorical devices. The manifold use of the trope of the double is witness to Unamuno's fertile imagination. The double appears in various guises: as self and image; as self and other; as self and mask; and as premonition of calamity. Moreover what applies at the intradiegetic level — more crudely at the level of the plot — applies too extradiegetically, that is, at the level of the composition. Unamuno is highly conscious of the fact that writing is both a writing *from* and a writing *for*. We could go as far as to say that the trope of the double in Unamuno's fiction is not so much a doubling as an undoubling — the author's own undoubling into the creating self and the created self; not simply the two selves whom Jean-Jacques Rousseau was aware of in his *Confessions*, the narrating self and the narrated self whose authenticity is suspect, but as it were one step beyond this, a creating self who strives for a particular effect and a created self who projects an autonomous image and has a personality all of its own. Philosophically we could say that this self acquires emergence, a separate quality of its own over and above those of its constituent parts. The stranger in the mirror that Unamuno found in his books functions as the author's double: it is, as he often emphasized, a phenomenon created by language, language offering its own reality beyond the world of material objects. An authorial projection will become as real as the author himself, and once projected cannot be reabsorbed. But as well as evoking the presence of a second self, writing implies another presence, the presence of a reader standing as it were on the other side of a two-way mirror. Writer and reader constitute the originating and inescapable double; they are not the same, but neither can function without the other. The writer is conscious of the presence, virtual though it may be, of the reader who will one day receive, absorb, and confer sense on the writing.

[17] On the dangers and complexities involved in trying to decide between Unamuno's contrary postures, in this case belief and unbelief, see Nicholas G. Round, 1986.

This reader, so persistently invoked in Unamuno's work, constitutes that other self whose very proximity yet inaccessibility breeds both fascination and anxiety, that self who like Joaquín's Abel is perceived as a potential source of love, hatred or indifference. The double in Unamuno is one more testimony to radical doubt.

CHAPTER 7

Philosophical Investigations

The Wittgensteinian title of this chapter is perhaps over-ambitious. Unamuno was not an analytic philosopher, his temperament being wholly unsuitable to such a profession. He was well aware of his limitations for sustained systematic deliberation, but this did not deter him from tackling important areas of human thought in his own inimitable way, questioning, challenging, overturning conventional ways of thinking and valuing the intuitive and heartfelt over the rationalistic and discursive. Unamuno's was always a philosophy in the making, never a completed system. To systematize meant to impose an artificial order which risked negating the inherent contradictions in man. Reason is a tool of our being, and behind it lies a driving force that is non-rational and of which we have little comprehension. Even the rationalist pursuits of analytic philosophers are sustained by something in their nature that is outside reason:

> La filosofía es un producto humano de cada filósofo, y cada filósofo es un hombre de carne y hueso que se dirige a otros hombres de carne y hueso como él. Y haga lo que quiera, filosofa, no con la razón sólo, sino con la voluntad, con el sentimiento, con la carne y con los huesos, con el alma toda y con todo el cuerpo. Filosofa el hombre. (*DSTV*, X, 297)

This sentiment has recently been echoed by Stephen Mulhall when he declares that 'the trouble with philosophy is that philosophers seem to have an almost inveterate tendency to forget that they are human beings too. For perfectly understandable reasons, philosophers — not specifically but including analytic philosophers — tend to forget that they are situated human beings' (quoted by Woessner, 2012: 170). All rational arguments after all must start from a premiss that was not argued in the first place, from an insight or judgment, from an intuition or experience of some kind. Professional philosophers can offer arguments *ad libitum*, but few can offer new insights, which are by their very nature rare and epiphanic. Kant's greatness as a thinker rests less on his lengthy systematization than on his realization that, to use his own words, 'reason has insight only into what it itself produces according to its own design' (Kant, 1998: 109), in other words that objects conform to our cognition and not the other way round. This probably helps to explain why Unamuno preferred to express his ideas via more literary or imaginative forms rather than through the traditional logic-based form of academic philosophers. Philosophical language aims at precision, poetic language aims at suggestion, and Unamuno often referred to himself as a poet. Indeed he went further, not only regarding the greatest philosophers as poets, but narrowing the distinction between the poet and the philosopher: 'poeta y filósofo son hermanos gemelos, si es que no la misma cosa' (*DSTV*, X, 280). This of course implies a very particular view of philosophy, the view that it consists of conceptualizing poetic intuitions; and to conceptualize means for Unamuno to think in words. If Unamuno did not see himself as a systematizer we should be wary of putting him in a straitjacket not of his making.[1]

Since Julián Marías published his influential book *Miguel de Unamuno* (1942), the novels have tended to be viewed — more especially in the Hispanic world — rather more as philosophical statements and rather less as narrative constructs. Unamuno himself may have encouraged this approach by insisting that great philosophical, historical, and theological treatises (including the Gospels) were novels, since he equated great writing in any discipline with poetry and poetry with creativity. This naturally invites us, conversely, to see his novels as treatises. All the same, it seems questionable to treat novels as philosophy or theology while forgetting altogether that their composition involves decisions of an aesthetic nature that have to do with the narrative genre — its origins, construction, and destination — and not simply with the ideas derived from a philosophical tradition that may very well inform the text. A novel has potentially a far more complex form than the most profound of philosophical treatises, including as it does generic aspects such as metaphor, irony, allegory, perspectivism, plotting strategies, narrative levels, character motivation, and time dilation/compression.

For Unamuno nonetheless all great works, irrespective of genre, were in one sense novels: '[...] la *Ética* de Spinoza, o la *Crítica de la razón práctica* de Kant, [...] dos obras imperecederas, son lo que son por haber brotado del corazón de sus autores, no de la cabeza' (VIII, 927). But the fact that Unamuno read philosophical treatises as works of the imagination, hence as autobiographies, does not mean, as Julián Marías seems to imply, that he approached such endeavours irrationally, or even non-rationally. It simply means that Unamuno held that mankind, including its best thinkers, are not simply driven by reason alone. And not just Unamuno. 'We also have to recognize', writes one of the most distinguished philosophers of our own day, 'that philosophical ideas are acutely sensitive to individual temperament, and to wishes. Where the evidence and the arguments are too meager to determine a result, the slack tends to be taken up by other factors. The personal flavour and motivation of each great philosopher's version of reality is unmistakable, and the same is true of many lesser efforts' (Nagel, 1986: 10). Though more soberly expressed, this comment is pretty much an exact parallel to Unamuno's declarations about philosophers in *Del sentimiento trágico de la vida* and elsewhere.

---

[1]   Which is not to say that Unamuno was an irrational mastodon. For an articulate defence against accusations of irrationality see his essay 'Sobre la consecuencia, la sinceridad' (VIII, 937–54). It is worth remembering too that human rationality is a modern invention dating from the seventeenth century (Descartes, Locke). For ancient philosophers reason was embedded in the cosmic order, not in man. As a classicist, Unamuno was fully familiar with the Platonic world view in which reason exists outside of man, and it is man who has to be brought to reason. In the modern world by contrast (notably so in Kant) reason is seen as a tool of the human mind which, as far as it goes, enables us to make sense of the cosmos.

It remains true of course that Unamuno read virtually all the great philosophers for their ideas and was to a substantial degree influenced by several of them. Early in his career he even saw himself as a philosopher in the making. But an attempt to write a philosophical treatise while still in his twenties and under the influence of Positivism, the 'Filosofía lógica', the draft of which survives in the Casa-Museo Unamuno, remained unfinished, unpublished, and forgotten. Not only was Unamuno too restless a mind to devote himself patiently to logical systematization, but he appears to have become too concerned with arresting the decline of the spiritual dimension of man in an increasingly secular age — a decline which he blamed on the inquisitorial dogmatism of the Catholic Church, its defence of indefensible doctrines[2] — to provide reasoned arguments in the tradition of analytic philosophy. Ortega y Gasset referred to him, unsurprisingly, as an 'energúmeno' for having denounced the new Spanish Europeanists as half-wits. *Del sentimiento trágico de la vida* is a quasi-philosophical and quasi-confessional exploration of his own incapacity to reconcile logical reason and longing for survival which ends in aporia or 'tragic sentiment', the recognition of a frustrating inability to resolve a personal conflict which he generalizes to mankind and which in the end is all that remains, a conflict which he raises to the status of a creative spur. In this, Unamuno was certainly more of a poet than a philosopher in the more traditional sense.[3] At the same time we should be prepared to recognize that there are certain driving ideas in his work which survive the many contradictions and inconsistencies to be found and which recur in a variety of guises with great frequency. Here I shall be concerned with exploring certain of those ideas as they inform his works of fiction, and indeed as they are re-shaped by them.

Unamuno has sometimes been criticized as a fabricator of contradictions or paradoxes, especially in the way he makes his fictional characters behave. The criticism is correct but uncomprehending. Unamuno uses characters to explore what are predominantly philosophical concerns. Indeed what the novel as medium allows Unamuno to do with a freedom that would be out of place in a philosophical treatise is to put forward paradoxical positions as peculiarly distinctive of the human situation. Nowhere is this more obvious than in his final novel, *San Manuel Bueno, mártir*, where all three co-protagonists uphold positions that are inherently contradictory yet deeply human. These paradoxical positions in which Unamuno invariably immerses his characters can be found from the start of his novelistic output, even if they tend to gain in complexity. We observe them in Ignacio Iturriondo's discomfiture as his bellicose enthusiasm for the Carlist besiegers of Bilbao enters into conflict with his love of the besieged city; in Pachico Zabalbide's

---

[2]   'La teología mata la fe', he writes in the unpublished 'Carta a Juan Solís' probably written in 1890 (Casa-Museo Unamuno, Caja N° 104/72).

[3]   Pedro Cerezo Galán comments on *Del sentimiento trágico de la vida* that 'se trata de una obra de inspiración básicamente poética' (Cerezo Galán, 1996: 375). It remains, nevertheless, the major source of Unamuno's guiding ideas. For a discussion of the poetic versus the logical approach in Unamuno see Cirilo Flórez Miguel, 1986. The debate over whether Unamuno's novels should be treated as philosophy is well illustrated by Francisco Martín, 2005 and José Luis Mora García, 2009.

contradictory pronouncements born of the unresolved clash between a mystical inclination and a persuasion to rationalism; in Don Avito Carrascal's antagonistic cerebral and instinctive compulsions; in Augusto Pérez's utterly ambivalent stance on self-determination; in Alejandro Gómez's expression of love through inexpressive silence; in Joaquín Monegro's violently oscillating disposition towards Abel; in Julio Macedo's self-affirmation through self-rejection; in Gertrudis's agitated interrogation of her motherly vocation; and in the unnamed letter-writer's double-edged fascination with his chess partner. All of these character-situations reveal a *sic-et-non* engagement with the business of living, as if the contract demanded a persistent re-negotiation. It is not so much that the characters themselves are disconcerting as that Unamuno uses them to explore what to him seems disconcerting about the human situation: the aspiration for certainty of knowledge where no prospect of such an attainment can be contemplated. What Unamuno wants to share with his readers is his perplexity in the face of a being whose longing to understand outweighs by far his capacity to explain. The author's explorations are the characters' predicaments, philosophy and fiction rolled into one.

There is in principle nothing to prevent art and philosophy from being profitably interwoven, and of course European existentialism has accustomed us to this phenomenon (we need only think of literary works by Jean-Paul Sartre or Gabriel Marcel), despite the reticence of colleagues working in university departments of philosophy; to which we might add such names as Nietzsche, Bergson, or the Wittgenstein of the *Philosophical Investigations* who are still regarded as philosophers even though their methods are scarcely those of mainstream philosophy. Unamuno was emphatically not a philosopher in the traditional sense of the word; nor did he wish to be. But perhaps he was a philosopher in a sense that has less to do with the discipline that is practised in university departments of philosophy and more to do with the mythic style of exploring and communicating ideas through the medium of imagined worlds, as was the case with much Greek tragedy, with which Unamuno was very familiar.[4] Unamuno's literary works are built around abstract themes, and his characters are perennially engaged in Socratic dialogues. But they face what are for them very real dilemmas. It is precisely this hybridity, the philosophical approach to literature or the literary approach to philosophy, to adopt a favourite trope of his, that lends his work that fascination or challenge which it still radiates after seven or eight decades of intense scrutiny. Whether Unamuno wrote novels to explore philosophical issues or whether he simply used such issues as the basis for imaginative works of literature is a moot point. What is important is the way in which ideas are conveyed, less through logical exposition and more through metaphorical exploration. We have already seen that the theme of identity, of the self and its awareness, which has of course been of major interest

---

[4] Martha Nussbaum has comprehensively shown that Greek epic poets and dramatists were regarded as thinkers and teachers dealing in their works with important ethical issues. Plato, who adopted a different method, looked upon them as serious rivals precisely because they dealt with the same topics that he himself dealt with in a more 'philosophical' way. If there is a difference, it is in the role accorded to the emotions in confronting ethical issues, much more marked in Greek tragedy than in Greek philosophy, as indeed is also the case in Unamuno. See Nussbaum, 2001: 12–18 and *passim*.

to philosophers, is at the very heart of Unamuno's interests as a creator of fictions. In what follows I shall look at Unamuno's fictional treatment of three other topics that have also aroused the interest of philosophers.

Freedom

It is well known that Unamuno's early thought, up to and including *En torno al casticismo* (1895) was heavily influenced by positive science, especially the writings of Herbert Spencer and Hippolyte Taine. It is equally clear that by about 1900 he had reacted strongly against this and from then on was to regret his earlier positivistic outlook and violently denounce Spencer and especially Taine as dangerous falsifiers. Nevertheless the deterministic ways of thinking that characterize Positivism left their mark on Unamuno, for not only does he return to the topic of freedom-versus-determinism philosophically or discursively, but he also transforms it into novelistic material in unexpected ways. Indeed the whole question of determined behaviour becomes one of the fundamental driving forces of his novelistic art, present in both the plot and the discourse beyond the plot.

Writing of himself in the third person — or of a former self or even an imagined self — Unamuno said in 1904:

> Antaño, largo tiempo ha, había sido un decidido determinista, ni siquiera toleraba que se le hablase del libre albedrío: tan irracional le parecía este supuesto. Pero luego, estudiando más el asunto, habíasele quebrantado aquella cerrada fe determinista; y ahora, cuando le encontramos arrellanado en el sillón de su celda, ante su manifiesto, ha echado la cuestión de determinismo o libre albedrío a la cilla de la metafísica, adonde raras veces baja. Ya no cree que la ciencia ha llegado a poner en claro tal cuestión, sino que se enreda siempre en una petición de principio. Mas lo que sí siente, lo siente más que lo piensa, es que por muy libre que uno sea dentro de sí, en cuanto tiene que exteriorizarse, manifestarse, hablar u obrar, comunicar con los prójimos, en cuanto tiene que servirse de su cuerpo o de otros cuerpos, queda atado a las rígidas leyes de ellos, es esclavo. Mis actos — piensa — no son nunca exclusivamente míos: si hablo, he de disponer de un aire que no es mío para que mi voz se produzca; y ni aun mis cuerdas vocales son en rigor mías, ni es mío el lenguaje de que he de valerme si quiero que me entiendan, y lo mismo me ocurre si escribo, si pego, si beso, si me bato. Y agrega: «Es que yo mismo ¿soy mío?» Y le vuelve zumbando la obsesión atormentadora. (VIII, 610)

From being an uncompromising determinist a long time before, this alter ego has since confined the whole question of determinism and free will to the store-room of metaphysics, we are told; all attempts at unravelling the issue scientifically get snarled up in a question-begging tangle. All he has left is the feeling that one's inner sense of freedom is no guarantee of freedom when it comes to action and expression. Unamuno here places the question of determinism in an ontological context, and more particularly in the context of self-expression. When we express ourselves in whatever way we choose, we may think we are making use of our freedom, but this inner sense of freedom could be deceptive, and the constraints that our actions face should make us think again. While self-expression can of course take a variety of forms, as Unamuno indicates, it is applicable in an immediate and forceful way to someone who makes a living through speaking and writing. The two basic questions that Unamuno often raised, the '¿por qué?' and the '¿para qué?', the causal and the purposive, acquire interesting applications when they are raised in the context of not just writing but the writing of fiction, of imagined worlds.

The Free Will-versus-Determinism debate is one of the most long-lived in philosophy and continues unresolved. The question of whether human beings enjoy freedom of action and of thought or whether we are part of a determinist system governed either by God or by natural laws has proved to be the most polemical among philosophers and religious thinkers since the Middle Ages. In Spain it provoked a state of civil war between Dominicans and Jesuits in the sixteenth and seventeenth centuries which only the intervention of Rome prevented from turning into a schism within the Spanish Church. In the nineteenth century Schopenhauer produced a prize essay on the topic, while in our own time the debate between Compatibilists and Incompatibilists, and the various ingenious gradations in between, has continued unabated. As a philosopher, Unamuno has not contributed to this debate in the manner of, say, a Sartre, but in his creative writing he has explored its possibilities to the full. Two novels in particular stand out, *Niebla* and *Abel Sánchez*.

The expression 'libre albedrío' appears in the opening paragraph of *Niebla*, when Víctor Goti says in his prologue that he is lacking in this attribute, adding that he believes Don Miguel is in the same position. From this moment onwards the novel becomes a mischievous game based on the dichotomy freedom/determinism, but a game which is well informed on the basics of the debate.[5] When the M. de U. of the post-prologue — we may call him Unamuno although he is more properly a literary puppet — questions the veracity of Goti's interpretation of Augusto's death, what this M. de U.'s argument comes down to is that if Augusto Pérez possessed free will, then he, M. de U., does not possess it, and if he, M. de U., does possess it, then Augusto Pérez does not. This M. de U. who speaks in the first person and who will later call himself 'el Dios de estos dos diablos nivolescos' (I, 624), thus enters into a totally paradoxical relationship with his creatures, a relationship with quasi-theological overtones. The intra-novelistic Unamuno denies that his creatures enjoy free will; they only speak for him, and he it is who decides for them. Yet what they are saying is that the one who does not enjoy free will is Unamuno, who has no power to decide for them. This obvious paradox brings to mind the position adopted by Jean-Paul Sartre to justify his atheism. Sartre, a stout

---

[5] In a pioneering essay which was to prove enormously influential, Geoffrey Ribbans placed the critical moment of the debate within the novel at the point of Unamuno's intervention in Chapter xxv: 'En adelante la obra será, no ya implícita sino manifiestamente, una discusión, en forma novelada, del problema de si el hombre goza de libertad o está predeterminado en su más mínimo movimiento' (Ribbans, 1971: 132). For my part, I believe the entire novel is, from the very beginning, an exploration of the dichotomy freedom/determinism. The intervention of the author at the end of Chapter xxv seems to be a comic or parodic version of the cosmological argument for the existence of God that Kant, in the *Critique of Pure Reason*, explains in A605/B633 and refutes in A613/B641 to A616/B644. This is the argument of the existence of God derived from the existence of his creatures.

defender of human freedom of action (man is condemned to be free, as he claimed in a masterly oxymoron), rejected the idea of God not because of a lack of proofs but because he found it incompatible with the idea of freedom in man. If, as he claimed, existence precedes essence, there can be no essence derived from God. For Sartre and existentialists in general to be human is to be free. The existence of God obviously implies a potential circumscription of the limitless freedom of a Sartrean being. But this much-vaunted freedom has the discomforting consequence of becoming pure contingency, something quite random and accidental, as can be observed in a well-known passage from *La Nausée*:

> The essential thing is contingency. What I mean is that, by definition, existence is not necessity. To exist is simply to *be there*. Those who exist appear, *are encountered*, but their existence could never be deduced. There are some people, I think, who have understood that; but they have tried to overcome this contingency by inventing a necessary being as their cause. No necessary being, however, can explain existence: contingency is not a mask, an appearance that can be dissipated; it is something that is absolute, and therefore perfectly gratuitous. Everything is gratuitous, those gardens, this town and I myself. (Sartre, 1938: 185)

This idea of human existence as pure contingency is also found in *Niebla*, especially in Chapters ii to vi, in which the word 'azar' is repeatedly employed, and not simply the word but the event as well, as in the case of the fall from the balcony of Doña Ermelinda's caged canary, which is a 'feliz accidente' according to Augusto Pérez but which Unamuno sardonically labels a 'canario providencial', providential, one assumes, in the sense that it is an unexpected event which the deity allows in order to give us the opportunity to react according to our own volition, which is precisely the position adopted by the scholastic tradition following the Christianization of Aristotle by St Thomas Aquinas. There is a moment when Unamuno seems to anticipate Sartre's philosophy: 'Dime Orfeo,' Augusto asks his wise but mute companion, '¿qué necesidad hay de que haya Dios ni mundo ni nada? ¿Por qué ha de haber algo? ¿No te parece que esa idea de la necesidad no es sino la forma suprema que el azar toma en nuestra mente?' (I, 516).[6] The difference between Sartre and Unamuno is that whereas Sartre is defending a particular thesis, Unamuno is simply exploring — in the particular case of *Niebla* in rather burlesque tone — various facets of human freedom, or the lack of it.

The influence of Kierkegaard in the fashioning of *Niebla*, and especially of *Either/Or*, has often been posited and is to a degree credible.[7] Freedom of choice

---

[6]   This is a repetition of what Unamuno had said in one of his key articles, '¡Plenitud de plenitudes y todo plenitud!' written in 1904 (VIII, 664). In that article he had said that absolute contingency (such as Roquentin is exemplifying in *La Nausée*) can only lead to absurdity and vertigo, what Sartre was to label nausea. The question 'Why is there something rather than nothing?' was made famous by Heidegger but can be traced back at least to Leibniz and is also formulated by Schopenhauer in *The World as Will and Representation* (1996: II, 579), where both Heidegger and Unamuno probably came across it.

[7]   See for example Ruth House Webber, 1964; Gemma Roberts, 1986; Jan E. Evans, 2005: 65–85; J. A. G. Ardila, 2008. It should be added by way of caution, however, that in the 1932–33 prologue to *San Manuel Bueno, mártir y tres historias más* Unamuno declared that he had left *Enter/Eller*

is certainly an ever-present theme in the work of the Danish thinker, but not so much its existence — which does not seem to bother Kierkegaard to the same extent that it has other thinkers — as its theological and moral consequences. For the young man in *Either/Or* what is daunting is choice, for it appears groundless, unexplainable. How to choose between endless possibilities becomes arbitrary and destabilizing, since there appears to be no justification for choosing one option rather than another. There is certainly something of this in *Niebla*, but not in any truly theological or moral sense, and the much-vaunted influence of *Either/Or* is far from clear. The issue becomes clearer if we bring to bear some of Kierkegaard's other works. In *The Sickness unto Death*, which places modern man between the two poles of freedom and necessity, not knowing where to find the limits of what one *has* to do and what one *can* do, the individual either feels compelled to take a particular course of action, or finds himself adrift and rudderless; in other words, we either lack possibility or we lack anchorage. In both cases self-grounding is denied us and the self breaks down. For Kierkegaard this raises deeply problematical issues of a moral kind, issues which he had already raised in *Fear and Trembling* in a recognizably theological setting. In his *The Concept of Anxiety* Kierkegaard also sees freedom of the will as necessary for the theological concepts of sin and guilt. There is no difference between good and evil in the abstract; such a difference exists only for freedom and in freedom, he writes. What concerns Kierkegaard — and this is altogether obvious in *The Concept of Anxiety* — is the nature of sin and the consequent issue of predestination. Unamuno does not appear to share any such preoccupation. We can consider for example the following declaration on determinism: 'El determinismo es una explicación metafísica que no vale ni más ni menos que la explicación opuesta, también metafísica, del libre albedrío. Más aún; suponiéndonos perfectos deterministas, hemos de declarar que por determinados que estén los actos de un hombre real, individual y concreto, son para nosotros los demás hombres indeterminables de antemano'.[8] Unamuno steers well clear of the good/evil dichotomy that worries Kierkegaard. For him the question boils down to whether we can know, or feel, ourselves to be free to choose.

What is left of course is uncertainty, an uncertainty that in *Niebla* is perfectly well reflected through the musings and antics of Augusto Pérez. For example, on two occasions we observe Augusto following a young woman without apparently having taken a decision to so do. There is no self-agency here, what philosophers call origination. Augusto, who wishes to carry out an experiment with women, ends up by being an object of their experiment. Naturally the experiment is that of Unamuno — the Unamuno of flesh and blood — with the novel genre, hence with his personage. Who leads whom? Does the author lead the personage or does the personage lead the author? Augusto and the intranovelistic Unamuno engage in an unlikely discussion about this, but the topic does have its serious or philosophical side. There are moments when Augusto sees himself as governed by a fate outside

---

unfinished and had only very recently resumed reading it. We do know from his correspondence that he began reading Kierkegaard in 1904 and was reading him again in 1908–09, but we do not know how far he got. See Unamuno, 1965: 302, and Unamuno, 1996: 316 and 330.

[8]   *Obras Completas* (Escelicer), 846–47.

his control, and regards the events in his life as predetermined. Yet he also thinks he has taken a decisive step: 'Los vientos de la fortuna nos empujan y nuestros pasos son decisivos todos' (I, 516), he declares to Orfeo, in another version of the popular Golden Age saying 'las estrellas obligan pero no fuerzan'. But this halfway house is not a comfortable one. Augusto vacillates, sometimes leaning towards belief in freedom because his situation demands a decision, sometimes retreating into a helpless determinism. As the narrator reminds us, Augusto becomes a human version of Buridan's ass, halfway between Eugenia and Rosario, unable to decide between one and the other, until one of them takes the decision for him, first in hitching, then in ditching him. But Augusto's real problem is not women but will: he does not appear to know whether he has any to exercise. For Buridan's ass either choice would have been arbitrary, but a choice is better than no choice. Here we are, philosophically speaking, at the core of the problem: that of knowing for certain whether our will is truly ours to exercise, rather than predetermined or simply random. Unamuno gives no clear answer, since the story of Augusto is a playful dissertation on the theme; but what he seems to be suggesting is that we do indeed enjoy free will so long as we do not think about it. We behave as if our acts were free, but as soon as our deliberations begin doubts supervene and we find ourselves lost. That in essence is Augusto's quandary. But what is perhaps most original about Unamuno's treatment of the theme is that he places what we call freedom in three distinct test-tubes and sets them on the boil: the test-tube of the passions, the test-tube of character or temperament, and the test-tube of literary composition. (One might even add the test-tube of religious belief, which according to Augusto is an inherited sentiment, as is the case of the former atheist and now believer Don Avito Carrascal). Let us consider these three aspects or contexts of free will.

The role of the passions in the Free Will debate is, as one might suppose, controversial. Do passions override our freedom of the will, or does freedom of the will enable us to indulge our passions? Clearly when other people hurt us (as happens to Augusto) we hold them responsible if they are in possession of their faculties. Do we apply the same criterion to ourselves when, led by our passions and inclinations, we hurt others? Once again Unamuno seems aware of this crucial question, but refrains from answering it. Augusto is prepared to break into the relationship of Eugenia with her *novio* but resents their action in breaking into his own relationship with Eugenia. His evaluation of his own actions is positive, but on the other hand he sees himself as victim of others' hostile actions. The question here is of course motivation.[9] What characterizes human agency is our ability to evaluate our motivation, to recognize the forces acting upon us and ascribe intention in the light of those forces. Unamuno appears to suggest in *Niebla* that the level of recognition varies according to the person. The picturesque Don Fermín, uncle of Eugenia and a determinist-anarchist, who somehow manages to believe both in freedom of action and in the deterministic laws that govern the destinies of men, persuades Augusto that knowledge is a physiological matter, not a psychological

---

[9] For a classic statement on how our emotions affect the Free Will debate see P. F. Strawson, 2003: 72–93.

one. 'Dime Orfeo', Augusto tells his dog, '¿cómo podéis conocer si no pecáis, si vuestro conocimiento no es pecado? El conocimiento que no es pecado no es tal conocimiento, no es racional' (I, 525).[10]

The idea of a purely physiological, non-reflective, existence is applied by Augusto to Rosarito after his frustrated attempt at 'conocimiento penetrante', as Don Fermín calls it: '¡Pobrecita! Pero... ¡con qué ingenuidad se dejaba hacer! Es un ser fisiológico, perfectamente fisiológico, nada más que fisiológico, sin psicología alguna' (I, 619). The implication of course is that Rosarito has no free will because she is ruled purely by physiological impulses. But to make of Rosarito a non-reflective creature, with no freedom of decision because she is ruled by passions, is a monumental error on the part of Augusto. Unamuno has indicated as much when he unveils Rosarito's thoughts after the sofa experience with Augusto: 'Cualquier día vuelvo yo a darme un rato así a beneficio de la otra prójima' (I, 619). This is sheer calculation, not that physiological, unthinking determinism that Augusto associates with the passions and which he fears. To achieve the sense of identity he craves for he needs to establish a relationship, but he does so intellectually, 'de cabeza sólo', as Víctor Goti explains to him, and not through the mediation of the passions, because this would imply a lack of agency. Here we reach the kernel of the debate, of whether the passions mark a lack of volition. There is no doubt that Eugenia is led by her passions in giving herself to the unscrupulous and cynical Mauricio; but she does so in a fully reflective and calculated manner. In that case, do the passions constrict our volition or, on the contrary, do they impel us to employ it in order to attain our desire? Indeed, is our volition a free act? I know of no philosopher who has been able to give a clear and definitive answer to this question, and of course Unamuno does not do so.[11] What is at any rate clear is that if for Buridan's ass any decision was arbitrary, that does not justify abstention. The decision, whatever it is, has to be taken; the justification will follow.

The second test-tube for freedom is that of character or temperament, an issue often raised by Unamuno and which revolves around the role played by inherited genes and family circumstances. Augusto is highly conscious of the influence of his mother, recently deceased, and what he seeks in looking for a wife is to recover his mother. In a novel such as *Niebla* in which the physical environment hardly counts, the importance which Unamuno gives to Augusto's life at his mother's side is conspicuous (especially obvious in Chapter v). This previous life under his mother's wing is the source of Augusto's present struggle in adapting to life without her. She had taken his decisions for him: 'si viviera mi madre, encontraría solución a esto' he tells himself (I, 509). We might here recall the hendecasyllabic verses that Augusto carries around in his wallet:

[10] 'Pecar' has of course been traditionally associated in the popular mind with the sexual act. Cf. Valle-Inclán: 'entramos, pecamos, y nos caminamos', as Séptimo Miau says to Mari-Gaila in *Divinas palabras* (Valle-Inclán, 1996: 75).
[11] Modern sociobiologists on the other hand do not hesitate to make pronouncements on the issue. They are convinced that all our decisions, including those that one would consider altruistic, are subject to biological motivations. What they do not explain is the biological motive behind their explanations.

> De la cuna nos viene la tristeza
> Y también de la cuna la alegría...

to which Unamuno adds through his personage: 'El hombre no hace sino buscar en los sucesos, en las vicisitudes de la suerte, alimento para su tristeza o alegría nativas. Un mismo caso es triste o alegre según nuestra disposición innata' (I, 491). Our temperament is something we carry around with us in our genes. There is here a deterministic orientation, but it is precisely at this juncture that Augusto's problem and consequent suffering are located: in his apparently inherent incapacity to take vital decisions, because, paradoxically, he fears becoming what he already is. He peers into the abyss of freedom and on feeling vertigo pulls back, a basic theme of European existentialism as it was soon to be propounded by Heidegger and Sartre, and in which anxiety is intimately bound to freedom of action. It is our sense of free agency that deprives us of security. If we are free to take any action and so are our fellow men, the world becomes an unpredictable, even threatening, place. That is the reality that Augusto does not wish to admit. He himself recognizes on more than one occasion that his character lies paradoxically in not having it. When circumstances call for a decision, he takes refuge in non-action. Even his way of justifying his own suicide is deterministic, not based on free choice: 'tengo mi carácter, mi modo de ser, mi lógica interior, y esta lógica me pide que me suicide' (I, 652). Determinism here becomes pure escapism, that is to say a way of evading a morbid self-depreciation. Augusto fails in his experiment with women, emerges snubbed and humiliated, sees himself as victim of a fate outside his control, and concludes that his predetermined path dictates his suicide. Interestingly, when he meets his creator he discovers, too late, that he has condemned himself by his own judgement.

It is clear that in transferring the debate over predestination onto a literary situation — I mean the situation of a novelist and his creatures, the third test tube — Unamuno can carry out, or simulate, experiments that cannot be carried out outside the pages of a book. Unamuno nevertheless insists, both in *Niebla* and in *Cómo se hace una novela*, in equating novel and life; in *Niebla* through Augusto, who, after hearing Víctor Goti's explanations about his novel, asks himself whether his own life might not be a *nivola*; and in *Cómo se hace una novela* through the narrator himself. The novel that Víctor Goti is in the process of writing, as he describes it, is not a predetermined artefact; but nor does it appear to be the product of the author's freedom of choice. It is pure contingency, written 'como se vive, sin saber lo que vendrá' (I, 571), or as Unamuno had said years previously, 'a lo que salga'. But we must be clear that this is what Unamuno had said before and not what the Unamuno who is writing *Niebla* is saying now. Indeed what this Unamuno, at any rate the intranovelistic Unamuno, is saying is rather different. 'Lo tengo ya escrito y es irrevocable' (I, 655), this Unamuno, sitting in his Salamanca office, says to Augusto Pérez. What this Unamuno means is that it is irrevocable for the entity called Augusto Pérez. But is it irrevocable for the entity called Miguel de Unamuno? For it is one thing to transplant the debate to the level of a fictional plot, that is, the debate over whether an author acts upon the characters thus depriving them of free will or whether the characters force the author to follow a particular pattern according to the demands of their make-up; and it is quite another thing to see the phenomenon from a perspective that is not merely authorial but genuinely existential, outside the limits of a novelistic invention with its plot, its personages and a sardonic novelist into the bargain. In the end, *Niebla* seems to turn into an exploration of the limits of our own freedom, but it is a simulacrum. We do not know who gets his own way, whether it is the Víctor Goti of the prologue or the M. de U. of the post-prologue, or indeed whether they are both wrong. But the real question can only be addressed to the real Miguel de Unamuno controlling the figures of Augusto Pérez, Víctor Goti and M. de U. Who or what was controlling the decisions of this Unamuno who was apparently deciding what these various characters said and did? That is the literary dilemma that the work presents: is the author of an imaginative work in full control of his invention? And if we treat the question allegorically, that is, as reflecting the position of God vis-à-vis his creation, Unamuno's treatment of the problem is even more suggestive. For if, according to the thesis first of Goti and then of Augusto, a novelist is not constrained by having to account for every detail of his creation, when transferred to the theological plane this must mean that neither does God have to account for every detail of the world He has created. In other words there are aspects of creation that are undetermined. If nothing else, this is an ingenious way of settling the never-ending debate over determinism. Let us recapitulate.

What does the story of Augusto Pérez tell us, philosophically speaking? The story revolves around Augusto's attempts to forge a character for himself as he emerges from the mists of non-existence. We need to bear in mind that this idea of making ourselves according to the decisions that we choose to take occupies a central role in existentialism and especially in Sartre. This is Sartre's famous 'existence precedes essence' according to which our essence (what we are or become) is brought about by our existence (what we choose to do). A human being is thus a life-project, as Unamuno maintained. The idea can be found much earlier in Western philosophy, notably so in Kant and Schopenhauer. It is equivalent to believing in the capacity for self-creation, according to which the character of a human being is in large measure his own work because he has the capacity of origination even in a universe governed by physical laws. In the first place, each one of us is the result of a biological inheritance and of early experiences when we are in the process of formation, as is the case of Augusto, a child overly protected by his widowed mother and who never learnt to take his own decisions, something Unamuno leaves very clear. How then will Augusto, now motherless, who appears at the door of his house as if newly-born to the world, go about his own self-formation? Now the possibility of fashioning or re-fashioning our character and personality depends to a degree, perhaps to a high degree, on what we find ourselves to be. We develop our personalities as we face and resolve the situations which require a response and which are a basic aspect of our lives. The need to make a choice or take a decision is what gives us our sense of being. Hence our intuitive conviction that we are responsible for what we do, that we are not simply the effect of causes which we do not control but that we are the causes of effects, originators in the philosophical significance of the term. If we identify ourselves with our actions — we should here recall that Augusto tells Víctor Goti that he needs to do something but does not know what — we are thereby identifying ourselves with our character, our being. And if we have an impulse that we do not wish to recognize as truly ours — for example the sudden sexual impulse which so concerns Augusto — that impulse that seems alien will be so in relation to the rest of our character. The implication is that the moral responsibility for what we do or fail to do (which is the case of Augusto with Rosarito) is intimately connected to what we are and to the responsibility for being the way we are. For if we do what we do because we are what we are, the responsibility for what we are is, from the point of view of character, ours and ours alone. And contrariwise, if the responsibility for what we are does not rest with us, then we cannot be held responsible for what we do. It is within these two extremes that the problem of freedom of action is situated. Augusto Pérez sets out to become a full being, to acquire a character and personality, and to that end he must face choices and take decisions, in other words he must act. But he does not know how to act because he does not know what he is.

Here we come up against the bothersome problem of regression. In order to assume responsibility for the way we are we need to have a previous nature that will allow us to make ourselves in a free and intentional manner. Where is this previous nature that confers those attributes, that enables us to take over our self-creation? And if in the last instance we cannot be responsible for what we are (that is, for our character, our personality, our motivations), can we be responsible for what we do? For the latter we would need to have a self or being that is independent of the characterological and motivational structures that make us what we are, a self with its own powers of decision, a self that would be, like God, *causa sui*, a necessary but unconditioned being. When Augusto Pérez addresses Unamuno in desperation with his cry of 'quiero vivir, vivir, y ser yo, yo, yo' (I, 654), Unamuno replies that it cannot be because there is no such thing. Who is right, Augusto or Unamuno? In general critics have seen this confrontation as offering an alternative choice: either we are free or we are predetermined. But the fundamental question posed by Unamuno seems a somewhat different one: if I am free to do what I want, am I also free to want what I do? Freedom and determinism may be incompatible, but volition and determinism are not. It is here that Augusto and the Salamanca professor do not agree. The former insists on exercising his volition, the latter insists on the lack of freedom of action on the part of the personage. They could both be right. Philosophically, there is no reason why we must see the question as a Kierkegaardian *Either/Or*. Indeed the position seemingly adopted by Unamuno is much closer to that of Kant. Kant held that freedom and determinism are to an extent compatible. In the third antinomy of the *Critique of Pure Reason* he affirms that both the thesis and the antithesis are true, that the determinist laws of nature do not conflict with our sense of acting undeterminedly (A542–558/B570–586). What is applicable in the realm of phenomena is not applicable in the realm of noumena. In the former the actions of a human being are empirically determined, but in the latter the actions are purely the result of an unconditioned choice of the human entity as a being-in-itself, of the intellect, or, what comes down to the same thing, of the innate capacity for self-determination. What Kant said, then, was simply that the existence of freedom of the will is something we take for granted but is not logically demonstrable, but nor is its non-existence demonstrable. Human freedom is mysterious, but Kant leaves open the possibility of its existence.[12] Unamuno seems to be adopting much the same posture towards the problem. Our conviction that we possess freedom of the will and that we are responsible for our actions and decisions is strongly intuitive, but rationally unprovable. Unamuno repeated the idea in an engaging little poem from the *Cancionero espiritual en la frontera del destierro* (1928):

> ¿Libre albedrío?
> Es como el río
> que se hace el cauce
> y el pie del sauce
> llega a besar;
> en el remanso
> no halla descanso;
> cuanto más fluye
> más se concluye;
> para en la mar. (V, 271)

Our sense of freedom of action, of our capacity to enact our own volition, is like the river that makes its own course. Once begun, the process becomes self-sustaining, inevitable even, until it reaches its natural end. Nothing tells us whether the course exists without the river.

The Free Will problem reappears in *Abel Sánchez* and does so squarely in the challenging context of human motivation. Here the debate centres around Joaquín Monegro's capacity or incapacity to change his psychological make-up. The character does indeed try to conquer his propensity to envy and hatred, and does so in two quite distinct and even contradictory ways. One is to try to fight his inclination, to assert himself via positive acts of generosity or self-sacrifice. The problem is that these actions do not appear to alter his personality, or at least to alter his perception of himself. The other way is to accept his personality as a given but to raise it to the status of a tragic role, to fulfil a destiny consciously and heroically, to be a Byronic Cain. In either case Joaquín is undermined by his own uncertainty about himself. It is here that once again we see the freedom and identity debates intersecting. Total freedom, freedom without any determining constraints, implies randomness, and is obviously incompatible with a definable personality. But a perfectly-defined personality implies no power of origination, effectively no free will. Unamuno places Joaquín in the maelstrom of the debate but does it in terms of personal ontology. The question facing Joaquín is not so much whether he has the capacity to act in an undetermined way — as Sartre contends that humans have — as whether he has the capacity to change what *he already is* through his actions. At a certain point he comes to believe that he does not. His response to Father Echevarría's encouragement to transform his hatred of others into a caring concern is stark:

---

[12] This applies to the *Critique of Pure Reason*. In the *Critique of Practical Reason* Kant insisted rather more forcefully on man's freedom of action, for without that freedom the categorical imperative would make little sense.

> — Pero debe cambiarlo [el odio] en noble emulación, en deseo de hacer en
> su profesión y sirviendo a Dios, lo mejor que pueda...
> — No puedo, no puedo, no puedo trabajar. Su gloria no me deja.
> — Hay que hacer un esfuerzo..., para eso el hombre es libre...
> — No creo en el libre albedrío, padre. Soy médico. (I, 727)

As a man of science, then, Joaquín does not believe in his own free will. What he is doing is applying naturalist causation to himself as agent. If events in the natural world are subject to the laws of causation which predetermine outcomes through a cause-and-effect connection, it would appear that human beings, as part of that natural world, are equally subject to those laws. Our genes and our circumstances make us what we are, and what we are, physically, emotionally, intellectually, governs what we do. Choices may exist, but they are fixed by heredity and environment. This is the classical position in which freedom of action and causal determinism are seen to be incompatible.

Unamuno of course does not leave things there. He shows Joaquín being motivated to take decisions, and moreover taking decisions which at times appear to cancel each other out. Above all Joaquín's sense of grievance, that is to say his obsession with the past, does not prevent him from planning for the future, which indicates a belief that the future is not fixed, that we can influence it, and that consequently naturalistic determinism leaves room for human agency based not merely on desires but also on unforced will. The very fact that Joaquín can and does act in opposite directions suggests that Unamuno is distinguishing between actions taken through the agency of our desires — voluntary but not free — and actions taken through the exercise of free will. Joaquín's sense of helplessness at one point leads him to deny freedom of the will, but only because he associates his consuming hatred, which he would like to exorcize, with a pre-existing cause: 'Y vi que aquel odio inmortal era mi alma. Ese odio pensé que debió de haber precedido a mi nacimiento y que sobreviviría a mi muerte' (I, 718). It is not simply that Joaquín is motivated by hatred but that he *is* hatred, or rather its embodiment. That is the only way in which he can explain his personality, a way which is symbolically deterministic to a very high degree.[13] Joaquín sees himself as a personification of Envy and hence of hatred for the other. But that is Joaquín's adopted position, especially his position as a man of science, in which every effect is the result of a cause or causes. It does not, however,

---

[13] Unamuno seems to be characterizing Joaquín's position in Schopenhauerian terms. According to Schopenhauer every man is what the Will has made him. His knowledge of himself is derived from the Will and not, as previously supposed, willing being derived from knowledge. According to the latter or conventional view, a man 'need only consider *how* he would best like to be, and he would be so; this is its freedom of the will. It therefore consists in man's being his own work in the light of knowledge. I, on the other hand, say that he is his own work prior to all knowledge, and knowledge is merely added to illuminate it. Therefore he cannot decide to be this or that; also he cannot become another person, but he *is* once for all, and subsequently knows *what* he is. With those other thinkers, he *wills* what he knows; with me he *knows* what he wills' (Schopenhauer, 1966: I, 293). Joaquín's view of himself fits into the Schopenhauerian paradigm perfectly, although this does not of course mean that Unamuno agrees with his position. Joaquín Monegro is an exploration of the problem of free will, not an exposition of it.

appear to be the position defended by Unamuno *qua* author; by which I mean that powerful as is Joaquín's assumed deterministic position we are allowed to glimpse alternatives that greatly enrich the debate.

First of all, Joaquín is inconsistent. He sees his attitude as causally predetermined; but he does not see others' attitudes in the same light. His resentment towards Abel and Helena arises because he considers that they behaved selfishly and inconsiderately when they could have behaved otherwise. And the same applies to Joaquín's view of Abel's relations with their grandson. Joaquín's reaction to Abel shows him as regarding Abel to be an originator of his actions. Unamuno seems to be pointing here to a common but curious phenomenon: we are prone to pleading 'force majeure' when we choose an unpopular course of action, but we are reluctant to grant the same self-justification to others. Joaquín's inconsistency undermines his deterministic stance.

Secondly, Unamuno makes Joaquín fully aware of the nature of decision-taking. He is no Buridan's ass, as is Augusto Pérez. He is capable of taking firm decisions, predetermined or otherwise, but is conscious that any choice involves not only affirmation but also renunciation. Several times during the course of the story (Abel's wedding, Abel's illness, Abel's painting) he takes a decision to act in a certain way while remaining highly conscious, even regretful, of not acting in the opposite way. This is of course a key issue in the Free Will debate. For freedom of the will implies not only that we are free to originate our decisions but also that we were free to take the opposite decision had we chosen to. If there is no alternative to taking a decision there is no free will.

Thirdly, and perhaps most importantly, causal determinism is a closed system, a way of explaining the cosmos in its entirety: it does not offer the choice of saying that one event is caused but another is not. Can this apply to human beings? Is a human being ever a closed or complete system? Augusto Pérez is very much a character in the making. Joaquín Monegro is less obviously so, but his self-questioning, self-analyses, and shifts of plan all suggest that his life-project is constantly evolving, that his personality is never complete, that it is, in other words, indeterminate. But whether this indeterminism of the person leads to self-determination is a much more problematical issue. Unamuno, like Kant before him and Sartre after him, believes in self-creation, and this pre-supposes a degree of operational freedom even within a causally determined natural world. The crucial distinction between desire-led decisions, which still allow us volition, and origination, or genuine Free Will decisions, is maintained in *Abel Sánchez* since Joaquín is clearly portrayed as perfectly capable of taking actions that do not concur with his emotional desires. The problem seems to be that these (generally altruistic) actions do not affect Joaquín's view of himself: he feels compelled not to act against his consuming self-loathing, as he himself appears to recognize at the end: 'Pude quererte, debí quererte, que habría sido mi salvación, y no te quise' (I, 791).[14] This is in a way an extraordinary declaration for it posits using freedom of the will to

---

[14] The sentiment seems straight out of Spinoza, who says that hatred can be cured by love (Spinoza, 1996: 93).

renounce that very freedom. If I opt out of a system based on freedom and choose to see my actions as causally conditioned and outside my control, am I a subscriber to a Determinist or to a Free Will system? At this juncture the distinction between freedom and determinism breaks down and the debate ends in aporia.

Joaquín's determinism, then, turns out to be far from absolute. Indeed we can see it as a position adopted in self-defence. Joaquín's problem is that, like Cain, he is obsessed by what he perceives to be others' dislike of him. This leads to a morbid and corrosive sense of self-disapproval. His deterministic stance allows him to argue that there is no alternative, that he has been predetermined to be the way he is. But Unamuno is not content to posit the deterministic thesis and leave it at that. For him the driving question was one of finality ('Pregunte más bien para qué nació', says Father Echevarría (I, 727)), and causal determinism applied to the human sphere puts paid to any search for finality; indeed the entire striving for knowledge — Joaquín aspires to be a medical researcher — becomes an illusion since we do not find things out by our efforts but are simply led by the hand of universal causation. In *Del sentimiento trágico de la vida* Unamuno does not question humanity's freedom of action, even if he does not speak of Kierkegaard's 'dizziness of freedom' or Sartre's 'nausea' and 'absurdity of freedom'. But he is not far from them either. For Unamuno freedom is an essential condition of the search for finality which is born from our sense of uncertainty. Uncertainty points to freedom, even if this freedom is a 'tragic' one. To ask what freedom is for makes no sense: if human freedom had a finality outside itself it would no longer be free. Sartre made this point too. He argued that freedom of choice cannot be justified because it is not derived from any prior reality. It serves rather as the foundation of the significations which we perceive in reality. No free choice, no significations (Sartre, 2003: 406). Total scepticism or total certainty would amount to a lack of freedom. Uncertainty on the other hand is perfectly compatible with freedom, and this freedom, although it might produce the vertigo and the anguish of which later existentialists speak, nevertheless opens the door to a redeeming feature of an existence over which initially we had no power of decision. As a Free Will proponent might say, we do not originate ourselves but we can (eventually) originate our actions. This is the lesson which the scientifically minded Joaquín, stuck in the rut of an outdated Positivism which prompts him to interpret the world and himself according to a causal order, does not understand, and he insists to himself, and to the imagined readers of his 'Confesión', that he is as he is because he was predestined to be so, like some organism programmed by Darwinian evolution, and that all he can do is to fulfil his fated role. But as Sartre and other existentialists pointed out, and as Unamuno had argued before them, our role is what we make of it. We are our own product. It is only on the character's deathbed — ironically the one circumstance in which freedom becomes irrelevant — that Unamuno allows Joaquín to accept that he was not wholly predetermined and that he could have affirmed his freedom and thereby redeemed his personality. Joaquín's final words bring him back, like some prodigal son, to his father's house, that is to say to the view that Unamuno had expressed in *Del sentimiento trágico de la vida*, the view that we are redeemed by our capacity to love: 'No te he querido. Si te hubiera querido me habría curado' (I,

790). These words of the dying Joaquín amount to a rejection of the determinism which he has sustained as justification of his misanthropy. To love is to give of oneself freely. For Unamuno, as for Gabriel Marcel after him, love of the other is what makes us not only free but deserving of eternity: 'El amor es quien nos revela lo eterno nuestro y de nuestros prójimos' (*DSTV*, X, 436). Freedom is ultimately the freedom to love or to reject, or as the existentialist closest to Unamuno put it, 'To love a being is to say: "Thou, thou shalt not die"' (Marcel, 1950: II, 153). Yet this injunction is of course possible because we die.

Finitude

Although finitude can be distinguished from death (the former is the quality of finiteness and the latter is the event that marks human finitude), when they are used with the Heideggerian sense of 'losing one's Being-in-the-world' (Heidegger, 1962: 281) the two terms are sufficiently close to be interchangeable. If death is 'the possibility of no-longer-being-able-to-be-there' (Heidegger, 1962: 294), my death is what signals my finitude, and my recognition of finitude all around me makes me anticipate my own death. Although one could establish a clinical difference, for all practical purposes my finitude is my death. But if my death is unique, death itself is not. Yet compared to subjects such as freedom, knowledge, morality, identity, language, or the arts, death as a topic worthy of systematic exploration has figured comparatively little in the work of philosophers. Interestingly, one of the few modern exceptions is Unamuno's one-time favourite philosopher, Schopenhauer, but Schopenhauer's whole discussion of death is driven by his obsession with the Will. The Will is the only dimension of us that can and must survive death, but since the Will is a universal undifferentiated force, we cannot survive as entities in any form: our intellect, that is our consciousness of world and self, must perish. What is indestructible about us is something quite other — the noumenon — of which we are but momentary manifestations. In a way Schopenhauer's view of death is an atheistic version of St Paul's apocatastasis, a return not to the godhead as fount of the universe but to the blind and timeless energy that is the essence of everything, both organic and inorganic. Unamuno found both versions unappealing, for both entailed a loss of self and a loss of what he deemed to be a necessary consciousness. The universe needs us as much as we need the universe: 'El mundo es para la conciencia' (*DSTV*, X, 284); and again: 'Si un día ha de acabarse toda conciencia personal sobre la tierra [...] y no ha de haber espíritu que se aproveche de toda nuestra ciencia acumulada, ¿para qué ésta?' (*DSTV*, X, 299). Of course, even positing the continuing presence of human consciousness does not solve the point at issue. The pressing question remains. Why should our finitude concern us personally? And what can we say about it? Death after all does not appear to form part of one's direct experience, despite affecting us all. 'The most formidable of evils, death, is nothing to us,' wrote Epicurus in his letter to Menoeceus, 'since, when we exist, death is not present to us; and when death is present, then we have no existence. It is of no concern, then, either to the class of the living or to the class of the dead; since for the one it has no existence, and the other has no existence itself' (Diogenes Laertius, 1853: X, §125). On the other hand, Socrates, far from dismissing death as irrelevant, saw it as the culmination of life. In his *Phaedo* Plato makes Socrates, on being condemned to death, inform his friends that they would be burying his body but not him. For Socrates, the most fundamental components of human existence were not material but spiritual. The common element — the body — could be destroyed; the individual element — the soul or psyche — could not. Death for Socrates was a separation, not an ending. Life was a 'learning to die', an anticipation of a purely spiritual or disembodied existence. Some twenty-three centuries later, this anticipation of death re-appeared in Heidegger's view of *Dasein* as *being-towards-death*. Heidegger and some other existentialists were concerned not so much with death itself as with what it means to live with the prospect of death. Death gives us urgency and resoluteness because the prospect of our death makes us aware of impending finitude. It also gives us our heightened sense of individuality, for no one can die another person's death.

Here we are concerned with the role that death is given in Unamuno's fiction and the broader implications of that role. In his book *Death in the Literature of Unamuno*, Mario J. Valdés offered an exhaustive account of death events in Unamuno and concluded that death is at the very heart of Unamuno's creativity because 'there is no survival as meaningful as the re-created word. In everything Unamuno writes he is sowing the seeds of his re-creation by others' (Valdés, 1966: 167).[15] In other words death is there to be survived, but the only possible survival is an aesthetic one. This of course coincides with what Unamuno said in some of his essays; but such a reading tends to overstate his self-centredness, for such a possibility of survival is open to very few. Unamuno's meditation on death via the characters of his fiction is altogether more suggestive and is not limited to the question of the author's survival. Indeed, he has in common with the existentialists that death is something to be confronted while alive, not something to be overcome in biological or literary posterity.

In his *Kant and the Problem of Metaphysics* Heidegger argues that Kant's three basic questions, what can I know?, what should I do?, and what may I hope?, are all attributable to man's finitude.[16] If we ask these questions it is because we are aware of our own temporality. Kant's attempt to place metaphysics on a sound footing was unconsciously an attempt to counter his own refutation of the ontological argument for the existence of God. Interestingly, some time before, Unamuno, in *Del sentimiento trágico de la vida*, had made a similar point about Kant, and without resorting to the linguistic abstruseness that characterizes most of Heidegger's writing. Unamuno's point is simply that Kant was asserting with one hand what he was denying with the other. He was not content to establish the limits of reason because 'era un hombre muy preocupado del problema. Quiero decir del único

---

[15] See also pages 34–36 of Valdés for an excellent exposition of the same idea.

[16] 'Not only does human reason betray its finitude by these questions, but also its innermost interest is concerned with this question. Finitude is not merely an accidental property of human reason; the finitude of human reason is finitization, i.e. "concern" about the ability to be finite. It follows that human reason is not finite only because it propounds these three questions, but on the contrary it propounds these three questions because it is finite' (Heidegger, 1962b: 224).

verdadero problema vital, del que más a las entrañas nos llega, del problema de nuestro destino individual y personal, de la inmortalidad del alma' (*DSTV*, X, 277). What could not be established by reason had therefore to be established by some other route. It is the awareness of our finitude and the concomitant recognition that we are not programmed to accept it that brings about both our moral sensibilities and our (apparently) consequential attribution of this categorical imperative to a divine source. For Unamuno, God is simply a consequence of our finitude rather than a guarantor of our immortality. Such a belief in God is not to be derided, since it appears to be inherent in man's own nature, or as Unamuno puts it, 'la razón construye sobre irracionalidades' (*DSTV*, X, 278). The essence of mankind, argues Unamuno, lies in its desire to live and to persist. This Unamuno has in common with the existentialists who were to follow shortly and for whom man was a being-in-time constantly anxious about his future. The essence of Being is to exist in an awareness of time that exposes man in a unique way to the horizon of death. Indeed it could not be otherwise, for existence implies finitude. Yet for some, notably Sartre, death is a contingent and meaningless event: 'Death is never that which gives life its meanings; it is, on the contrary, that which on principle removes all meaning from life. If we must die, then our life has no meaning because its problems receive no solution' (Sartre, 2003: 560). For others though, what would be meaningless would be a life without end, for such a life would become an endless postponement in which nothing would be worth doing at any given moment. As Gabriel Marcel wrote, 'the fact that one vanishes is constitutive of existence. In the absence of this fact I would be, *qua* being, a duration without end and would not exist' (Marcel, 2002: 241).

Seen phenomenologically, death marks the end of an individual's possibilities of action. We constantly project ourselves into the future, we act in expectation of being around later today, tomorrow, next month, next year, or whenever. One's life is a series of possibilities until death puts an end to any further possibilities. What we are looking forward to is, in the last resort, a negative, not a possibility but the lack of one. 'More primordial than man' wrote Heidegger, 'is the finitude of the Dasein in him' (Heidegger, 1962b: 237). Heidegger, who referred to death in a well-known paradox as 'the possibility of an impossibility', regarded death as an expectation rather than as a fact, since we cannot experience it when we are alive: 'Dying is not an event; it is a phenomenon to be understood existentially' (Heidegger, 1962a: 284). If to be alive is to experience, death is the cessation of experience, which implies that death cannot be experienced. This, however, is not Unamuno's point, although it was certainly Epicurus's. What Unamuno emphasizes is a foreboding, a sense of nothingness or helplessness, which becomes in turn a source of anxiety. This anxiety is the price we pay for the heightened self-awareness that consciousness of death confers, what Karl Jaspers in his *General Psychopathology* referred to as the ultimate 'limit situation', where our coping resources may begin to fail. Nor is it entirely a non-event, *pace* Heidegger. To a degree death can be experienced as a personal event through the death of a loved one, both through witnessing the occurrence and through experiencing the loss, for although death severs communication, the dead person retains an existential presence in me to the extent that I am aware of the essence of his being even after his empirical death. This is of course analogous to Unamuno's idea of living on in others and making others live on in us, which appears not just in *Del sentimiento trágico de la vida* but also and very obviously in novels such as *La tía Tula* and *San Manuel Bueno, mártir.* Even so, as Karl Jaspers concedes, awareness of my impending death must remain a source of anxiety for me.

Anxiety in the face of death is certainly portrayed in several Unamunian novels, notably so in *La novela de Don Sandalio, jugador de ajedrez.* The letter-writer, who has come to a resort to convalesce, is suffering from a heart ailment, as diagnosed by the doctor who visits him, but his illness is as much of the mind as of the body, 'más de aprensión que de enfermedad' (II, 364). The repeated use of certain symbols — dying tree, dying waves, dead leaves, house in ruins — suggests that his 'aprensión' is a fear of death. It is this apprehension that makes him contemptuous of the trivialities of everyday existence: he cannot tolerate the superficial inanities of those who 'se mueren sin darse cuenta de ello' (II, 373). His only consolation lies in watching the 'hiedra también heroica' taking the place of the death-defying tree (II, 353). Through these various symbols the letter-writer, a lonely and ailing figure, appears to anticipate the end of his life just as the autumnal season is moving inexorably towards winter. The approach of death makes him restless, unsociable, and self-centred. As we can see in his sporadic and reluctant visits to the club, he craves human fellowship yet at the same time shuns it. He experiences the existential loneliness of knowing that he has to face death on his own. He sees himself as a Robinson Crusoe on a desert island, hankering after companionship yet terrified by its presence. He allays his fears by creating his own Man Friday in the person of Don Sandalio, and in his creation he reveals the nature of his predicament. 'No viene al Casino más que a jugar al ajedrez', he says of Don Sandalio, 'y lo juega, sin pronunciar apenas palabra, con una avidez de enfermo' (II, 355), as if it were the last game of his life. The chess game which the letter-writer plays with Don Sandalio with such intensity encapsulates the ever-present threat of death, death which can supervene at any moment as if by checkmate. The symbolic function of the game of chess as a desperate struggle for survival comes through clearly in the nightmare which the letter-writer recounts and in which, significantly, he is playing white and is being devoured by the black pieces. Anyone who can face death with equanimity is, like the idealized Don Sandalio, a 'jugador heroico' (II, 360), or a 'roble heroico' (II, 359), but the letter-writer himself falls short of this ideal. He has not reached the state of self-possession and serene contemplation that Don Sandalio demonstrates in his game. His anxiety takes the form of flight, of aimless wanderings in the woods and on the beach. The beach represents solitude, 'la playa de mi soledad' (II, 359), the existential loneliness of the individual as he faces the sea, a symbol, like the lake in *San Manuel Bueno, mártir,* of the impenetrable mystery of death. The death of Don Sandalio, as we saw in the previous chapter, is a death-experience, a premonition or revelation of the letter-writer's own death. The unexpected news sends him on a dizzy flight, 'como sonámbulo' (II, 371). Don Sandalio's death fills him, he says, with a deep despair and creates in him a 'vacío inmenso' (II, 371), the same void which encompasses him as he sits in the hollow tree now surrounded by dead leaves, the void, that is, of eternal nothingness. Wherever he turns, he sees only death and decay staring at him. *La novela de Don Sandalio*, then, can be seen as a novel not so much about death as about the obsession with death, an obsession that is threatening to engulf the letter-writer's mind and personality. Struggling to come to terms with his own approaching death and full of pity for himself and hatred of those who live seemingly oblivious of their fate, he takes refuge in a flight from reality that leads him into a private world charged with symbols, omens and enigmas. What Unamuno appears to be suggesting is that whereas a heightened awareness of death can lead to a fuller life, as in the cases of Father Manuel Bueno or Gertrudis, an excessive preoccupation with one's finitude will interfere with our capacity for action and threaten the usefulness of our lives.

The only constructive solution to anxiety is to regard it as a test of one's resolve in the face of the ultimate ignorance. It is not so much death as non-knowledge that poses the challenge. If we accept it as non-knowledge, putting aside all spurious proofs of immortality, then we need neither to cling to hopes of survival nor to dismiss death as meaningless. Its meaning lies precisely in forcing us to acknowledge that we cannot know, that this incapacity to penetrate the veil is part of our innermost humanity. For Unamuno this was the ultimate acceptance of the uncertainty of the human situation. This uncertainty was also the necessary prelude to genuine faith, because 'el que afirma su fe a base de incertidumbre, no miente ni puede mentir' (*DSTV*, X, 432). If death represents the prospect of the loss of our self-consciousness, then life represents the struggle to assimilate this prospect. This, at any rate, is what Unamuno and several of the later existentialists had in common. Yet the ultimate ignorance is not one with which Unamuno was easily reconciled. In his short story 'Don Martín o de la gloria' he made the eponymous character express his sentiment in typical sardonic style:

> — ¿A que no sabe usted — me dijo — una de las cosas que más terrible me hacen la visión de la nada de ultratumba? Pues es el pensar que ni siquiera he de saber el secreto, si es que fuera ése; que si muero y no hay más allá nada, no he de tener el consuelo de saberlo; que en la nada no hay ni conciencia de ella... Morirse, morirse para no saber el secreto de la muerte... entonces, ¿para qué morir? ¡Esto es terrible joven! (II, 501)

What horrifies Don Martin is the thought that he may not learn the secret of death, which robs death of any point. Don Martín's horror of posthumous ignorance — a state of non-awareness cannot be aware of itself — smacks of self-deflation, of Unamuno laughing at his own obsessive preoccupation with whether or not his consciousness could survive bodily death. If so, it is a little light relief from what was a recurrent theme in his writing.

In the prologue added to the second edition of *Amor y pedagogía* (1931), Unamuno tells of a Jesuit who accused him of dwelling obsessively on death and suicide and thereby encouraging the latter through his obsession (I, 302). This Jesuit was obviously a dedicated reader and one with a keen eye for Unamunian inclinations, though not a spiritual fellow-traveller. Death, both through natural causes and through suicide, is indeed an extremely frequent phenomenon in Unamuno's fiction. In the thirteen works which form the basis of this study (that is, excluding the short stories) there are twenty-six deaths among the fictitious characters with roles of some significance. Only one work, *Una historia de amor*, is free from an actual death, although even here the co-protagonist, Liduvina, painfully recalls the death of her blue-eyed young brother who used to call her Ina. But this one exception among Unamuno's novels is precisely about a symbolic death, the death (and resurrection) of love. Of the two dozen-plus deaths in the other twelve works four are suicides (those of Apolodoro, Juan, Alejandro Gómez, and Julio Macedo) and two are either ambiguous or unexplained (those of Augusto Pérez and Don Sandalio). Unamuno, then, pursues his characters to the end. But the end is not really seen as completion but more usually as protest, as self-assertion, as entreaty, or even as injustice. Death is not completion because our life-project needs to be articulated, that is to say it needs self-interpretation. But this can never be completed because articulation itself, as Wittgenstein taught, will always require further explanation (Wittgenstein, 2009: §87, 45e).

The process that Unamuno portrays seems rather that of a struggle to assimilate an event that cannot be fully grasped. In his study and edition of *Paz en la guerra*, Francisco Caudet tries to apply Kermode's idea of ending as catharsis or purification to the return of Pedro Antonio and Josefa Ignacia to the former's native village after the loss of their son in the war. The word *purificación* does indeed appear, but it is questionable whether it represents purgation through loss. The process that Unamuno portrays seems rather that of a struggle to assimilate an event that cannot be fully grasped. The real ending of the novel is not in Pedro Antonio's return to his native village (he will in any case soon go back to Bilbao) but in his and Josefa's attempts to come to terms with the death of Ignacio, which initially they find hard to accept: 'Ni el padre ni la madre estaban convencidos del todo de la muerte del hijo; podía ser equivocación; y a diario le esperaban al amanecer sin darse mutua cuenta de su esperanza, y a diario desesperaban de volver a verle' (I, 236). Ignacio becomes for them 'una sombra invisible', 'una común esperanza', 'un hijo espiritual vivo' (II, 268). Pedro Antonio replaces the attempt to recover his son by the attempt to recover his loans to the Carlist cause, a clear case of displacement, which causes his cousin Don Pascual to comment that 'nos han vencido porque no nos hemos purificado aún' (I, 274). Back in Bilbao, Josefa Ignacia goes surreptitiously to a church and there, in a side-chapel, seeks solace by shedding her tears in front of a statue of Our Lady of Solitude, who 'mirando al cielo, tenía en el regazo al Hijo muerto y desnudo, con los flácidos brazos pendientes, abandonado a la voluntad del Padre celestial' (I, 275). No catharsis, no sense of an ending here; at best a sublimation of pain, at worst a desperate questioning of a divine power who shows no pity. The death of Josefa Ignacia, brought about by a consuming sorrow ('se acordaba cada día más de su difunto hijo, a quien no lograba representárselo muerto' (I, 283)), in its turn has its effect on Pedro Antonio. At first the struggle to accept another death returns to haunt him:

> En adelante duróle largo tiempo el desasosiego por la falta de su Pepiñasi; ¿dónde estaba?, ¿qué era de ella?, ¿por qué no había venido ya, como otros días, a comer?, ¿iban a estar esperándola así? Algo le faltaba, algo había roto el nexo de su vida humilde. Y cada vez que se presentaba a su mente, asociada a la falta de su mujer, la imagen de la muerte, se le ablandaba el pecho. (I, 284)

What is the image of death here, save the sense of irrecoverable loss, the sense not of an ending but of an absence? Eventually peace returns, but it is an opting out, a peace that is achieved at the expense of devaluing the hustle and bustle of ordinary life and seeing human existence *sub specie aeternitatis*. In a long poetic meditation that ill befits the workhorse character of Pedro Antonio as depicted earlier, Unamuno makes him assimilate the death of his son and wife through a process of converting his memories into a reflection of the imperturbability of nature, 'la naturaleza inocente y desinteresada'. And he continues:

> Vive [Pedro Antonio] en lo profundo de la verdadera realidad de la vida, puro de toda intencionalidad trascendente, sobre el tiempo, sintiendo en su conciencia serena como el cielo desnudo la invasión lenta del sueño dulce del supremo descanso, la gran calma de las cosas eternas, y lo infinito que duerme en la estrechez de ella. Vive en la verdadera paz de la vida, dejándose mecer indiferente en los cotidianos cuidados: al día, mas reposando a la vez en la calma del desprendido de todo lo pasajero: en la eternidad; vive al día en la eternidad. (I, 286)

This poetic meditation on time borders on the mystical. Pedro Antonio does in the end achieve reconciliation with death but only through converting daily life into an eternal moment, a 'vida profunda', an underlying existence that can have no end. Pedro Antonio at last appears free from anxiety. But in this respect this early Unamunian character is something of an exception and his terminal equanimity will not be repeated.[17] Future characters will not reconcile themselves so readily to the fact of death, although they too will seek in some way to overcome their temporality. Indeed Unamuno's fiction can be seen as a meditation on human transience and perhaps too on the quest for some form of noumenal survival, that is to say survival in a disembodied form whose presence can be apprehended but only through the imaginative faculty. Gertrudis is very clear on this: hers is a quest for endurance in others because she believes in the rightness of her mission. Joaquín on the other hand could be said to represent the opposite: he advocates total obliteration, because he sees his life as destructive. Life begets an attraction/repulsion syndrome. What makes us want to live, our feelings, emotions, acute self-awareness, is also what may make us want to die.

There has been a general tendency to see Unamuno's literature as his own quest for survival in disembodied form, for his personality to endure through others, specifically through his readers.[18] But while there is undoubtedly an element of this, it is too easy to conclude that Unamuno was writing for posterity. In his early short story, 'El héroe' (1889), Unamuno writes ironically of the hero that 'se preocupaba en dar al escrito aquel tono que convenía para cuando muerto y descubierta su

---

[17] The artificiality of the final pages of *Paz en la guerra* is stark. Unamuno is determined to end his novel with the idea of inner peace within an outer struggle as the closing words indicate ('paz en la guerra misma') and to this end he is prepared to sacrifice both historical accuracy (Spain was to enjoy no inner peace but only an uneasy and corrupt political truce broken by external wars in North Africa, the Philippines, and Cuba) and fictional consistency. Pedro Antonio has not been depicted as the kind of character who can withdraw from life or achieve the degree of spiritual serenity he enjoys at the end. Almost right up to the end he has been depicted as restless.

[18] The most articulate and persuasive comment to this effect is that of Ciríaco Morón Arroyo, 1964: 235–36.

correspondencia se publicara o como medio de apreciar a un genio o como extraño modelo de un amor gigantesco' (II, 746). Here Unamuno is having a dig at so-called Erostratism. And at about that same time he was writing to a friend: 'son muchos los que, yendo para grandes hombres, en sus íntimos propósitos miran y remiran cuanto escriben a su novia o al amigo o al prestamista en previsión de que muertos, ellos lo publiquen. Esta condenada literatura, al acentuar el egoísmo, ha hecho que nos convirtamos todos en teatro de nosotros mismos, y vivamos representando un papel' (Unamuno, 1996: 54). Writing for posterity, then, is pure theatre, mere hypocrisy. This is, admittedly, an early sceptical comment, and Unamuno could have changed his mind. But the ambiguity remains.[19] In the story 'Una visita al viejo poeta' we are made aware of the paradox that the poet's ideas have been absorbed by the community whereas he himself has been forgotten. He has been forgotten precisely because his ideas are no longer his: they have become a natural part of others' existence. The poet has fulfilled his role, but as a result he is now symbolically dead, cast aside. Indeed if we are to believe Don Martín in 'Don Martín o de la gloria', the situation for the writer is even more hopeless. Don Martín embodies the phenomenon of a writer no longer recognizing his own work because, as he says, it was written by his reading public. His work has become a part of the national consciousness and therefore goes unnoticed: 'Mi espíritu se desparrama y difunde en el de mi pueblo [...], pero es perdiéndolo yo. Yo no soy mío' (II, 499). To live on through literary fame is not worth it, says the ageing writer as he feels life ebbing away. One is not one's legend after all. But the narrator, whose last conversation with Don Martín he is recalling, does not agree with his view of literary glory as merely a cake to be shared among consumers. The narrator, who is also a writer, does not thank Don Martín for his vision of an embracing nothingness, for arguing that life is worth far more than posthumous fame. Unamuno, in this particular instance, does not take sides, but limits himself to drawing a contrast between living through one's body and living through one's work. Is then the work of the writer to be seen as 'la concreción [...], la presencia viva de la persona, aun después de que ésta haya muerto'? (Morón Arroyo, 1964: 235). We must of course accept that the works of a great writer, artist, composer, etc., perdure, and, in perduring, the spirit or creativeness that was infused in them perdures too. So long as those works continue to speak to us (are in accord with our own ways of thinking), we, as living beings, can envision the mind or even perhaps experience the same thoughts that the mind contained. But we must not confuse this with the survival of consciousness in any shape or form, with 'la presencia viva' of the writer. It is not the consciousness of the artist that is present but *our* consciousness of him with no possibility of interplay, for works of art do not respond to our views of them in the same way that living beings do, and if there is no reciprocity Unamuno's idea of our sense of self as derived from others' views of us breaks down. Unamuno in any case believed that a writer's work became the reader's work as soon as the writer had passed it on. The author's survival through writing is thus no more than a mirage. Indeed Unamuno himself

[19] The idea of achieving immortality through art re-appears in Chapter III of *Del sentimiento trágico de la vida* (DSTV, X,162–66), but Unamuno seems almost to regret this struggle, 'lucha mil veces más terrible que la lucha por la vida' (164), rather than approve of it.

admitted as much when he pointed out that responses to artistic works change through time.[20]

Unamuno's writing cannot therefore simply be taken as a naive attempt to surmount finitude. Such a quest would be little more than self-deception. For as we saw in Chapter 1 his distinction between the physical and the mental realms is an essentially historical one, historical in the sense that it is ideas, including of course ideas of persons, that survive the decay of physical processes so long as there are physical brains to generate and propagate them.[21] The individual's problem lies not in how to survive death but in how to live with it, how to come to terms with the expectation that something as apparently solid as our sense of self is to be taken away from us. What we constantly find illustrated in Unamuno's fiction is a concern for self as manifested in relation to others, and this is a matter of life as much as of death: of life because the death of others deprives us of part of our self, and of death because we will no longer have others. The dying Gertrudis does not so much fear death itself as the loss of her children, all the more because they were not biologically hers. She belongs with them. Ángela Carballino, in losing first her father, then her mother, then Don Manuel, and finally her brother, has already lost a great part of her life. Her death is, as it were, already happening even as she writes. The letter-writer in *La novela de don Sandalio*, who has lost his *hogar*, his family, is already experiencing death as a premonition. For Augusto Pérez the death of his mother will turn out to be a disconcerting and irreplaceable loss. For Tulio Montalbán the death of his wife is tantamount to the destruction of his self, as it is of course for Alejandro Gómez. While deaths are events within the fiction, death for Unamuno's characters is not so much an event as an expectation, whether long-awaited or recently discovered, but a presence or encounter nonetheless. Nowhere is this presence of finitude more intensely — because poetically — represented than in *San Manuel Bueno, mártir*, where Father Manuel sees in the submerged waters of the lake his beloved village of Valverde de Lucerna which he will leave behind just as others did before him. In his eyes that village is already a mythical entity, and it is that entity to which the dead may belong. In Unamuno's fiction, then, a character's life is indelibly marked by finitude, their own and others'. If they carry with them 'a sense of an ending', it is more as epiphany than as catharsis.

The novels almost invariably end in death. If there is an aftermath, as in *La tía Tula* or *San Manuel Bueno, mártir*, that aftermath is governed by the preceding death. In the traditional realist novel the plot had been strongly geared towards the outcome or dénouement, a compositional technique which is at its most evident in detective fiction, a sub-genre that emerged in the nineteenth-century. In the Unamunian

---

[20] We might bear in mind too what he states unequivocally in *Del sentimiento trágico de la vida*: 'Todo eso de que uno vive en sus hijos, o en sus obras, o en el universo, son vagas elucubraciones con que sólo se satisfacen los que padecen de estupidez afectiva' (*DSTV*, 115). In the essay 'Salvar el alma en la historia' (*Obras Completas* (Escelicer) VII, 998–1003), Unamuno argues that what is important is one's mission in life, not one's renown in posterity. The label of *erostratismo* that is often assigned to Unamuno does not appear to be justified.

[21] Spinoza makes this same point. The idea of Peter exists in Peter's mind and in Paul's. But Peter's idea of his own nature ends with the end of his body, whereas 'Paul's mind will still regard Peter as present to itself, even though Peter does not exist' (Spinoza, 1996: 46).

novel, the traditional dénouement or unveiling is usually replaced by the death of the protagonist, so that the latter event becomes a compositional technique as much as the dénouement was in the nineteenth-century novel. For Unamuno a fictional character is a life, a creative flicker in the night of nothingness, for no sooner has the character created himself and his public role than the curtain cuts him off from his audience. Unamuno's approach to his characters' lives is existential through and through. They are existences driven by temporality and anxiety, defined by relationships, bounded by a reality which they struggle to control, unsettled by motives which they cannot understand. Death is presented as the only conceivable outcome of a coming into existence that is wholly arbitrary, a mere random consequence of a biological occurrence. There is no 'who' in birth; identity is a self-creation, an art, as we see symbolized in Abel's/Joaquín's portrait of Cain. Gertrudis 'creates' her children, Ángela 'creates' her Don Manuel, Avito 'creates' his Apolodoro, the letter-writer 'creates' Don Sandalio, and Augusto 'creates' the dog Orfeo, and through creating others they engage in self-creation, because it is through others that we acquire our sense of self. It is this self-creation, the work that takes up our lives, that is brought to an end. It is not a simple matter of biological death but of a creative or artistic death, the death of our creative faculties, or, *mutatis mutandis*, the death of the character as the death of his fiction, not a case of *ars longa, vita brevis*, but of *artis finis, vitae finis*.

The Jesuit priest's accusation of morbidity or of inducement to suicide is nevertheless misplaced. Unamuno does not devalue life and celebrate death. The coming into existence may be an arbitrary and gratuitous occurrence, but once it happens it acquires its own importance. If for Unamuno death is an injustice, as he himself tells us in *Del sentimiento trágico de la vida* (*DSTV*, X, 487) following Senancour's *Obermann* ('Man is perishable. That may be; but let us perish resisting and if it is nothingness that awaits us, do not let us so act that it shall be a just fate'), it is because when we rise to the challenge of a meaningless gift of life (the unanswerable '¿por qué?') and provide our own meaning (the answer to '¿para qué?'), this creative response is ultimately cast aside. We cannot endure even as an artistic form, for the latter forms have a limited shelf life, dependent as they are on the creative continuity of other minds. Lázaro Carballino, on his death bed, puts it rather pointedly: 'No siento tanto tener que morir [...] como que conmigo se muere otro pedazo del alma de Don Manuel. Pero lo demás de él vivirá contigo. Hasta que un día hasta los muertos nos moriremos del todo' (II, 343). For Don Manuel life is a living death, indeed he does not separate the two, and helping people to die or to overcome their sense of loss is the mark of his ministry. The gift of life carries with it the gift of death, as Derrida, after Patočka, has termed it, although it is doubtful if Unamuno would have approved of such nomenclature.[22] If eternal life is in human terms inconceivable, as Unamuno states in *Del sentimiento trágico de la vida*, since it would be tantamount to deleting time, then death is a necessary adjunct to birth. In a writer as rich in binary oppositions as Unamuno, the birth–death binary should be the most natural of all. Yet in a way it is not. Unamuno seldom gives details of his

---

[22] I refer of course to the English translation, *The Gift of Death* (Derrida, 1996).

characters' birth, presumably because it does not form part of one's consciousness. At most he offers vague memories of childhood, often involving the loss of one of the parents, usually the father. Augusto Pérez and Ángela Carballino, brought up by their mothers, have but a faint memory of their father, and Gertrudis not even that. Don Manuel Bueno has a mother, but no father, while Abel and Joaquín grow up with each other, not with parents, of whom there is no mention.[23] The disappearance of the father seems to be a recurrent motif in Unamunian ontology, leading one to suspect that the binary life–death is symbolically associated with the mother–father binary. Since Unamuno himself lost his father before he was six and was brought up by his mother and grandmother it might be more prudent to see this as an unconscious reflection of experience rather than as some kind of theological proposition in which Mother (Earth) is the life-giver and Father (God) the death-giver. At any rate we should recall Gertrudis's insistence on the father beseeching forgiveness from the mother at the moment of birth: the father takes, the mother gives. It is perhaps for this reason that the death of children so appals Father Manuel Bueno, not simply because he is the symbolic father of Valverde de Lucerna but also because a young life destroyed is a life unfulfilled, the height of pointlessness in a pointless existence which he struggles to combat. The death of a child undermines the 'para qué', the conferment of purpose on our life-project. To fulfil a life-project one needs to bring it to some sort of climax, and in this sense death could be said to offer, if not completion, then at least a degree of fulfilment and closure, as indeed it does in part for some Unamunian characters (Gertrudis, Don Manuel, Lázaro Carballino, who die, if not willingly, at least with a sense of achievement); but premature interruption is an arbitrary sentence that turns life into an empty, even ironic, gift. If this is so, what are we to make of those who die by their own hand?

There are, as noted above, a surprising number of suicides in Unamuno's fiction (not just those of major characters but of many subsidiary figures mentioned in passing in *Amor y pedagogía, Niebla, Abel Sánchez, San Manuel Bueno, mártir,* and *La novela de don Sandalio,* as well as in the short stories). How does Unamuno present these deaths? What we usually find in the lead-up to suicide is an absence, an emptiness, a nothingness. The self-assertive Alejandro Gómez is not afraid of death but of life, a life without that other who has made him what he is. Similarly Julio Macedo has tried to replace the Elvira that he knew and has failed to do so. The outcome is identical: life without the other can only be a living death. Apolodoro, too, though the victim of his father's foolish experiment, fails to find the other on whom he has pinned his hopes, as of course does Augusto Pérez, who resolves to kill himself because, as he puts it to Unamuno, 'mi lógica interior [...] me pide que me suicide' (I, 652), by which is meant, presumably, that his self-image has been shattered, that his dignity has been stolen from him. The one exception to this pattern, if exception it be, would appear to be Juan, whose suicide is foretold, almost

---

[23] In the case of Don Manuel there is something of an inconsistency in the story since on the one occasion when he mentions his father he says he died at nearly ninety. Don Manuel is twenty-seven years older than Ángela, yet Ángela knew his mother, alive during his ministry, but not his father. The chronology does not quite add up.

mandated, by Raquel: 'Si quieres, pues, matarte, mátate' (II, 232). Furthermore, as we saw in the previous chapter, Juan is suffering from alienation. In one respect he is a clear inversion of the cases of Alejandro Gómez and Julio Macedo, whose self-possession and sang-froid as they contemplate self-destruction is almost eerie. Nevertheless Juan's case still fits the same pattern, graphically so, since not only does he descend into the mental abyss ('abismo') of nothingness but physically throws himself down a precipice. Why does he kill himself? Unamuno makes it clear that his two women have taken possession of his identity, have sucked every ounce of autonomy and agency out of him. Like Augusto, he feels deprived of his self-respect. Killing himself thus becomes a way of recovering what is uniquely his own, of re-asserting his selfhood. Whether Juan, or anyone else, can experience death as his own is of course debatable, but this is not Unamuno's point. For Unamuno suicide is a willed act, an assertion rather than a negation of self. Rather than seeing suicide conventionally as evasion, Unamuno seems to see it instead as an attempt to recover something lost. Even Apolodoro's pitiful 'dimito' is his first-person-singular response to his father's coercive designs. He wants, like Don Juan, to escape the clutches of an embrace that is denying him the opportunity to create himself. Federico, his rival for the hand of Clarita, has his own theory of suicide. On seeing a corpse floating in the river, he comments: 'alguno a quien aterraba la muerte [...] Sólo se suicida el que odia la muerte' (I, 390). 'Odiar la muerte' is to live with the anxiety of death, which paradoxically makes death the cure for the disease. It is the ultimate defiance of uncertainty.

Suicide for Unamuno, then, is a paradox, the paradox of an inability to reconcile oneself to annihilation, to loss of selfhood. This paradoxical attraction of the abyss of nothingness is perfectly expressed by Father Manuel Bueno in highly poetic language, as Lázaro tells his sister quoting the priest's very words:

> ¡Y cómo me llama esa agua que con su aparente quietud — la corriente va por dentro — espeja al cielo! ¡Mi vida, Lázaro, es una especie de suicidio continuo, un combate contra el suicidio, que es igual; pero que vivan ellos, que vivan los nuestros! [...] Aquí se remansa el río en lago, para luego, bajando a la meseta, precipitarse en cascadas, saltos y torrentera, por las hoces y encañadas, junto a la ciudad, y así remansa la vida aquí en la aldea. Pero la tentación al suicidio es mayor aquí, junto al remanso que espeja la noche de estrellas, que no junto a las cascadas que dan miedo. (II, 333–34)

The imagery is eloquent. The turbulent river (of life) broadens into a calm mysterious lake whose stillness mirrors the unreachable yet beckoning sky. Rather than as solution, suicide is presented as bewitchment, as a temptation to bring forward the final encounter rather than surrender passively to its relentless approach. Far from a 'passing away', it is a 'passing into'. Indeed even Unamunian characters who die natural deaths are not usually allowed simply to fade away in a normal process of a gradual cessation of bodily functions. In the case of characters who appear to die from natural causes Unamuno's presentation is dramatic, at times even, one could say, melodramatic.

In only one case is the actual process of the passage from life to death described, and it is done in what today would be considered conventional terms. That case is the early one of Ignacio in *Paz en la guerra*. Shortly before he is hit by an enemy bullet, and after witnessing the death of another soldier, Ignacio wonders what death entails: '¿Morir? ¿Qué es eso? — pensaba, no pudiendo concebirse muerto —. ¿Y si muero?' (I, 214). A few pages later it is indeed Ignacio's turn to die, and Unamuno makes an attempt to capture the onset of death subjectively. The process of dying is seen as a rapid action-replay in reverse of certain memories of Ignacio's life reaching back to infancy, until the loss of blood makes his mind fall into unconsciousness. At this point the narrator is forced to move out of Ignacio's consciousness and look at him from the outside, as part of the battle scene, and his death merits but a brief poetic utterance: 'Junto a él resonaba el fragor del combate, mientras las olas del tiempo se rompían en la eternidad' (I, 223). Although in the later case of Apolodoro's death there is a brief reference to asphyxia, Ignacio's dying is the only one that is described in some detail. Unamuno will never again attempt to describe the moment of clinical death from the inside, faithful to his belief that it is impossible for anyone to imagine the state of death: 'No podemos concebirnos como no existiendo' (*DSTV*, X, 305).[24]

Rosa's death in *Amor y pedagogía* is seen from the outside: through the grotesque and unsympathetic pseudo-scientific pronouncements of her father, Don Avito; through the embarrassed sensibility of her brother, Apolodoro; and through the deep distress of her suffering mother, Marina. Her death merits exactly two-and-a-half lines. The only association with clinical death is made through the verb 'estertorar', death-rattle. In *Niebla*, Augusto's death is more dramatic but equally rapid: he wakes up as if from a dream shouting the name of Eugenia, and tries to sit up in bed only to fall back dead. In *Abel Sánchez*, Abel, realizing he is having a heart attack, utters a final laconic '¡Me muero!' and breaths his 'último respiro' (I, 787). Joaquín's death throes are not even described. After a melodramatic outburst, he simply falls silent and hours later 'rendía su último cansado suspiro' (I, 791). Ramiro's death in *La tía Tula* is described with an equally conventional phrase, 'rindió el espíritu con el último huelgo' (I, 866). His first wife Rosa's death is referred to as an 'agonía lenta' (I, 826), but is not described. His second wife's death is not described either, nor is Gertrudis's in any direct sense; her death is poetic: 'Y se apagó como se apaga una tarde de otoño cuando las últimas razas del sol, filtradas por nubes sangrientas, se derriten en las aguas serenas de un remanso del río en que se reflejan los álamos' (I, 895). In the case of *San Manuel Bueno, mártir*, the death scene is pure theatre, with no attempt at a realistic portrayal. Don Manuel, crucifix in hand and with Blasillo next to him, in what is an obvious echo of the Crucifixion, dies in front of the whole congregation while the Creed is being recited: 'todo el pueblo sintió que

---

[24] The thought reappears in the fiction in various forms of expression. For example, in the already cited story 'Don Martín, o de la gloria' Don Martín says to his young interlocutor: 'Joven, intente usted una noche, estando acostado, concebirse como no existiendo, y verá usted, verá usted, que hormigueo le da en el alma' (II, 501). As for Ignacio's psychological experience of dying as a rewinding, this has a more purely philosophical or abstract counterpart in one of Augusto Pérez's dialogues with his other self, the dog Orfeo: 'Cuando morimos nos da la muerte media vuelta en nuestra órbita y emprendemos la marcha hacia atrás, hacia el pasado, hacia lo que fue. Y así, sin término, devanando la madeja de nuestro destino, deshaciendo todo el infinito que en una eternidad nos ha hecho' (I, 517).

había entregado su alma a Dios', while Blasillo likewise 'había entregado su alma a Dios' (II, 340). Death has become symbolic or otherworldly. What we observe in following these various deaths from first to last is a gradual mythologizing process, from an early attempt at describing the experience of a biological shutdown right through to a symbolic or mystical passage from the known to the unknown, from time to timelessness. If in Gertrudis finitude becomes a disembodied presence in the family, in Don Manuel finitude finally becomes universal consecration.

Against finitude, then, Unamuno counterposes eternity in another of his binary oppositions, a way of reasoning for which the later structuralists were to become notorious. In effect it is a way of thinking in which any concept is made to acquire meaning only by virtue of its opposite. It is a thoroughly linguistic, even poetic, manner of presenting ideas. Temporality/eternity is for Unamuno another version of the physical/mental, material/spiritual divide in which he sees humanity immersed. The opposing tendencies cannot be split off from each other, even if we give preference to one or other. We are conscious of our finitude because of our hankering for eternity, or perhaps it is the other way round, our concern over our finitude giving rise to just such a hankering. In *Del sentimiento trágico de la vida* Unamuno uses our sense of finitude to explain the pursuit of religious or eternal values, but in the fiction we are just as likely to encounter the reverse image, a sense of finitude emanating from our desire for a continuation of life. This is precisely the case of Father Manuel Bueno. His desire for permanence does not appear to lead to religious belief, since we are told he has no belief in a transcendent or supernatural existence. What he does possess is an awareness of the endurance of nature, besides which the individual human being is ephemeral.

> Otra vez — me decía también mi hermano — , cuando volvíamos acá, vimos a una zagala, una cabrera, que enhiesta sobre un picacho de la falda de la montaña, a la vista del lago, estaba cantando con una voz más fresca que las aguas de éste. Don Manuel me detuvo y señalándomela dijo: 'Mira, parece como si hubiera acabado el tiempo, como si esa zagala hubiese estado ahí siempre, y como está, y cantando como está, y como si hubiera de seguir estando así siempre, como estuvo cuando empezó mi conciencia, como estará cuando se me acabe. Esa zagala forma parte, con las rocas, las nubes, los árboles, las aguas, de la naturaleza y no de la historia.' (II, 334)

The passage vividly illustrates the opposition/conjunction of finitude and permanence. Don Manuel is highly conscious of his beginning and his end. At the same time this consciousness of himself is acknowledged as a mere ripple in the timelessness of eternity. He visualizes the goatgirl standing motionless on the mountain crag as frozen in time, as part of nature, as outside history. It is precisely our history that makes us transient, whereas it is nature, of which we too are a part, that gives us a kind of eternity.[25] Nature, in the symbolic form of mountain

---

[25] Cf. Lord Byron: 'I live not in myself, but I become / Portion of that around me; and to me / High mountains are a feeling, but the hum / of human cities torture' (*Child Harold's Pilgrimage*, Canto 3, LXXII). This need to commune with nature is exactly the feeling earlier expressed by Ángela with reference to her oppressive stay in the city; but she identifies the lake and the mountain with the priest.

and lake, reminds Don Manuel of his own impermanence, yet paradoxically offers a source of consolation. Twenty-seven years earlier Unamuno had expressed much the same sentiment through the schoolmaster Don Casiano in 'El maestro de Carrasqueda':

> Mira, Ramonete: nada muere, todo baja del río del tiempo al mar de la eternidad y allí queda... El universo es un vasto fonógrafo y una vasta placa en que queda todo sonido que murió y toda figura que pasó; sólo hace falta la conmoción que los vuelva un día... Las voces perdidas y muertas resucitarán un día y formarán coro, un coro inmenso que llene el infinito... Me voy de esta España, de la terrestre, de la que fluye, a la otra España, a la España celestial... Ya sabes que el cielo envuelve a la tierra... ¡Habla y enseña aunque no te oigan...! Soy una voz que se apaga en el desierto... ¡Adios, hijo mío! (II, 523)[26]

The biblical tone of the dying schoolmaster's words is unmistakeable. As he fades away from the river of time into the sea of eternity, he enjoins his disciple to carry on preaching his message of hope, that our efforts in life are not lost but are part of a vast and universal canvas.

Unamuno's novels are in a deep sense biographies of the characters they portray. Irrespective of time span, the fictions take the characters from an initial or growing self-awareness to a final expiration. In between they have had to cope with the realization of transience. Learning to live is a learning to die. Death, whether self-inflicted or not, is seldom if ever portrayed as a routine event, as a straightforward cessation of biological activity. It is rather a climax, a form of judgment, a pronouncement, not of divine pleasure or displeasure, but rather on the life lived. Some lives end in despondency, some in regret, some in self-assertion, some in triumph tempered by doubt. Death is thus not only a prelude or a looking-forward but also a looking back, a self-assessment. It is, too, and notably so, a final confrontation with the self one has created or passively accepted. It appears to be the one truly authentic moment in Unamunian ontology. We reach the culmination of our self-consciousness when we know it is about to end.

Yet it is not easy to abandon that 'living-for-tomorrow' that has been ingrained in us throughout our lives. Acceptance that the world will continue without us as if nothing had changed does not come easily. Hence Unamunian characters often make pronouncements on their deathbeds that refer to a future they will not know. It is a last desperate effort to assert their presence in their absence, a kind of 'do this in memory of me', whether we think of Gertrudis issuing instructions to her successor as lay abbess; or of Father Manuel asking Lázaro and Ángela to continue his pastoral mission, to look after his poor sheep, as he pointedly says; or of Augusto Pérez vengefully predicting Unamuno's death; or even, most tragically, of Joaquín Monegro proclaiming yet again his self-destructive propensity for hatred instead of love. If death cannot be experienced, dying can be, and is, for Unamunian characters, a final opportunity to assert their right to be what they are, to assert, that

---

[26] In the schoolmaster's lifelong dedication to the children of the village and to its agricultural activities, in his biblical teachings, in his very public death in the school, and in the discipleship of young Ramonete who later tried to give him public recognition with an official medal, 'El maestro de Carrasqueda' (1903) is a distant but very clear precedent of *San Manuel Bueno, mártir*.

is, their irreplaceability. It is precisely finitude, Unamuno seems to be saying, that gives a life its meaning. Dying is the ultimate singularity: no one can die in another's place. Unamuno treats death not as a general but as a personal phenomenon. It is not the biological fact, what constitutes clinical death, that interests him but the implications of the 'I die'. Death may be a perfectly natural phenomenon, but it can never be natural for me because I have been accustomed to live. To overlook death and its impenetrability is to ignore one essential dimension of life. Death-awareness is very much a part of Unamuno's conception of character, no doubt because it reflects his view that it explains many aspects of human belief and behaviour. As in Heidegger, it is the anticipation of death that characterizes authentic living. Unamuno's characters, like their creator, may see death as an injustice, but they do not see it as absurd (unlike some existentialists such as Sartre). Death is the necessary confirmation of our temporality, and it is our temporality that gives our life-project meaning. It is our transience that makes possible the determination to *eternizarse*, to rise above a purely biological existence. Unamuno's novels are, in a very central way, a meditation on death, but on death as challenge rather than defeat. In the end we come back to Unamuno's preoccupation with personality, for our sense of finitude serves to enhance our self-awareness, our continuing search for identity. But for this search we need to enlist the aid of those who surround us.

Community

We exist among others. A self can never achieve an identity independently of other selves. From Plato onwards, many important thinkers have held that the social structure is the natural and necessary structure of all existence. Everything living is in some way or other social, from multicellular organisms right up to the human species. Human beings help to make one another what they are, contributing as they almost invariably do to one another's existence. From an individual's point of view a community is a collection of others who share his or her outlook and thereby give solidity to his or her presence and sense of self. This idea is central in Unamuno's concept of the self, as it is indeed in most existentialist thinkers. 'Under what conditions [do] I become conscious of myself as a person'?, asks Gabriel Marcel; to which he replies, 'these conditions are essentially social' (Marcel, 2010: 12). I have a *here* and a *now* which is given to me as well as a sense of difference. There is a boundary between me and not-me which establishes my profile, but what is there inside this boundary? What can I say usefully about myself to fill that void within my boundary? The answer, according to Unamuno, Sartre, or Marcel, is practically nothing, nothing at any rate which will firm up my existence in space and time. For this I need the confirmation of others. This is what Marcel refers to as 'this paradox, by virtue of which even the most self-centred among us looks to others and only to others for his final investiture' (Marcel, 2010: 11). The paradox of course is that my subjectivity, which is so important to me, is not enough to satisfy my sense of existing; my presence demands to be recognized, that is, to be experienced by others. To be meaningful, an I requires a Thou, as Martin Buber powerfully argued (Buber, 2004). Only when others experience my presence can I truly acquire a secure sense of existence, of selfhood. In his short story 'El espejo de la muerte' Unamuno reverses the process. Matilde loses her will to live because she feels others do not sustain her. When she tackles her increasingly distant boyfriend she looks at him 'como a espejo' (II, 6), that is, trying to find herself in him, but encounters only evasion, as if the mirror did not reflect. During the *romería*, José Antonio averts his gaze while the other young men ignore Matilde and chase the other girls. Abandoned by her own community of others, Matilde now refuses to look in her real mirror and dissipates into oblivion. She has lost her sense of presence because she is absent for others. In this simple story Unamuno draws attention to the phenomenon of ontological reinforcement, of one's dependence on others to boost one's self-recognition. Similarly, in *Niebla*, it is only when he feels the target of others' derision rather than respect that Augusto feels the full impact of his existential anguish and consequent need to destroy himself. 'No se existe sino para los demás' (I, 662), sentences the doctor called in to examine Augusto's corpse.

The idea of community is an Unamunian constant, and it is to be found at various levels: at the level of the family, of the institution, of the village, of the region, of the nation, and of course of the reader (the latter in the way Unamuno constantly tries to construct a community of virtual readers as we saw in Chapter 4).[27] It might at first seem something of a paradox that a writer as obsessed as Unamuno with the nature of his own self should confer such importance on the idea of community; but the fact is that for Unamuno life is, or ought to be, a communitarian activity, something on which he placed a good deal of emphasis. The Unamunian concept of community starts by being based on language, and it is as such that it appears in *En torno al casticismo* and in many earlier essays, but it develops into a more spiritually driven notion, as we see in *La tía Tula*. Indeed I would go so far as to say that the idea of human existence as fundamentally communitarian is far more pronounced in Unamuno than in Heidegger or Sartre; for it is surprising that in spite of the Heideggerian *being-with-others* and the Sartrean *being-for-others*, these thinkers have very little to say on what a community is or what it is to live in community, and the little they have to say tends to be negative. Even the theologian Rudolf Bultmann, strongly influenced by Heidegger, has nothing positive to say about the Christian community, and complains that the Church represents, as does society in Sartre, a danger for the individual because it has the power to wrest authenticity from him.[28] For Kierkegaard too, the other represents a potential distraction from the narrow path to God, a notion that we certainly do not find in Unamuno. Apart perhaps from the Jewish writer Martin Buber, who in his well-known 1922 work *I and Thou* explored human reciprocity and inter-relationship, the only existentialist thinker who had important things to say about communal existence was Gabriel Marcel, a convert to Catholicism, which might suggest that this interest in the role of the community in our lives has something to do with the Catholic doctrine of the communion of saints, which can be regarded as a kind of hypothetical version of the historical transmission of communal consciousness as well as of continuity;

---

[27] Stephen G. H. Roberts has given us an excellent account of community seen from a socio-political perspective. See Roberts, 2007.

[28] See Bultmann, 1955, and the discussion in Macquarrie, 1973: 202–11.

of continuity because that community that exists through the 'communion' or communication among its members is formed by the living and the dead in the city of God. This concept of a corporate personality to which the living and the dead are attached is something which Christianity inherited from Judaism: the idea which we find in St Paul is a continuation of the Jewish notion of community, which perhaps explains why we find it in both Martin Buber and Gabriel Marcel. The Catholic doctrine of the communion of saints is of course a mystical construction, not a rational or political one, but one nonetheless which is explained perfectly clearly in the encyclical of Pope Leo XIII *Mirae Caritatis*, as well as in the commentary on that encyclical to be found in the *Catholic Encyclopaedia*.

In Unamuno this historical transmission from generation to generation has a primordially linguistic basis (as in Herder and Humboldt), for it is from language that a community springs, since speech is a communitarian activity. The idea of a linguistically based community, which Unamuno invokes frequently whenever he refers to his much-desired pan-Hispanism,[29] acquires in late works clearly religious hues, although this religiosity is not of an orthodox kind. In fact Unamuno had already indicated in an essay of 1900, 'La fe' (VIII, 333–46), that his concept of communal life was fundamentally religious: life with others, he had written in this work, should take the form of a religious community, an idea that many years later he would develop novelistically. This quasi-religiosity of communal life consists in self-realization through others. Living through others does not mean obliterating one's self but, on the contrary, interacting through what I can only call a process of lending and borrowing, what Unamuno vaguely terms 'imposición mutua' in *Del sentimiento trágico de la vida*. It amounts to making one's presence felt while feeling the presence of others. Unamuno treats this as a lay vocation, since he speaks of the need to implement this outlook in every profession and in all walks of life. He sees this less in terms of sacrifice and more in terms of creation. Gertrudis sacrifices her reproductive instinct in order to create a family community, and Ángela Carballino does the same out of fidelity to Don Manuel and his community. We are here very close to Gabriel Marcel's 'creative fidelity', a fidelity to others that has to transcend particular circumstances and temporality. But these Unamunian characters do not arrive at their decisions easily or out of an intellectual conviction, for if there is one thing about them that the novelist makes clear it is that they have to fight their doubts to persevere in their communitarian enterprise. They also show that they possess that capacity that Marcel called *disponibilité*, the ability to express themselves through others rather than through contemplative withdrawal. Against Sartre's opinion that individual freedom and interpersonal relations are incompatible, Marcel argues that it is precisely freedom that makes such relationships possible (Marcel, 2002: 30–32, 51–52). It is the freedom that I possess that enables me to make myself available to others. It is in this transcending towards others that Marcel, unlike Sartre, locates a more authentic existence. According to Sartre, 'I am an existent in the midst of other existents; but I cannot "realize" this existence in the midst of others' (Sartre, 2003; 568–69). The other is a hindrance to one's

---

[29] For Unamuno's pan-Hispanism see Stephen G. H. Roberts, 2000 and 2004.

self-fulfilment, and to seek to live through interpersonal relationships leads to an inauthentic mode of being. According to Marcel, on the other hand, it is my openness to others, my availability or *disponibilité*, that makes my own personal existence meaningful. This participation in communal life is for Marcel a necessary condition for the achievement of a fully human status. Fidelity to the other, and hence reciprocity, is the consummation of personal liberty. In his exploration of the theme of community in his novels, Unamuno would seem to occupy a half-way position between Sartre and Marcel. On the one hand, the community exists because we create it ourselves and devote ourselves to it; on the other, this devotion is not wholly disinterested. Let us look at Unamuno's treatment of the theme in two of his novels.

In *La tía Tula*, Gertrudis appears as the founder of a community (Unamuno suggests the comparison with St Teresa),[30] and in *San Manuel Bueno, mártir* Ángela (a modern Mary Magdalene) becomes the continuator and upholder of the community founded by Father Manuel Bueno (whom she sees as a latter-day Jesus Christ). What function do these communities serve? In effect they serve to provide cohesion, solidarity, what Spanish sociologists call *religación*. This rootedness or sense of belonging helps to overcome temporal barriers, the consciousness of degeneration and finitude which we observe all around us. Both Gertrudis and the parish priest of Valverde de Lucerna place great value on the idea of transmission and continuity: the community that each of them has created must be superior to the longevity of their founders. The expiry of the latter must be transcended. Before she dies, Gertrudis transfers her responsibility as Mother Superior of the community to Manolita in what is clearly a rite of apostolic succession. The goal of that religio-domestic community has been to sustain the family's solidarity and inculcate in the new generations a perennial allegiance to truth, justice, and fraternity, but above all a sense of togetherness. Unamuno does not end the story with the death of Gertrudis, but continues it for another two chapters in order to emphasize the continuity of her work and her presence in the family even after her empirical death. From beyond the grave Gertrudis continues to exercise her influence, sowing peace and co-existence whenever discord threatens. Her memory is sacred, for if Gertrudis dies physically she does not die spiritually, or, as Unamuno indicates, her noumenal presence survives her bodily presence: '¿Murió la tía Tula? No, sino que empezó a vivir en la familia, e irradiando de ella, con una nueva vida más entrañada y más vivífica, con la vida eterna de la familiaridad inmortal' (I, 896). Hers, then, is a radiant presence at the heart of her community. She is the community and the community is her in a mutually supportive relationship.

When I said a moment ago that on the question of communal life Unamuno seems to occupy a halfway space between the atheist Sartre and the believer Marcel it was Gertrudis I had in mind, for if, on the one hand, there is no doubt that Gertrudis gives herself totally to her own, on the other, we cannot but see Gertrudis's quest for spiritual perdurance as a substitute for biological procreation. And whatever psychological motives we may choose to discern in Gertrudis's

---

[30] For the religious symbolism of the novel, David G. Turner, 1974: 92–106, is still the most reliable study.

behaviour, the salient fact of the story is that she is not bequeathing her genes but her moral philosophy. But is this a meaningful quest? 'To be dead is to be a prey for the living. [...] the one who tries to grasp the meaning of his future death must discover himself as the future prey of others', wrote Jean-Paul Sartre (2003: 564). If this is true, to be a future prey is what Gertrudis is aiming for. Yet it is questionable whether that is how Unamuno, or even his fictional character, sees it. Gertrudis, and by implication Unamuno, see it in terms of continuity rather than in terms of appropriation and victimization. It is true that the final beseeching cry, 'que no se den cuenta de que me he muerto' (I, 891), which Gertrudis on her death-bed twice directs at Manolita, suggests a desire to impose her presence not just on the others as she has been doing all along, but also on a fate that seems to condemn us to ultimate oblivion. And yet the way Gertrudis's exhortation to Manolita is formulated — 'Let them not realize that I am no longer here' — reveals not so much a concern for self as a concern for others. In other words what is sacred for Gertrudis is not her person but her precept, the sense of togetherness she has instilled in her adopted family and which she now urges Manolita to carry on fomenting. The domestic community founded by Gertrudis and to which she devotes her life can thus be seen not simply as a substitute for her aspiration to immortality, which is hardly a Christian stance, but also as a testament to her faith in enduring values that reach beyond the realm of the physical. Gertrudis shows no great concern with one's prospects in the next life, whether by way of punishment or reward. Her concern is very much with preserving the spirituality of this one. Irrespective of whether she herself aspires to live on in the memory of her adoptive children, this preservation of spiritual values requires that she does her best to ensure the presence in the community of the living spirit of those who have predeceased her, Ramiro and his two wives, who are constantly invoked when she speaks to their children and whose portraits are prominently displayed. For Gertrudis therefore what is important is to ensure that the dead continue to form an integral part of the community over which she presides, and when she dies it is Manolita, her successor, who takes over responsibility for maintaining alive the spiritual reality of Gertrudis: 'Ella era la historia doméstica; por ella se continuaba la eternidad espiritual de la familia' (I, 897). Unamuno's characteristic phrase, 'eternidad espiritual' is a giveaway, the triumph of mind over matter. This spiritual presence is not subject to physical decay; it is inherent in the community itself, a permanent bond between the family militant and the family triumphant. The parallel with the Catholic doctrine of the communion of saints could hardly be clearer, even if we are dealing here with a secular or profane equivalent. In our next case, however, the sacred and the profane are irremediably mixed.

In the preceding chapter I argued that Father Manuel Bueno's position as perceived by Ángela was logically untenable. To hold religious belief to be valid for others and not for oneself is a contradiction which robs the idea of valid belief of any reliable application. There is, however, a different way of approaching Father Manuel's position which bypasses this logical contradiction. This puts to one side the criterion of validity — of whether belief in X is valid or invalid, since it cannot be both — and looks instead at the effects of the position adopted. Religious belief is clearly not just about hope in personal survival after death. What has made religion throughout the ages meaningful is its communality. The word religion, which shares its etymological root with the Latin *religare*, to bind, to bundle, implies something that holds together. It is a more powerful form (usually, though not invariably) of tribalism or nationality because it — or at least some versions of religion — has come to transcend the particular language that created it and to appeal to a diversity of linguistic communities; but it is still closely tied to language and plays a similar role.[31] It is its ability to bond its followers that gives a religion its significance, rather than any promises it makes to an individual about his or her immortality. Such guarantees of perdurance, which in any case have not been offered by all religions, are today received, and have been for some time, with widespread scepticism; yet people still continue to belong to church communities and in some degree to practise a religion. In his book *Christian Atheist*, Brian Mountford argues persuasively that what brings people to a religion is the sense of belonging that they find. 'What we are describing', he writes, 'is a territory between faith and reason, between embedded religious culture and secularism, physics and metaphysics, gospel and organised religion, the temporal and the absolute, that it is proper to occupy; that in fact that is the territory where most people live' (Mountford, 2011: 17).[32] It is somewhere in this territory too that we can place Father Manuel Bueno as Ángela Carballino has revealed him. The uncomplicated allegiance of his parishioners to the Church of Valverde de Lucerna provides them with a sense of belonging, a solidarity of outlook that encompasses life and death, possession and loss. This is what Don Manuel refers to as 'unanimidad de sentido' (II, 330), as if recognizing that it is not in the particularities of belief that the value of religion lies but in providing a collective identity and sense of purpose, a sense of purpose that is shared not just by the doubter Ángela and the unbeliever Lázaro but of course by Don Manuel himself, even if he does not share the theological underpinnings. The contradiction that is there if we see Don Manuel's position solely in terms of adherence to a particular set of beliefs melts away when we see it in terms of communal identity, for Don Manuel is very much a part of that corporate existence. Don Manuel's story, however, starts a little earlier.

As was pointed out in Chapter 5, we find in *San Manuel Bueno, mártir* an interesting parallel with *La tía Tula*. Don Manuel, like Gertrudis, did not have a religious vocation. He became a priest to help his widowed sister and serve as father to his orphaned nephews. Instead of begetting a family himself he adopts one. The idea of community, then, begins with the family, and from there it extends to the whole village of Valverde, which encompasses the village of today and that of yesterday, the village by the lake and that submerged in its waters, one adjacent to the other. When Ángela's mother is close to death Don Manuel tells the dying

---

[31] For the linguistic origins of myths and religions see F. Max Müller, 1866 and 2002. Unamuno was familiar with Müller's writings.

[32] In an interview with anthropologist Nigel Hamway the latter explains how he can be an atheist and an Anglican at the same time (Mountford, 2011: 13–17). For him it is not a matter of reconciling opposing beliefs but of accepting religion as an anthropological category, as part of the human story.

woman that she is not departing for another world but that she will continue to be in this one, next to her children, because that is where God is to be found. In the same way that Gertrudis names Manolita her successor, Don Manuel, on sensing the approach of death, asks Lázaro to continue his mission as Joshua continued that of Moses. And the narrator confirms that 'Lázaro continuaba la tradición del santo' (II, 341). When Lázaro dies, Ángela, without her master and her brother, submerges herself in the soul of her village, of that village created by Father Manuel and continued by Lázaro, or as she says in quasi-mystical language, 'no vívia yo ya en mí, sino que vivía en mi pueblo y mi pueblo vivía en mí' (II, 343). The departed are described as 'muertos de vida' (II, 343), an oxymoron borrowed from the mystics and which invokes the continuing presence of the dead members in the collective consciousness of the villagers, in precisely the same way as it is invoked in the domestic community created by Gertrudis. Generations may pass, Unamuno implies, but their spirit remains, precisely because the village is itself a collective spirit, or as Unamuno writes of his symbolical Valverde de Lucerna, 'no era un coro, sino una sola voz' (II, 318). Life acquires meaning only through the community, and as we saw in Chapter 3 meaning for a community is invested in its language, its 'voz'. Communal identity is located precisely at the intersection between language and religion.

On two occasions, Unamuno, through his narrator, makes Father Manuel utter the phrase 'unanimidad de sentido', which at a time dominated by an invasive subjectivism after the collapse of nineteenth-century ways of thinking (Positivism, determinism, scientism), is especially significant, above all in light of the view of Unamuno as an insatiable egocentric, still occasionally encountered. To be a community is to have 'unanimidad de sentido', to share a collective outlook, and that is where Don Manuel's faith is firmly located, and not in some future reward. This idea of community that Unamuno is sustaining in *San Manuel Bueno, mártir*, may also be seen to have theological implications. For it is no longer a case of a God who is a mere consequence of a 'quiero que Dios exista' (IX , 53) of the 1907 essay 'Mi religión'. Father Manuel's God is fully a social God, not a God of the individual or an individual God.[33] Unamuno seems here to be harking back to Genesis 1. 27, which tells us that God created man in his own image, a view found in St Augustine's *On the Psalms*, promulgated in the Catholic catechism, and re-emphasized by Unamuno's contemporary, the Christian existentialist Nikolai Berdyaev. Given that man is overwhelmingly a social creature, it must follow from the Bible that God must be too, and indeed this idea is found starkly expressed in *Del sentimiento trágico de la vida*: 'Dios [es] un producto social' (*DSTV*, X, 297). But if God is a social God, then clearly he must participate in our own society in some way or other. Father Manuel's view of God as a part of, and not apart from, the community of Valverde de Lucerna far from being an atheistic denial of God's existence seems entirely in keeping with the Biblical concept of God implied by Genesis. The God of the Old Testament is a communitarian God. He exists for

---

[33] A social God must not of course be confused with the 'reinado social de Jesucristo' which in *La agonía del cristianismo*, Chapter VII, Unamuno denounces as a convenient politicization of Christianity by conservative forces and especially the Jesuits.

and through his creation, the peak of which is mankind. Unamuno's incursion into theology, if such it is, is perfectly intelligible and coherent. God, irrespective of the (for us) insoluble question of His objective existence, is part of our collective consciousness.[34] In the end it matters not whether He made us or we made Him, since we have a symbiotic relationship and we cannot be separated. As Father Manuel says, 'Dios, hija mía, está aquí como en todas partes, y le verá usted desde aquí. Y a todos nosotros en Él, y a Él en nosotros' (II, 327).[35]

The Church visible and the Church invisible, above and below the waters of the lake, thus co-exist alongside each other in a communion that transcends physical and temporal barriers. All who belong are drawn to the centre: Don Manuel, who returns from the seminary, Ángela, who returns from her city school, Lázaro, who returns from America, the disgraced daughter of Tía Rabona, who returns from the city, the sick and possessed, who come to bathe in the waters of the lake, and the labourers who come in from the fields. All converge on their community. The taking of communion in public on the part of Lázaro is of course highly symbolic. It signifies much more than an induction into the club led by Don Manuel; it establishes his participation in a community that stretches beyond the immediate confines of the present and the visible, as Ángela's words make very clear: '¡Ay, Lázaro, Lázaro!, ¡qué alegría nos has dado a todos, a todos, a todo el pueblo, a todo, a los vivos y a los muertos, y sobre todo a mamá, a nuestra madre!' (II, 329). Ángela here invokes the presence of the entire community, both alive and departed, including their dead mother, as witnesses to Lázaro's full membership of the spiritual community that is Valverde.

Just as Gertrudis names Manolita as successor to the leadership of the domestic community, so Father Manuel names Lázaro as his successor, a Joshua who is to take over from Moses, or as Ángela sees him a St Peter to continue the work of Jesus Christ.[36] The idea of apostolic succession is once again present. When Lázaro

---

[34] God is, according to Unamuno, an emotional need, not a rational necessity. 'Dios y el hombre se hacen mutuamente [...], y si cada cual de nosotros, en el empuje de su amor, en su hambre de divinidad, se imagina a Dios a su medida, y a su medida se hace Dios para él, hay un Dios colectivo, social, humano, resultante de las imaginaciones todas humanas que le imaginan. Porque Dios es y se revela en la colectividad', he had written in *Del sentimiento trágico de la vida* (*DSTV*, X, 410).

[35] Bénédicte Vauthier interprets this as a sign of panentheism (the belief that God inheres in every part of the universe but is ontologically greater than the universe), which, she argues, makes of Don Manuel a Krausist. For her, *San Manuel Bueno, mártir* is an ironic denunciation of Menéndez y Pelayo for his rabid attack on the Krausists. The irony, according to Vauthier, lies in the fact that Don Manuel is a Krausist yet is about to be beatified by the Catholic Church (Vauthier, 1998). Vauthier sees irony where there is probably none. For there is nothing heterodox about Father Manuel's declaration, which is far from uncommon in Catholicism. Indeed there is a whole Christian tradition of seeing God through nature. St Augustine, for example, said in his *De Trinitate* that God's presence is observed in nature, and in his commentary on Psalm 26 he said that God's mind inheres in nature much as an artist's mind inheres in his work. Father Manuel's words echo those found in *Del sentimiento trágico de la vida*, VIII, 416, which in turn are based on Acts of the Apostles 17. 24–28, as Nelson Orringer has pointed out in his edition of *DSTV* (Unamuno, 2005: 331, n. 86).

[36] The connection with St Peter is of course made through the reference to the cock crowing on the day of Lázaro's communion (Matthew 26. 34 and 74; Mark 14. 30, 68 and 72).

dies he becomes another link between the living and the dead, 'otra laña más entre las dos Valverdes de Lucerna, la del fondo del lago y la que en su sobrehaz se mira' (II, 343), despite his unbelief in a personal afterlife. Lázaro of course has his own reasons for becoming a communicant which have nothing to do with personal survival and a great deal to do with social commitment, but, as we observe, he is not required by Don Manuel to sacrifice his deepest beliefs or unbeliefs, any more than Don Manuel sacrifices his. A true community, Unamuno seems to suggest, does not need to erase individual diversity. Indeed the danger of depersonalization, of removing personal choice and substituting impersonal codes and materialistic ends, may come from collectivism rather than community, as Don Manuel seems to suggest when Lázaro proposes founding a Catholic agrarian collective. If he dissuades Lázaro from going down such a road it is not on economic or political grounds, but rather on the grounds that such institutions can breed confrontations whereas his community of Valverde exists to promote contentment, unselfishness, and a sense of purpose, or as he adds, 'que se consuelen de haber nacido, que vivan lo más contentos que puedan en la ilusión de que todo esto tiene una finalidad' (II 335), a sentiment later repeated by Lázaro to her sister, 'hay que hacer que vivan de la ilusión' (II, 341), in a similarly ambiguous phrase, since 'ilusión' means both mirage and hope. This teleology can only truly exist communally, where the other becomes the sense of purpose of the one. If Unamuno is actually proposing Father Manuel as an ideal of hope, he has moved a considerable way from Kierkegaard, for Kierkegaard, we must remember, had little regard for a communal spirit and saw the other as a potential obstacle on the individual's path to God. If anything, Don Manuel's position is exactly at the other end of the scale: we will only find God in the other.

Lázaro, then, is not called upon to abandon his socialist ideals, but comes round to Don Manuel's way of thinking anyway. To instate 'progressive' views is to misread the nature of the real problem, for what is required first is 'fe en el contento de la vida' (II, 341). To impose dogmatic belief and dogmatic unbelief are equally harmful. Towards the end of the novel Lázaro, explaining how Father Manuel won him over to his cause, says to his sister:

> — Él me hizo un hombre nuevo, un verdadero Lázaro, un resucitado — me decía — . Él me dió fe.
> — ¿Fe? — le interrumpía yo.
> — Sí, fe, fe en el consuelo de la vida. Él me curó de mi progresismo. Porque hay, Ángela, dos clases de hombres peligrosos y nocivos; los que convencidos de la vida de ultratumba, de la resurrección de la carne, atormentan, como inquisidores que son, a los demás para que, despreciando esta vida como transitoria, se ganen la otra; y los que no creyendo más que en este mundo [...] esperan no sé qué sociedad futura y se esfuerzan en negarle al pueblo el consuelo de creer en otro. (II, 341)

The faith that Lázaro discovers, the one Father Manuel has pointed to, is a faith that is beyond both dogmatism and scepticism. It is faith in the solace of life, a faith that acknowledges both the material and the spiritual dimension of the human community. God thus becomes, in Father Manuel's religious sociology, the collective belief of the community, what gives the village, in his own words, 'unanimidad de sentido'.[37] Time and again Unamuno insisted that human nature is profoundly social. Our identity, as we have seen, arises from others. So does our language, and hence our ideas. To think is to engage in a dialogue with others, or with our own other when there are no others. To dialogue is to interact linguistically. The God of the community of Valverde is the God created by the dialogue between Don Manuel and Lázaro, as is clearly shown in the communion scene. This God is a God at the service of the community; He is its inter-communal dialogue. It goes without saying that this is a relative, not an absolute God, because each one can believe in Him in his or her own way, as we observe in the differing positions adopted by Lázaro, Ángela, Blasillo, the possessed women, the simple villagers, and Father Manuel himself. God is to be found, to use the narrator's own phrase, 'en el lago espiritual de nuestro pueblo' (II, 318); God is that lake precisely because He exists and reveals himself in 'la colectividad' rather than in the individual's own preferences. For Unamuno as for Father Manuel — and this is the one point on which they do coincide — the sense of God and the sense of community are inseparable. We do not know what Don Manuel's personal religious beliefs are, but we do know *what he stands for*. Written in 1930, a time when uncertainty and fear gripped Spain, a time of political indecision and social insecurity, *San Manuel Bueno, mártir* emphasizes the importance of social binding, of that communal outlook that the parish priest Don Manuel and the anticlerical socialist Lázaro Carballino — representatives of that divided Spain which in real life was *not* to learn how to live in peaceful coexistence — instigate and accomplish in their parishioners. These two central preoccupations that Unamuno entertained throughout his life, his country and his perdurance, come poetically together in this highly suggestive farewell to the novel genre.

Conclusion

In her book *Crossfire: Philosophy and the Novel in Spain, 1900–1934*, Roberta Johnson has called the Unamunian novel a 'representational philosophical novel', a work that is truly a novel and yet is self-consciously philosophical in intent' (Johnson, 1993: 103). It is this dual approach to novel writing, what Johnson herself refers to as 'a bold new hybridity', that indeed characterizes Unamuno's approach to the genre, an approach that was to be followed decades later by such well-known examples as *La Nausée* (1938), *L'Étranger* (1942), and *Der Mann ohne Eigenschaften* [*The Man without Qualities*] (1942). It is both a way of creating fiction and of exploring imaginatively some pretty central problems of metaphysics. Whether we are free, what death means for us, and how our existence is primarily communal, are three topics that loom large in Unamuno's fiction.

That Unamuno was familiar with the philosophical debate about freedom of the will seems clear enough; less clear, however, is just where he stands on this,

---

[37] As indicated earlier, in *Del sentimiento trágico de la vida* Unamuno had given us a glimpse of his other version of God, not the personal God but the social God: '[...] si hay sentimiento y concepto colectivo, social, es el de Dios, aunque el individuo lo individualice luego. [...] la teología es necesariamente colectiva' (*DSTV*, X, 400).

although from the point of view of novelistic theory what matters is that he saw the topic as a promising one for exploitation through narrative. While environmental determinism à la Taine is still detectable in his first novel, *Paz en la guerra*, from *Amor y pedagogía* onwards the issue of determinism is presented in a much more abstract way, and the two novels in which the theme is most prominent are not at all concerned with historical and physical factors. The debate is presented almost exclusively in terms of self-identity. The question facing both Augusto Pérez and Joaquín Monegro is whether they are in control of their being or whether they are merely passive reactors to what happens to them. Unamuno's exploration of the topic through his fictional characters suggests that he does not question the idea of freedom of choice, but that he sees indeterminism as bringing its own problems. For Augusto Pérez those problems have to do largely with control. Controlling one's decisions does not necessarily mean controlling one's life. His plans do not work out. For Augusto this is incomprehensible and demoralizing, and ultimately leads to fatalism and despair. But as Gabriel Marcel wrote in his *Metaphysical Diary*, 'the possibility of despair is bound up with liberty' (Marcel, 1965a: 104); despair in a fully determined world would make no sense. Augusto's error, Unamuno suggests, is that of coming to think that his decisions do not count, or are not his, simply because the outcomes are not predictable. But this of course is the inescapable drawback of free will, that genuine freedom and predictability are incompatible. On this one point at any rate Unamuno is clear and consistent. We are free to make of ourselves what we will but always within the constraints imposed by other people's freedom. In the case of Joaquín the question is even more complex because his inclination towards determinism appears to be willed, but it is the source of this willing that is the real point at issue. Joaquín's pathological resentment is such as to surpass all rational explanation, and hence he comes to regard it as innate, as predetermined. Yet this does not stop him from setting that resentment aside when it comes to taking magnanimous decisions. What these altruistic decisions do not do, however, is stop or even attenuate those feelings of resentment. Joaquín is a good physician of others, but not of himself. He can control his actions while yet remaining prey to his misanthropic feelings. Here Unamuno is hinting strongly at the idea of a split personality, one part of which *acts* freely and the other of which *feels* compulsively. Joaquín can control the way he acts but not the way he feels. Unamuno is approaching the Free Will debate from his fundamental view of man as governed by both reason and emotion. Our reason tells us that we are free to choose what we do or refrain from doing; we enjoy no such freedom of choice when it comes to our emotions. Neither a free-wheeling determinist nor a determined free-willer, Unamuno's exploration of the theme is inconclusive yet persuasive.

Whereas freedom is a topic that was central to all existential philosophizing, death is rather less ubiquitous. Sartre argues, in opposition to Heidegger, that death, 'far from being my peculiar possibility, is a *contingent fact* which as such on principle escapes me and originally belongs to my facticity'. In other words death is so far removed from my experience that I might as well ignore it. I can neither discover anything about it nor take up an attitude towards it. 'Death is a pure fact, as is birth; it comes to us from outside and it transforms us into the outside. At bottom it is in no way distinguished from birth, and it is the identity of birth and death that we call facticity' (Sartre, 2003: 566). Unamuno would most probably not have agreed. For him, as for Heidegger, death is an ever-present possibility for the individual, and because he identifies himself through others he knows that what has already happened to others awaits him. There is something forced or artificial about Sartre's argument, for birth and death, far from being the same, are clearly distinguishable. Unless we equate existence with non-existence, at birth we are not being deprived of anything. At death we are being deprived of existence, of our being and of our-being-with-others. Most people, one imagines, would be happy to see their lives extended forward, for death to be postponed, perhaps indefinitely. How many of those same people would wish their lives to be extended backwards, to have their births pushed back?[38] To equate birth and death is to devalue life, something Unamuno never did, not even at his most Schopenhauerian, at moments when life's purpose seemed impenetrable.[39] For Unamuno death is not so much a fact as a mystery: we do not know why something that is freely given is taken away. And he is very clear that it is not existence in the abstract that we are in danger of losing, but our awareness of existing, which is the only thing that counts. By existing we contribute to existence, and it is this active participation that, *contra* Sartre, who sees absurdity everywhere, makes life meaningful. In other words existence needs us, fully conscious beings. That is why death, for Unamuno, is hard to accept. For him, existence without consciousness is of no value. And that too is why his fictional characters strive heroically to express their own being in the face of death.

This being can only be expressed through others, for it is others who receive our presence as we receive theirs. And this leads straight into the concept of community. For Unamuno the teacher, his community was composed of his pupils, and for Unamuno the writer, of his imagined readers. Are we justified to see in his teaching or in his writing an expectation of ontological survival on his part? I think not. Community for Unamuno is a 'living in' rather than a 'living on', a part of that 'moral invasiva' which he advocates in *Del sentimiento trágico de la vida*. It is through interaction with others that we become fully conscious of ourselves as persons; and it is this same sentiment of living through others that we find in the works of fiction. The concept of community that comes through powerfully in *La tía Tula* and *San Manuel Bueno, mártir* is not one that emphasizes survival as against annihilation, but rather one that emphasizes retention as against loss. It is the living who retain the presence of the dead. The hope is the hope of the living that they will not lose their dead forever. In promoting a sense of communion between the living and the dead in his community of Valverde de Lucerna, Father Manuel Bueno is not promising the resurrection of the departed. His business is with the living, not with the dead. His role is to combat the sense of loss both of those who are dying and about to lose their loved ones, and of those who have lost them in remaining behind. Ángela's role in the community does not stop her from experiencing a terrible sense of loss, but it does ensure that the loss is shared, that

---

[38] A point made by Thomas Nagel, 1979: 7–8, and 1986: 229.
[39] 'Me gustaría desnacer, no morir' (II, 171), Unamuno makes his character Julio Macedo declare, thereby denying that the pre-existent and the post-existent states are the same.

the bond with the living is also a bond with the dead. For the latter's existence in our lives cannot be denied. Gabriel Marcel had his own aphoristic way of expressing the sentiment: 'To say of the dead, "they no longer exist", is not only to deny them, but to deny oneself, and perhaps to deny absolutely' (quoted in Blackham, 1961: 76). Our sense of loss is thus paradoxically a recognition of presence.

CONCLUSION

A Theory of the Novel?

For Unamuno writing was a form of self-discovery. But because that self or nuclear 'I' becomes cognizable only through writing it must be considered first and foremost a linguistic phenomenon. Whether there is an underlying 'real' self that is objectified in an author's work is unknown and perhaps unknowable. We can only know it as a mental construct. The same applies to a linguistic community's identity across time: this corporate identity is enshrined above all in its literature because that is what survives and where we can recognize it. This accords the activity of reading a crucial place in crystallizing that sense of identity that lies latently or potentially in the writing. Both are creative and inseparable activities, because each exists for the other. This exactly mirrors the notion of personality, which is a form of reading an individual, as well as of reading how an individual is read by others. The self appears as a text, that is to say as an interpretation, and it exists only as interpretation. The inner and outer worlds are inter-dependent. Reading is the outer world of writing in the same way that personality is the outer form of an inner self. Both living and writing are subject to this double dimension, the view from inside and the view from outside, the subjective and objective, the 'I' and the 'You' in conflict and collaboration. The novel thus becomes for Unamuno the expression of this double-sided view of existence: a living in my world and a living in the world of others. Whatever one may think of Unamunian ontology, with its constant struggle for cognition and recognition, the fact remains that his poetics of fiction is both coherent and consistent with his view of man as a constitutionally divided being trying to make sense of two seemingly different kinds of worlds.

Immanuel Kant famously identified the three most pressing questions of philosophy as God, freedom, and immortality. One could adjust this very slightly and say that for Unamuno the three pressing questions were: (1) identity (which includes the I–You, self–community relationship); (2) freedom (which includes the problem of agency and self-determination); and (3) death (which revolves around the teleological question of one's purpose and role in life). These three preoccupations are of course closely intertwined, but what is truly interesting is the way in which they have invaded his conception of the novel as an artistic genre. The first theme, identity, is reflected in the pervasive idea of writing and reading as creative acts that confer individual and collective personhood. The second theme, freedom, revolves around the debate of who, in a text, imposes decisions, outcomes, and interpretations in the tripartite command author-character-reader. The third theme, the prospect of death and consequent search for purpose, manifests itself in the constant hermeneutical challenge posed by the text, a time-bounded artefact that demands collaboration at every reading. A novel thus appears as a microcosm in which the author, the text, and the reader are caught in a web in which mutual dependencies are inextricably and transformingly at work.

Unamuno held strongly to the view that modern materialism — the materialism associated with nineteenth-century Positivism — fails to do justice to the spiritual or non-material dimension of the human entity, with its constant striving for knowledge, enduring values, and artistic self-expression. He did not object to materialist explanations of the surrounding world, including the human body together with its brain. What he objected to was materialist reductionism; and he countered this modern trend by positing the dominance of mind — or soul as he preferred to call it from his position as Professor of Greek — over body. A human person was for him an embodied soul. If Nature has given us consciousness, a consciousness that we know and value above all else, there must be a reason. From this simple premiss he approached the task of creative writing as a manifestation of the human desire to transcend our transient material circumstances and reach out for a more permanent form of identity. He did this primarily by abandoning the causal '¿por qué?' question and substituting the teleological or purposive '¿para qué?' question. For Unamuno writing became a search for purpose, whether mankind's or an individual's. His fictional output partakes of this basic goal by becoming a medium of exploration of fundamental questions concerning our make-up and our role. But this questioning about roles encompassed the medium itself, as well as those who participate in it, authors, readers, and characters.

Largely as a result of the pervasive influence of Unamuno's religious philosophy as expounded in *Del sentimiento trágico de la vida*, his fictional corpus has been turned by the academy into a bleak and tragic statement on the human situation. While some works are sombre and disturbing, notably so *Abel Sánchez*, if we take his work as a whole, humour, both black and white, is far from absent, as we observe in *Amor y pedagogía* and *Niebla*, which are veritable tragicomedies or 'bufo trágico' as Víctor Goti describes the genre in the latter novel, and *Un pobre hombre rico*, which exploits a farcical story with elements of *grand guignol*, or even the sad but teasing story of Don Sandalio the chess player which thrives on the mischievous technique of non-disclosure. We should not discard the humour and entertainment value of Unamuno's fiction, often revealed in racy dialogues, pithy remarks, and a certain penchant for incongruities reminiscent of Schopenhauer's 'Theory of the Ludicrous' (Schopenhauer, 1966: I, 58–61 and II, 91–101).[1]

While the entertainment value is there, it is clear nevertheless that the novel was, for Unamuno, much more than a literary genre aimed at filling moments of leisure. Ciríaco Morón Arroyo expresses this well when he says that Unamuno's symbolic art is not aimed primarily at synaesthetic effects but rather 'pretende fundir en la obra de arte las más hondas procupaciones del hombre' (Morón Arroyo, 2003: 164). Fictional writing was in a very real sense both a cognitive and a preceptive tool

---

[1]   For a study of the grotesque in Unamuno see Antonio Vilanova, 1989.

that may reasonably be studied alongside Unamuno's more purely discursive essays as the revelation of a philosophy in the making, an exploration of possibilities and not a completed system. This is entirely in accordance with his expressed view. In response to Jules Verne, who had manifested pessimistic views on the state of the novel, Unamuno wrote in 1902: 'Muy lejos de decaer el papel de la novela, ábrensele a ésta cada vez nuevos y más amplios horizontes, y puede asegurarse que las novelas son hoy el canal más importante por donde llega al público el pensamiento sociológico, ético, religioso, y filosófico de los maestros'.[2] Like Bakhtin and Lukács after him, Unamuno regarded the novel as the very expression of contemporaneity, a channel through which to reach an even greater audience than he could reach in the lecture room or the Athenaeum. Through the novel he addressed fundamental problems related to our constitution and our situation, the problematic nature of our freedom, how our need to exercise our decision-making capacity is a source of anxiety, how that raises questions about our identity and our future, how that identity is intimately tied to the beings who surround us, that is, reciprocally connected to seeing and being seen, and how this idea of inter-dependency leads in turn to the idea of a living community, of a way of life expressed through others, and how if this is universally applied, recognized by each and every one of us, we can achieve that 'unanimity of meaning' of which Don Manuel Bueno speaks and whose maximum expression is a social God. In Unamuno's fiction, psychology, sociology, and theology are rolled into one. If Baroja called the novel 'un saco donde cabe todo' and Pérez de Ayala 'un breve universo', Unamuno could well have called it 'un universo donde cabe todo un hombre', a universe, that is, which aspired to encapsulate man in all his complexity, contradiction, and anxiety.

That is the broad outlook that underlies Unamuno's fiction. But his conception of the novel as an artistic genre is both more specific and more derivative. Indeed it is his familiarity with English and German writers of the late eighteenth and early nineteenth centuries that informs his ideas on writing. In other words, Unamuno's notions are essentially Romantic. But whereas Romantic theory applied above all to poetry, Unamuno applies it equally to compositions in prose. For this he has to ascribe to prose some of the qualities more typically perceived in poetry, and while he does not go very far in specifying what these qualities are, he does at any rate make it clear that a novelist who has the capacity to share in the sentiments of his characters is the one who will create poetically. 'Una novela es un poema. Cuando lo es, claro. Y cuando no lo es, tampoco es novela' (*Alrededor*, 94). The greatest novels, like the greatest autobiographies, were for Unamuno poems precisely because they entailed a use of language to evoke inner worlds. Poets are seen as creative writers who are capable of using language in such a way as to summon hidden worlds from the depth of their being, irrespective of the genre they happen to be utilizing.

In common with the Romantics, Unamuno entertained an expressivist concept of literary creation, that is to say, the notion that writing is the outward expression of an inner state. For the Romantics the source of art in general and poetry in particular was no longer nature, nor even nature refracted through the artist's mind;

---

[2]   From 'El porvenir de la novela', *Obras Completas* (Escelicer), VII, 1281.

art was quite simply the creation of the mind itself.[3] The idea that true nature lies within and not without, that by being faithful to our sentiments and outlook we are being faithful to nature, goes back to Herder, was taken up by the German Romantics of the late eighteenth century, and greatly expanded upon by the English Romantics. In Romantic literary theory, the idea that underlies literary creation is that the poet's mind acts not as a mirror of nature outside, but as a projector of nature inside. The poet thus becomes the centre of the poetic universe, not an interpreter or mediator but an originator. Expressivism is really self-expressivism. This, too, becomes Unamuno's position. His starting point was to place the author at the centre of the work, and in his essays he repeatedly distinguished between authentic and inauthentic writing, a distinction which hinged on an author's use of language: it can be used parrot-fashion or it can be used creatively. Authentic expression involves using words in a way — what Unamuno calls the poetic way — the aim of which is to reveal an inner world which competes with, modifies, or greatly expands upon the world of logical reasoning. To transmit such a sensation the writer has to do so 'por emoción estética, por obra de arte' (VIII, 666). It is only through the creative use of language that a writer can convey what Unamuno calls 'revelaciones sustanciales', such as those achieved by writers of the stature of Shakespeare or Calderón (VIII, 667).[4]

For Unamuno, then, any form of expression is the voice of the writer's inner nature, and to have the capacity to listen to it is to have the capacity to express it. This, too, was a central tenet of Romanticism: that the work cannot be separated from the spirit that produced it. Expression was seen to be integral to what was expressed, inseparable from it. Whether poet or novelist, the result is the same: self-creation. 'Todo poeta, todo creador, todo novelador — novelar es crear — , al crear personajes se está creando a sí mismo, y si le nacen muertos es que él vive muerto' (II, 382). To express is to create because what is expressed did not truly exist prior to its formulation. There can be no radical distinction between what is expressed and the manner of its expression, for the artist's nature is in his art; and his art is a manifestation of his life. This manifestation is itself a defining quality of a life, a mind. Art becomes self-articulation. In this Unamuno is simply following the views of Herder — who saw literature as the spirit of its progenitors — and of those nineteenth-century thinkers of language, such as Schleiermacher and Humboldt, who, building on Herder's insight, saw linguistic expression as a window into the soul of the speaker or writer.

Unamuno does not reject the rational language of science or traditional western philosophy; but he sees such language as dealing or aspiring to deal in abstractions, whereas the language of poetry is based on personal experience, hence the appeal to the poet's own. A novel is thus autobiographical in the sense that it arises from personal experience — what the writer knows, perceives, feels, and above all discovers. And if poetic expression represents the writer's experience or state of

---

[3] The shift from the mimetic to the expressivist was well documented by M. H. Abrams, 1953.

[4] The position adopted by Unamuno can be observed in his essay '¡Plenitud de plenitudes y todo plenitud!' (VIII, 655–71) in which he advocates a poetic, i.e. creative, approach to life, something he has in common with his Russian contemporary Nikolai Berdyaev.

mind, then in that sense it is at least as true as science. This inevitably leads to another and much more dubious assumption, that of sincerity. The title of one of Unamuno's essays, 'Sobre la consecuencia, la sinceridad', tells well enough where his priorities lie, and the content of the article where his anxieties are located; but Unamuno offers little guidance on how a reader might discriminate between authentic and inauthentic writing except through the presence of a vibrant or an affected style. Style for Unamuno is crucial because it is the connecting link between him and his readers. It is through the author's style that readers form their impression of him. But the idea of using style to impact the reader is deceptive. In Romantic theory the reader as addressee, who had been very much present in the imaginative literature of the seventeenth and eighteenth centuries as the essential receptor of the work, is replaced by the poet himself. 'All poetry is in the nature of soliloquy', in the words of John Stuart Mill (quoted in Abrams, 1953: 25).[5] Given that in Unamuno the presence of a reader is frequently invoked, there would seem to be a clear difference of emphasis here. But the invocation of a reader does not by itself establish a clear difference from Romanticism. Unamuno's reader is a creation of his: not the assumed real audience who will be reading his novels but a ghostly entity that represents more than anything a defence of his unconventional approach to the genre. This hypothetical reader who reads as Unamuno would like to be read is no more than a critical version of himself, a part of that unfolding of himself into writer and reader that he often invokes through various metaphors (the mirror, the book, the double). So instead of Mill's soliloquy what we have is a 'monodiálogo'. What counts in both cases is not simply the external world (and its readers), but the internal world, which includes these writers' apprehension of their own image as an external object. For Unamuno that internal image needs to be objectified, confirmed, and it is in that process that he brings his readers back to fulfil their function.

Unamuno's frequent invocation of a reader is part and parcel of his attempt to cultivate a new type of fiction. The real reader is of course the depository of reading conventions, and such conventions are likely to get in the way of an appreciative reading of radically unconventional works. Just as for Wordsworth and Shelley the poet had to act as a kind of teacher whose task was to enlighten the understanding of the readers, especially in a moral sense, so for Unamuno the novelist has to be an educator who strives, or should strive, to teach his readers how to read in such a way as to grasp the complexities, contradictions, and enigmas of the person. As experiences, reading and writing become inseparable, both sharing in the creative act of conferring significance to the text. The novel begins as the manifestation of a vision of a particular consciousness, which is instantiated in the very act of writing; but it is the act of reading that ultimately confers sense on the writing, is indeed already implicit in it, for to write is necessarily to read. The function of a reader, or rather of reading, is to structure the text, because the text demands a response, a

---

[5] Abrams comments: 'The purpose of producing effects upon other men, which for centuries had been the defining character of the art of poetry, now serves precisely the opposite function: it disqualifies a poem by proving it to be rhetoric instead. [...] there is in fact something singularly fatal to the audience in the romantic point of view' (Abrams, 1953: 25).

filling out, a completion. What Unamuno is saying about the role of the reader is essentially what a number of post-structuralist theoreticians were to say over half a century later: that the structure or 'meaning' of narrative is created, not unveiled, by the readers and their baggage.

In one important sense Unamuno's theory of the novel reduces to a theory of reading. The reader is immanent in the text no less than the author. To write is to prefigure the reading; indeed to write is to engage in a dialogue with a reader. Reading is not seen as a future event but as a fully concurrent one. It is a necessary adjunct to writing for the simple reason that language is directed at another. Writing is a writing for, the famous 'para qué' that Unamuno always saw as the key question facing man, a matter of ends rather than of beginnings. His approach to creative writing is thus intimately connected to his theory of personal identity. An I implies a Thou, and to be aware of oneself is to engage in a perpetual dialogue with the self we carry within us, a self derived from others, what Unamuno called 'el otro'. If this awareness of myself becomes as it were my second person with whom I must always dialogue and who will exercise a shaping influence upon me, when I become a writer that second self will take the form of the reader who will be watching, questioning, moulding every word I write, every decision I take. To create is to create for, and just as he saw the conscious mind as the mark of identity of the universe, so Unamuno saw the reader as co-creator, inhering in the writing act and conferring significance upon it. Existing in a symbiotic relationship, God and man, self and other, writer and reader are but different facets of the two-dimensional world, the inner and outer, that we inhabit. Our role as readers is the same as our role as humans: to confer meaning.

Unamuno goes beyond Saussure's view that the meaning of a sign is merely a matter of convention. He suggests that meaning can never be fully realized: texts, which are after all conjunctions of words, have to be made to mean. Like language itself, an Unamunian text does not mean but is rather an invitation to meaning. Unamuno is only too conscious that as a writer he reveals himself linguistically, but since language is not something that possesses a stable or physical structure, neither does he. This is where Unamuno really does go beyond the Romantic notion of *poiesis*. While he struggles to capture his creative self in a distinctive style, he recognizes that his literary persona is reader-dependent. It is not of course that Unamuno was a post-structuralist; his position was after all a predictable development of the nineteenth-century hermeneutic tradition which he had absorbed: to be understood texts have to be interpreted, but all interpretation is necessarily performed from a point of view, and that point of view is crucial to the understanding of the text, as Schleiermacher had made clear. The ultimate point of view is that of the reader, whatever shaping forces are at work. It is not that meaning is undecidable, as some extreme post-structuralists have argued; it is simply that we decide as we read. And not only as we read a text, but as we 'read' any artistic creation. Abel's painting of Cain acquires its significance and fame *after* Joaquín's speech, not before. Indeed only after hearing Joaquín's interpretation did it dawn on Abel what his painting was all about. Meaning does not inhere; it is conferred. Just as God needs us, conscious humans, to give meaning to His creation (as Unamuno argues in *Del sentimiento trágico de la vida*), so any artistic creator needs a conscious observer for his work to acquire meaning. Our role should be purposive, teleological, whether as human beings in the real world or as receptors of imagined worlds. Hence Unamuno's constant appeals to an imagined reader.

A narrative comes to be whatever it is in the act of reading, and of course in the act of writing criticism. What Unamuno abhorred was academic criticism based on so-called scientific facts; what he sought was a creative engagement, one that could never, by its very nature, attain the last word. But this does not bring about the 'death of the author', as Barthes would have it. What it does mean in Unamunian terms is that the author-in-the-text needs a reader if he is to engage in meaningful dialogue. As a linguistic form the novel lacks meaning until an interlocutor steps in. That interlocutor will be in the first place 'the reader in the writer', as Unamuno sees him, and then the external reader who takes up the text but who will remain an unknown quantity in nearly all cases. The text is seen in terms of possibilities, realized only in the act of reading. What is especially significant in Unamuno is that this search, initiated by the novelist himself and contrived by the reader, is reflected, crystallized even, in the search of the fictional characters themselves: the characters strive to find their own meaning in their life-project, they are as it were readers of their own lives, and even on occasion readers of their own writing (Joaquín, Ángela, Don Sandalio, Julio Macedo).

At the heart of Unamuno's fiction-making lies the struggle of the central character — sometimes of more than one — to come to terms with him or herself. This is of course where the characters owe their outlook to their creator's own psychological make-up and life-concerns. They constitute an exploration of authorial preoccupations and in that sense reflect his inner nature, although the parallel ends here, and incautious critics who have seen the characters as simulacra of the author or fictional alter egos are choosing to ignore Unamuno's warning: '«¡Es que Augusto Pérez eres tú mismo...!» — se me dirá — ¡Pero no! Una cosa es que todos mis personajes novelescos, que todos los agonistas que he creado, los haya sacado de mi alma, de mi realidad íntima [...] y otra cosa es que sean yo mismo' (II, 196), a warning repeated in his well-known 1933 article 'Almas sencillas', following the publication of *San Manuel Bueno, mártir y tres historias más*, which had prompted some commentators to identify Unamuno with the priest Don Manuel. Because these explorations often are by their nature highly complex, revolving around topics such as identity, authenticity, belief, free will, etc., the characters who embody these concepts ('Un concepto puede llegar a hacerse persona', writes Unamuno (II, 195)) are more often than not contradictory, opaque, hard to fathom, and often subject to irreconcilable forces. This perhaps helps to explain why Unamuno's fictional characters do not evoke empathetic reactions in the same way that so many nineteenth-century characters do. What they cry out for is explanation. Why do they behave as they do? The challenge to explain is very clearly there, but explanation is what Unamuno seems to pre-empt, even to sabotage by invoking readers who prefer enigmas to solutions. Unamuno's narratives are by no means as puzzling as Kafka's; with a couple of exceptions in his short stories, there are no unexplained events. It is only his characters that pose the problem. But since the narratives revolve around their personalities and dilemmas we cannot avoid confronting the behavioural issues posed.

As we saw in Chapter 1, Unamuno prizes the mental over the physical. What truly characterizes human beings is not their physical appearance but their mental qualities. 'Lo que llamamos espíritu me parece mucho más material que lo que llamamos materia; a mi alma la siento más de bulto y más sensible que a mi cuerpo' (VIII, 660), he had written in '¡Plenitud de plenitudes y todo plenitud!', eight years before he developed the idea in *Del sentimiento trágico de la vida*. We cannot explain the mental by reducing it to the physical; but we might explain the physical by subordinating it to the mental, or according it a sustaining function. Curiously enough, this is a quasi-Schopenhauerian view. What Unamuno is doing is replacing Schopenhauer's blind Will of Nature with a purposive striving that he identifies with 'alma' or 'espíritu'. It is through our minds rather than through our bodies that we express our real human natures. It is this mental striving that is reflected in the urges and impulses of Unamuno's personages, from Pachico's desperate search for inner peace and Augusto's anguished search for a role, through Joaquín's Byronic ambition, Tula's demotion of sex as a distasteful deflection from our true calling, Ángela's sublimation of her maternal instincts, to Lázaro's idealistic socialism and Father Manuel's fraternal solidarity with his country folk. Even where no spiritual dimension is present, as in the widow Raquel or Carolina the Marqués de Lumbría's daughter, there is an evident desire to transcend the limitations imposed by material circumstances, sterility in the first case, the removal of primogeniture in the second.

The central issue that emerges from Unamuno's concept of character is the probably unanswerable question of whether the characters' actions are conditioned by their personalities or whether their personalities arise from their actions. Indeed in some cases outward behaviour and inner predisposition appear to be irreconcilable. But whether explicable or not, facets of personality is the one thing that Unamuno's novels are certainly about, giving the lie to that type of contemporary critical wisdom which, emulating changes in the psychology profession's conception of character, has derided character-analysis as superficial and irrelevant. Unamuno's narratives are about minds, and minds do not exist in a disembodied state. They need a visible or, in the case of fiction, a conceptual presence. No critical approach to Unamuno's novels can cast the concept of character aside and yet say anything worthwhile about them. It is not, of course, a matter of simply explaining actions in terms of some pre-established notion of character, but of knowing what a character *stands for*. Unamuno's characters, like Dostoyevski's, are placed in situations in which they find themselves virtually incapable of understanding their own motivations. They are a challenge to themselves no less than to the reader. To see Gertrudis as a monster or Father Manuel Bueno as a liar is surely to miss the point of Unamuno's use of these characters.[6]

---

[6] These views are not uncommon even among top Unamuno scholars. The views I have just quoted can be found in Paul R. Olson, *The Great Chiasmus* and Thomas R. Franz, *Unamuno's Paratexts*, among many others. There is a potentially fascinating book waiting to be written on critical responses to Unamuno's fictional characters.

For Unamuno, then, characters in novels are devices, symbols. If we try to describe them exclusively in terms of their character traits we will usually end up with contradictions, or else with expressions of our own likes and dislikes leading to an impoverished judgemental view. Instead we need to consider their function within the scheme of things, and the scheme of things almost invariably has to do with freedom, decision, moral responsibility, finality, memory, anxiety, belief, mutuality, self-knowledge. We need to get to grips with what a character really is, both epistemologically and ontologically. Indeed *Niebla* is in one major respect precisely about this very question: what makes a fictional character? What is it about such characters that makes us readers accept their 'reality' beyond their world of words? Why do we react to them, judge them, and confer on them some element of self-determination? Can they force themselves upon authors as they take shape? Are the characters' decisions the novelist's, or are novelists led to their apparent decisions by (their conception of) the characters? And where precisely on the axis creator–reader is the character to be located? These questions may not be answered, but they are certainly raised and cannot be dismissed by rejecting the notion of character as a delusion or even by labelling a character according to one's sympathetic or anti-pathetic reaction. For Unamuno the characters of fiction have a noumenal reality that can be as imposing as an actual or historical one. They have a life, and that life must be given a purpose. The Unamunian keyword here is identity, both the individual's and the community's, with an inevitable interaction. Where does a character's identity come from and how is it expressed? This is so fundamental to Unamuno's work that it is even reflected in his notion of the novel as an ongoing interaction between himself and his community of readers, an interaction that gives him an identity. He even allows for the fact that our self-identity may be an illusion, that what is real is our search for it because our identity is in our purpose; and this is equally true of his fictional characters. In this respect the truth of narrative and its characters is congruent with the truth, or falsity, of language. It is as true or as false as we make it, as Unamuno often suggests in his paratexts.

It is Unamuno's use of the characters as agents of exploration, as test-tube creatures, that explains his 'organic' view of the novel: 'Una novela, para ser viva, para ser vida, tiene que ser, como la vida misma, organismo y no mecanismo' (VII, 616–17). Here Unamuno is associating writing a novel with developing one's identity and self-awareness, and in the case of a writer this is understandably so: writing can indeed be seen as a process of self-discovery and self-affirmation. But once again Unamuno is adopting a view of literature derived from the Romantics. For the idea of a literary composition growing organically as a plant grows from a seed was heavily promoted in the late eighteenth and early nineteenth centuries, probably as a reaction to the pervasive influence of Newtonian mechanics for the previous one hundred years. In England Coleridge denounced the mechanistic approach to existence and championed art as a living organism that grows out of the creative imagination of the artist, but already before him the Germans, Herder, Goethe, Schelling, and A. W. Schlegel had taken the 'organic turn'. Unamuno clearly must have encountered the idea of art as organism in at least some of the Romantic writers whom he frequented, and the idea obviously had its appeal in its promise of reconciling reason and feeling through biological metaphors.[7] But the organic view must not be confused with the Unamunian distinction between *viviparismo* and *oviparismo*. The view of the novel as a living organism is of course consonant with *viviparismo*, the idea that the novel grows naturally or 'makes itself' as it goes along, to take Victor Goti's definition in *Niebla*; but it is just as compatible with *oviparismo*, the planned work, since what counts in organicism is not whether the work is pre-planned or written spontaneously but whether it follows rules already laid down or develops its own rules in the writing. Many of Unamuno's novels had a long gestation, existed in note form, and went through several drafts, so they were clearly not viviparous. But with the exception of *Paz en la guerra*, they did not conform to the patterns laid down by the nineteenth-century realist and naturalist novels. Hence Unamuno's predilection for the organic label.

The organic unity of the work of art, in which form and content are inseparable because both grow together, derived of course from the imagination of the poet; hence the theory of immanence in the work of art. It was K. W. F. Schlegel who, following Herder, most clearly enunciated the doctrine of the poet as creator by analogy with God and His creation, an analogy repeated insistently more than a century later by Unamuno's Russian contemporary Nikolai Berdyaev: just as God creates man in His own image, so does man's own creativity inhere in his creations. The Author is immanent in his work. Poets are thus seen as creators in a divine sense, that is to say, creators out of nothing other than themselves. What counts is not the work's fidelity to anything outside of itself, but its inner consistency, its own vitality as conferred by its creator. The corollary is creative freedom (or the urge to freedom), a concept which applies to Romantics and Existentialists alike, and which can be seen to be operative in many Unamunian characters in the way they strive to express themselves and search for significance, and even sometimes in the way they seek to assert themselves in a bid to overcome their sensed lack of freedom. Once mimesis is abandoned as the mainstay of art, the imagination takes over as the driving force of creativity. And in the case of a writer this will inevitably involve adjusting prevalent generic conventions and received forms of expression. For Unamuno, 'la realidad poética' is to be found in the inner man, and the inner man, the real entity, 'es un símbolo' (II, 195). This concurs with what was perhaps the chief linguistic innovation of Romanticism, namely the introduction of the symbol as the manifestation of something that lies undetected or unnamed, as representative of that which can be intuited but not logically defined.

The work, whether poem or novel — and Unamuno does not distinguish between the two — articulates an inner domain which, in Unamuno, is strongly associated with 'querer ser', a self-remaking. This explains why even in third-person novels Unamunian characters engage in 'monodiálogos' or dialogues with themselves: to explore this inner domain or self-striving necessarily involves a first-person stance. It is not enough to describe from outside; digging down to the roots of our being is an inside job. But it is here that Unamuno departs from the Romantic theory of

---

[7] As indicated in Chapter 4, the influence of organicism in Unamuno has been well studied by Francisco La Rubia Prado, 1996, although he subsequently applies it rather too rigidly to some of the novels. See Also Marta E. Altisent, 1996.

the primacy of the creative imagination and the immanence of the artist. For the Romantics the artistic self was a coherent entity. For Unamuno there is no such coherence. Indeed we can go so far as to see his fiction as an exploration of precisely this problem, the problem of understanding what the self is, if it is anything at all, and how it manifests itself. Here we need to complete the earlier quotation in which Unamuno warns us that his characters are not simply himself: '[...] y otra cosa es que sean yo mismo. Porque, ¿quién soy yo mismo? ¿Quién es el que se firma Miguel de Unamuno? Pues... uno de mis personajes, una de mis criaturas, uno de mis agonistas. Y ese yo último e íntimo y supremo, ese yo transcendente — o inmanente — ¿quién es? Dios lo sabe...' (II, 196). Miguel de Unamuno the writer is but another personage, a creation. And the creative self that lies below must remain an unknown quantity, sensed, tantalizing, but unreachable. In this respect — incomplete knowledge of the self — Unamuno is no God, whatever that other Don Miguel might have said in *Niebla*.

The problem is, then, that although the artist may be immanent in his work and in his creatures there is no way of identifying that artistic self except as a reflection of the work. The producer turns out to be a product, the originator a mere consequence. And not even his own product, but rather his readers'. This indeed is what Augusto Pérez suggests to Don Miguel, that he loses control of his own work, an idea that Unamuno also expressed elsewhere: 'Cien veces he dicho que no admito en todo caso la interpretación que un autor da a su propio escrito. El pensamiento, ya lo he dicho, es social, es colectivo, y una vez expresado, es de cualquiera que se apropie su expresión.'[8] This, too, is a Romantic notion, as Frank Kermode reminded us in *Romantic Image*: 'Even the author has no business to interfere with or explain his work. If it were merely mechanical he could take it back to the drawing board; but as it is organic, he can only talk about it as everybody else can. Such notions have been commonplace since Coleridge' (Kermode, 1971: 110).

But what has radically altered is the Romantics' view of the harmony of the artistic self, a natural harmony at one with the spirit of nature that was capable of visions of beauty and synthesis. By the end of the nineteenth century few writers held on to the Romantic belief that the inner world of man was a natural and harmonious world because we carried the spirit of nature within us. Instead man was seen as the product of conflicting forces, biological, cultural, educational, as well as of primitive impulses and unconscious anxieties. That a harmonious and coherent self could arise from such formative diversity was altogether unlikely, and hence there arose the view of the human individual as 'plusieurs personnes superposées' (Proust) or 'all bits' (Lawrence). Fragmentation threatens the integrity of the self and thereby undermines the concept. However attractive he found the Romantic concept of immanence, Unamuno's preoccupation with getting to the root of his being, of what makes a human entity human and distinctive, goes well beyond the Romantic notion of self-articulation via artistic creation. For he has raised the question that has no answer: which self inheres in the work of art? Even if that self were there, it could not exist objectively but only subjectively among

[8]   *Obras Completas* (Escelicer), IX, 873.

the population of consumers. One cannot define one's self. The only self capable of being defined is the self one would wish to be. This Unamunian 'querer ser' is in the last resort a defensive mechanism, a consolation prize. Unable to locate a root self, or to locate a dominant self among the many selves, Unamuno invented the 'querer ser' as the being that would ensure our 'salvation', as he famously expressed it: 'Y por el que hayamos querido ser, no por el que hayamos sido, nos salvaremos o perderemos' (II, 194). The originator's real self cannot survive because it cannot be known objectively, only surmised, even by the artist himself. And as we saw in the section on Finitude in the preceding chapter, contrary to what is often said, Unamuno was not even convinced that art represented a credible bid for incorporeal or noumenal survival.

The Unamunian novel thus becomes not so much an expression of the self as an exploration of selves, both emergent and potential. Unamuno, like Michel Foucault after him, did not after all appear to believe that personality has hidden depths that can be trawled for the truth. What it has is possibilities, both realized and unrealized. In other words, we are what we do. Our personality is in our actions, rather than the other way round. Since writing is an action, writings may confer identity or identities, they help define the writer rather than reflect a prior and unchanging self. Unamuno's view of artistic creation bears comparison with Heidegger's as exposed in his essay *The Origin of the Work of Art*. In the same way that he held that Being manifested itself through beings, Heidegger believed that the artist was the agent through whom Art manifested itself. The true artist did not 'learn' or 'copy' his art, he 'disclosed' it, in the same way that the language of poetry is inventive and discloses new dimensions of Being (Heidegger, 1975: 15–86).

In his work, then, the novelist may be said to be inventing his being or self. This view clearly implies an unfolding into the writing self and the written self, a phenomenon Unamuno refers to as the mirror effect of writing, of a stranger staring back. This unfolding or apparent objectification of the writer's self, which Unamuno says he found disturbing, in turn becomes a principle of composition observed in his persistent and varied used of the literary trope of the double, which can be treated psychologically as indicating a split personality, but which is also a reflection of the simple if unsettling truth that a person necessarily exists subjectively and objectively, and that each of those existences impacts on the other. Far from being novels about solitary individuals cut off from society, Unamuno's fiction is built on the principle that it is the community's view of one that dominates one's view of oneself. One's self-image is not dependent simply on self-observation, but also and even more on observing other's reactions to one. The 'who am I?' question that looms so large in Unamuno's novels, in which the characters invariably undergo some kind of identity crisis as they search for their roles in life, is not one that can be answered by a few circumstantial facts such as name, address, age, and occupation. The drastic disorientation and uncertainty that Unamuno inflicts upon his personages reduces to the question of where one stands in relation to others, of how we respond subjectively to our objective existence in the community. The pursuit of personal identity which is such a central feature of Unamuno's fiction cannot be carried out in isolation, and those characters who try to isolate themselves or flee from others' intrusion invariably fail. 'El hombre ni vive solo ni es individuo aislado' (*DSTV*, X, 294). It is clearly not enough to define personal identity in terms of self-awareness (very obvious, for example, in *Niebla*), and Unamuno's novels suggest that there are two fundamental reasons for this. Firstly, a self necessarily exists among other selves, and it is that community of other selves that enables one to find out who and what one is, although this, it should be said, is converted by Unamuno into a source of both enrichment and perplexity, as his metaphor of multiple mirrors obviously indicates. One's public selves can become a source of anxiety as well as of reassurance. Secondly, a self has to stand for something, as Unamuno insists time and again in those essays of a spiritual or educational cast. A character's beliefs, attitudes, allegiances, or values only make sense in the context of a community's outlook, irrespective of whether those beliefs etc. are in consonance or conflict with the encompassing framework. In Unamunian ontology what this comes down to is in a sense quite radical, and certainly goes beyond the original Romantic theory of the creative self. For in effect what comes through in Unamuno's fiction is that a stable, knowable self is just that, a fiction; or at any rate that if it exists it is inapprehensible. The novelist creates his artistic role just as his personages create theirs. Self-interpretation does not lead to the discovery of a deep-lying, governing self, but merely to a statement of preferences. To try to explain our preferences, our self-perception, is to engage in a game of Russian dolls.

There is, finally, one point about Unamuno's fictional explorations of identity which, though already hinted at, is important enough to bear repetition. Unamuno sees his characters, and by extension his fellow-humans, as creatures inhabiting a world of words. In part no doubt this stems from Unamuno's training as a philologist, but the issue of interest here is just how closely the ontological and linguistic preoccupations are related to each other in his novels. If the Romantics placed the poet's self at the heart of the creative impulse, Unamuno, even more relentless in the pursuit of that elusive inner self, places language at the core of creativity. It almost seems as if it is language rather than self that is the creative force, or at any rate that language and identity go hand in hand, for a person's identity is seen to be constructed principally through language. We observe this at work in Unamuno's repeated recourse to dialogue, often of a terse and dramatic kind. Unamunian characters will often express themselves as if their personality, even their very existence, depended on their words. It is Unamuno's view that our experiences, thoughts, and memories, in themselves incoherent, shapeless, ungraspable, are given meaningful shape only through language, and it is thus in a very real sense language that defines us, and that is as far as we can go. When Derrida, in his masterwork *Of Grammatology*, argued that to regard language as giving us unmediated access to realities outside of itself was a deep-seated illusion, he was only repeating what Unamuno had said on numerous occasions ('inventar lo que no hay' to quote the dog Orfeo). For Unamuno language is more than a representation; it becomes our reality, whether true or false. It is not about something 'out there', but about the utterer. Language is really about the speaker, or more importantly (because the words endure), about the writer. Words have a noumenal existence; objects pass, words remain because they are the soul of matter: 'Las cosas se van, quedan las palabras, sus almas.'[9] Here Unamuno is going beyond the Romantic idea of immanence by ascribing such immanence not just to the poet's creativity but to the very nature of language. Central to Unamuno's theory of writing is that language acts upon us in certain ways, that it forces us to think in particular terms, or as he puts it, 'toda filosofía es, pues, en el fondo, filología' (*DSTV*, X, 518). What characterizes great writers is their awareness of their own enslavement by words and their ability to turn the tables by breaking out of conventional ways of expression and therefore conventional ways of thinking, and thereby to forge new relationships and visions. One of the consequences of such an attitude to language is that the idea of a persistent, unchanging self becomes untenable. For Unamuno every new piece of writing entailed a new self-disposition or self-discovery.

But language of course belongs to a community, indeed a community is so closely identified with its language as to be scarcely conceivable without it. It is from the community that the individual absorbs it. This only serves to reinforce the sense in which an individual is in the first place a creation of his or her community. A person is constituted both by others' views and by the concomitant mediation of language. Because language can easily become conventionalized, ossified, Unamuno sought to convey or invoke experience through a highly personal, or as he preferred to call it 'poetic', use of language. Hence his injunction to young writers to find their own expression. Language was not to be left to waste away at the representational or mimetic level; it had to be interpretative, epiphanic, enabling us to see beyond the surface of things, to turn inwards and transfigure the world through the writer's vision. At the same time Unamuno was all too conscious of the inescapable truth that language will always antecede the writer and is to a large degree constrained by convention, so there is bound to be a gap between it and what it is meant to invoke. Unamuno many times declared a deep mistrust of words, a paradox in the case of someone who throughout his life devoted himself to language in different forms. Perhaps this may explain why he felt obliged to admit that one's personal identity or self was ultimately unknowable. For if 'nombrar es crear', if language is a form of utterance that acquires its own separate existence, we may be creating what is not there beyond the deceptive world of words, as Augusto Pérez tells his dog Orfeo and as Orfeo will faithfully repeat. This helps explain too why in Unamuno's view — certainly in Augusto Pérez's view as he tells Don Miguel in the famous interview, repeating what Víctor Goti had earlier told him — the author is ultimately displaced by the reader, by the legend. Humanity, too, is its own invented story. If in some ways Unamuno's novels can be seen to explore traditionally important philosophical and psychological issues, in others they closely prefigure the fictions of Jorge Luis Borges. The reality behind Unamuno's worlds of the mind must remain shrouded in mist. For him the novel became yet another reflection of the radical uncertainty of the human situation.

---

[9] *Obras Completas* (Escelicer), IV, 467.

SELECT BIBLIOGRAPHY

The critical bibliography on Unamuno has acquired such vast proportions that it is now virtually unmanageable. Any listing which would aim to cover not even every item but simply a majority of them would itself be the size of a substantial book. The bibliography below includes works which have been cited during the course of this study. To those works on Unamuno which have been cited I have added a very small number of items which, although I have not had occasion to cite, seem to me of potential relevance to our appreciation of Unamuno as a writer of fiction and which other researchers in this area might wish to consult. Clearly, however, this listing neither is nor aspires to be anything like complete.

Dates are those of the editions used.

Works by Unamuno

UNAMUNO, MIGUEL DE (1890?). 'Carta a Juan Solís', unpublished manuscript (Casa-Museo Unamuno, Caja N° 104/72)

——(1965). *Cartas inéditas de Miguel de Unamuno*, recopilación y prólogo de Sergio Fernández Larraín (Santiago de Chile: Zig-Zag)

——(1966). *Obras Completas*, 9 vols (Madrid: Escelicer)

— —(1971). *Epistolario y escritos complementarios Unamuno-Maragall*, prólogo de Pedro Laín Entralgo, epílogo de Dionisio Ridruejo (Madrid: Seminario y Ediciones)

——(1985). *Niebla*, ed. by Mario J. Valdés (Madrid: Ediciones Cátedra)

——(1991). *Epistolario inédito*, ed. by Laureano Robles, 2 vols (Madrid: Austral)

——(1993). *Artículos en 'Las Noticias' de Barcelona (1899–1902)*, ed. by Adolfo Sotelo Vázquez (Barcelona: Editorial Lumen)

——(1994). *Artículos en 'La Nación' de Buenos Aires (1919–1924)*, recopilación y estudio de Luis Urrutia Salaverri (Salamanca: Ediciones Universidad de Salamanca)

——(1995a). *Abel Sánchez*, ed. by C. A. Longhurst (Madrid: Cátedra)

——(1995b). *Obras Completas*, ed. by Ricardo Senabre, 10 vols (Madrid: Biblioteca Castro)

——(1996). *Epistolario americano (1890–1936)*, ed. by Laureano Robles (Salamanca: Ediciones Universidad de Salamanca)

——(1998). *Alrededor del estilo*, ed. by Laureano Robles (Salamanca: Ediciones Universidad de Salamanca)

——(1999). *Paz en la guerra*, ed. by Francisco Caudet (Madrid: Cátedra)

——(2005). *Del sentimiento trágico de la vida en los hombres y en los pueblos y Tratado del amor de Dios*, ed. by Nelson Orringer (Madrid: Tecnos)

Works on Unamuno

ALAS, ADOLFO, ed. (1941). *Menéndez y Pelayo, Unamuno, Palacio Valdés: epistolario a Clarín* (Madrid: Ediciones Escorial)

ALTISENT, MARTA E. (1996). 'Unamuno y la metáfora organicista de la creación literaria', *Letras de Deusto* 26: 75–93

ÁLVAREZ CASTRO, LUIS (2005). *La palabra y el ser en la teoría literaria de Unamuno* (Salamanca: Ediciones Universidad de Salamanca)

——(2006). 'El personaje-escritor en la narrativa breve de Unamuno: metaliteratura y autobiografía' *Cuadernos de la Cátedra Miguel de Unamuno*, 42.2: 13–38

——(2012). '¿Quién mató a Augusto Pérez? Control hermenéutico y chantaje existencial en *Niebla*, de Unamuno', *Revista de Estudios Hispánicos*, 46: 25–47

ANDERSON, REED (1974). 'The Narrative Voice in Unamuno's *San Manuel Bueno, mártir*', *Hispanófila*, 50: 67–76

ARDILA, J. A. G. (2008). 'Nueva lectura de *Niebla*: Kierkegaard y el amor', *Revista de Literatura*, 70: 83–115

——(2010). 'Unamuno y Cervantes: narradores y narración en *Niebla*', *Modern Language Notes*, 135: 348–68

——(2011). 'The Origin of Unamuno's *Mist*: Unamuno's Copy of Kierkegaard's *Diary of the Seducer*', *Modern Philology*, 109: 135–43

——(2012a). 'Unamuno, el monólogo interior y el flujo de conciencia: de William James y *Amor y pedagogía* a Knut Hamsun y *Niebla*', *Hispanic Review*, 80: 445–66

——(2012b). 'Unamuno, Freud y Strindberg: los sueños en *Amor y pedagogía* y *Niebla*', *Neophilologus*, 96: 47–64

AZAR, INÉS (1970). 'La estructura novelesca de *Cómo se hace una novela*', *Modern Language Notes*, 85: 184–206

BATCHELOR, R. E. (1972). *Unamuno Novelist* (Oxford: Dolphin)

BIGGANE, JULIA (2000). 'Yet another Other: Unamuno's *El Otro* and the Anxiety for Influence', *Bulletin of Hispanic Studies* (Glasgow), 77.5: 479–91

——(2005). 'Introjection, Loss and the Politics of Possession in Unamuno's *San Manuel Bueno, mártir*', *Hispanic Review*, 73: 329–49

——(2009). 'Miguel de Unamuno's *Cómo se hace una novela*: Confession, Abjection, Religious Economy', *Modern Language Review*, 104: 1018–37

BLANCO AGUINAGA, CARLOS (1961). 'Sobre la complejidad de *San Manuel Bueno, mártir*', *Nueva Revista de Filología Española*, 15: 569–88

——(1964). 'Unamuno's *Niebla*: Existence and the Game of Fiction', *Modern Language Notes* 79: 188–205

BONADDIO, FEDERICO (2011). '*San Manuel Bueno, mártir* and the Art of Hagiography', *Bulletin of Spanish Studies*, 88.7–8: 247–57

BUTT, JOHN (1981). *Miguel de Unamuno: 'San Manuel Bueno, mártir'*, Critical Guides to Spanish Texts (London: Grant & Cutler/Tamesis)

CEREZO GALÁN, PEDRO (1996). *Las máscaras de lo trágico: filosofía y tragedia en Miguel de Unamuno* (Madrid: Trotta)

CIFO GONZÁLEZ, MANUEL (1989). 'El espacio y el tiempo en la estructura narrativa de *Niebla*', in *Actas del Congreso Internacional Cincuentenario de Unamuno*, ed. by Dolores Gómez Molleda (Salamanca: Ediciones Universidad de Salamanca): 425–28

——(2003). 'Literatura y vida: algunas consideraciones acerca del simbolismo en *Niebla*', in *Miguel de Unamuno: estudios sobre su obra. I*, ed. by Ana Chaguaceda Toledano (Salamanca: Ediciones Universidad de Salamanca): 61–80

COBB, CHRISTOPHER H. (1972). 'Sobre la elaboración de *Abel Sánchez*', *Cuadernos de la Cátedra Miguel de Unamuno*, 22: 127–47

COLLINS, MARSHA S. (2002). 'Orfeo and the Cratyline Conspiracy in Unamuno's *Niebla*', in *Hispanic Modernisms*, ed. by Nelson R. Orringer, *Bulletin of Spanish Studies*, 79.2–3: 285–306

CRIADO MIGUEL, ISABEL (1986). *Las novelas de Miguel de Unamuno: estudio formal y crítico* (Salamanca: Ediciones Universidad de Salamanca)

DÍAZ-PETERSON, ROSENDO (1986). 'Sobre el dinamismo científico de *Niebla*', in *Volumen-Homenaje Cincuentenario a Miguel de Unamuno* (Salamanca: Casa-Museo Unamuno): 383–93

——(1987). *Las novelas de Unamuno* (Potomac, MA: Scripta Humanistica)

DÍEZ, RICARDO (1976). *El desarrollo estético de la novela de Unamuno* (Madrid: Playor)

DURAND, F. (1969). 'The Search for Reality in *Nada menos que todo un hombre*', *Modern Language Notes*, 84: 239–47

EVANS, JAN E. (2005). *Unamuno and Kierkegaard* (Lanham, MD: Lexington Books)

FALCONIERI, J. V. (1964). '*San Manuel Bueno, mártir* — Spiritual Autobiography: A Study in Imagery', *Symposium*, 18: 128–41

FERNÁNDEZ, ANA M. (1991), *Teoría de la novela en Unamuno, Ortega y Cortázar* (Madrid: Pliegos)

FERNÁNDEZ, PELAYO H. (1966), *El problema de la personalidad en Unamuno y en San Manuel Bueno, mártir* (Madrid: Mayfe)

FLÓREZ MIGUEL, CIRILO (1986). 'Unamuno filósofo: poética *versus* lógica', in *Volumen-Homenaje Cincuentenario a Miguel de Unamuno* (Salamanca: Casa-Museo Unamuno): 597–616

FOSTER, D. W. (1973). *Unamuno and the Novel as Expressionistic Conceit* (Puerto Rico: Inter-American University Press)

FRANZ, THOMAS R. (1980). 'Parenthood, Authorship, and Immortality in Unamuno's Narratives', *Hispania*, 63: 647–57

——(1990). *Parallel but Unequal: The Contemporizing of Paradise Lost in Unamuno's 'Abel Sánchez'* (Valencia: Albatros Hispanófila)

——(2003).'*Niebla' inexplorada: midiendo intersticios en el maravilloso texto de Unamuno* (Newark, DE: Juan de la Cuesta)

——(2006). *Unamuno's Paratexts: Twisted Guides to Contorted Narratives* (Newark, DE: Juan de la Cuesta)

FRIEDMANN, EDWARD (1980). 'From Concept to Drama: The Other Unamuno' *Hispanófila*, 23: 29–39

——(2007). 'Qixotic Inscriptions: Unamuno's Theory of the Novel', in *Framing the Quixote: 1605–2005*, ed. by Alvin F. Sherman Jr. (Provo, ID: Brigham Young University): 151–76

GLENDINNING, NIGEL (1978). 'The Social Dimension of *San Manuel Bueno, mártir*, *Vida Hispánica*, 26.2: 21–24

GORDON, M. (1986). 'The Elusive Self: Narrative Method and Its Implications in *San Manuel Bueno, mártir*', *Hispanic Review*, 54: 147–61

GREENFIELD, SUMNER M. (1979). 'La iglesia terrestre de San Manuel Bueno', *Cuadernos Hispanoamericanos*, 348: 609–20

GULLÓN, RICARDO (1964). *Autobiografías de Unamuno* (Madrid: Gredos)

ILIE, PAUL (1961). 'Unamuno, Gorky, and the Cain Myth: Toward a Theory of Personality', *Hispanic Review*, 39: 310–23

——(1967). *Miguel de Unamuno: An Existential View of Self and Society* (Madison: University of Wisconsin Press)

——(1987). 'Language and Cognition in Unamuno', *Revista Canadiense de Estudios Hispánicos*, 11: 289–314

IMIZCOZ BEUNZA, TERESA (1996). *La teoría poética de Miguel de Unamuno* (Pamplona: Ediciones Universitarias de Navarra)

Johnson, Roberta (1993). *Crossfire: Philosophy and the Novel in Spain, 1900–1934* (Lexington: University of Kentucky Press)

Jurkevich, Gayana (1990). 'Unamuno's Gestational Fallacy: *Niebla* and "escribir a lo que salga"', *Anales de la literatura española contemporánea*, 15: 65–81

——(1991). *The Elusive Self: Archetypal Approaches to the Novels of Miguel de Unamuno* (Columbia and London: University of Missouri Press)

Kirsner, Robert (1953). 'The Novel of Unamuno: A Study in Creative Determinism', *Modern Language Journal*, 37: 128–39

La Rubia Prado, Francisco (1996). *Alegorías de la voluntad: pensamiento orgánico, retórica y deconstrucción en la obra de Miguel de Unamuno* (Madrid: Libertarias Prodhufi)

——(1999). *Unamuno o la vida como ficción* (Madrid: Gredos)

Livingstone, L. (1941). 'Unamuno and the Aesthetic of the Novel', *Hispania*, 25: 442–50

——(1967). 'The Novel as Self-Creation', in *Unamnuo, Creator and Creation*, ed. by Barcia and Zeitlin (Berkeley and Los Angeles: University of California Press): 92–115

Longhurst, C. A. (1999). 'The Turn of the Novel in Spain: From Realism to Modernism in Spanish Fiction', in *A Further Range: Studies in Modern Spanish Literature from Galdós to Unamuno*, ed. by Anthony H. Clarke (Exeter: University of Exeter Press): 1–43

——(2003). 'Teoría de la novela en Unamuno: de *Niebla* a *Don Sandalio*', in *Miguel de Unamuno. Estudios sobre su obra. I*, ed. by Ana Chaguaceda Toledano (Salamanca: Ediciones Universidad de Salamanca): 139–51

——(2008). 'La transparencia del ser: Unamuno y Martín-Santos', in *Miguel de Unamuno. Estudios sobre su obra. III*, ed. by Ana Chaguaceda Toledano (Salamanca: Ediciones Universidad de Salamanca): 47–58

——(2011). 'Unamuno, Schleiermacher, Humboldt: A Question of Language', *Hispanic Review*, 79: 573–91

López de Abiada, José Manuel (1988). 'Autobiografía, ficción y ontogenia novelística en *Cómo se hace una novela*', *Revista de Literatura*, 50: 149–55

Lozano Marco, Miguel Ángel (1989). 'Consideraciones sobre *Una historia de amor*, relato unamuniano', in *Actas del Congreso Internacional Cincuentenario de Unamuno*, ed. by Dolores Gómez Molleda (Salamanca: Ediciones Universidad de Salamanca): 505–08

Luby, Barry J. (2008). *The Uncertainties in Twentieth and Twenty-First Century Analytic Thought: Miguel de Unamuno, the Precursor* (Newark, De: Juan de la Cuesta)

Marcos, Luis Andrés (2008). 'El lector unamuniano como clave filosófica', in *Miguel de Unamuno: estudios sobre su obra. III*, ed. by Ana Chaguaceda Toledano (Salamanca: Ediciones Universidad de Salamanca): 89–97

Marías, Julián (1942). *Miguel de Unamuno* (Buenos Aires: Espasa-Calpe)

Martín, Francisco José (2005). 'Filosofía española y novela unamuniana', in *Miguel de Unamuno: estudios sobre su obra. II*, ed. by Ana Chaguaceda Toledano (Salamanca: Ediciones Universidad de Salamanca): 155–64

Martín, Rebeca (2007). '«El que se enterró». Germen de *El otro* o el misterio del doble de Miguel de Unamuno', *Cuadernos de la Cátedra Miguel de Unamuno*, 44.2: 113–24

Mermall, Thomas (1990). 'The Chiasmus: Unamuno's Master Trope', *PMLA*, 105: 245–55

Minter, Gordon (2000). '*Amor y pedagogía*: An Object Lesson in Biography', in *Spain's 1898 Crisis: Regenerationism, Modernism, Post-Colonialism*, ed. by Joseph Harrison and Alan Hoyle (Manchester: Manchester University Press): 81–90

Moncy, A. (1963). *La creación del personaje en las novelas de Unamuno* (Santander: Isla de los Ratones)

Mora García, José Luis (2009). 'La Generación del 98: entre literatura y filosofía', in *Miguel de Unamuno: estudios sobre su obra. IV*, ed. by Ana Chaguaceda Toledano (Salamanca: Ediciones Universidad de Salamanca): 421–31

Morón Arroyo, Ciríaco (1964). '*San Manuel Bueno, mártir* y el "sistema" de Unamuno', *Hispanic Review*, 32: 227–46

——(1989). 'Ser y escribir: consistencia de Unamuno y paradojas de la realidad', in *Actas del Congreso Internacional Cincuentenario de Unamuno*, ed. by Dolores Gómez Molleda (Salamanca: Ediciones Universidad de Salamanca): 331–43

——(2003). *Hacia el sistema de Unamuno: estudios sobre su pensamiento y creación literaria* (Palencia: Ediciones Cálamo)

Navajas, Gonzalo (1985). 'The Self and the Symbolic in Unamuno's *La tía Tula*', *Revista de Estudios Hispánicos* 19.3: 121–37

——(1992). *Unamuno desde la posmodernidad: antinomia y síntesis ontológica* (Barcelona: PPU)

Nicholas, Robert L. (1987). *Unamuno, narrador* (Madrid: Castalia)

Olson, Paul R. (1969). 'The Novelistic Logos in Unamuno's *Amor y pedagogía*', *Modern Language Notes*, 84: 248–68

——(1984). *Unamuno: 'Niebla'*, Critical Guides to Spanish Texts (London: Grant & Cutler/ Tamesis)

——(1986). 'Sobre las estructuras de *Niebla*', in *Volumen-Homenaje Cincuentenario Miguel de Unamuno* (Salamanca: Casa-Museo Unamuno): 423–34

——(1987). 'Unamuno's Break with the Nineteenth-Century: Invention of the *Nivola* and the Linguistic Turn', *Modern Language Notes*, 102: 307–15

——(2003). *The Great Chiasmus: Word and Flesh in the Novels of Unamuno* (West Lafayette: Indiana University Press)

Orringer, Nelson (1985). *Unamuno y los protestantes liberales* (Madrid: Gredos)

——(1986). '*Niebla* y Dios: una desconocida fuente teológica', in *Volumen-Homenaje Cincuentenario Miguel de Unamuno* (Salamanca: Casa-Museo Unamuno): 435–56

——(2003). 'La visión del paraíso perdido en el pensamiento y la novela de Unamuno', in *Miguel de Unamuno: estudios sobre su obra. I*, ed. by Ana Chaguaceda Toledano (Salamanca: Ediciones Universidad de Salamanca): 163–84

Øveraas, Anne Marie (1989). 'La literatura en *Niebla*: ¿Augusto pseudo-agonista?', *Actas del Congreso Internacional Cincuentenario de Unamuno*, ed. by Dolores Gómez Molleda (Salamanca: Ediciones Universidad de Salamanca): 561–67

——(1993). *Nivola contra novela* (Salamanca: Ediciones Universidad de Salamanca)

Palomo, Pilar (1986). 'La estructura orgánica de *Niebla*: nueva aproximación', *Volumen-Homenaje Cincuentenario Miguel de Unamuno* (Salamanca: Casa-Museo Unamuno): 457–73

Parker, A. A. (1967). 'On the Interpretation of *Niebla*', in *Unamuno, Creator and Creation*, ed. by Barcia and Zeitlin (Berkeley and Los Angeles: University of California Press): 116–38

Ramsden, H. (1974). *The 1898 Movement in Spain: Towards a Reinterpretation* (Manchester: Manchester University Press)

Renart, J. Guillermo (1987). 'Problemas semióticos de la narrativa ideológica de personaje: *Tulio Montalbán y Julio Macedo* de Unamuno', *Revista Canadiense de Estudios Hispánicos*, 11: 377–402

Ribbans, Geoffrey (1971). *Niebla y soledad* (Madrid: Gredos)

——(1986). 'El autógrafo de parte de *La tía Tula* y su significado para la evolución de la novela', *Volumen-Homenaje Cincuentenario Miguel de Unamuno* (Salamanca: Casa-Museo Unamuno, 1986): 475–93

——(1987) 'A New Look at *La tía Tula*', *Revista Canadiense de Estudios Hispánicos*, 11: 403–20

——(1989). 'Dialéctica de lucha y ambigüedad en la novelística unamuniana', in *Actas del Congreso Internacional Cincuentenario de Unamuno*, ed. by Dolores Gómez Molleda (Salamanca: Ediciones Universidad de Salamanca): 153–64

Roberts, Gemma (1986). *Unamuno: afinidades y coincidencias kierkegaardianas* (Boulder, CO: Society of Spanish and Spanish-American Studies)

ROBERTS, STEPHEN G. H. (2000). 'Unamuno, Spanishness and the Ideal Patria: An Intellectual's View', *Journal of the Institute of Romance Studies*, 8: 125–36

——(2004). 'Hispanidad: el desarrollo de una polémica noción en la obra de Miguel de Unamuno', *Cuadernos de la Cátedra Miguel de Unamuno*, 39: 61–80

——(2007). *Miguel de Unamuno o la creación del intelectual español moderno* (Salamanca: Ediciones Universidad de Salamanca)

RÓDENAS DE MOYA, DOMINGO (2009). 'Humorismo polémico en *Un pobre hombre rico o el sentimiento cómico de la vida*', in *Miguel de Unamuno. Estudios sobre su obra. IV*, ed. by Ana Chaguaceda Toledano (Salamanca: Ediciones Universidad de Salamanca): 407–18

RODGERS, EAMONN (2011). 'Faith, Creed, and Scripture in *San Manuel Bueno, mártir*', *Bulletin of Spanish Studies*, 88.7–8: 259–69

ROUND, NICHOLAS G. (1974). *Unamuno: 'Abel Sánchez'*, Critical Guides to Spanish Texts (London: Grant and Cutler/Tamesis)

——(1986). 'On the Logic of Unamuno Criticism: The Problem of Belief', in *Volumen-Homenaje Cincuentenario a Miguel de Unamuno* (Salamanca: Casa-Museo Unamuno): 683–705

——(1989a). 'Lectura intertextual de *Nada menos que todo un hombre*', in *Actas del Congreso Internacional Cincuentenario de Unamuno*, ed. by Dolores Gómez Molleda (Salamanca: Ediciones Universidad de Salamanca): 595–98

——(ed.) (1989b). *Re-Reading Unamuno* (Glasgow: University of Glasgow)

SÁNCHEZ CALVO, ARSENIO (1989). 'Miguel de Unamuno, novelista innovador', in *Actas del Congreso Internacional Cincuentenario de Unamuno*, ed. by Dolores Gómez Molleda (Salamanca: Ediciones Universidad de Salamanca): 617–19

SENABRE, RICARDO (1989). 'Los arquetipos temáticos en la literatura unamuniana', in *Actas del Congreso Internacional Cincuentenario de Unamuno*, ed. by D. Gómez Molleda (Salamanca: Ediciones Universidad de Salamanca): 165–79

SHAW, DONALD L. (1977). 'Concerning Unamuno's *La novela de don Sandalio, jugador de ajedrez*', *Bulletin of Hispanic Studies*, 54.2: 115–23

SINCLAIR, ALISON (1987). 'Definition as the Enemy of Self-Definition: A Commentary on the Role of Language in Unamuno's *Niebla*', in *Words of Power: Essays in Honour of Alison Fairlie*, ed. by Dorothy Gabe Coleman and Gillian Jondorf (Glasgow: University of Glasgow): 187–225

——(1999). 'Boundaries and Black Holes: The Physics of Personality and Representation in Unamuno', in *A Further Range: Studies in Modern Spanish Literature from Galdós to Unamuno*, ed. by Anthony H. Clarke. (Exeter: University of Exeter Press): 238–57

——(2001). *Uncovering the Mind: Unamuno, the Unknown and the Vicissitudes of Self* (Manchester: Manchester University Press)

SUMMERHILL, STEPHEN J. (1985). '*San Manuel Bueno, mártir*, and the Reader', *Anales de la Literatura Española Contemporánea* 10: 61–79

——(1992). 'Theory and Practice of the Novel in Unamuno: The Case of *Dos madres*', *Revista Hispánica Moderna*, 45: 15–34

TORO, FERNANDO DE (1981). 'Personaje autónomo, lector y autor en Miguel de Unamuno', *Hispania*, 64: 360–65

TURNER, DAVID G. (1974). *Unamuno's Webs of Fatality* (London: Tamesis)

VALDÉS, MARIO J. (1966). *Death in the Literature of Unamuno* (Urbana and London: University of Illinois Press)

——(1972). 'Metaphysics and the Novel in Unamuno's Last Decade, 1926–1936', *Hispanófila*, 15: 33–44

——(1982). 'Unamuno: The Point of Departure', in *Shadows in the Cave: A Phenomenological Approach to Literary Criticism Based on Spanish Texts* (Toronto: Toronto University Press): 3–14

VAUTHIER, BÉNÉDICTE (1998). 'Huellas del ideario (religioso) krausista en *San Manuel Bueno, mártir*', *Cuadernos de la Cátedra Miguel de Unamuno*, 33: 145–89

——(1999). *'Niebla' de Miguel de Unamuno: a favor de Cervantes, en contra de los cervantófilos. Estudio de narratología estilística* (Bern: Peter Lang)

——(2003). 'Ejercicio(s) de estilo(s) en *Amor y pedagogía* de Miguel de Unamuno: el *Ars magna combinatoria* del gran mixtificador unamuniano', in *Miguel de Unamuno. Estudios sobre su obra. I*, ed. by Ana Chaguaceda Toledano (Salamanca: Ediciones Universidad de Salamanca): 113–22

——(2004). *Arte de narrar e ironía en la obra narrativa de Miguel de Unamuno* (Salamanca: Ediciones Universidad de Salamanca)

VILANOVA, ANTONIO (1989). 'La teoría nivolesca del bufo trágico', in *Actas del Congreso Internacional Cincuentenario de Unamuno*, ed. by Dolores Gómez Molleda (Salamanca: Ediciones Universidad de Salamanca): 189–216

WEBBER, RUTH HOUSE (1964). 'Kierkegaard and the Elaboration of Unamuno's *Niebla*', *Hispanic Review*, 32: 118–34

WYERS, FRANCES (1973). 'Unamuno's *Niebla*: From Novel to Dream', *PMLA*, 88: 209–18

——(1976). *Miguel de Unamuno: The Contrary Self* (London: Tamesis)

Other works cited

ABRAMS, M. H. (1953). *The Mirror and the Lamp* (Oxford: Oxford University Press)

AZORÍN (José Martínez Ruiz) (1972). *La voluntad*, ed. by E. Inman Fox (Madrid: Castalia)

BAROJA, PÍO (1946). *Obras Completas*, 8 vols (Madrid: Biblioteca Nueva)

BLACKHAM, H. J. (1961). *Six Existentialist Thinkers* (London: Routledge and Kegan Paul)

BLEICH, DAVID (1978). *Subjective Criticism* (Baltimore, MD: Johns Hopkins University Press)

BRENTANO, FRANZ (1995). *Psychology from an Empirical Standpoint*, ed. by Linda L. McAlister (London: Routledge)

BRUGGER, PETER *et al.* (1994). 'Heautoscopy, Epilepsy, and Suicide', *Journal of Neurology, Neurosurgery, and Psychiatry*, 57: 838–39

BUBER, MARTIN (2004). *I and Thou*, trans. by Ronald Gregor Smith (London: Continuum)

BULTMANN, RUDOLF (1955). 'Forms of Human Community', in *Essays: Philosophical and Theological* (London: SCM Press): 291–304

BYRON, LORD (1912). *Child Harold's Pilgrimage*, Canto III (Oxford: Clarendon)

CAMUS, ALBERT (1942). *L'Étranger* (Paris: Gallimard)

CULLER, JONATHAN (1975). *Structuralist Poetics: Structuralism, Linguistics and the Study of Literature* (Ithaca, NY: Cornell University Press)

DERRIDA, JACQUES (1976). *Of Grammatology*, trans. by G. C. Spivak (Baltimore, MD: Johns Hopkins University Press)

—— (1996). *The Gift of Death*, trans. by David Wills (Chicago, IL, and London: University of Chicago Press)

DIOGENES LAERTIUS (1853). *Lives of the Eminent Philosophers*, trans. by C. D. Yonge (London: Henry G. Bohn)

DOSTOYEVSKI, FYODOR (1997). *The Double*, trans. by Constance Garnett (Mineola, NY: Dover Publications)

DURÁN, MANUEL (1957). 'La técnica de la novela y la generación del 98', *Revista Hispánica Moderna*, 23: 14–27

EAGLETON, TERRY (1996). *Literary Theory: An Introduction* (London: Arnold)

ECO, UMBERTO (1979). *The Role of the Reader: Explorations in the Semiotics of Texts* (Bloomington: Indiana University Press)

FERNÁNDEZ CIFUENTES, LUIS (1982). *Teoría y mercado de la novela en España: del 98 a la República* (Madrid: Gredos)

FEYERABEND, PAUL (2001). *Conquest of Abundance* (Chicago, IL, and London: University of Chicago Press)

FISH, STANLEY (1972). *Self-Consuming Artifacts: The Experience of Seventeenth-Century Literature* (Berkeley: University of California Press)

——(1980a) 'Affective Stylistics', in *Reader-Response Criticism: From Formalism to Post-Structuralism*, ed. by Jane P. Tompkins (Baltimore, MD, and London: Johns Hopkins University Press): 70–100

——(1980b). *Is there a text in this class? The Authority of Interpretive Communities* (Cambridge, MA: Harvard University Press)

FOUCAULT, MICHEL (1986). 'What is an author?', in *The Foucault Reader*, ed. by P. Rainbow (Harmonsworth: Penguin): 101–20

FREUD, SIGMUND (1966). *The Psychopathology of Everyday Life*, trans. by Alan Tyson (London: Ernest Benn)

GADAMER, HANS-GEORG (1979). *Truth and Method*, trans. and ed. by Barden and Cumming (London: Sheed and Ward)

GANIVET, ÁNGEL (1961). *Idearium español*, in *Obras Completas*, I (Madrid: Aguilar)

GIDE, ANDRÉ (1955). *Les Faux-monnayeurs* (Paris: Gallimard)

GOLDKNOPF, DAVID (1972). 'The Confessional Increment: A New Look at the I-Narrator', in *The Life of the Novel* (Chicago, IL, and London: University of Chicago Press): 25–41

HEIDEGGER, MARTIN (1962a). *Being and Time*, trans. by John Macquarrie and Edward Robinson (Oxford: Blackwell)

——(1962b). *Kant and the Problem of Metaphysics*, trans. by James S. Churchill (Bloomington: Indiana University Press)

——(1975). *The Origin of the Work of Art*, in *Poetry, Language, Thought*, trans. by Albert Hofstadter (New York: Harper Collins): 15–86

HOLLAND, NORMAN (1968). *The Dynamics of Literary Response* (Oxford and New York: Oxford University Press)

——(1975). 'Unity, Identity, Text, Self', *PMLA*, 90: 813–22, reproduced in *Reader-Response Criticism*, ed. by Jane P. Tompkins (Baltimore, MD, and London: Johns Hopkins University Press): 118–33

HUMBOLDT, WILHELM VON (1999). *On Language: On the Diversity of Human Language Construction and its Influence on the Mental Development of the Human Species*, trans. by Peter Heath, ed. by Michael Losonsky (Cambridge: Cambridge University Press)

HUXLEY, ALDOUS (1935). *Point, Counterpoint* (London: Chatto and Windus)

ISER, WOLGANG (1974). *The Implied Reader* (Baltimore, MD, and London: Johns Hopkins University Press)

JAMES, WILLIAM (1950). *The Principles of Psychology*, 2 vols (New York: Dover Publications)

JASPERS, KARL (1997). *General Psychopathology*, trans. by Hoenig and Hamilton (Baltimore: Johns Hopkins University Press)

JAUSS, HANS ROBERT (1970). 'Literary History as a Challenge to Literary Theory', *New Literary History*, 2 (Autumn): 7–37

——(1982). *Towards an Aesthetic of Reception* (Hemel Hempstead: Harvester Wheatsheaf)

KANT, IMMANUEL (1998). *Critique of Pure Reason*, trans. by Paul Guyer and Allen W. Wood (Cambridge: Cambridge University Press)

KERMODE, FRANK (1971). *Romantic Image* (Glasgow: Collins Fontana)

——(1979). *The Genesis of Secrecy* (London: Harvard University Press)

KIERKEGAARD, SOREN (1954). *Fear and Trembling and The Sickness unto Death*, trans. by Walter Lowrie (New York: Doubleday)

——(1959). *Either/Or*, trans. by D. F. and L. M. Swenson, 2 vols (New York: Doubleday)

——(1981). *The Concept of Anxiety*, trans. by Reidar Thomte (Princeton: Princeton University Press)

LAING, R. D. (1990). *The Divided Self* (London: Penguin)

LAWRENCE, D. H. (1955). *Kangaroo* (London: William Heinemann)

MAILLOUX, STEVEN (1982). *Interpretive Conventions: The Reader in the Study of American Fiction* (Ithaca, NY: Cornell University Press)

MACQUARRIE, JOHN (1973). *An Existentialist Theology: A Comparison of Heidegger and Bultmann* (Harmondsworth: Penguin Books)

MARCEL, GABRIEL (1950). *The Mystery of Being*, 2 vols (London: Harvill)

——(1965a). *A Metaphysical Diary*, in *Being and Having* (London: Collins/Fontana)

——(1965b). *Being and Having* (London: Collins/Fontana)

——(2002). *Creative Fidelity*, trans. by Robert Rosthal (New York: Fordham University Press)

——(2010). *Homo Viator: Introduction to a Metaphysics of Hope*, trans. by Emma Craufurd and Paul Seaton (South Bend, IN: St Augustine's Press)

MOUNTFORD, BRIAN (2011). *Christian Atheist: Belonging without Believing* (Winchester and Washington: O Books)

MUSIL, ROBERT (1997). *The Man without Qualities*, trans. by Sophie Wilkins and Burton Pike (London: Picador)

MÜLLER, F. MAX (1866). *Lectures on the Science of Language* (London: Longmans Green)

——(2002). *The Essential Max Müller: On Language, Mythology and Religion*, ed. by J. R. Stone (New York: Palgrave Macmillan)

NAGEL, THOMAS (1979). *Mortal Questions* (Cambridge: Cambridge University Press)

——(1986). *The View from Nowhere* (New York and Oxford: Oxford University Press)

NOONAN, HAROLD (1989). *Personal Identity* (London and New York: Routledge)

NUSSBAUM, MARTHA (2001). *The Fragility of Goodness: Luck and Ethics in Greek Tragedy and Philosophy*, rev. edn (Cambridge: Cambridge University Press)

ORRINGER, NELSON, ed. (2002). *Hispanic Modernisms*, Bulletin of Spanish Studies, 79.2–3

PARFITT, DEREK (1984). *Reasons and Persons* (Oxford: Oxford University Press)

PLATO (1997). *Complete Works*, ed. by John M. Cooper and D. S. Hutchinson (Indianapolis, IN: Hackett)

PÉREZ DE AYALA, RAMÓN (1976). *Belarmino y Apolonio* (Madrid: Cátedra)

POE, EDGAR ALLAN (1884). *Tales*, ed. by J. H. Ingram (Leipzig: Tauchnitz)

PRINCE, GERALD (1982). *Narratology* (Berlin and New York: Mouton)

PROUST, MARCEL (1990). *À la Recherche du temps perdu. Le Temps retrouvé* (Paris: Gallimard, Collection Folio Classique)

RABINOWITZ, PETER (1987). *Before Reading: Narrative Conventions and the Politics of Interpretation* (Ithaca, NY: Cornell University Press)

RODGERS, EAMONN (1992). 'The Reception of Naturalism in Spain', in *Naturalism in the European Novel: New Critical Perspectives*, ed. by Brian Nelson (New York and Oxford: Berg): 120–34

SARTRE, JEAN-PAUL (1938). *La Nausée* (Paris: Gallimard)

—— (2003). *Being and Nothingness*, trans. by Hazel E. Barnes (London and New York: Routledge, 2003)

SCHLEIERMACHER, FRIEDRICH (1998). *Hermeneutics and Criticism*, trans. and ed. by Andrew Bowie (Cambridge: Cambridge University Press)

SCHOPENHAUER, ARTHUR (1966). *The World as Will and Representation*, trans. by E. F. J. Payne, 2 vols (New York: Dover Publications)

——(1970). *Sobre la voluntad en la naturaleza*, trans. by Miguel de Unamuno (Madrid: Alianza)

——(1999). *Prize Essay on the Freedom of the Will*, trans. by Eric F. J. Payne, ed. by Gunter Zöller (Cambridge: Cambridge University Press)

SEARLE, JOHN R. (1997). *The Mystery of Consciousness* (New York: New York Review of Books)

SPERRY, R. W. (1968). 'Hemisphere Deconnection and Unity in Conscious Awareness', *American Psychologist*, 23: 723–33

SPINOZA, BENEDICT (1996). *Ethics*, trans. by Edwin Curley (London: Penguin Books)

STRAWSON, GALEN (2009). *Selves: An Essay in Revisionary Metaphysics* (Oxford: Oxford University Press)

——(2010). *Mental Reality* (Cambridge, MA: MIT Press)

STRAWSON, P. F. (2003). 'Freedom and Resentment', in *Free Will*, ed. by Gary Watson (Oxford: Oxford University Press): 72–93

VALLE-INCLÁN, RAMÓN DEL (1966). *Divinas Palabras* (Madrid: Austral)

VAN FRAASSEN, BAS C. (2002). *The Empirical Stance* (New Haven, CT, and London: Yale University Press)

WITTGENSTEIN, LUDWIG (1961). *Tractatus Logico-Philosophicus*, trans. by D. F. Pears and B. McGuinness (London: Routledge and Kegan Paul)

——(2009). *Philosophical Investigations*, trans. by G. E. M. Anscombe, P. M S. Hacker, and Joaquim Schulte (Oxford: Blackwell)

WOESSNER, MARTIN (2012). 'Angst across the Channel: Existentialism in Britain', in *Situating Existentialism*, ed. by Jonathan Judaken and Robert Bernasconi (New York: Columbia University Press): 145–79

ONOMASTIC INDEX

The index lists names of all authors referred to, and includes explicit mentions of literary and philosophical works under the appropriate author. Titles of books and articles on Unamuno are not included in the index; they will be found in the bibliography under the author.

SUBJECT INDEX

High-frequency terms, such as writer, reader, and their derivatives are not referenced in the subject index, nor in general are those which are identified in the contents page.